# 汽车英语阅读

郑殿旺　　陈庆新　主编
李荣菲　　许洪国　主审

哈尔滨工业大学出版社
哈　尔　滨

## 内 容 提 要

本书以培养学生汽车专业英语阅读能力为主要目标,全书共分六章。主要内容为:汽车基本组成、汽车发动机、汽车底盘、汽车车身、汽车计算机控制系统和汽车设计,其中选编了有关汽车运用、修理和维护方面的文章,包括课文、词汇、注释、练习等。本书既注重学生专业英语学习,又考虑介绍有关的专业知识。

本书可作为高等院校汽车、内燃机及相关专业的专业英语阅读课教材,也可供汽车爱好者在学习英语及汽车技术方面参考之用。

**图书在版编目(CIP)数据**

汽车英语阅读/郑殿旺等主编.—哈尔滨:哈尔滨工业大学出版社,1998.10(2018.8 重印)
ISBN 978-7-5603-1348-1

Ⅰ.汽… Ⅱ.郑… Ⅲ.汽车工程-英语-阅读教学-高等学校-教材 Ⅳ.H319.4

中国版本图书馆 CIP 数据核字(2008)第 008155 号

| | |
|---|---|
| 责任编辑 | 徐欣颖 |
| 封面设计 | 卞秉利 |
| 出版发行 | 哈尔滨工业大学出版社 |
| 社　　址 | 哈尔滨市南岗区复华四道街 10 号 邮编 150006 |
| 传　　真 | 0451-86414749 |
| 网　　址 | http://hitpress.hit.edu.cn |
| 印　　刷 | 肇东市一兴印刷有限公司 |
| 开　　本 | 850mm×1168mm 1/32 印张 13.375 字数 381 千字 |
| 版　　次 | 1998 年 10 月第 1 版 2018 年 8 月第 6 次印刷 |
| 书　　号 | ISBN 978-7-5603-1348-1 |
| 定　　价 | 38.00 元 |

(如因印装质量问题影响阅读,我社负责调换)

# 前　言

国家教育部颁布的大学英语教学大纲把专业英语阅读列为必修课而纳入英语教学计划，强调通过四年不断线的教学使学生达到顺利阅读专业刊物的目的。根据这个精神，我们编写了这本《汽车英语阅读》教材，以满足高等院校汽车和内燃机及其他有关专业学生的专业英语教学的需要和从事上述专业工程技术人员学习英语的要求。

本书主要内容包括了汽车结构中的各主要系统。重点放在较详细地介绍汽车电子燃油喷射、汽车排放控制、汽车自动变速系统及其他电控新结构和新技术。全书共分六章：第一章为汽车基本组成，第二章为汽车发动机，第三章为汽车底盘，第四章为汽车车身，第五章为汽车计算机控制系统，第六章为汽车设计。

本书由郑殿旺副教授、陈庆新副教授主编。参加编写的有：清华大学张俊智，吉林工业大学王云鹏，哈尔滨工业大学赵桂范，西安公路交通大学高利，重庆交通学院李伟，山东农业大学王会明，山东工程学院王云松，佳木斯大学工学院鲁立刚、姚喜贵、张磊、王宇、刘远军、孙玉芝、邢恩辉等同志。全书由李荣菲、许洪国主审。对书中的不足之处，恳请广大读者批评指正。

作　者
1998 年 4 月

# Contents

**Chapter 1　The Basic Components of an Automobile** ……… (1)
　1.1　Automobile Construction ……………………………… (1)
　1.2　Layout of an Automobile ……………………………… (5)
**Chapter 2　Engine System** ……………………………………… (15)
　2.1　Engine ……………………………………………………… (15)
　　2.1.1　Reciprocating Engine ………………………… (16)
　　2.1.2　Engine Blocks ………………………………… (26)
　　2.1.3　Crankshaft …………………………………… (37)
　　2.1.4　Pistons ………………………………………… (42)
　　2.1.5　Valves ………………………………………… (51)
　2.2　Supplyment Systems …………………………………… (65)
　　2.2.1　Fuel Systems ………………………………… (65)
　　2.2.2　Induction Systems …………………………… (75)
　　2.2.3　Exhaust Systems …………………………… (81)
　2.3　Cooling and lubrication Systems ………………………… (88)
　　2.3.1　Cooling Systems ……………………………… (88)
　　2.3.2　Lubrication Systems ………………………… (95)
　2.4　Gasoline Fuel Injection Systems ……………………… (109)
　　2.4.1　Electronic control Systems ………………… (109)
　　2.4.2　Fuel Injection ………………………………… (126)
　2.5　Emission Control Systems ……………………………… (144)
　2.6　Electrical System ………………………………………… (157)
　　2.6.1　Charging System …………………………… (157)
　　2.6.2　Starting System …………………………… (163)
　　2.6.3　Igniting System …………………………… (167)
**Chapter 3　Chassis System** …………………………………… (181)
　3.1　Clutch ……………………………………………………… (181)
　3.2　Manual Transmission …………………………………… (192)
　3.3　Automatic Transmissions ……………………………… (202)
　　3.3.1　Hydraulic Control Systems ………………… (204)

· I ·

    3.3.2    Torque Converters ............................... (215)
    3.3.3    Planetary Gear Systems ...................... (226)
  3.4    Drive Axles ................................................ (244)
    3.4.1    Axles ................................................. (244)
    3.4.2    Drive Shafts ..................................... (251)
  3.5    Suspension Systems ................................... (260)
  3.6    Steering Systems ...................................... (273)
    3.6.1    Manual Steering Gears ...................... (277)
    3.6.2    Front-End Alignment ........................ (282)
  3.7    Brake Systems .......................................... (291)
    3.7.1    Air Brake System ............................. (293)
    3.7.2    Hydraulic Brake System .................... (300)
**Chapter 4    Automobil Body** ................................... (313)
  4.1    Body Construction .................................... (313)
  4.2    Frame ...................................................... (316)
**Chapter 5    Computerized Automotive-Control Systems** ... (324)
  5.1    Computerized Engine-Control Systems .......... (324)
    5.1.1    Electronic Fuel Injection Systems ............ (324)
    5.1.2    Computerized Ignition ........................ (329)
    5.1.3    Electronically Controlled Emission Systems ... (335)
    5.1.4    Idle-Speed Control ............................ (344)
    5.1.5    Electronically Controlled Transmissions ... (346)
    5.1.6    System Diagnosis and Service ............... (350)
  5.2    Other Automotive Electronic Systems ............ (360)
    5.2.1    Electronic Antilock Braking Systems ....... (360)
    5.2.2    Active Computerized Suspension Systems ... (367)
    5.2.3    Air Bag Restraint Systems ................... (375)
    5.2.4    Self-Diagnosis Systems ....................... (381)
**Chapter 6    Automobile Design** ................................ (389)
  6.1 The Design Objective .................................. (389)
  6.2 The Design of the Basic Components .............. (392)
  Measuring Systems ......................................... (402)
  Metric Tables ................................................ (404)
  Index ........................................................... (405)

# Chapter 1
# The Basic Components of an Automobile

## 1.1 Automobile Construction

The automobile consists of five basic mechanisms, or components. These are:

1. The engine, which is the source of power, including the fuel, lubricating, cooling, and electric systems
2. The frame, which supports the engine, wheels, steering and brake systems, and body
3. The power train, which carries the power from the engine (through the clutch, transmission, drive shaft, differential, and axles) to the car wheels
4. The car body
5. Car-body accessories, including heater, lights, windshield wipers, and so forth.

The engine is the source of power that makes the car move. It is usually called an internal-combustion engine because gasoline is burned inside the engine cylinders, or combustion chambers. This is in contrast to external-combustion engines (such as steam engines), where the combustion takes place outside the engine. The burning of gasoline in the engine cylinders produces the power. The power is then carried from the engine through the power train to the car wheels so that the wheels turn and the car moves.

The fuel system plays a vital part in the power-producing process since it supplies the gasoline to the engine cylinders. In each engine cylinder, a mixture of gasoline vapor and air enters the cylinder, the piston pushes up into the cylinder to compress the mixture, and then an electric spark ignites the compressed mixture so that the piston is forced downward. Of course, in the engine the piston is not blown completely out of the cylinder, the piston simply moves up and down in the cylinder-up to compress the mixture, down as the mixture burns. The piston straight-line motion must be changed to rotary motion before it can be used to make the car wheels rotate. A connecting rod and a crank on the engine crankshaft make this change.

The engine valves get the burned gasoline vapor out of the engine cylinder and bringing fresh charges of gasoline vapor and air into the cylinder. There are two openings, or ports, in the enclosed end of the cylinder, each containing a valve. The valves are accurately machined plugs on long stems. When they are closed, or seated (that is, moved up into the ports), the ports are sealed off and gas cannot pass through the ports. When the valve is open, gas can pass through the port.

The valves are opened by cams on the engine camshaft. The cam has a high point, or lobe; every time the cam rotates, the lobe comes around under the valve lifter and move it upward. The lifter then carries this upward movement through the pushrod to the rocker arm. The rocker arm pivots on its support and pushes down on the valve stem, causing the valve to move down, that is, to open. After the cam has turned enough to move the lobe out from under the lifter, the heavy valve spring pulls the valve back into its seat. The spring is attached to the upper end of the valve stem by a spring retainer and lock. There is a cam for each valve (two cams per cylinder) on the engine camshaft. The camshaft is driven off the crankshaft by gears or by sprockets and a chain.

When the entire cycle of events requires four piston strokes (two crankshaft revolutions), the engine is called a four-stroke-cycle engine, or a four-cycle engine. The four strokes are intake, compression, power, and exhaust.

On the intake stroke, the intake valve is open. The piston moves down, pulled by the rotation of the crankshaft. This piston movement creates a partial vacuum in the cylinder, and air rushes into the cylinder past the intake valve to "fill up" this vacuum. As the air moves toward the cylinder, it must pass through the carburetor. There it is charged with gasoline vapor. Thus, it is a mixture of air and gasoline vapor that rushes into the cylinder as the piston moves down on the intake stroke.

After the piston moves down to the bottom dead center on the intake stroke, the intake valve closes. The lobe on the cam controlling the intake valve has moved out from under the valve lifter. Since the other valve is also closed, the upper end of the cylinder is sealed. Now, as the piston is pushed up by the rotating crankshaft, the mixture of air and gasoline vapor that has been drawn into the cylinder is compressed. By the time the piston has moved up to the top dead center, the mixture is compressed to a seventh or an eighth of its original volume. That is like taking a gallon of air and compressing it to a pint. The result is high pressure in the cylinder.

About the time the piston reaches the top dead center on the compression stroke, an electric spark occurs at the cylinder spark plug. The spark plug is essentially two heavy wire electrodes; the spark jumps between these electrodes. The spark is produced by the ignition system. It ignites, or sets fire to, the compressed air-gasoline-vapor mixture. Rapid combustion takes place; high temperatures and pressures result. At this instant, the downward pressure on the top of the piston may amount to as much as 2 tons. This powerful push forces the piston down, and a power impulse is transmitted to the crankshaft through the connecting rod and the crank.

The piston is forced down by the pressure of the burning gasoline vapor during the power stroke. When the piston reaches the bottom dead center, the exhaust valve opens. Now, as the piston starts back up again, it forces the burned gases from the cylinder. By the time the piston has reached the top dead center the cylinder is cleared of the burned gases. The exhaust valve closes and the intake valve opens. Then, the piston starts back down again on the next intake stroke. The four cycles, or piston strokes, are continuously repeated while the engine is running.

# NEW WORDS

| | | |
|---|---|---|
| mechanism | ['mekənizəm] | n. 机械装置,机构,结构 |
| lubricate | ['ljuːbrikeit] | vt.;vi. 使润滑,给…涂上油,给…上油;起润滑作用 |
| accessary | [æk'sesəri] | n.;adj. 附件,附属品;附属的,附加的 |
| windshield | [wind'ʃiːld] | n. 挡风玻璃 |
| wiper | [wipə] | n. 刮水器,滑动片 |
| combustion | [kəm'bʌstʃən] | n. 燃烧,有机体的氧化 |
| contrast | ['kɔntræst] | n. 对比,对照,对照之下形成的悬殊差别 |
| vital | ['vaitl] | adj. 极其重要的,必不可少的 |
| ignite | [ig'nait] | vt. 点燃,点火于,使燃烧,使灼热 |
| blown | [bləun] | adj. 吹胀的,吹制的 |
| enclose | [in'kləuz] | vt. 关闭住,围住,围起 |
| lobe | [ləub] | n.;adj. 凸角,耳垂;有裂片的 |
| rocker | ['rɔkə] | n. 摇轴,摇杆,摇臂,摇摆器,震荡器 |
| pivot | ['pivət] | n. 枢,枢轴,支枢,支点 |
| sprocket | ['sprɔkit] | n. 链轮齿,齿轮柱 |
| stroke | ['strəuk] | n. 冲程,行程 |
| pint | ['pint] | n.;adj. 品脱(英美干量或液量名);小的 |
| electrode | [i'lektrəud] | n. 电极,电焊条 |

# PHRASES AND EXPRESSIONS

| | |
|---|---|
| consist of | 由…组成,由…构成 |
| take place | 发生,产生,举行 |
| come around | 旋转,前来,苏醒过来 |
| and so forth | 等等 |
| power train | 动系,传动系 |
| windshield wiper | 挡风玻璃,刮水器 |

  play a vital part      起重要作用
  four-stroke-cycle      四冲程循环
  at this instant       在这一瞬间，在这一刹那间

## NOTES TO THE TEXT

  1. The fuel system plays a vital part in the power-producing process since it supplies the gasoline to the engine cylinders。
  燃油系统在动力产生的过程中起重要作用，主要是由于它向发动机气缸内提供汽油。
  since 引导的状语从句在句中做原因状语；the fuel system 在句中做主语；play a vital part in 在句中起着重要作用。
  2. The cam has a high point, or lobe; every time the cam rotates, the lobe comes around under the valve lifter and more it upward.
  凸轮有一最高点，即凸角；每一次，凸轮旋转，凸角旋转到挺杆的下部，使其向上移动。
  every time 做为连词，每当…时，引导时间状语从句，修饰后句中谓语动词 comes。
  3. The lobe on the cam controlling the intake valve has moved out from under the valve lifer。
  控制进气阀的凸轮上的凸角在阀挺柱向下回转。
  controlling the intake valve 现在分词短语做定语，修饰 the cam，has moved … 现在完成时，做谓语。

## 1.2 Layout of an Automobile

  The layout of different types of vehicles is different. A private car which is to carry upto eight persons is generally four seats.
  The layout of a car is shown in (Figure1-1). It shows the position of the main parts of an automobile. It consists of engine located at the front of the vehicle, followed by a clutch, gear box, propeller shaft, universal joint, differential, back axle etc. The radiator is located in front of the engine. Various other parts of the vehicle

shown in the layout are dynamo, horn, steering box, fan, timing gear, carburettor, air filter, gear control, steering wheel, cylinder, petrol tank, rear axle, back axle. The drive from the gear box is conveyed through a short shaft to the front universal joint of the propeller shaft. From the propeller shaft it is conveyed to the rear universal joint through a sliding splined type of joint. The bevel gear of the short shaft is driven by the rear universal joint. This bevel gear meshes with a larger bevel gear which drives the two rear axle shafts through a differential gear.

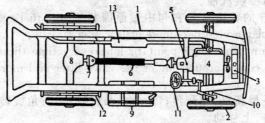

Figure1-1  Layout of a car
1-Frame; 2-Wheels; 3-Radiator; 4-Engine; 5-Clutch and gearbox; 6-Propeller shaft; 7-Universal joint; 8-Differential, Rear Axle; 9-Fuel tank; 10-Front axle; 11-Steering; 12-Road springs; 13-Exhaust/silencer

    The layout also consists of independent front-wheel springing with quarter-elliptic leaf springs, steering column bevel-gear control and hydraulic braking system.

    The wheels which are four in number are fitted below the car chassis to support the load of the vehicle and passengers as well as to run the car. They are fitted with hollow rubber tyres filled with air in rubber tubes under sufficient pressure necessary for carrying the load. The shocks caused by road irregularities are absorbed by them. By fitting springs between the wheels and the vehicle allowing the vertical movement of wheels in relation to vehicle, greater part of unevenness of road surfaces is taken care of.

    Front axle is used for steering front wheels carried on stub axles swivelling upon king pins at the axle extremities.

Steering arms and a track rod link the two stub axles together for swivelling them by a steering wheel about the king pins. The steering wheel linked to one of the stub axles by a shaft, a gear box and a suitable linkage is operated by the driver's hand wheel. Previously the axle-a onepiece beam was used to support the vehicle through springs. An arrangement known as independent front suspension has replaced the axle and spring arrangement. Under the control of springs, the wheels are free to rise and fall vertically independently of each other.

For fixing rear wheels, a tube like shaft enclosing driving shafts with suitable bearings for rotating the wheels is used. It is enlarged at the center for enclosing the final drive gears used for providing main speed reduction between the engine and the driving wheels. The change of direction of the drive from the fore and aft line of the propeller shaft to the transverse line of the axle shafts is also provided by this tube known as rear axle.

When going round a curve, the inner wheel has to travel a smaller distance in comparison to the outer wheel. But both the rear wheels would rotate at the same speed if they are connected by a shaft. This rotation of both the wheels would result in slipping of one or both of them on the road surface causing excessive tyre wear as well as severe twisting loads on the shaft. Moreover, the two wheels of the exactly similar diameter (which is not usually so) can only turn at the same speed without slip on the straight road. Tyres fitted on the opposite sides may be of different states of wear and even tyre of same nominal diameter made by different or same manufacturer may differ in actual dimensions or may not be exactly similar. Due to change of rolling radius (the distance from the wheel center to the ground) the effective size of the tyre may be altered by different inflation pressure also.

Each wheel is provided with its own separate halfshaft connected by a differential gear and meeting at about the center of the axle. The wheels are free to rotate at different speeds although they are provided with equal drive by the differential gear.

For preventing the transmission of shock from uneven road surfaces to the vehicle, springs are used to support the vehicle on the axle.

In order to allow for the vertical movements of the wheels relative to the frame as well as to allow the parts of the shaft to operate at different angle, another increasingly used arrangement is used. It consists of mounting the final-drive gears and the differential gear in a casing attached to the frame with independently sprung wheels attached to them by means of shafts through devices called universal joints.

Power unit consists of an internal combustion engine. It is usually mounted at the point end of the car. The clutch and the gear box are placed immediately behind it. The three components, engine, clutch and gear box are assembled into a single unit.

For connecting the output shaft of the gear box to the rear axle, a long shaft known as propeller shaft is used. This shaft is either enclosed in a tubular casing or kept exposed or opened with a universal joint fitted at each end for allowing the changes in the shaft alignment with the rise and fall of the rear axle due to road surface variations. Universal joints cannot be eliminated even if the final drive gears are fixed to the frame with the wheel springing independently. Neither the misalignment resulting from the flexing of the vehicle structure over bumpy road surfaces can be avoided nor the precise alignment of shaft can be ensured without them.

For controlling the movement of the vehicles or to stop them, efficient braking system is a necessity for a vehicle. Brakes attached to each of the four wheels are of two types. In the initial type, a pair of shoes carried on a stationary plate is expanded in contact with a rotating drum mounted on the wheels to arrest the motion of the drum. In the modern type of brakes, one or more pairs of pads are carried in a caliper attached to the axle or wheel supporting linkage. The sides of the disk mounted on the wheel are griped by these pads. By applying pressure on a pedal, the brakes are applied. A hand lever acting through a separate linkage and locked in the on position is used.

For operating the brake, either mechanical or hydraulic system is used. Mechanical system requiring gearing system for mechanical and hydraulic fluid for the hydraulic brakes are used.

## NEW WORDS

| | | |
|---|---|---|
| propeller | [prə'pelə] | n. 传动轴,推进器 |
| radiator | ['reidieitə] | n. 散热器,水箱 |
| dynamo | ['dainəməu] | n. 发电机,精力充沛的人 |
| spline | [splain] | vt. 开键槽子,用花键(或方栓)联接 |
| bevel | ['bevəl] | n.;adj. 斜截,斜面;倾斜的,斜角的 |
| stub | [stʌb] | n. 粗短立柱 |
| tyre | ['taiə] | n. 轮箍,轮胎,车胎 |
| swivel | ['swivl] | n. 链的转节,转环,旋轴,旋轴接头 |
| extremity | [iks'tremiti] | n. 末端,终极,尽头 |
| track | [træk] | n. 跨距,轮距 |
| fore | [fɔː] | adv.;adj. 在前面,在前头;先前的 |
| aft | [ɑːft] | n.;adv.;adj. 尾部;在后面,在后头;先后的 |
| transverse | ['trænzvəːs] | adj. 横向的,横断的,横截的 |
| dimension | [di'menʃən] | n. 尺寸,尺度,线度 |
| inflation | [in'fleiʃən] | n. 充气,膨胀 |
| casing | ['keisiŋ] | n. 汽车外胎,包装厢 |
| tubular | ['tjuːbjulə] | adj. 管的,管形的,(声音)像从管中发出的 |
| eliminate | [i'limineit] | vt. 排除,消除,消灭 |

## PHRASES AND EXPRESSIONS

| | |
|---|---|
| propeller shaft | 传动轴 |
| universal joint | 万向节,万向接头 |
| steering box | 转向器壳体,转向机 |
| timing gear | 正时齿轮 |
| air filter | 空气滤清器 |
| stearing wheel | 转向轮 |
| in relation to | 关于,至于,对…来说 |

fit … with　　　　　　在…安装…,对…提供设备,与…适应
fill … with　　　　　　充满,装满,盛满
attach to　　　　　　　与…联在一起,系在一起,安装在一起

## NOTES TO THE TEXT

1. The wheels which are four in number are fitted below the car chassis to support the load of the vehicle and passengers as well as to run the car .
两个车轮安装在车底架下面以支承车及乘客、并驱动车。
to support … 是不定式短语做目的状语；as well as 是并列连词,它后面的 to run the car 与前面的 to support 并列做目的状语。

2. They are fitted with hollow rubber tyres filled with air in rubber tubes under sufficient pressure necessary for carrying the load.
它们与橡胶轮胎相适应,橡胶轮胎中充满了由橡胶管在一定的有效压力下充入的空气,这个压力对承担负载是必要的。
fitted with 与…适应,是 fit 的被动语态做谓语；filled with 充满着,是过去分词短语做定语。

3. This rotation of both the wheels would result in slipping of one or both of them on the road surface causing excessive tyre wear as well as severe twisting loads on the shaft.
两个车轮的旋转会导致一个或多个车轮在路面上的滑动,导致额外的车轮磨损以及轴上严重的扭转负荷。
would 情态动词,会,可能；result in 导致,是句中的谓语；slipping 及 causing 是动名词做 result in 的宾语。

## EXERCISES

I . Answer the following questions according to the text：

1. What are the five basic mechanisms, or components of a automobile?
2. Why is a engine usually called internal-combustion engine?
3. What's the function of the fuel system?
4. By what are the engine valves opened?
5. When does an electric spark occurs at the cylinder spark

plug?

6. What are the cars consisted of?

7. How are the greater part of unevenoess of road surface is taken care of?

8. What's the function of rear axle?

9. Why the rear wheels are not connected by one shaft?

10. Why the universal joints is used in a car?

11. Why do the vehicles need efficient braking system?

II. Completing the sentences: The sentences below are incomplete. After each sentence there are four words or phrases, only one of which will correctly complete the sentence, selecting the proper word or phrase to complete it correctly:

1. A 6×4 tractor has ____.
   A. six axles and four drive axles
   B. six wheels and four axles
   C. six wheels and four driven wheels
   D. six axles and four driven wheels

2. ____ of the following would you most likely find on a class 8 truck.
   A. leaf springs
   B. twin countershafts in the transmission
   C. a 24-volt starter
   D. all of the above

3. All safety glasses should have ____.
   A. side protectors    B. safety glass
   C. steel rims         D. A and B only

4. Airtight containers are used to hold ____.
   A. oil rags      B. shop parts
   C. gaskets       D. solvent

5. ____ of the following is considered dangerous exhaust.
   A. water         B. carbon monoxide
   C. carbon dioxide   D. nitrogen

6. ____ of the following is a symptom of carbon monoxide poisoning:
   A. headaches and tiredness

B. nausea and ringing in the ears
C. fluttering heart
D. all of the above
7. ____ of sound can be damaging to the ears.
A. 90 to 100 decibels      B. 30 to 40 decibels
C. 10 to 20 decibels       D. 0 to 5 decibels
8. When working in the truck repair shop, it is important to ____.
A. put oil rags in the proper container
B. leave tools greasy for later clean up
C. let the shop foreman put tools away
D. let the service manager fix the vehicle

III. Choose a phrase from the list for each space in the passage below:

1. are classified as          6. are divided into
2. be provided with           7. are subdivided into
3. such as                    8. according to
4. aside from                 9. are equipped for
5. are classified

The automobile is a self-propelled transport vehicle. According to their application, automobiles ____ trucks, passenger, and special-purpose vehicles. Cargocarriers include trucks, truck tractors, trailers, pole trailers, and semitrailers. The trucks may ____ beds to transport different goods or with special-purpose bodies ____ dump bodies to transport loose and viscous cargo, tank bodies for liquids, refrigerator vans for perishables, etc. ____ a body type, trucks ____ according to their load-carrying capacity and cross-country capability.

The passenger vehicles ____ into cars seating from one to six men , and buses. The buses ____ city and intercity ones. Tourist buses make a separate group. ____ to their length buses are classified as minibuses (up to 5m), small (up to 7.5m), medium (up to 9m), large (up to 12m), and articulated (over 16.5m).

The special-purpose automobiles ____ performing particular tasks. Among them are fire and garbage trucks, ambulances, tower, water tank, repair trucks, etc.

Ⅳ. Translate the following sentences into Chinese:

1. The engine burns its fuel within the engine proper, as compared to a steam engine where the fuel is burned externally.

2. The fuel system takes a correctly proportioned mixture of gasoline and air to burn and develop the power needed to push the piston down the cylinder.

3. The ignition system furnishes a spark to each spark plug when its cylinder is full of the compressed air-fuel mixture.

4. The lubrication system provides a constant flow of filtered oil to all moving parts of the engine.

5. The coolant of the cooling system picks up the excess combustion heat as it is circulated through the block and heads by a centrifugal-type pump, delivered to the radiator where it is cooled, and then returned to the water pump for recirculation.

6. The drive line consists of mechanisms and units which transmit torque from the engine to the drive wheels and change torque and rpm in magnitude and direction.

7. The clutch is a friction device used to connect and disconnect a driving force from a driven member.

8. A transmission is a speed and power changing device installed at some point between the engine and driving wheels of the vehicle.

Ⅴ. Translate the following passage into Chinese:

Corrosive wear is attributed to the action of corrosive media (acids, alkalis, oxygen) on the part surface.

Fatigue wear is caused by multiple alternating loads. Most automobile parts are subject to several types of wear simultaneously.

The mating parts have definite clearances established during the design and manufacture of mechanisms and units. As the parts wear, the clearances increase, the parts reach the limit of size at which they continue to operate normally and then additional loads imposed by excessive wear disrupt normal functioning. The clearance grows progressively which may finally lead to breakage of the parts and ruining of the entire unit or mechanism. Besides, excessive wear of parts of the steering system, brakes, power line may cause a traffic accident.

Deviation of the technical condition of an automobile (trailer) or its units from the established norms is called defect.

Disabling of an automobile resulting in the interrupted haulage is called failure.

# Chapter 2  Engine System

## 2.1 Engine

Modern automotive engines are called internal combustion engines because fuel burns inside the engine. The engine converts the burning fuel's thermal energy to mechanical energy (Figure 2-1).

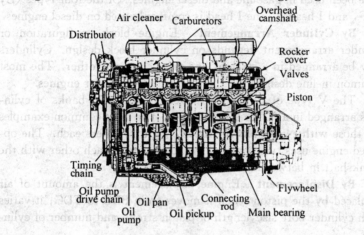

Figure 2-1  Cutaway of an in-line, six cylinder engine using an overhead camshaft

**By Cycles**  Two-stroke and four-stroke-cycle engines are being used.

**By Cooling Systems**  Liquid-cooled engines and air-cooled engines are being used. Liquid-cooled engines are the most common in the diesel industry.

**By Fuel System**  Gasoline, diesel and propane fuel systems are currently used in a wide variety of engines.

**By Ignition Method**  Gas engines use the spark (electrical) ignition system. The electrical ignition system causes a spark across the spark plug electrodes in the cylinder at the end of the compression stroke, which ignites the vaporized fuel and air mixture.

Diesel engines use the heat from compressing the air to ignite the fuel when it is injected into the cylinder at the end of the compression stroke. Since diesel engine compression ratios are much higher than gasoline engine compression ratios, sufficient heat is generated by compressing the air to ignite the fuel upon injection.

**By Valve Arrangement** Four types of valve arrangements have been used in gasoline and diesel engines. Of the four types (L, T, F, and I heads), the I head is commonly used on diesel engines.

**By Cylinder Arrangement** Engine block configuration or cylinder arrangement depends on cylinder block design. Cylinders may be arranged in a straight line one behind the other. The most common in-line designs are the four-and six-cylinder engines.

The V type of cylinder arrangement uses two banks of cylinders arranged in a 60° to 90° V design. The most common examples are those with two banks of three to eight cylinders each. The opposed engine uses two banks of cylinders oppsite each other with the crankshaft in between.

**By Displacement** Engine displacement is the amount of air displaced by the piston when it moves from BDC to TDC; it varies with cylinder bore size, length of piston stroke, and number of cylinders.

**By Engine Speed** Engines are classified as low, medium, high, and super high speed.

### 2.1.1 Reciprocating Engine

Except for the wankel rotary engine, all production automotive engines are the reciprocating, or piston, design. Reciprocating means "up and down" or "back and forth". It is this up-and-down action of a piston in a cylinder that gives the reciprocating engine its name. Almost all engines of this type are built upon a cylinder block, or engine block. The block is an iron or aluminum casting that contains the engine cylinders. The top of the block is covered with the cylinder head, which forms the combustion chambers. The bottom of the block is covered with an oil pan, or oil sump. A major exception to this type of engine construction is the air-cooled Volkwagen engine. It is representative of the horizontally opposed air-cooled engines used by Porsche, Chevrolet (Corvair), and some other automobile manufacturers in years past.

Power is produced by the inline motion of a piston in a cylinder. However, this linear motion must be changed to rotating motion to turn the wheels of a car or truck. The piston is attached to the top of a connecting rod by a pin, called a piston pin or wristpin (Figure 2-2). The bottom of the connecting rod is attached to the crankshaft. The connecting rod transmits the up-and-down motion of the piston to the crankshaft, which changes it to rotating motion. The connecting rod is mounted on the crankshaft with large bearings called rod bearings. Similar bearings, called main bearings, are used to mount the crankshaft in the block (Figure 2-2).

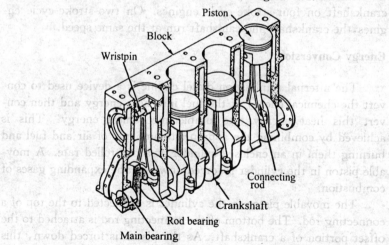

Figure 2-2  The crankshaft changes the reciprocation motion pistons rotating motion

The crankshaft changes the reciprocating motion of the pistons to rotating motion.

The combustible mixture of gasoline and air enters the cylinders through valves. Automotive engines use poppet valves. The valves can be in the cylinder head or in the block. The opening and closing of the valves is controlled by a camshaft. Lobes on the camshaft push the valves open as the camshaft rotates. A spring closes each valve when the lobe is not holding it open. The most common arrangements of engine cylinders and valves are discussed later. The basic single-cylinder engine consists of a cylinder (engine block), a movable piston inside this cylinder, a connecting rod attached at the top end to the piston and at the bottom to the offset portion of a crankshaft, a camshaft to operate the two valves (intake and exhaust), and a cylinder head. A flywheel is attached to one end of the crankshaft. The other end of the crankshaft has a gear to drive the camshaft gear. The camshaft gear is twice as large as the crankshaft gear. This drives the camshaft at half the speed of the crankshaft on four-stroke-cycle engines. On two-stroke-cycle engines, the crankshaft and camshaft run at the same speed.

**Energy Conversion**

The internal combustion diesel engine is a device used to convert the chemical energy of the fuel into heat energy and then convert this heat energy into usable mechanical energy. This is achieved by combining the appropriate amounts of air and fuel and burning them in an enclosed cylinder at a controlled rate. A movable piston in the cylinder is forced down by the expanding gases of combustion.

The movable piston in the cylinder is connected to the top of a connecting rod. The bottom of the connecting rod is attached to the offset portion of a crankshaft. As the piston is forced down, this force is transferred to the crankshaft, causing the crankshaft to rotate. The reciprocating (back and forth or up and down) movement of the piston is converted to rotary (turning) motion of the crankshaft, which supplies the power to drive the vehicle.

In general an average air-fuel ratio for good combustion is about 15 parts of air to 1 part of fuel by weight. However, the diesel engine always takes in a full charge of air (since there is no throttle plate in most systems), but only a small part of this air is used at low or idle engine speeds. Air consists of about 20 percent oxygen while the remaining 80 percent is mostly nitrogen. This means that, for every gallon of fuel burned, the oxygen in 9,000 to 10,000 gallons of air is required.

**Four-Stroke Cycle**

Gasoline by itself will not burn, it must be mixed with oxygen (air). This burning is called combustion and is a way of releasing the energy stored in the air-fuel mixture. To do any useful work in an engine, the air-fuel mixture must be compressed and burned in a sealed chamber. Here the combustion energy can work on the movable piston to produce mechanical energy. The combustion chamber must be sealed as tightly as possible for efficient engine operation. Any leakage from the combustion chamber allows part of the combustion energy to dissipate without adding to the mechanical energy developed by the piston movement.

The 4-stroke engine is also called the Otto cycle engine, in honor of the German engineer, Dr. Nikolaus Otto, who first applied the principle in 1876. In the 4-stroke engine, four strokes of the piston in the cylinder are required to complete one full operating cycle: two strokes up and two strokes down. Each stroke is named after the action it performs-intake, compression, power, and exhaust:

1. **Intake Stroke**   As the piston moves down, the vaporized mixture of fuel and air enters the cylinder past the open intake valve.

2. **Compression Stroke**   The piston returns up, the intake valve closes, the mixture is compressed within the combustion chamber, and ignited by a spark.

3. **Power Stroke**   The expanding gases of combustion force the piston down in the cylinder. The exhaust valve opens near the bot-

tom of the stroke.

4. **Exhaust Stroke** The piston moves back up with the exhaust valve open, and the burned gases are pushed out to prepare for the next intake stroke. The intake valve usually opens just before the top of the exhaust stroke.

This 4-stroke cycle is continuously repeated in every cylinder as long as the engine remains running.

**Two-Stroke-Cycle**

The two-stroke-cycle diesel engine completes all four events (intake, compression, power, and exhaust) in one revolution of the crankshaft or two strokes of the piston.

A series of ports or openings is arranged around the cylinder in such a position that the ports are open when the piston is at the bottom of its stroke. A blower forces air into the cylinder through the open ports, expelling all remaining exhaust gases past the open exhaust valves and filling the cylinder with air. This is called scavenging.

As the piston moves up, the exhaust valves close and the piston covers the ports. The air trapped above the piston is compressed since the exhaust valve is closed. Just before the piston reaches top dead center, the required amount of fuel is injected into the cylinder. The heat generated by compressing the air ignites the fuel almost immediately. Combustion continues until the fuel injected has been burned. The pressure resulting from combustion forces the piston downward on the power stroke. When the piston is approximately halfway down, the exhaust valves are opened, allowing the exhaust gases to escape. Further downward movement uncovers the inlet ports, causing fresh air to enter the cylinder and expel the exhaust gases. The entire procedure is then repeated, as the engine continues to run.

**Comparison of Two-Cycle and Four-Cycle Engines**

It could be assumed that a two-cycle engine with the same

number of cylinders, the same displacement, compression ratio, and speed as a four-cycle engine would have twice the power since it has twice as many power strokes. However, this is not the case, since both the power and compression strokes are shortened to allow scavenging to take place. The two-cycle engine also requires a blower, which takes engine power to drive.

About 160 degrees out of each 360 degrees of crankshaft rotation are required for exhaust gas expulsion and fresh air intake (scavenging) in a two-cycle engine. About 415 degrees of each 720 degrees of crankshaft rotation in a four-cycle engine are required for intake and exhaust. These figures indicate that about 44.5% of crank rotation is used for the power producing events in the two-cycle engine, while about 59% of crank rotation is used for these purposes in the four-cycle engine. Friction losses are consequently greater in the four-cycle engine. Heat losses, however, are greater in the two-cycle engine through both the exhaust and the cooling systems. In spite of these differences, both engine types enjoy prominent use worldwide.

## Engine Displacement and Compression Ratio

Two frequently used engine specifications are engine displacement and compression ratio. Displacement and compression ratio are related to each other, as we will learn in the following paragraphs.

## Engine Displacement

Commonly used to indicate engine size, this specification is really a measurement of cylinder volume. The number of cylinders is a factor in determining displacement, but the arrangement of the cylinders or valves is not. Engine displacement is calculated by multiplying the number of cylinders in the engine by the piston displacement of one cylinder. The total engine displacement is the volume displaced by all the pistons.

The displacement of one cylinder is the space through which the piston's top surface moves as it travels from the bottom of its stroke (bottom dead center) to the top of its stroke (top dead center). It is the volume displaced by the cylinder by one piston stroke. Piston displacement can be calculated as follows:

1. Divide the bore (cylinder diameter) by two. This gives you the radius of the bore.
2. Square the radius (multiply it by itself).
3. Multiply the square of the radius by 3.1416 (pi or $\pi$) to find the area of the cylinder cross section.
4. Multiply the area of the cylinder cross section by the length of the stroke.

You now know the piston displacement for one cylinder. Multiply this by the number of cylinders to determine the total engine displacement. The formula for the complete procedure reads:

$R^2 \times \pi \times stroke \times No.$ of cylinders = displacement

**Compression Ratio**

This specification compares the total cylinder volume to the volume of only the combustion chamber (Figure 2-3). Total cylinder volume may seem to be the same as piston displacement, but it is

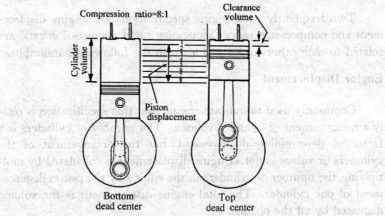

Figure 2-3 Compression ratio is the ratio of the total cylinder volume to the clearance volume

not. Total cylinder volume is the piston displacement plus the combustion chamber volume. The combustion chamber volume with the piston at top dead center is often called the clearance volume.

Compression ratio is the total volume of a cylinder divided by its clearance volume. If the clearance volume is one-eighth of the total cylinder volume, the compression ratio is 8 (8 to 1). The formula is as follows: $\dfrac{\text{Total volume}}{\text{Clearance volume}}=$ Compression ratio.

In theory, the higher the compression ratio, the greater the efficiency of the engine, and the more power an engine will develop from a given quantity of fuel. The reason for this is that combustion takes place faster because the fuel molecules are more tightly packed and the flame of combustion travels more rapidly.

But there are practical limits to how high a compression ratio can be. Because of the unavailability of high octane fuel, most gasolineburning engines are restricted to a compression ratio no greater than 11.5 to 1. Ratios this high, however, create high combustion chamber temperatures. This in turn creates oxides of nitrogen ($NO_x$), a primary air pollutant. In the early 1970s, compression ratios were lowered to around 8 to permit the use of lower octane, low-lead or unleaded fuel, and to reduce $NO_x$ formation. Advances in electronic engine controls in the 1980s have allowed engineers to raise compression ratios to the 9 and 10 to 1 range for optimum performance and economy.

## NEW WORDS

| | | |
|---|---|---|
| automotive | [ˈɔːtəməutiv] | adj. 汽车的,自动推进的,机动车的 |
| convert | [kənˈvəːt] | vt. 转变,转换,变化,转化 |
| thermal | [ˈθəːməl] | adj.;n. 热的,热量的,温泉的;上升暖气流 |
| piston | [ˈpistən] | n. 活塞,(铜管乐器的)直升式活塞 |
| cylinder | [ˈsilində] | n. 气缸,圆筒,圆柱体,量筒 |
| representative | [ˌrepriˈzentətiv] | adj.;n. 代表性的,表现的;代表,典型 |

| | | |
|---|---|---|
| rotate | [rəu'teit] | vi. 转动,旋转,循环 |
| camshaft | ['kæmʃɑːft] | n. 凸轮轴 |
| offset | ['ɔːfset] | vt. 抵销,弥补,偏置 |
| throttle | ['θrɔtl] | n. 节流阀,风门,油门,喉门 |
| nitrogen | ['naitrədʒən] | n. 氮,氮气 |
| gallon | ['gælən] | n. 加仑 |
| leakage | [liːkidʒ] | n. 渗漏,泄漏,漏出物,漏出量 |
| dissipate | ['disipeit] | vt. 消除,消耗,浪费 |
| principle | ['prinsəpl] | n. 原理,原则,法规 |
| scavenge | ['skævindʒiŋ] | vt. ;vi. 扫气,清除;清除污物 |
| chamber | ['tʃeimbə] | n. 房间寝室,腔,室 |
| prominent | [prɔminənt] | adj. 突起的,突出的,杰出的 |
| specification | [spesifi'keiʃən] | n. 规格,规范,说明书 |
| diameter | ['daiæmitə] | n. 直径,对径,放大镜,放大倍数 |
| multiply | ['mʌltiplai] | v. 增加,增多,增值,使…相乘 |
| formula | ['fɔːmjulə] | n. 公式,程式,处方,惯用语句 |
| restrict | [ri'strikt] | vt. 限制,限定,约定 |
| optimum | ['ɔptiməm] | n. 最佳条件,最适度,良性 |
| molecule | ['mɔlikjuːl] | n. 分子,微小颗粒 |

## PHRASES AND EXPRESSIONS

| | |
|---|---|
| convert into … | 把…转化成 |
| internal combustion engine | 内燃机 |
| reciprocating engine | 往复式发动机 |
| the wankel rotary engine | 旋转式发动机 |
| the combustion chamber | 燃烧室 |
| four-stroke-cycle | 四冲程 |
| poppet valve | 气门(提升阀) |
| Otto cycle engine | 奥托发动机 |
| in one revolution of | 在…的一个变化中 |
| intake stroke | 进气冲程 |
| intake valve | 进气门 |
| compression ratio | 压缩比 |
| heat losses | 热量损失 |

engine displacement　　　　　　发动机排量
exhaust valve　　　　　　　　　排气门
bottom dead center　　　　　　下止点
top dead center　　　　　　　　上止点

## NOTES TO THE TEXT

1. The connecting rod transmits the up-and-down motion of the piston to the crankshaft, which changes it to rotating motion.

连杆把活塞的上下运动传递给曲轴,曲轴把直线运动转变成旋转运动。

which changes it to rotating motion 为非限制定语从句,修饰 crankshaft; change … to … ,把…变成,在从句中做谓语; transmit … to … 把…传到,把…送到做主句的谓语。

2. However, the diesel engine always takes in a full charge of air (since there is no throttle plate in most systems), but only a small part of this air is used at low or idle engine speeds.

然而,柴油机总是充满大量的空气(因为绝大多数柴油机没有节气门),只是在低速或急速时才需要少量空气。

take in a full charge of 完全控制;由 but only 连接两个并列分句,构成整个句子,前一分句的主语是 the diesel engine;后一分句采用被动语态,主语是 a small part of this air; at low … 介词短语做状语。

3. It could be assumed that a two-cycle engine with the same number of cylinders, the same displacement, compression ratio, and speed as a foure-cycle engine would have twice the power since it has twice as many power strokes.

假设二冲程发动机与四冲程发动机具有相同的缸数,排量,压缩比和速度,则前者与后者相比具有两倍的作功次数,同样就应具有两倍的功率。

It could be assumed that … 是形式主词句型,that… 引导主语从句,在此从句中 a two-cycle engine, the same displacement, compression ratio, speed 做并列主语; would have twice 做谓语, since 引导原因状语从句。

## 2.1.2 Engine Blocks

The block (Figure 2-4) serves as a rigid metal foundation for all parts of an engine. It contains the cylinders and supports the crankshaft and camshaft. In older engines, the valve seats, ports, and guides are built into the block. Accessory units and clutch housing are bolted to it. Note that the crankcase is formed with the block.

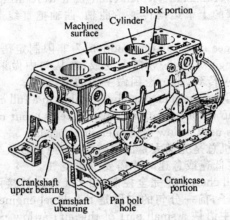

Figure 2-4   Typical block construction for a four cylinder valve-in-head engine

Blocks are made of either cast iron or aluminum. In some of the small, one cylinder engines, the material is die cast metal. Die cast metal is a relatively light, soft metal especially suited to the die casting process.

Blocks are commonly formed in two ways. One method is to pour molten cast iron, or aluminum, into a mold made of sand. A core is placed within the mold to form the cavities and passageways within the block. After the casting has cooled, it is removed from the mold, and the sand core is dissolved and washed out.

The second method is to use a mold of metal and force molten aluminum, or die-cast metal, into the mold under pressure. The pressure casting process has several advantages. It produces a block free of air bubbles(called voids), gives sharp corners, and a high degree of accuracy can be maintained. This reduces machining operations to a minimum. The same mold can be used over and over.

All parts of the aluminum or die cast block that are subjected to wear will have metal inserts either pressed in place or actually cast into the block.

The lighter the block (providing it has sufficient strength) the better. A more modern process, called precision thin wall casting, controls core size and placement much more accurately than the older casting process. This permits casting the blockolder casting process. This permits casting the block walls much thinner, thereby effectively reducing the weight. Since wall thicknesses are more uniform, block distortion during service is less severe.

The cylinder block is the main supporting structure to which all other engine parts are directly or indirectly attached. Two basic types of block construction are used: the en-bloc and the fabricated, welded steel types.

The block is formed by pouring the molten metal into a mold with a sand-based core. When the metal has cooled and hardened, the mold and sand core are removed. Removing the sand core leaves openings for cylinders, water jackets, crankcase, and bearing bores. Rough holes in the side of the block through which the sand core was supported are machined and closed with soft metal plugs. These core hole plugs are also known as expansion plugs or frost plugs. They are either of the dished type or the cup type.

Oil galleries are either cast in the block or drilled and plugged during the machining process.

Oil galleries are required to provide lubrication for bearings and cam followers as well as other engine parts. Two-cycle engines have air passages, called air boxes, in the block to provide air for induction.

Block mating surfaces are carefully machined to provide good sealing surfaces for attaching cylinder heads, gear covers, oil pans, and flywheel housings. Main bearing caps are installed and align bored, as are the camshaft bearing bores. This ensures that the shafts can rotate freely without any binding.

Particular attention is paid to such items as the block deck surface, cylinder liner counterbores, and crankshaft centerline to deck surface dimensions. The cylinder centerline must also be at exactly 90 degrees to the crankshaft centerline to ensure that pistons can move freely without creating side stresses on the pistons, rods, and cylinders.

Cam follower bores are machined at right angles to the camshaft bearing bores. Separate cam follower housings bolted to the block are used in many engines. Holes are drilled and threaded to allow parts to be attached.

**Cylinder Liners**

Cylinder liners (Figure 2-5) are used to permit engine rebuilding without the expense of cylinder block replacement. If the cylinder block is in good condition, the cylinders can be restored to like-new condition by replacing the cylinder liners. Cylinder liners are also known as cylinder sleeves.

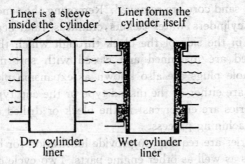

Figure 2-5  Cylinder liner types

Several different types of cylinder liners are used in diesel engines. These include the dry, wet, water-jacketed, and ported types. Some small diesel engine designs do not use cylinder liners. In these cases cylinder blocks are reconditioned by reboring cylinders to oversize and installing new oversize pistons, or by replacing the block.

**Dry Cylinder Liners**

The dry cylinder liner does not come in contact with the engine coolant. Dry liners are relatively thin walled steel and are supported full-length by the linerbore of the cylinder block. Some designs are a press fit in the cylinder block, while others are a looser slide in fit. Press fit liners are usually replaced when worn with the loose fit type. This requires resizing the bores in the block to a slightly larger diameter. All cylinder liners in the block must be of the same type and fit. Dry liners usually have a flanged top that fits into the counterbore in the block deck. The liners are held in place tightly by the cylinder head and are sealed at that point by a gasket or sealing ring.

**Wet Cylinder Liners**

In this design the liner forms part of the water jacket. The liner is of thick wall design to withstand all combustion pressures and is usually of cast iron alloy construction. Liner-to-block seals are provided at both top and bottom to prevent coolant leakage into the combustion chamber and crankcase. Wet liners also have a flanged top that fits into the couterbore in the block deck. Wet liners are held in place by the cylinder head and are sealed at the top by a gasket or seal ring similar to the dry liner.

**Water-Jacketed Cylinder Liners**

This type of liner is used in many of the larger diesel engines with fabricated engine frames or blocks. They are of double-wall construction with space between for coolant circulation. Coolant enters the liner jacket at one end and exits at the other.

Jacketed liners may be cast integrally or they may be a two-piece design in which the liner is installed in a separate water jacket. Seals are required at the top and bottom. Each jacket is provided with a coolant drain plug at the bottom.

Some cylinder liners are designed with a counterbore at the top inside circumference of the liner just above piston ring travel. This prevents the formation of a cylinder ridge as the liner wears due to piston ring friction. The counterbore is slightly larger in diameter than the rest of the liner.

**Ported Cylinder Liners**

Two-cycle diesel engines are equipped with ported cylinder liners. Ports are required to provide the cylinder with air for scavenging and combustion. These ports are precisely designed and positioned to provide the desired port timing and air flow characteristics. Seals are required above and below the ported area to seal the air passages from engine coolant and lubricant.

**Cylinder Liner Material**

Cylinder liner materials must be able to withstand the extreme heat and pressures developed by the engine. At the same time friction and wear must be kept at a minimum. Fine-grained cast iron or steel are commonly used. The wear surface of many liners is plated with finely porous chrome or treated chemically to improve wear resistance and lubrication.

**Cylinder Heads**

The cylinder head forms the top or lid for the engine cylinders. It contains thes that open and close the intake and exhaust ports that lead from the combustion chamber to the exhaust manifold and from the intake manifold to the combustion chamber. It also contains the valve guides that keep the valves in position, the valve seats, water passages, provision for mounting fuel injectors, threaded holes for attaching valve operating parts, and other accessories as well as a number of non-threaded holes for attaching the cylinder head to the block. Machined surfaces allow for positive sealing of combustion chambers and other openings with the proper gaskets in between.

Some in-line diesel engines use a single-cylinder head assembly that serves all cylinders, usually up to six. A cylinder head for each pair of cylinders is also used on some engines. Large engines normally use a separate cylinder head for each cylinder.

Cylinder heads are usually of cast iron alloy construction. The casting process is similar to that used for casting engine blocks. Internal passages are created by a sand core during casting, after which the sand is removed. Other openings and surfaces are machined. Particular attention is given to provide adequate coolant flow over the exhaust seat areas and may include coolant nozzles that direct coolant at the hottest areas.

Cylinder head problems include cracking that causes fluid or pressure leaks either internally or externally, rust and scale buildup in the water jackets resulting in poor heat conduction, warpage, valve guide and bridge guide wear, and valve seat wear or damage.

A stamped steel, cast iron, or aluminum cylinder head cover and gasket are used to cover the valve and injector operating parts and to prevent oil leakage and entry of dirt.

**Cylinder Head Gaskets**

Cylinder head gaskets are designed to provide a positive seal between the head and engine block. One of the primary jobs of the gasket is to prevent any escape of combustion pressures from the cylinders. Very high pressures occur in the cylinder and no leakage must be allowed. Other jobs include sealing and metering coolant flow, sealing lubrication passages, and the like.

Materials used in head gaskets include steel, copper, asbestos, fiber, synthetic rubber, and silicone. Gasket materials must be compatible with the fluids and gases they are required to seal and must not deteriorate from contact with them. Gaskets are also subject to a wide range of temperature and pressure extremes, as well as to metal expansion and contraction. In spite of all these hazardous conditions, properly installed gaskets last a very long time.

## NEW WORDS

| | | |
|---|---|---|
| rigid | ['ridʒid] | adj. 刚硬的,硬式的, |
| accessory | [æk'sesəri] | n. ;adj. 附件,附属品;附属的,附加的 |
| crankcase | ['kræŋkeis] | n. 曲轴箱 |
| mold | [məuld] | n. ;vt. 模型,铸造;用模子做,浇铸 |
| cavity | ['kæviti] | n. 坑,洼,腔 |
| passageway | ['pæsidʒwei] | n. 通道,走廊 |
| bubble | ['bʌbl] | n. ;v. 气泡,水泡;吹泡,冒泡 |
| void | [vɔid] | n. ;adj. 空的,没有的;空处,空虚 |
| accuracy | ['ækjurəsi] | n. 准确,精确,准确度,(机)精度 |
| distortion | [dis'tɔːʃən] | n. 变形,畸变,曲解,歪曲 |
| fabricate | ['fæbrikeit] | vt. 配制,捏造,伪造 |
| fly wheel | ['flaihwiːl] | n. 飞轮 |
| sleeve | [sliːv] | n. ;vt. (机)套,筒;给…装套筒 |
| coolant | ['kuːlənt] | n. 冷却剂 |
| gasket | ['gæskit] | n. 垫密片,衬垫圈 |
| alloy | ['ælɔi] | n. ;vt. ;vi. 合金;合铸;熔合 |
| integrally | [ˌintigrəli] | adv. 总体的,完整地 |
| ridge | [ridʒ] | n. ;v. 脊,隆起部;装脊,起皱 |
| port | [pɔːt] | n. 口,气门,水门 |
| lubricant | [ˌluːbrikənt] | n. 润滑剂,润滑料 |
| porous | ['pɔːrəs] | adj. 多孔的,疏松的,有孔的,能渗漏的 |
| nozzle | ['nɔzl] | n. 喷油嘴,管嘴,喷嘴 |
| crack | [kræk] | v. 裂开,爆裂,断裂,使…开缝 |
| compatible | [kəm'pætəbl] | adj. 相容的,可共存的,谐和的 |

## PHRASES AND EXPRESSIONS

cast iron      铸铁

| | |
|---|---|
| over and over | 反复,一遍遍地 |
| crankshaft center line | 曲轴轴线 |
| at right angles | 在适当角度 |
| dry cylinder liner | 干式气缸衬套 |
| in contact with | 与…接触 |
| wet cylinder liner | 湿式气缸衬套 |
| water jacket | 水套 |
| cast iron alloy construction | 铸铁合金结构 |
| seal ring | 密封环 |
| in spite of | 尽管,不管,不顾 |
| as well as | 至于,关于 |
| a stamped steel | 特种钢,模锻钢 |
| total cylinder volume | 总排量 |
| clearance volume | 余隙容积 |
| cylinder water | 气缸壁 |

## NOTES TO THE TEXT

1. The block is formed by pouring the molten metal into a mold with a sand-based core.
　　机体的形成是将金属浇注到有砂芯的模型中。
　　pouring… into… 浇注,灌;the block 做主语,is formed 被动语态做谓语,by pouring… 是介词短语做方式状语。

2. The dry cylinder liner does not come in contact with the engine coolant.
　　干式缸套不直接与发动机的冷却液接触。
　　come in contact with … 与…有关,做此句中的谓语。

3. Gasket are also subject to a wide range of temperature and pressure extremes, as well as to metal expansion and contraction.
　　缸垫必须能适应一定范围的高温高压,以及金属的膨胀和收缩。
　　as well as … 不但…而且…,是并列连词,连接二个并列句,be subject to 经受,易受…,在二个句中分别做谓语。

# EXERCISES

Ⅰ. Answer the following questions according to the text:

1. Do you list the strokes in a four-stroke cycle engine in their proper order?

2. Do you list the strokes needed in the two-stroke cycle engine? Do you explain the sequence of events during these strokes?

3. What are the basic differences between four-stroke cycle and two-stroke cycle engines?

4. What is meant by bore and stroke?

5. How is compression ratio figured?

6. What are cylinder sleeves?

7. What must be done to gasoline to speed up the burning rate?

Ⅱ. Completing the sentences: The sentences below are incomplete. After each sentence there are four words or phrases, only one of which will correctly complete the sentence, selecting the proper word or phrase to complete it correctly:

1. The four-stroke cycle operates in which order ____.

A. intake, exhaust, power, compression

B. intake, power, exhaust, compression

C. compression, power, intake, exhaust

D. intake, compression, power, exhaust

2. Compression ratio is ____.

A. piston displacement plus clearance volume

B. total volume times number of cylinders

C. total volume divided by clearance volume

D. stroke divided by bore

3. In carburetor engines, the air-fuel mixture is ____ by a spark.

A. developed      B. produced

C. ignited      D. blown out

4. Engines can be divided into ____ by the number of piston strokes in one complete cycle.

A. two groups      B. three kinds

C. four classes    D. six
   5. According to the method of ignition of the airfuel mixture, engines are divided into ____.
   A. gas engine and steam engine
   B. gasoline engine and dieseel engine
   C. external combustion engine and compression ignition en-gine
   D. internal combustion engine and diesel engine
   6. In the standard engine, each cylinder has ____.
   A. one valve    B. two valves
   C. three valves    D. four valves
   7. Because of its fuel injection system, a diesel engine ____.
   A. needs no carburetor or distributor
   B. has a constant fuel mixture
   C. is inefficient
   D. operates only in a two-stroke configuration

Ⅲ. Choose the words or a phrase from the list for each space in the passage below:
   1. requires
   2. due to
   3. to wear out
   4. affecting
   5. are also subject to
   6. wear out
   7. as soon as
   8. Furthermore
   9. wear on
   10. such as

   Satisfactory performance of the modern powerplant ____ the maintenance of the engine, its accessories, and subsystems to keep them in a condition equivalent to new. But ____ a vehicle leaves the dealer's showroom floor and the owner places it into service, the vehicle begins ____. As a rule, this process continues for the life of a properly maintained automobile for about 150,000 miles.
   Some of the wear on the key components ____ engine performance is very predictable. For instance, friction causes ____ the engine's bearings, cylinder walls, pistons, and rings. In the standard ignition system, spark plugs and breaker points in the distributor deteriorate with use. ____, some of the distributor's mechanical parts ____ the distributor shaft, bearings, driving gear, breakerplate bearings, and internal electrical connections may ____ or become defec-

tive. Both the high-and low-ten-sion wirings ____ deterioration due to oxidation, heat, oil deposits, and age; their terminals can become loose or corroded. In the fuel system, the fuel pump may require replacement ____ a ruptured diaphragm. Also the carburetor may malfunction because of deposits in its circuits due to dirty fuel or air filters.

Ⅳ. Translate the following sentences into Chinese:

1. From the above it will be realised that the fundamental difference between petrol and diesel engines is that in the petrol engine the source of heat for igniting the charge, namely, an electric spark, is generated outside the engine, and is taken, as it were, into the waiting charge at the required instant.

2. Anyone familiar with the working of the ordinary petrol engine is aware that the motive power is produced by igniting above the piston in each cylinder a mixture of petrol vapour and air, the resultant combustion of which causes an expansion of gases exerting pressure on the top of the piston.

3. In crosshead-type engines, the piston fastens to a vertical piston rod whose lower end is attached to a sliding member called a "crosshead", which slides up and down in guides.

4. Incidentally, the ratio of the total volume of the cylinder above the piston when it is in its lowest position to that of the combustion or clearance space when it is at its highest position is known as the compression ratio, and in modern commercial vehicle petrol engines varies from about 6:1 to 8:1.

5. It is true, of course, that the ratio of surface to volume is greater in the case of the compressed charge, but as the total surface is less than it would be with combustion carried out in a large portion of the cylinder volume, the resulting opportunities for heat transmission are less.

6. The casting for the engine block is normally rather intricate, since it contains not only the engine cylinders, but the water jackets that surround them.

Ⅴ. Translate the following passage into Chinese:

Diesel engines differ from gasoline-burning engines in other ways. Instead of a carburetor to mix the fuel with air, a diesel uses a precision injection pump and individual fuel injectors. The pump delivers fuel to the injectors at a high pressure and at timed intervals. Each injector measures the fuel exactly, spraying it into the combustion chamber at the precise moment required for efficient combustion. The injection pump and injector system thus perform the fuel delivery job of the carburetor and the ignition timing job of the distributor in a gasoline engine.

The air-fuel mixture of a gasoline engine remains nearly constant-changing only within a narrow range-regardless of engine load or speed. But in a diesel engine, air remains constant and the amount of fuel injected is varied to control power and speed. The air-fuel mixture of a diesel can vary from as little as 85:1 at idle, to as rich as 20:1 at full load. This higher air-fuel ratio and the increased compression pressures make the diesel more efficient in terms of fuel consumption than a gasoline engine.

Like gasoline engines, diesel engines are built in both 2-stroke and 4-stroke versions. The most common 2-stroke diesels are the truck and industrial engines made by the Detroit Diesel Allison Division of General Motors. In these engines, air intake is through ports in the cylinder walls, aided by supercharging. Exhaust is through valves in the head. Crankcase fuel induction cannot be used in a 2-stroke diesel.

### 2.1.3 Crankshaft

The crankshaft is one of the major moving parts of the engine. It is the only connection between the power-producing parts of the engine and the drive train. It is designed to transmit all the power the engine is able to produce and must be able to do so trouble free for many thousands of hours of operation (Figure 2-6).

As the name implies, the crankshaft consists of a series of cranks offset from the crankshaft centerline. Inline engine crankshafts usually have one crank for each cylinder, while V-type engines normally have one crank for each pair of cylinders. The crankshaft converts the reciprocating motion of the pistons and connecting rods to rotary motion of the crankshaft.

Modern diesel engine crankshafts are usually constructed of one-piece forged alloy steel. Forged crankshafts are much stronger than the cast steel crankshafts usually used in automobile engines. The forging method forms the crankshaft in a process where very high pressure is applied to the metal to create the desired shape and stress direction. Some large engines use a crankshaft built up from two forgings by bolting them together at the two flanged ends. Bearing surfaces or even the entire crankshaft are induction hardened to reduce the wear rate.

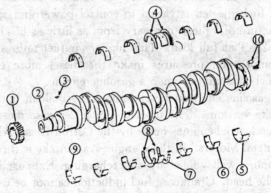

1. Crankshaft gear
2. Crankshaft
3. Woodruff key
4. Upper thrust flanges
5. Lower rear main bearing shell
6. Lower intermediate main bearing shell
7. Lower center main bearing shell
8. Lower thrust flanges
9. Lower front main bearing shell

Figure 2-6   Crankshaft and main bearings

The major portion of the crankshaft consists of the main and connecting rod journals. Connecting rod journals are also known as crank pins. The rod journals are connected to the main journals by two webs also called cheeks or arms. The crank pin and its two connecting arms are known as a crank throw.

The entire crankshaft is supported in the cylinder block by means of friction bearings at each of the main bearing journals. In some large engines the crank pins and main journals are hollow to reduce weight. Drilled lubrication passages connect the main and rod journals. These passages are usually chamfered at the journal surface to aid in oil distribution and prevent bearing damage from sharp edges. Endwise movement of the crankshaft is controlled by a flanged main bearing or by thrust washer-type bearing inserts that bear against machined surfaces on the crankshaft at one of the main bearing journals. Machined surfaces are also provided for oil seals to prevent oil leakage past the ends of the crankshaft.

Many crankshafts are equipped with counter-weights designed to offset the weight of the crank pin and connecting rod during rotation. Counter-weights may be an integral part of the crankshaft or they may be attached to it by means of capscrews.

A machined section at one end of the shaft provides the means for mounting accessory drive gears, a vibration damper, and at the other end a flywheel or torque converter mounted to the crankshaft flange. Keyways provide the means for maintaining a positive drive connection to the gears, vibration damper, and pulley. The crankshaft may also have a threaded hole at the end for a retaining bolt.

Smooth engine operation depends to a large extent on evenly spaced power impulses being transmitted to the crankshaft. Uniform crankshaft rotation can result only if power impulses are evenly spaced at alternating ends of the shaft as much as possible. The precise positioning of the crank throws is designed to achieve these results. In some cases, however, successive firing of cylinders cannot be avoided, especially in 2-, 3- and 4-cylinder engines.

On inline engine design, the crank throws are spaced radially an equal number of degrees apart. A six-cylinder, four-cycle, in-line engine has the crank throws spaced exactly 120 degrees apart. This results from dividing 720 degrees by 6, the number of cylinders. This means that cylinders are paired with respect to their radial position. In a firing order of 1-5-3-6-2-4, for example, the pairs are 1 and 6, 2 and 5, 3 and 4. When pistons 1 and 6 are at TDC and number 1 is beginning the power stroke, then number 6 is beginning the intake stroke. In other words, each pair of cylinders is 360 degrees apart in the four-stroke cycle of events.

In V-type engine design the concept is not quite as simple, since the angle formed between the cylinder banks must be considered. This is so since cylinders fire in opposite banks. When angles used do not divide evenly into 720 degrees, radial positioning of crank throws must be staggered to achieve even cylinder firing. In the 60 degree V6 design crank throws can be evenly spaced, since 60 divides evenly into 720 degrees. In the 65 degree V6 design this is not the case, since 65 does not divides evenly into 720. Three of the crank pins must be offset 5 degrees from the other three to provide even firing.

The number and arrangement of crank throws on a crankshaft depends on engine design factors such as the operating cycle (two-or four-stroke), cylinder arrangement (in line, V, or opposed), the angle formed between banks of cylinders on V engines, and the number of cylinders.

## NEW WORDS

| | | |
|---|---|---|
| crankshaft | [kræŋk'ʃa:ft] | n. 曲轴 |
| transmit | [trænz'mit] | vt. 传播,传达,播送 |
| offset | ['ɔ(:)fset] | n. ;v. 分支,偏置;抵销,补偿 |
| reciprocate | [ri'siprəkeit] | vt. ;vi. 使(机件)往复移动;互换,报答 |
| forge | [fɔ:dʒ] | n. ;v. 锻工车间;锻造,做锻工 |
| bolt | [boult] | n. ;v. (门、窗的)插销(和 U 形钉),螺栓;栓住 |
| flange | [flændʒ] | n. ;vt. (机)凸缘,法兰(盘);给…装凸缘 |
| journal | ['dʒə:n] | n. 轴颈,日志,航海日记 |
| web | [web] | n. ;vt. (机)连结板,金属薄条片;使落入圈套 |
| cheek | [tʃi:k] | n. 颊板,中型箱,机械(或器具)上两侧 |

|          |            | 成对的部件 |
|----------|------------|-----------|
| hollow   | ['hɔlou]   | adj.;adv.;vt. 凹的,空虚的;完全;变空 |
| damper   | ['dæmpə]   | n. 风档,调节器,阻尼器,减震器 |
| stagger  | ['stægə]   | v.;n. 摇晃,蹒跚;(机)铆接 |
| bank     | [bæŋk]     | n.;v. 岸,堤,堆积,使…倾斜 |
| uniform  | ['ju:nifɔ:m] | adj.;n. 一样的,相同的,一致的;制服 |
| chamfer  | ['tʃæmfə]  | n.;vt. 倒棱,倒角,斜切,在…上开槽 |
| pulley   | ['pulə]    | n. 皮带轮,滑轮,滑车,辘轳 |

## PHRASES AND EXPRESSION

| a series of | 一系列,连续 |
| be applied to | 适用于,致力于 |
| a firing order | 发火顺序 |
| be known as | 据知,众所周知 |
| piston pin | 活塞销 |
| by means of | 依靠,用 |
| prevent…from | 阻止…,制止…,防止… |
| ring cap | 活塞环开口 |
| be equipped with | 用…装备 |
| to a large extent | 在很大程度上 |

## NOTES TO THE TEXT

1. As the name implies, the crankshaft consists of a series of cranks offset from the crankshaft centerline.
   顾名思义,曲轴是由一系列相对于曲轴中心线偏置的曲拐组成。
   As 引导方式状语从句,从句中 the name 做主语,implies 做谓语;主句中 the crankshaft 为主语,consists of 为谓语。

2. Many crankshafts are equipped with counterweights designed to offset the weight of the crank pin and connecting rod during rotation.
   很多曲轴都配置平衡块以抵消曲柄销和连杆在转动时产生的惯性力。

be equipped with … 配备,装备;此句谓语是被动语态,be equipped with;designed to 是过去分词短语做定语,修饰 counterweights。

3. The number and arrangement of crank throws on a crankshaft depends on engine design factors such as the operating cycle (two-or four-stroke), cylinder arrangement (in line, V, or opposed), the angle formed between banks of cylinders on V engines, and the number of cylinders.

曲轴上的曲拐数目和布置依赖于很多因素:如循环工作类型(二或四冲程),气缸布置(直列,V型,对置式),V型发动机相对倾斜的气缸角度和气缸数目等。

depend on 依赖于,依靠,做句中谓语。此句主语是 the number and arrangement;such as 引导 fact 的同位语。

## 2.1.4 Pistons

The piston is literally a sliding plunger that rides up and down in the cylinder. It has several jobs to do in proper sequence (Figure 2-7).

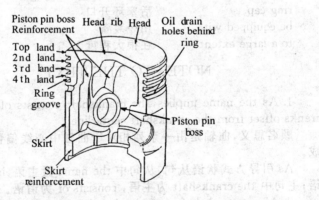

Figure 2-7 Construction details of piston and piston terminology

The piston must move down through the cylinder to produce a

vacuum to draw a fuel charge into the cylinder. It then travels up in the cylinder and compresses the mixture. When the mixture is fired, the pressure of the expanding gas is transmitted to the top of the piston. This drives the piston back down through the cylinder with great force, transmitting the energy of this firing stroke to the crankshaft. The piston then travels up through the cylinder, and exhausts the burned fuel charge.

The overall job the piston performs is a difficult one indeed. A piston is subjected to intense heat from the burning air-fuel mixture. It must change directions at "blurring speeds". It is "hounded" by friction against the cylinder walls. In addition to all this, the piston receives the tremendous thrust of power on the firing stroke. That a piston not only survives these forces, but will do so for many thousands of miles of driving, is a tribute to the engineering skill of engine manufacturers.

Pistons are usually made of aluminum. Often, aluminum pistons are tin-plated to allow a good breaking-in job when the engine is started. Aluminum pistons can be forged, but are more commonly cast.

The aluminum piston is light and, for most purposes, this gives it an advantage over the cast iron type. A piston must change its direction of travel at the end of every stroke. At engine speeds sometimes in excess of 5 000 revolutions per minute (rpm), it is obvious that the lighter the piston is, the more efficient it will be.

Cast iron is a good material for pistons used in a slow speed engine. It has excellent wear characteristics and will perform admirably in an engine suited to its needs. Pistons which are designed to operate in silicon aluminum cylinders are iron-plated aluminum.

The piston head is subjected to the direct heat of the exploding fuel. This heat can raise the temperature of the piston crown (very top) somewhat above 600°F (316°C). The temperature will lower as you go down the piston. The bottom of the skirt will be about 300°F (149°C).

The temperatures will vary according to engine design and work application. As the bottom of the skirt is the coolest, some pistons have the skirt slightly wider at the bottom. The top area of the skirt would be a trifle smaller in diameter.

It is obvious that the piston head is by far the hottest part of the piston. As a result, it expands more. In order to avoid having the head grow tight in the cylinder, the piston head is turned to a smaller diameter than the skirt of the piston (not cam ground) The head will generally be .030 to .040 in. (0.76 to 1.02 mm) smaller than the skirt.

Some pistons have flat-topped heads. Others are dome shaped. Still others have irregular shapes designed to help in exhausting burned gases, and also to assist in creating a rapid swirling to help break up gasoline particles on the compression stroke. One type forms the shape of the combustion chamber in the head of the pistons, thus allowing the use of a flat surfaced cylinder head.

**Piston Pins**

Pistons are fastened to connecting rods by means of steel pins. These pins, called piston pins, pass through one side of the piston, through the rod upper end, then on through the outer side of the piston (Figure 2-8).

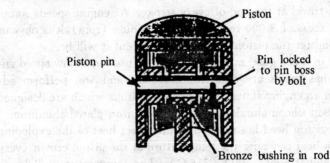

Figure 2-8  Piston pin locked to one pin boss allows rod to oscillate on pin

The piston pin is usually hollow, to reduce weight. It is also casehardened to provide a long wearing surface. Casehardening is a process that hardens the surface of the steel but leaves the inner part fairly soft and tough to prevent brittleness. This hardness penetrates from .004 in. (0.10 mm) up to any depth desired. However, there would be little advantage in making the hard shell any deeper than a few thousandths of an inch. Piston pins are ground to a very accurate size and are highly polished.

## Piston Rings

Piston rings provide a dynamic seal between the piston and the cylinder wall. Their purpose is to prevent combustion pressures from entering the crankcase and crankcase oil from entering the combustion chamber. They also control the degree of cylinder wall lubrication.

The general classification of piston rings includes compression rings and oil control rings. Some manufacturers refer to the top compression ring as a fire ring. Some diesel engines use only two piston rings, one compression ring at the top and one oil control ring just below the compression ring. Other designs use three, four, five, or even more rings perpiston, as shown in the illustrations. Rings may be chrome-faced, copper oxide-coated or plasma-faced (Figure 2-9).

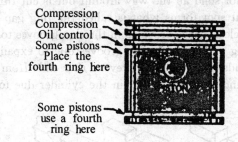

Figure 2-9 Location of compression and oil control rings

Compression rings are required to seal against combustion and compression pressures. Oil control rings are required to control cylinder wall lubrication. Both types of rings may be designed to scrape excess oil from the cylinder walls. Piston ring design therefore requires that rings be installed correctly. Lower rings on Detroit Diesel two-cycle engines also serve to prevent scavenging air from entering the crankcase.

Some combustion gases and unburned fuel (hydrocarbons) will inevitably pass the rings and reach the crankcase. If the rings, pistons, cylinders, and fuel and lubrication systems are in good condition, this will be minimal.

Since engine oil from the lubrication system helps seal the rings, any decrease in lubrication system efficiency will affect the rings' ability to seal and will increase ring and cylinder wear.

Counterbores and chamfers on compression rings assist the rings to slide over the oil on the cylinder walls during upward movement of the piston and scrape the oil off the cylinder walls on downward movement. Tapered-face and barrel-face ring designs are also used for this purpose.

The ring is built so it must be squeezed together to place it in the cylinder. This will cause the ring to exert an outward pressure, thus keeping it tightly against the cylinder wall.

The ring is not solid all the way around but is cut through in one spot. This cut spot forms what is called the ring gap (Figure 2-10). Ring side clearance is provided in the ring grooves to prevent rings from sticking or binding in the grooves due to expansion. A gap at the ring ends is provided to prevent ring ends from butting and causing the ring to become tight in the cylinder due to expansion.

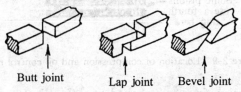

Butt joint   Lap joint   Bevel joint

Figure 2-10   Types of piston ring gap joints

During operation, piston rings are subjected to dynamic pressures, friction, heat, constant change of direction and speed, and inertia. Since there is some side clearance between the ring and the land, the piston ring moves up and down in the ring groove on the different strokes of the engine. Due to ring pressure against the cylinder wall and the inertia of the piston ring, the ring tends to stay behind when the piston changes direction. This causes the ring to move up and down in the groove and eventually causes ring groove wear. The ring itself also wears, increasing ring side clearance even further. When clearance is excessive, ring breakage can occur.

Another factor concerning ring and groove wear is cylinder condition. When a cylinder wears, it becomes tapered (larger diameter at the top of ring travel than at the bottom of ring travel). As a result, the piston rings are forced deeper into the ring grooves as the piston moves down in the cylinder. As the piston moves up in the cylinder, ring tension causes the ring to expand to fit the worn part of the cylinder. The rings continuously expand and contract in the ring grooves as the piston moves up and down in the worn cylinder.

When the ring is in the cylinder, the cut ends must not touch. When the ring heats up, it will lengthen. Since it cannot expand outwardly, it will close the gap.

## Connecting Rods

As the name implies, connecting rods are used to connect pistons to the crankshaft (Figure 2-11).

The upper end of a rod oscillates (swings back and forth), while the lower or big end bearing rotates (turns).

As there is very little bearing movement in the upper end, the bearing area can be reasonably small. The lower (big) end rotates very fast, and the crankshaft journal turns inside the connecting rod. This rotational speed tends to produce heat and wear. To make the rod wear well, a larger bearing area is required.

The upper end of the rod has a hole through it for the piston pin. The lower end must be split so the rod can be installed on the crankshaft journal.

The upper and lower halves of the lower end of the rod are bolted together. The upper and lower halves should be numbered and when installed, the numbers should be on the same side. This prevents turning the cap around when installing the rod.

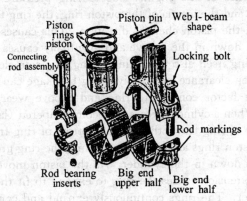

Figure 2-11  Typical connecting rod forged steel rod used in conjunction with aluminum piston

Turning the connecting rod cap around would make the rod bearing hole out-of-round. In making rods, the upper and lower halves are bolted together and the holes are bored to an accurate size. The hole may be slightly off-center. If the caps are crossed, the upper hole half may not line up with the lower hole.

The piston-and-rod assembly (in conjunction with the cylinder and valves) acts as a pump on the intake and exhaust strokes. On the power stroke, it transmits the pressure of expanding gases to the crankshaft, forcing it to turn.

The connecting rod is attached to the crankshaft at one end (big end) and to the piston at the other end (small end). The tapered I-beam type of connecting rod is the most common. The big end of the rod is split so that it can be connected to the crankshaft. The cap and yoke are a matched pair, and their relationship must not be altered. Both rod and cap are numbered. Special precision connecting rod bolts and nuts keep the cap in proper alignment with the rod. Some connecting rods have an oil spurt hole in the yoke or at the cap mating surface to provide cylinder wall lubrication. Notches in the yoke and cap provide proper bearing positioning. The small end of the connecting rod is attached to the piston by a piston pin. In some cases the small end of the rod is clamped to the pin or has a bushing in it to allow pin and rod oscillation. In other designs the pin is bolted to the rod. Connecting rods are usually drilled to provide lubrication to the piston pin and also to spray oil into the bottom of the piston for piston cooling on some designs.

The connecting rod undergoes high loads and speeds as well as constant change of direction. Overloading the engine can cause bent connecting rods and bearing failure. The big end of the connecting rod can also become out-of-round as a result of high loads and high mileage or extended hours.

Connecting rods are normally made of alloy steel. They are drop-forged to shape, then machined. The customary shape uses I-beam construction.

Some rods are built of aluminum. Generally these are for small engines designed for light duty. Small engines often utilize the rod material for both upper and lower bearing surfaces. Special aluminum rods for high speed, high performance engines can be purchased from specialty machine shops.

## NEW WORDS

| | | |
|---|---|---|
| literally | ['litərili] | adv. 字面上，照字义，逐地 |
| plunger | ['plʌndʒə] | n. 柱塞，活塞，短路器 |
| vacuum | ['vækjuəm] | n. ;adj. 真空，真空度；真空的，利用真空的 |
| blur | [blə:] | vt. 弄模糊，涂污，抹掉，涂掉 |
| hound | [haund] | vt. ;n. 追逐，使追逐；猎狗 |
| tremendous | [tri'mendəs] | adj. 可怕的，惊人的，极大的，非常的 |

| | | |
|---|---|---|
| explode | [iks'pləud] | vt.;vi.;adj. 爆炸,破除;突发;分解的 |
| crown | [kraun] | n. 花冠,冕,隆起,根颈 |
| trifle | ['traifl] | n. 小事,细故,琐事 |
| dome | [dəum] | n. 圆顶屋,圆盖,(机)汽室 |
| swirl | [swə:l] | v.;n. 打漩,涡动,漩涡,纷乱 |
| caseharden | ['keis'ha:dn] | vt. 使…表面硬化 |
| polish | ['pɔliʃ] | v.;n. 磨光,擦亮,琢磨;润饰 |
| shell | [ʃel] | n.;vt.;vi. 壳,外壳,剥…的壳;脱落 |
| hydrocarbon | ['haidrəu'ka:bən] | n. 烃,碳氢化合物 |
| squeeze | [skwi:z] | vt.;vi.;n. 压榨;挤;压榨,压力 |
| groove | [gru:v] | n.;vt. 槽,沟;开槽于 |
| inertia | [i'nə:jiə] | n. 惯性,惯量,惯性调节器 |
| breakage | ['breikidʒ] | n. 破损,破断片,破损物,损耗 |
| oscillate | ['ɔsileit] | vi.;vt. 摆动,波动,使摆动,使动摇 |
| conjunction | [kən'dʒʌŋkʃən] | n. 连结,结合,同时发生 |
| yoke | [jəuk] | n.;vt. 轭状物,轭;给…上轭,配合 |
| alignment | [ə'lainmənt] | n. 队列,一直线,定线,准线 |
| spurt | [spə:t] | vi.;n. 冲刺,奋进;喷出,进出 |
| clamp | [klæmp] | vt.;n. 夹住,夹紧;夹钳,夹子 |
| mileage | ['mailidʒ] | n. 每里运费 |
| utilize | ['ju:tilaiz] | vt.;adj.;n. 利用;可利用的;利用 |
| penetrate | ['penitreit] | vt.;v. 穿过,透过;穿入,刺入 |
| customary | ['kʌstəməri] | adj. 通常的,惯例的,习惯的 |

## PHRASES AND EXPRESSIONS

| | |
|---|---|
| piston skirt | 活塞裙部 |
| oil film | 油膜 |
| in addition to | 除…之外 |
| connecting rod | 连杆 |
| flat-topped | 平顶 |
| compression stroke | 压缩冲程 |

| piston rings | 活塞环 |
| in some cases | 在某种情况下 |
| cylinder wall | 缸壁 |
| be subjected to | 使受到,使遭遇 |

## NOTES TO THE TEXT

1. That a piston not only survives these forces, but will do so for many thousands of miles of driving, is a tribute to the engineering skill of engine manufacturers.

活塞不仅要承受这些力,而且需在远行的成千上万里都如此,这是发动机制造厂家工程技巧上的贡献。

that 引导的是主语从句,that … driving 在整个句子中做主语,is 是谓语,a tribute 是表语,to …manufacturers 是动词不定式短语做状语;而主语从句中由 not only … but (also) 并列连词连接二个并列句充当全句的主语。

2. The aluminum piston is light and, for most purposes, this gives it an advantage over the cast iron type.

铝活塞较轻,而且大多数情况下,这使铝活塞比铸铁活塞更具有优势。

这是两个并列的分句,用 and 连接,for … purpose 是插入语。

3. Due to ring pressure against the cylinder wall and the inertia of the piston ring, the ring tends to stay behind when the piston changes direction.

由于活塞环压紧在气缸壁上,总是在活塞改变方向后再变化。

due to … 由于,应归于,引导原因状语从句;to stay 动词不定式做宾语,when … 为时间状语从句。

## 2.1.5 Valves

Each engine cylinder ordinarily has two valves. However, some racing and automobile engines use four valves per cylinder.

Exhaust valves are made of heat resistant metal, because the head of a valve operates at temperatures up to $1300℉ (704℃)$. It is obvious that the steel used in valve construction must be of high quality.

In order to prevent burning, the valve must give off heat to the valve guide and to the valve seat. The valve must make good contact with the seat, and must run with minimum clearance in the guide.

Some valves have special hardfacing on the face areas to increase their useful life. Others use hollow stems filled with metallic sodium (Figure 2-12). At operating temperature, the sodium becomes a liquid and splashes up into the head. This draws the heat into the stem where it transfers to the valve guide.

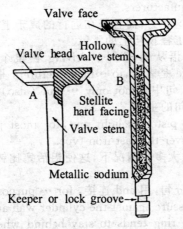

Figure 2-12  A-Valve with special hard facing to lengthen useful life; B-special heat resistant valve utilizing a hollow stem partially filled with metallic sodium

The valve stem passes through the valve guide in the port, and the valve head close the port when the valve is seated. The valve seat is located at the combustion chamber end of the ports. The valve spring is located on the spring seat and keeps the valve seated until the camshaft causes the valve to open against spring pressure. The spring is held in place by a spring retainer that is locked to the valve stem by two split locks. The valve stem seal is located on the valve stem to prevent engine oil from entering the combustion chamber or exhaust manifold through the valve guide.

Intake and exhaust valves are designed to operate over a long period of time with relatively little attention or problems. Valve heads are sufficiently heavy for good heat capacity, yet light enough not to cause valve float very readily. Valve face and seat angles can be 30°, 45° or 60°. Seating angles are required to provide a positive seal. The wiping action of angled seating surfaces helps clear minor carbon particles that could prevent proper sealing. The wedging action of the angled surfaces also contributes to better sealing. Valves are made of high-grade steel alloy for long service life.

Intake and exhaust valve materials include alloy steel valves with an aluminized face and chrome stem, Silchrome valve with an aluminized face, stainless steel, austenitic steel with aluminized face and chrome stem, and SAE 21-2 steel with a nickelplated face. Exhaust valves with sodium-filled stems are sometimes used for better valve cooling. At operating temperature, the sodium is liquefied. Valve movement causes the sodium to transfer heat from the head of the valve to the valve stem and then to the valve guide.

Exhaust valve temperature may reach approximately 1300° to 1500°F (704° to 815°C). This means that they are in fact running red-hot. Good heat transfer therefore is essential.

Mechanical lifters are usually made of cast iron. The bottom part that contacts the camshaft is hardened. Some lifters are hollow to reduce weight. A screw is placed in the top to adjust clearance between end of valve stem and lifter.

The hydraulic valve lifter performs the same job as the mechanical lifter. The major difference is that the hydraulic lifter is self-adjusting, operates with no lifter-to-rocker arm clearance and uses engine oil under pressure to operate. Hydraulic lifters are quiet in operation.

To operate, engine oil under pressure enters the hydraulic lifter body. The oil passes through a small opening in the bottom of an inner piston, into a cavity beneath the piston. The oil raises the piston up until it contacts the push rod (the oil pressure is not high enough to open the valve).

When the cam raises the lifter, pressure is applied to the inner piston. The piston tries to squirt the oil back through the small opening but cannot do so as a small check ball seals the opening.

As the cam raises, the lifter becomes solid and lifts the valve. When the cam lowers, the lifter will be pushed down by the push rod. The lifter will then automatically adjust to remove clearances (Figure 2-13).

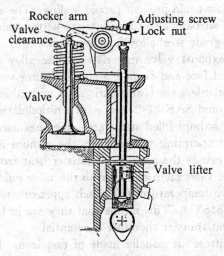

Figure 2-13  Rocker arm with adjustment screw used to set proper valve clearance or "lash"

## Camshafts

The camshaft assembly includes the camshaft, bearings, and drive mechanism. The camshaft and drive assembly are required to control the opening and closing of the valves. In some cases the camshaft also operates the injectors.

The design of the camshaft and drive results in valves being opened and closed at a controlled rate of speed as well as at a precise time in relation to piston position. This also applies to injector operation on engines where injectors are engine camshaft-operated (injector timing).

Camshafts are of forged steel construction for strength and are induction-hardened or heat-treated for wear resistance and long life.

Four-stroke-cycle engines have two cam lobes per cylinder when injectors are not engine camshaft-operated. On four-stroke-cycle engines with engine camshaft-operated injectors, the camshaft is designed with three lobes per cylinder, one intake cam lobe, one exhaust cam lobe, and a third lobe operating the injector.

The two-stroke-cycle diesel engine has three lobes per cylinder: one lobe to operate the unit injector, and two lobes to operate the two or four exhaust valves per cylinder (There are no intake valves).

The cam lobe converts the rotary motion of the camshaft to reciprocating motion of the cam follower.

Endwise movement of the camshaft is limited by a thrust plate located between the bearing journal and the drive gear or sprocket. The thrust plate is bolted to the engine. On some engines there is no thrust plate to hold the camshaft in place. This design uses a thrust pin installed in the block, which engages a groove in the camshaft. The design of the cam lobe contour has a major effect on engine performance. The amount of valve opening, the amount of time that the valve remains open (duration), the time when the valves open and close (valve timing), and the speed at which valves open and close are determined by cam lobe design. Camshafts are usually driven by gears marked for correct timing with the crankshaft. Some smaller diesel engines have a chain-or cog belt-driven camshaft. A V-type engine with two camshafts may have one camshaft turning clockwise and the other turning counterclockwise (Figure 2-14).

**Camshaft Bearings**

Camshaft bearings are of the bushing type or split type and are similar in construction to crankshaft bearings. On some engines the camshaft bearings are all of equal diameter. On other engines the front camshaft bearings and journal are the largest, and the remaining bearings and journals are of progressively smaller diameter, with the smallest at the rear of the engine. This sizing makes it easier to remove and install the camshaft. Camshaft bearings are lubricated from oil galleries in the block or cylinder head.

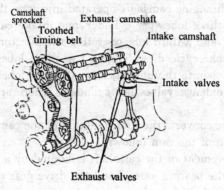

Figure 2-14  Dual overhead camshaft driven by a toothed drive belt

## Flywheel and Harmonic Balancer

A flywheel is required to stabilize the speed fluctuations of the crankshaft resulting from power impulses of the engine cylinders.

The flywheel stores energy during the power stroke and releases it during the non-power-producing strokes of the engine. The flywheel has an important speed-governing effect since it limits the speed increase or decrease during sudden changes in engine load. In many cases the flywheel provides a convenient means for mounting a large ring gear used for starting purposes. It also provides the frictional drive surface for a clutch type mechanical drive (Figure 2-15). Engine timing marks are often located on the flywheel.

These degree markings indicate the TDC piston position usually for No. 1 cylinder and are used to determine fuel injection timing.

Flywheels are made from cast iron alloys, cast, or rolled steel. Provision for mounting is provided by the flywheel web in the center area. The precisely machined opening in the center ensures centering of the flywheel with the rotating axis of the crankshaft. The radial positioning of the flywheel is maintained by unevenly spaced mounting bolt holes or by a dowel pin. This relationship must be maintained for timing marks to be valid.

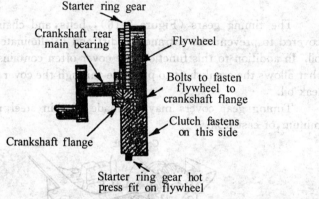

Figure 2-15  Heavy flywheel is bolted to the crankshaft flange

Flywheel designs include the flat and the recessed types. The recessed type reduces the overall size of the clutch and flywheel assembly. On engines equipped with hydraulic drive mechanisms, the torque converter serves the purpose of the flywheel and clutch assembly.

The starter ring gear is a shrink fit on the flywheel, and it may also be welded to it as well. The ring gear is heated prior to installation. Heating the ring gear increases its diameter, allowing it to slip easily over the flywheel mounting surface.

## Oil Pan

The oil pan acts as a reservoir for oil, and it also serves as a dust shield for the bottom of the engine. It is attached to the bottom of the block with cap screws.

The pan is generally made of thin steel stamped to shape. Plastic may also be used.

## Timing Gear Cover

The timing gears (Figure 2-16), belts, and chains must be covered to prevent the entrance of dirt and to eliminate the loss of oil. In addition to this function, the cover often contains an oil seal that allows the crankshaft to protrude through the cover and yet not leak oil.

Timing gear covers may be made of thin steel, plastic, aluminum, or cast iron.

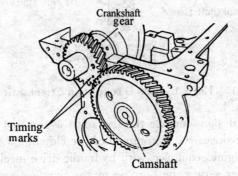

Figure 2-16  Timing gear drive for camshaft also requires alignment of timing marks

## Gaskets and Seals

In an engine where machined parts fit together, gaskets are

used to make the joints tight and to prevent leakage of oil, water, and/or gasoline.

The cylinder heads must seal in the water of the cooling system and must also contain the pressure of the exploding fuel. Thin steel, copper, and asbestos gaskets are used between the head and engine block.

It is very difficult to machine metal parts to the degree of accuracy necessary for leakproof joints. As the engine expands and contracts during warmup and cooling periods, there are minute shifts in the fastened parts. This, coupled with vibration, will loosen many parts to the point of leakage.

Gasket material is somewhat resilient (soft and springy) and will adapt itself to expansion and contraction. It will also conform to irregularities in the surfaces of the mating parts.

## NEW WORDS

| | | |
|---|---|---|
| sodium | ['səudjəm] | n. [化]钠 |
| splash | [splæʃ] | v. 溅，飞溅，泼，泼出 |
| capacity | [kə'pæsiti] | n. 容量，容积，能量 |
| stainless | ['steilis] | adj. 没有污点的，不锈的，纯洁的 |
| nickel | ['nikl] | n. [化]镍 |
| approximate | [ə'prɔksimit] | adj.;vt.;vi. 近似的；大约的；使接近；近于 |
| screw | [skru:] | n. 螺旋，螺丝，螺丝钉 |
| adjust | [ə'dʒʌst] | vt. 整顿，调整，调节 |
| hydraulic | [hai'drɔ:li:k] | adj. 水力的，水力学的，水压的，液压的 |
| squirt | [skwə:t] | v.;n. 喷，喷出；喷水 |
| sprocket | ['sprɔkit] | n. 链轮 |
| duration | [djuə'reiʃən] | n. 耐久，持久，期间，持续 |
| cog | [kɔg] | n. (机)嵌齿，(齿轮)轮牙，大齿 |
| reservoir | ['rezərwa:] | n. 储蓄器，储器，蓄水池 |
| shield | [ʃi:ld] | n. 盾，护罩，挡板，盾状物 |
| resilient | [ri'ziliənt] | adj. 有弹性的，弹回的，恢复活力 |

| | | |
|---|---|---|
| | | 的 |
| harmonic | [ha:'mɔnik] | adj. ;n. 谐和的,和声的,和睦的;泛音 |
| fluctuation | [ˌflʌktju'eiʃən] | n. 波动,涨落,起伏 |
| stabilize | [steibilaiz] | vt. ;vi. 稳定;安定 |
| propane | ['prəupein] | n. [化]丙烷 |
| configuration | [kən'figju'reiʃən] | n. 构形,形象,位形,组态 |

## PHRASES AND EXPRESSIONS

| | |
|---|---|
| drive mechanism | 驱动机构 |
| camshaft bearing | 凸轮轴承 |
| heat resistant metal | 耐热钢 |
| hollow stem | 中空导杆 |
| combustion chamber | 燃烧室 |
| transfer····from···to··· | 把····从····传递到···· |
| bearing journal | 轴颈 |
| thrust plate | 推力盘 |
| oil galleries | 油道 |
| timing gear | 正时齿轮 |
| leakproof joints | 防漏接合 |
| adapt···to | 使适应,使适合 |
| conform to··· | 与····一致,使符合 |

## NOTES TO THE TXET

1. In order to prevent burning, the valve must give off heat to the valve guide and to the valve seat.

为了防止气门烧坏,气门必须把热量传给气门导杆和气门座。

give off 发出,传递,在句中做谓语;in order to 引导目的状语。

2. When the cam raises the lifter, pressure is applied to the inner piston. The piston tries to squirt the oil back through the small opening but cannot do so as a small check ball seals the opening.

当凸轮顶起挺柱时,压力作用在内部柱塞上。柱塞趋向把机油从进路压回,但因有一个单向阀将开口密封,所以机油不会倒流。

apply to 应用,使用;when 引导时间状语从句;as a small ···,

as 引导原因状语从句。

3. In an engine where machined parts fit together, gaskets are used to make the joints tight and to prevent leakage of oil, water, and/or gasoline.

发动机在机械相接触处放置垫圈来密封其接合处,以防止机油、水和汽油泄漏。

fit together 结合在一起;在 In an engine … together 短语中包含一个 where machined part … 引导定语从句修饰先行词 engine。

## EXERCISES

Ⅰ. Answer the following questions according to the text:
　1. Do you state the purpose of the crankshaft?
　2. Why are piston rings needed?
　3. What is the purpose of the connecting rod?
　4. Why are ring side clearance and ring gap clearance required?
　5. What is the purpose of the intake and exhaust valves?
　6. What is the speed of the camshaft in relation to that of the crankshaft?
　7. What three functions are performed by the flywheel?

Ⅱ. Completing sentences: The sentences below are incomplete. After each sentence there are four words, only one of which will correctly complete the sentence, selecting the proper word to complete it correctly.

　1. As the camshaft ____, each cam lifts the tappet together with the push rod.
　　A. rotaion　　　　B. rotating
　　C. rotates　　　　D. roary

　2. Valves are opened by ____.
　　A. camshaft lobes　　B. connecting rods
　　C. the crankshaft　　D. valve springs

　3. The connecting rod is attached to the piston by the ____.
　　A. rod cap　　　　B. piston pin
　　C. cap bolts　　　D. cap bearing

　4. The timing gear is locked on the camshaft with a key and

____ a bolt with a washer.

A. is linked  B. is secured by
C. attached to  D. is connected with

5. The crankshaft takes the forces ____ the pistons via the connecting rods and converts them into torque.

A. transmitted from  B. absorbed by
C. giving to  D. applied to

6. The crankshaft consists of crankpins and main journals, ____, and counterweights.

A. flywheel  B. timing gear key
C. crank webs  D. the fan drive pulley

7. The rear end of crankshaft ____ for bolting the flywheel.

A. has a hole  B. is flanged
C. is drilled  D. has a socket

8. The periodic gas pressure and ____ taken by the crankshaft may cause it to suffer wear and bending.

A. centrifugal forces  B. thrust forces
C. twisting force  D. inertia forces

Ⅲ. In each case, choose one of the four words that best matches the definition given below:

1. shaft containing lobes or cams which operate engine valves

A. revolving shaft  B. camshaft
C. crankshaft  D. driving shaft

2. a liner or tube interposed between piston and cylinder wall

A. cylinder sleeve  B. washer
C. gasket  D. nipple

3. main shaft of an engine which, in conjunction with connecting rods, changes reciprocating motion of pistons into rotary motion

A. differential shaft  B. final drive shaft
C. crankshaft  D. cardan shaft

4. a heavy wheel in which energy is absorbed and stored by means of momentum

A. gearing wheel  B. sprocket wheel
C. automobile tyre  D. flywheel

5. a valve which permits a fluid or gas to enter a chamber and

seals against exit
  A. by-pass valve
  B. differential valve
  C. intake valve
  D. exhaust valve

6. journal for bearing in small end of an engine connecting rod which also pass through piston walls
  A. piston ring
  B. piston pin
  C. bearing
  D. bearing journal

7. largest single part of an engine, basic or main mass of metal in which cylinders are bored
  A. piston
  B. crankcase
  C. cylinder block
  D. engine frame

8. a wheel with one or more rows of teeth for fitting into and turning a chain
  A. sprocket
  B. chain
  C. driving wheel
  D. driven wheel

Ⅳ. Choose the words or a phrase from the list for each space in the passage below:

1. mating
2. as well as
3. to spray
4. so that
5. as a result of
6. is attached to
7. matched
8. both…and
9. in some cases
10. is bolted to

The connecting rod ____ to the crankshaft at one end (big end) and to the piston at the other end (small end).

The tapered I-beam type of connecting rod is the most common. The big end of the rod is split ____ it can be connected to the crankshaft. The cap and yoke are a ____ pair, and their relationship must not be altered. ____ rod ____ cap are numbered. Special precision connecting rod. bolts and nuts keep the cup in proper alignment with the rod. Some connecting rods have an oil spurt hole in the yoke or at the cap ____ surface to provide cylinder wall lubrication. Notches in the yoke and cap provide proper bearing positioning. The small end of the connecting rod is attached to the piston by a piston pin. ____ the small end of the rod is clamped to the pin or has a bushing in it to allow the pin and rod oscilation. In other designs the pin ____ the rod. Connecting rods are usually drilled to provide lubrication to the piston pin and also ____ oil into the bottom of the piston for piston cooling on some designs.

The connecting rod undergoes high loads and speeds ____ constant change of direction. Overloading the engine can cause bent connecting rods and bearing failure. The big end of the rod can also become out-of-round ____ high loads and high mileage.

Ⅴ. Translate the following sentences into Chinese:

1. The principal force an engine crankshaft must resist is the bending action of the connecting rod thrust when the piston is at top center.

2. The connecting rod, in essence, is a bar or shut with a bearing at each end, whose purpose is to transmit the piston thrust to the crankshaft.

3. Connecting rods are generally fabricated from a high-quality steel in the form of a bar with ring-shaped heads at its ends, the heads being known as the connecting rod big end and small end and serving to attach the rod to the crankpin and the gudgeon pin of the piston, respectively.

4. Inlet valves offer no serious problems as to suitable material because, although they are exposed to the heat of combustion, they are well cooled by the current of air which flows over them when they are open.

5. To take care of the greater expansion in the high-temperature zone, the crown is machined on a slight taper, the diameter being greatest where the crown meets the skirt and becoming less toward the top.

6. One form of VCR piston has been developed that provides improved starting, better idling and improved output per cubic inch of displacement.

7. It may be forged in one piece, including the cams themselves, that is, "integral" cams, or the camshaft may consist of a steel shaft with seperate forged-steel or cast-iron cams keyed on.

Ⅵ. Translate the following passage into Chinese:

An engine valve is a device designed to open a passage when

moving in one direction and to close it when moving in the opposite direction. Each cylinder of a four-stroke-cycle diesel or gasoline engine is commonly equipped with an intake (admission) valve and an exhaust valve. The purpose of the intake valve is to allow the air-fuel mixture (gasoline engines) or air (diesel engines) to enter the cylinder. After the combustion process has been completed, the burned gases are permitted to escape from the cylinder through the exhaust valve. To obtain sufficient valve area, some truck engines have two intake and two exhaust valves.

Two-stroke-cycle diesel engines have two exhaust valves in each cylinder, but no intake valves. Because the two-stroke-cycle design is not an efficient airpump, a blower is used to force air into the cylinder through air intake ports located around the circumference of the cylinder liner. The air enters the cylinder when the ports are uncovered by the piston at the bottom of its stroke. The incoming air scavenges the engine by forcing exhaust gases out through the open exhaust valves.

## 2.2 Supplyment Systems

### 2.2.1 Fuel Systems

Fuel and air must be delivered to the carburetor or fuel injection system before the air-fuel mixture can be created. This is the job of the fuel system. The system contains:
1. The fuel storage tank
2. Fuel delivery lines
3. Evaporative emission controls
4. The fuel pump
5. The fuel filters
6. Air cleaners and filters
7. Thermostatic air cleaner controls.

**Tanks and Fillers**

The automobile fuel tank is made of two corrosion-resistant steel halves, which are ribbed for additional strength and welded together. Exposed sections of the tank may be made of heavier steel for protection from road damage and corrosion.

Some cars, sports utility vehicles, and light trucks may have an auxiliary fuel tank. A few of these auxiliary tanks have been made of polyethylene plastic. Greater use of composites in fuel tank construction seems likely in the future.

Tank design and capacity are a compromise between available space, filler location, fuel expansion room, and fuel movement. Some latemodel tanks deliberately limit tank capacity by extending the filler tube neck into the tank low enough to prevent complete filling. A vertical baffle in this same tank limits fuel sloshing as the car moves.

Regardless of its size and shape, a fuel tank must have the following:

1. An inlet or filler tube through which fuel can enter the tank
2. A filler cap
3. An outlet to the fuel line leading to the fuel pump
4. A vent system.

Despite the care generally taken in refining, storing, and delivering gasoline, some impurities get into the automotive fuel system. Fuel filters remove dirt, rust, water, and other contamination from the gasoline before it can reach the carburetor or injection system (Figure 2-17).

The useful life of all filters is limited, although Ford specifies that its filters used with injection systems should last the life of the vehicle. If fuel filters are not cleaned or replaced according to the manufacturer's recommendations, they will become clogged and restrict fuel flow.

Several different types of fuel filters are used, and some systems may contain two or more. Filters can be located in several places within the fuel system.

**Carburetor**

All carburetors must perform three vital functions. They must break up the liquid gasoline into a fine mist, change the liquid into a vapor, and distribute the vapor evenly to the cylinders. These three principles of atomization, vaporization, and distribution of fuel are important principles of carburetion.

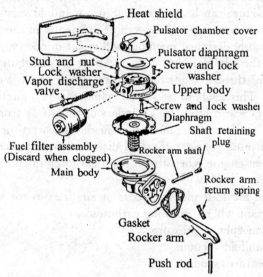

Figure 2-17  This entire filter assembly

Gasoline must be atomized, or broken up, into a fine mist if the fuel is to be properly vaporized. Atomization takes place as the fuel travels from the carburetor discharge nozzles into the moving stream of air.

Vaporization starts as the atomized fuel passes the throttle and enters the intake manifold. Complete vaporization cannot occur unless the fuel is hot enough to boil. Vaporization is affected by the

following factors:
1. Temperature—vaporization increases as the fuel is heated.
2. Volatility—the greater the volatility of the fuel, the lower the temperature at which it will vaporize and the faster it will vaporize.
3. Pressure—a decrease in pressure causes fuel to vaporize faster at a lower temperature.

Low volatility, cold intake air, or a cold manifold can cause poor vaporization. As you learned before, thermostatic air cleaners and heated intake manifolds are ways in which the problems of a cold air-fuel mixture can be overcome. Since manifold vacuum creates a low-pressure area, fuel vaporizes more efficiently in the intake manifold. A poorly designed manifold will result in poor vaporization.

The throttle plate has a direct effect on distribution, since the angle of the throttle sends the mixture against one side of the intake manifold. This tends to feed some cylinders a rich mixture and other cylinders a lean mixture. Cylinders farther away from the carburetor may get less of the mixture than those nearest the carburetor. Engineers must consider the fuel distribution or metering requirements of an engine when they design carburetors and intake manifolds.

There are four measurements of air pressure, or vacuum, that are important when discussing carburetors:
1. Atmospheric pressure
2. Manifold vacuum
3. Venturi vacuum
4. Ported vacuum.

Atmospheric pressure is the pressure of the air outside the carburetor. It is always present, and varies within a narrow range, depending upon altitude and atmospheric conditions.

Manifold vacuum is the low pressure beneath the carburetor throttle valve. Manifold vacuum is produced by the engine and is always present when the engine is running. Manifold vacuum decreases as the throttle valve is opened.

Venturi vacuum is the low-pressure area created by airflow through the venturi restriction in the carburetor barrel. Venturi vacuum increases with the speed of the airflow through the venturi. It is present whenever the throttle valve is open and increases as the throttle is opened.

Ported vacuum—the low-pressure area just above the throttle valve—is present whenever the throttle is opened to expose the port in the lower portion of the carburetor barrel to manifold vacuum. Ported vacuum is absent at idle, high at small throttle openings, and decreases as the throttle is opened farther. Vacuum taken from this point often is used to operate distributor vacuum advance units and other vacuum-operated devices. Small ports, or holes, in the side of the carburetor are connected to hoses, which are connected to the vacuum devices.

**Fuel Pump**

The fuel pump and the fuel lines deliver gasoline from the tank to the carburetor or injection system. The fuel pump moves the fuel with a mechanical action that creates a lowpressure, or suction, area at the pump inlet. This causes the higher atmospheric pressure in the fuel tank to force fuel to the pump. The pump spring also exerts a force on the fuel within the pump and delivers it under pressure to the carburetor or injection system. All pumps, except electric turbine pumps, develop this mechanical action through a reciprocating, "push-pull" motion.

While all pumps deliver fuel through mechanical action, they generally are divided into two groups:
1. Mechanical (driven by the car engine)
2. Electrical (driven by an electric motor or vibrating armature).

The most common type of fuel pump used by domestic and foreign automakers on carbureted engines is the single-action, diaphragm-type mechanical pump (Figure 2-18). The rocker arm is driven by an eccentric lobe on the camshaft. (On some overhead-cam 4-cylinder engines, the eccentric lobe may be on an accessory shaft.) The pump makes one stroke with each revolution of the camshaft. The eccentric lobe (often called simply, "the eccentric") may be part of the camshaft.

In some applications, the rocker arm is driven directly by the eccentric. Other engines have a pushrod between the eccentric and the pump rocker arm. The most common examples of this arrangement are the small-block Chevrolet V-8 and some 4-cylinder Ford engines. The fuel intake stroke begins when the rotating camshaft eccentric pushes down on one end of the pump rocker arm. This raises the other end, which pulls the diaphragm up (Figure 2-18), and tightens the diaphragm spring. Pulling the diaphragm up creates a vacuum, or low-pressure area, in the fuel chamber. Since there is a constant high pressure in the fuel lines, the inlet check valve in the pump is forced open and fuel enters the fuel chamber.

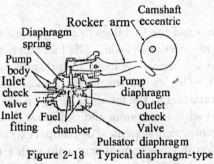

Figure 2-18 Typical diaphragm-type

As the camshaft eccentric continues to turn, it allows the outside end of the rocker arm to "rock" back up. Along with the push given by the diaphragm spring, this allows the diaphragm to relax back down. This is the start of the fuel output stroke. As the diaphragm relaxes, it causes a pressure buildup in the fuel chamber. Sometimes called a turbine, roller cell, roller vane, or rotary vane pump, the impeller pump. Figure 2-19 is driven by a small electric motor which draws fuel into the pump, then pushes it out through the fuel line to the carburetor or injection system. Since this type of pump uses no valves, the fuel is moved in a steady flow rather than the pulsating motion of all other electrical and mechanical pumps.

An electric fuel pump is quite efficient. It has a couple of advantages not offered by the mechanical type pump.

The electric pump will fill the carburetor merely by turning on the key. Another feature is the electric pump's adaptability to most any location. This allows the pump to be mounted away from the heat of the engine to reduce the chance of vapor lock. Some electric pumps are run submerged inside the fuel tank.

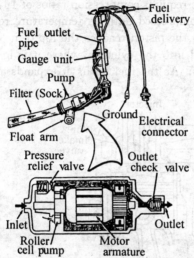

Figure 2-19   An impeller-type electric fuel pump

The basic difference between the electric and the mechanical pump is that the electric pump uses an electromagnet (a magnet produced by electricity flowing through a coil) to operate a metal bellows that alternately forms a vacuum and then pressure. Some electric pumps use an electromagnet to work a regular diaphragm. Other models drive either a vane or impeller type pump with a small electric motor.

## Diesel Engine

In 1892, a German engineer named Rudolf Diesel perfected the compression-ignition engine that bears his name. The diesel engine uses heat created by compression to ignite the fuel, so it requires no spark ignition system.

The diesel engine requires compression ratios of 16:1 and higher. Incoming air is compressed until its temperature reaches about 1,000°F (538°C). As the piston reaches the top of its compression stroke, fuel is injected into the cylinder, where it is ignited by the hot air (Figure 2-20). As the fuel burns, it expands and produces power.

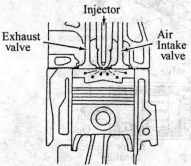

Figure 2-20  Diesel combustion occurs when fuel is injected into the hot, highly compressed air in the cylinder

The diesel engine must produce the power needed to drive the vehicle or tractor under varying conditions of speed, load, and environment.

The size of the engine required is determined by the size and type of the vehicle and the load and performance requirements of the unit.

Both two-stroke-cycle and four-stroke-cycle engines are in common use. Multi-cylinder reciprocating piston diesel engines with two, three, four, five, six, eight or more cylinders are produced.

Regardless of the type of engine being used, the demands placed on the engine to perform are rigorous. Speed and load requirements in many types of service are constantly changing during operation. Seasonal and regional temperature extremes are also encountered. All of these factors are considered in engine desing, operation, and service.

The diesel engine is easily recognized by the absence of such components as spark plugs, ignition wires, coil, and distributor, common to gasoline engines.

The diesel fuel system must provide the right amount of clean fuel to each cylinder at the correct time and must atomize the fuel adequately for good combustion. This must be achieved without entry of air into the fuel system. Injection of fuel into the cylinder must take place for a controlled period of time and must prevent leakage of fuel from the injector during non-injection time. Combustion must be controlled to limit exhaust emissions within pollution standards.

There are four basic types of diesel fuel injection systems to consider. These are (1) the multiple pump system, (2) the pressure time system, (3) the unit injector system, and (4) the distributor pump system.

The multiple pump system is used on many four-stroke-cycle engines such as Mack, Perkins, J. I. Case, Ford, Deere & Company, Fiat-Allis, International Harvester, Caterpillar, etc.

The pressure time system is used by the Cummins Engine Company, Inc. on its engines, which are used in many different manufacturers' products.

The unit injector system is used by Detroit Diesel Allison; for example, on its engines, both two-stroke and four-stroke, which are also used in many different manufacturers' products.

The distributor pump system is used on various makes of four-stroke engines.

# NEW WORDS

| | | |
|---|---|---|
| carburetor | [ˈkɑːbjuretə] | n. 化油器,增碳器 |
| filter | [ˈfiltə] | n. ;vt. ;vi. 滤器,滤波器;过滤;滤过 |
| thermostatics | [θəːməsˈtækiks] | n. 静热力学 |
| corrossion | [kəˈrəuʒən] | n. 腐蚀,侵蚀,溶蚀 |
| utility | [juːˈtiliti] | adj. ;n. 实用的,经济的;效用,实利 |
| deliberately | [diˈlibəritli] | adv. 慎重地,故意,从容地 |
| vertical | [ˈvəːtikəl] | adj. 竖,竖式的,垂直的 |
| baffle | [ˈbæfl] | n. ;vt. ;vi. 挡板,阻遏体;阻碍;徒作挣扎 |
| vent | [vent] | n. ;vt. 通风孔,排气道;给…开口 |
| refine | [riˈfain] | vt. 精炼,精制,提纯 |
| impurity | [imˈpjuəriti] | n. 不纯,不洁,杂质,混杂物 |
| contamination | [kənˈtæmineiʃən] | n. 污,沾污,染污 |
| specify | [ˈspesifai] | vt. 指定,详细,说明,列举 |
| clog | [klɔg] | n. 障碍,障碍物,木底鞋 |
| atomization | [ˈætəmaizeiʃən] | n. 雾化,原子化 |
| distribution | [ˈdistriˌbjuːʃən] | n. 分配,配给,区分,分类 |
| altitude | [ˈæltitjuːd] | n. 高度,高处,高地,高级 |
| barrel | [ˈbærəl] | n. 筒,圆筒,枪管 |
| armature | [ˈɑːmətjuə] | n. 盔甲,电枢,转子,衔铁 |
| domestic | [dəˈmestik] | adj. 本国的,国内的,国产的 |
| diaphragm | [ˈdaiəfræm] | n. 膜片,隔板,光圈,振动膜 |
| eccentric | [ikˈsentrik] | adj. ;n. 偏心的,离心的;偏圆,偏心轮 |
| pulsate | [pʌlˈseit] | vi. 振动,搏动,有节奏地鼓动 |
| adaptability | [əˌdæptəˈbiliti] | n. 适应性,改编 |
| submerge | [səbˈmədʒ] | vt. ;vi. 浸没,淹没;没入水中 |
| electromagnt | [iˈlektrəuˈmægnit] | n. 电磁体(铁) |

## PHRASES AND EXPRESSIONS

| | |
|---|---|
| corrossion-resistant | 耐腐蚀 |
| auxiliary fuel tank | 辅助油箱 |
| fuel pump | 燃油泵 |
| fuel line | 油道 |
| electric turbine pump | 电动叶片泵 |
| windshield wiper | 雨刷 |
| break up | 分裂,解散 |
| divide … into | 分成…,分开 |
| back up | 支持,阻塞 |
| needle valve | 针阀 |

## NOTES TO THE TEXT

1. The automobile fuel tank is made of two corrosion-resistant steel halves, which are ribbed for additional strength and welded together.

汽车油箱由两片耐腐蚀的钢片组成,并有加强筋焊在油箱上用以增强油箱的强度。

which 引导的非限制性定语从句修饰 two corrosion-resistant steel halves; is made of … 由 … 组成,在句中做谓语。

2. The unit injector system is used by Detroit Allison, for example, on its engines, both two-stroke and four-stroke, which are also used in many different manufacturers products.

单体喷射系统用在底特律柴油机上,举例说,它可用在二冲程发动机上,也可装在四冲程发动机上,同时,它还可应用在许多不同制造者制造的产品上。

该句中 is used 是被动语态,是表示被动;which 引导的是非限制性定语从句,修饰 system。

**2.2.2. Induction Systems**

The induction system must provide the engine with an adequate supply of clean air at the proper temperature for good combustion (and for scavenging cylinders on two-stroke-cycle engines) for all operating speeds, loads, and operating conditions. Up to 1 500 cubic feet of air per minute or more may be required, depending on engine size and load.

On a naturally aspirated four-stroke-cycle engine, the system includes the air cleaner, a precleaner (if used), the intake manifold, and the connecting tubing and pipes. On the two-stroke-cycle, the system also includes a blower for scavenging air and for combustion.

On a turbocharged engine, additional air is supplied by means of a turbocharger, which is exhaust gas-driven. On a supercharged engine a mechanically driven blower is used to provide additional air supply.

An air shut-off valve may be included to allow engine intake air to be shut off completely for emergency engine shutdown.

An intercooler or aftercooler may also be included in the induction system. Since cooler air is more dense, a greater amount of air is in fact supplied if the air is cooled. The intercooler is mounted to cool the intake air after it leaves the discharge side of the turbocharger and before it enters the engine (before it enters the blower on two-stroke-cycle diesels). The aftercooler is mounted in the two-stroke-cycle diesel engine block so that it will cool intake air after it leaves the blower and before it enters the cylinder ports.

**Air Cleaners**

The air cleaner and filter have three primary functions:
1. They clean the air before it is mixed with fuel.
2. They silence intake noise.
3. They act as a flame arrester in case of a backfire (Figure 2-21).

In 1957, engineers at the Lincoln-Mercury Division of Ford Motor Company were searching for ways to improve driveability under cold weather conditions. They discovered that driveability improves when the air cleaner is used to provide warm air to the carburetor at low temperatures. It also allows more efficient carburetor

adjustments, which in turn:
1. Reduce exhaust emissions without reducing engine performance
2. Permit leaner air-fuel ratios
3. Give better fuel economy
4. Reduce carburetor icing in cold weather.

Since then, the air cleaner has become a separate emission control system for intake air temperature control. It also has become a part of other emission controls, such as the PCV system.

The automotive engine burns about 9 000 gallons (34 065 liters) of air for every gallon of gasoline at an air-fuel ratio of 14.7 to 1. With many of today's engines operating on even leaner ratios, the quantity of air consumed per gallon of fuel is closer to 10 000 gallons (37 850 liters). This equals 200 000 gallons (757 000 liters) of air with every 20 gallons (76 liters) of fuel.

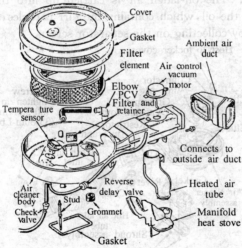

Figure 2-21 Typical air cleaner assembly

Although the basic airborne contaminants—dust, dirt and carbon particles—are found whenever a car is driven, they vary in quantity according to the environment. For example, engine air intake of abrasive carbon particles will be far greater in constant bumper-to-bumper traffic. Intake of dust and dirt particles will be greater in agricultural or construction areas.

A dry type air cleaner draws air through a specially treated paper. The paper is pleated accordion style. Figure 2-22 illustrates a modern filter of this type having a series of ducts (passages) and a thermostat designed to furnish heated air to the cleaner during engine warm-up. The air is drawn from around the exhaust manifold. When the engine is heated the thermostat will close off the source of heated air.

In the oil bath air cleaner shown, air is drawn through the inlet and down through the center tube. At the bottom of the tube, the direction of air flow is reversed and oil is picked up from the oil reservoir cup. The oil-laden air is carried up into the separator screen where the oil, which contains the dirt particles, is separated from the air by collecting on the separator screen.

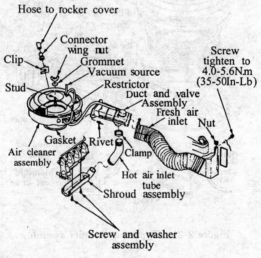

Figure 2-22 Modern air cleaner with paper type air filter element

A low-pressure area is created toward the center of the air cleaner as the air passes a cylindrical opening formed by the outer perimeter of the central tube and the inner diameter of the separator screen. This low pressure is caused by the difference in air current velocity across the opening.

The low-pressure area, plus the effect of gravity and the inverted cone shape of the separator screen, causes the oil and dirt mixture to drain to the center of the cleaner cup. This oil is again picked up by the incoming air, causing a looping cycle of the oil; however, as the oil is carried toward another cycle, some of the oil will overflow the edge of the cup, carrying the dirt with it. The dirt will be deposited in the outer area surrounding the cup. Oil will then flow back into the cup through a small hole located in the side of the cup. Above the separator screen, the cleaner is filled with a wire screen element, which will remove any oil that passes through the separator screen. This oil will also drain to the center and back into the pan. The clean air then leaves the cleaner through a tube at the side and enters the intake system.

**Intake Manifold**

The intake manifold is of cast-iron or cast-aluminum alloy construction. It is designed to direct air from the air cleaner or turbocharger to each cylinder intake port on four-stroke-cycle engines. On the two-stroke-cycle engine, it directs air from the air cleaner or turbocharger to the blower inlet opening.

## NEW WORDS

| | | |
|---|---|---|
| induction | [inˈdʌkʃən] | n. 吸入,感应,感应现象 |
| cubic | [ˈkjuːbik] | adj. ; n. 立方体的,立方的;三次曲线,三次方程 |
| scavenge | [ˈskævindʒ] | vt. 清除,(机)(从内燃机气缸里)扫气 |
| aspirate | [ˈæspərit] | n. ; vt. ; adj. 气音;送气发音;送气音的 |

| | | |
|---|---|---|
| adjustment | [ə'dʒʌstmənt] | n. 调整,调节,修正 |
| abrasive | [əb'reisiv] | n. ;adj. 腐蚀剂,研磨料;有研磨作用的 |
| contaminant | [kən'tæminənt] | n. 污染物,污染 |
| velocity | [vi'lɔsiti] | n. 速度,速率,迅速,周转率 |
| thermostat | ['θəːməstæt] | n. 恒温器,根据温度自动启动的装置 |
| drain | [drein] | vt. ;vi. ;n. 喝干;排水;排出管 |
| overflow | ['əuvə'fləu] | v. 泛滥,横流,溢水 |

## PHRASES AND EXPRESSIONS

| | |
|---|---|
| in case of | 假如,万一 |
| spark ignition system | 火花点火系统 |
| air cleaner | 空气滤清器 |
| turbocharged engine | 涡轮增压发动机 |
| supercharged engine | 增压发动机 |
| airborne contaminaties | 空气中的污染物 |
| oil reservoir cup | 燃油储存杯 |

## NOTES TO THE TEXT

1. The induction system must provide the engine with an adequate supply of clean air at the proper temperature for good combustion for all operating speeds, loads, and operating conditions.

进气系统必须向发动机提供足够充分的清洁空气以达到某一温度下良好的燃烧,以便适应车辆的各种工况和操纵条件。

must 必须,情态动词,此句谓语由情态动词加上 provide 构成;with 引导的介词短语做方式状语,at the proper…conditions 也是介词短语做状语,表明状况。

2. Although the basic airborne contaminant—sdust, dirt and carbon particles—are found whenever a car is driven, they vary in quantity according to the environment.

尽管在空气中有悬浮的灰尘,杂质和碳颗粒—在汽车行驶时随处可见,但它们的数量仍是随环境而变化的。

although 尽管,引导让步状语从句,whenever 引导时间状语从句,they vary in quantity… 是主句。

## 2.2.3 Exhaust Systems

### Exhaust Ststem Types

The exhaust system routes engine exhaust gases to the rear of the car, quiets the exhaust noise, and, in most cases, reduces the pollutants in the exhaust. The system design varies according to engine design. The three major types are:

1. Inline   2. Single V-type   3. Dual V-type

### Inline

When an engine's cylinders are arranged in line, all of the exhaust valves are on the same side of the engine. An exhaust system pipe connects to this side of the engine at the exhaust manifold. The single pipe connects to one or more units that may include a muffler, a resonator, and a catalytic converter.

### Single V-Type

A V-type engine has exhaust valves on both cylinder banks. There are two ways in which these valves can be connected to a single exhaust pipe:

1. There can be a Y-pipe behind the engine.
2. There can be a crossover pipe beneath the engine.

### Dual V-Type

Some V-type engines have two separate exhaust systems, one for each cylinder bank. The systems are similar to the single systems used on an inline engine.

### Exhaust System Components

Major parts of the exhaust system include:

1. Manifolds   2. Pipes   3. Mufflers   4. Resonators   5.

Catalytic converters
**Pipes**

The flow of exhaust gases from the engine should be as smooth as possible. If there are restrictions in the flow, there will be backpressure at the engine. Backpressure is the pressure resisting the flow of exhaust from the cylinders. Too much backpressure will not allow all the exhaust to leave the combustion chamber before the next stroke starts. This preheats and leans the incoming air-fuel mixture, hurting efficiency. It can also cause engine mechanical failures such as burned valves. Exhaust system pipes should be as strgight as possible, without sharp turns and restrictions. Pipes must also be able to withstand the constant presence of hot, corrosive exhaust gases and undercar hazards such as rocks.

The exhaust pipes on many late-model cars are formed with an inner and an outer skin. Occasionally, the inner skin will collapse and form a restriction in the system. From the outside, the exhaust pipe will look normal even when the inside is partially or almost completely blocked. Close inspection is necessary to locate such a defect.

**Mufflers and Resonators**

The muffler is an enclosed chamber that contains baffles, small chambers, and pipes to direct exhaust gas flow. The gas route through the muffler is full of twists and turns (Figure 2-23). This quiets the exhaust flow but also creates backpressure. For this reason mufflers must be carefully matched to the engine and exhaust system.

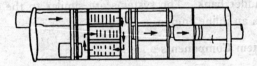

Figure 2-23  Exhaust gases must twist and turn to travel through this muffler

Some mufflers consist of a straight-through perforated pipe surrounded by sound-deadening material, usually fiberglass. These "glass-pack" mufflers, as they are often called, reduce backpressure but are not nearly as quiet as conventional mufflers.

Some engines also add resonators to the system. These are small mufflers specially designed to "fine tune" the exhaust and give it a pleasant, quiet, "resonant" tone.

**Catalytic Converters**

In order to meet tightening exhaust emission standards, carmakers turned to the catalytic converter in 1975. These were oxidation converters that changed HC and CO to harmless $CO_2$ and $H_2O$. Reduction converters first appeared on some 1978 cars which also help eliminate $NO_x$ emissions.

In the simplest arrangement, one catalytic converter is installed in the exhaust system between the manifold and the muffler. Many cars, however, use two converters. Some cars have converters bolted directly to the exhaust manifold.

Catalytic converters are simple. The catalyst combines with the exhaust gases, and causes a chemical reaction to take place. This amounts to a "realignment" of molecules that results in less emissions to the atmosphere. Catalytic converters have no moving parts and never need adjusting. Most converters have a guaranteed lifespan of 50,000 miles, and may outlast the car. The pellets in early General Motors converters can be removed and replaced by removing a plug in the bottom of the unit. Tetraethyl lead, the gasoline octane booster (Figure 2-24) will coat or "poison" the catalyst and reduce its efficiency. This may make converter replacement necessary.

The link between a converter and a well-tuned engine is important. An engine that is misfiring or improperly tuned can also destroy a catalytic converter, because the converter cannot accept exhaust temperatures above 1 500°F (815°C). Neither will it work right if the air-fuel mixture is too rich. Two spark plugs misfiring in succession for a prolonged time will raise the temperature in the converter and shorten its life.

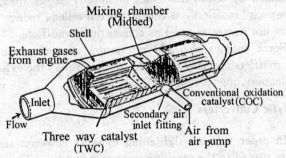

Figure 2-24 Three-way, dual bed monolith catalytic converter

## Exhaust System Effects on Performance, Economy, and Emissions

The main effect of the exhaust system on the engine is the backpressure it creates. Too much backpressure will restrict the flow of exhaust gases from the cylinders and hurt engine performance.

## NEW WORDS

| rea | [riə] | vt. 竖起,举起,建立 |
| muffler | ['mʌflə] | n. 消声器,围巾,厚手套 |
| catalytic | [ˌkætə'litik] | adj. 催化的 |
| resonator | ['rezəneitə] | n. 谐振器,共鸣器 |
| dual | ['djuəːl] | adj.;n. 双,二元的;双数 |
| component | [kəm'pəunənt] | adj.;n. 组成的,合成的;(组成)部分 |
| corrosive | [kə'rəusiv] | adj.;n. 腐蚀性的;腐蚀的;腐蚀剂 |
| deaden | ['dedn] | vt. 使…无感觉,削弱,缓和 |
| eliminate | [i'limineit] | vt. 删除,淘汰,消除 |
| pellet | ['pelit] | n. 丸子,小团团,小子弹,弹丸剂 |
| prolong | [prə'lɔg] | vt. 延长,拉长,拖长 |
| fiberglass | ['faibə'glaːs] | n. 玻璃纤维 |
| octane | ['ɔktein] | n. [化]辛烷 |

## PHRASES AND EXPRESSIONS

| | |
|---|---|
| exhaust manifold | 排气歧管 |
| crossover pipe | 交叉管 |
| catalytic converter | 催化转化器 |
| similar to … | 类似的,相似的 |
| sharp turns | 急转弯 |
| straight-through perforated pipe | 直通式穿孔管 |
| a realignment of molecules | 分子的重新组合 |

## NOTE TO THE TEXT

1. Neither will it work right if the air-fuel mixture is too rich.
如果混合气太浓转换器也不会正常工作。
if 引导条件状语从句,neither 为否定词前置,此句为倒装句;主句的主语是 it,做谓语的是 will work。

2. Some mufflers consist of a straight-through perforated pipe surrounded by sounddeadening material, usually fiberglass.
许多消声器由直通的带孔管道,管道通常由消声材料组成,消声材料通常是纤维玻璃。
consist of 由…组成,做句子的谓语,some mufflers 为主语,surrounded 过去分词短语做后置定语,修饰 pipe。

## EXERCISES

I. Answer the following questions according to the text:
1. Can you list four features of a good gasoline?
2. What is a dual or double-barrel carburetor?
3. What are carburetor jets?
4. Can you name the parts that make up a fuel delivery system?
5. Can you name three elements commonly used to filter fuel?
6. Can you list the major components of a diesel fuel supply system as found on a diesel engine?
7. Can you list the major components of the induction system of (a) a naturally aspirated engine and (b) a turbocharged engine?

8. How is the air heated in the heating system of a vehicle?

9. What is the primary function of a catalytic converter?

II. Fill in the blank in each sentence with one of the four words or phrases which correctly complete the sentence:

1. All automobiles have some form of ____ supply system.
   A. water    B. fuel    C. air    D. oxygen

2. The purpose of this system is to store and then to supply a clean, Continuous, and ____ amount of fuel to the carburettor.
   A. sufficient    B. adequate
   C. inadequate    D. considerable

3. The vertical baffle plate ____ the fuel from sloshing around in the tank as the vehicle moves.
   A. provides    B. protects    C. projects    D. prevents

4. Two-tank combination ____ the vehicle with a greater driving range without the need for refueling.
   A. provides    B. protects    C. projects    D. prevents

5. The tube itself can be made as one piece and attached ____ the tank.
   A. flexibly in    B. rigidly to
   C. vertically on    D. horizontally with

6. ____ the style of construction of the filler tube, all late-model vehicles requiring unleaded fuel have a special filler tube.
   A. Because    B. Regardfully
   C. Without regard to    D. Regardless of

III. Choose the words or a phrase from the list for each space in the passage below:

1. are connected          6. delivery
2. against                7. either…or
3. in addition            8. where
4. is least likely        9. depending on
5. along with             10. in order to

Many components of the fuel system ____ together with lines and hoses. These lines and hoses carry the fuel from the tank to the fuel pump, from the pump to the carburettor, return excess fuel to the tank, and carry fuel vapors. ____ the type of installation, these lines can be ____ rigid ____ flexible.

The fuel lines that fasten to the vehicle body, frame, or engine are formed from seamless steel tubing. ____ , some lines may have a steel spring covering at certain points for protection ____ damage. The tubing is held in place by clips and against, road hazards such as flying stones, where vibration ____ to harden it , and away from the exhaust system ____ to minimize the possibility of creating a vapor lock.

In all sections of the fuel system ____ flexibility is necessary, a section of synthetic rubber hose is installed. These hoses ____ their clamps connect two rigid lines or connect a rigid line to some other component within the fuel system. The diameter of a flexible fuel ____ hose is 5/16 to 3/8 inch while a fuel return or vapor hose is usually 1/4 inch.

Ⅳ. Translate the following sentences into Chinese:

1. Only by doing this can the engine operate at uniform speed with a uniform power output from each cylinder.

2. The receiving unit mounted on the dash board indicates the amount of fuel in the tank on a caliberated gauge by the amount of current received from the sending unit.

3. In addition, the linkages, assist devices, and various controls on all carburetors can vary widely, even between two automobiles of the same make and model but with different engines.

4. This simply means that the carburetor not only must provide a ratio to meet power demands, caused by such things as light-speed variations and changing engine load conditions, but also provide reasonable fuel economy and minimum exhaust emissions.

5. A diesel engine fuel system consists of a fuel tank, a primary filter, a secondary filter, a fuel supply pump with a hand primer, an injector pump with a speed governor and automatic injection timing clutch, nozzle holders with nozzles, low-and high-pressure fuel lines.

6. When the plunger moves down forced by the spring, the fuel under a slight pressure created by the fuel supply pump flows through the longitudinal inlet passage in the body filling the space above the plunger.

Ⅴ. Translate the following passage into Chinese:

The carburetor is the all-important device that converts air and gasoline into an air-fuel mixture that can be burned in the cylinders. Carburetors must operate under all types of conditions and in all temperatures. Although there are dozens of carburetor designs available, all operate on the same basic principle of pressure differential. Pressure differential is the difference in air pressure between the relatively high pressure of the atmosphere outside the engine, and the low pressure of the carburetor and intake manifold. A partial vacuum is created by the downward stroke of the piston, which draws air in through the manifold and the carburetor.

For a carburetor to operate efficiently, the gasoline must be properly atomized, vaporized, and distributed to the cylinders through the intake manifold.

In spite of different designs, most carburetors have the same seven basic systems of passages, ports, jets, and pumps. Venturis, or restrictions, help speed the airflow through the throat, and throttle valves help control the rate of flow.

Most carburetors made since 1979 are of a tamperproof design in which the idle mixture and choke adjustment are set at the factory and sealed according to U.S. government regulations. This was done to prevent unauthorized adjustments that would affect emissions.

## 2.3 Cooling and Lubrication Systems

### 2.3.1 Cooling Systems

When the air-fuel mixture in a combustion chamber burns, the cylinder temperature can soar to 6 000℉ (3 316℃). During the complete 4-stroke cycle, the average temperature is about 1 500℉ (816℃). About one-third of this heat energy is turned into mechanical energy by the engine. The remaining two-thirds must be removed from the engine so that the engine can operate efficiently. If the heat energy remains, several things will happen:

    1. The engine oil temperature will increase, affecting engine lubrication.

    2. The incoming air-fuel mixture will become too hot, making it expand and reduce engine efficiency.

    3. Metal engine parts will expand, eventually causing the engine to seize.

Where does the extra heat energy from combustion go? About half of it is absorbed by the metal in the engine, which is then cooled by the cooling system. The other half remains in the combustion gases, and exit through the exhaust system.

**Cooling System Function**

We have said that about one-third of the total heat energy from combustion is absorbed by the engine's metal. This is both good and bad:

    1. It is good because an engine that is too cool will have poor fuel vaporization, poor lubrication, excessive acids in the blowsy gases, and high HC emissions.

    2. It is bad because an engine that is too hot will have weakened metal, poor volumetric efficiency, poor lubrication, high oxides of nitrogen ($NO_x$) emissions, and in extreme cases may exhibit harmful detonation or pre-ignition.

Obviously, there must be a "just-right" engine operating temperature that will minimize these problems. This temperature is slightly different from engine to engine, depending on the design. Early engines ran at about 180°F (82°C). Late-model engines run as high as 230°F (110°C). These temperatures will vary depending on driving conditions.

**Cooling System Operation**

Most automotive engines use a liquid cooling system (Figure 2-25). Liquid coolant constantly circulates through the engine, absorbing heat from the engine block and cylinder head. The coolant is then circulated outside of the engine and exposed indirectly to the air. The air absorbs heat from the coolant, so that the coolant can go back into the engine and absorb more heat. The greater the difference in temperature between the coolant and the air, the more heat will be absorbed by the air.

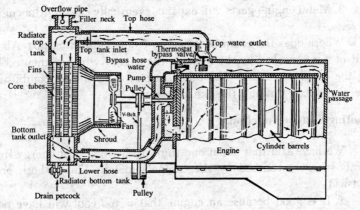

Figure 2-25   A typical liquid cooling system

## Circulation Patterns

Within the engine, coolant circulates in passages called water jackets (Figure 2-25). Outside the engine, the coolant circulates through hoses and the radiator. To keep the engine running at its ideal temperature, there are two patterns of coolant circulation. The two patterns are controlled by the thermostat, which is a temperature-sensitive valve that opens and closes a passage between the engine and the radiator.

## Circulation When Cold

When the engine is cold, it must be warmed quickly to its ideal temperature. With the cooling system in full operation, it would take a long time for this to happen. To speed the warm-up, the thermostat is closed when the coolant is cold. This keeps the coolant in the engine from circulating through the radiator. The coolant, does however, circulate inside the engine, so the coolant warms uniformly. Because there is no heat transfer between the coolant in the engine and the air passing the radiator, the heat of combustion quickly warms the engine.

**Circulation When Warm**

As the coolant within the engine gets warm, the thermostat opens. This allows full coolant circulation between the engine and the radiator. The operating temperature of the engine is determined by the thermostat, which opens between 180° and 210°F (82 and 99°C)—depending on its design. The amount of coolant in the system and the size of the radiator determine the cooling capacity of the system.

**Cooling System Components**

A typical liquid cooling system, includes the:
1. Water jackets
2. Thermostat-controlled bypass
3. Core, or freeze, plugs
4. Radiator
5. Water pump
6. Radiator fan
7. Thermostat
8. Radiator pressure cap
9. Coolant hoses
10. Drive belt
11. Coolant recovery system.

The following paragraphs describe these parts:

**Thermostats**

The thermostat is a temperature-sensitive flow control valve located in the thermostat housing at the front of the engine. The thermostat remains closed until the engine reaches operating temperature. As the temperature increases, the thermostat opens. This allows coolant to be circulated through the radiator for cooling. When the engine coolant falls below operating temperature, the thermostat closes once again. Coolant circulation is restricted to the engine block and cylinder heads and the cab's interior heater when the thermostat is closed. A bypass provides the passage for coolant return to the pump.

Many V-type engines have two or more thermostats, one or two for each bank of cylinders.

Semi-blocking thermostats are used in the rapid warm-up cooling system.

In this warm-up system enough coolant to vent the system is by-passed to the radiator top tank by means of a separate external deaeration line and then back to the water pump without going through the radiator cores. As the coolant temperature rises above 170°F., the thermostat valves start to open, restricting the by-pass system, and permit a portion of the coolant to circulate through the radiator. When the coolant temperature reaches approximately 185°F., the thermostat valvesare fully open, the by-pass system is completely blocked off, and all of the coolant is directed through the radiator.

A defective thermostat which remains closed, or only partially open, will restrict the flow of coolant and cause the engine to overheat. A thermostat which is stuck in a full open position may not permit the engine to reach its normal operating temperature. The incomplete combustion of fuel due to cold engine operation will result in excessive carbon deposits on the pistons, rings, and valves.

Properly operating thermostats are essential for efficient operation of the engine. If the engine operating temperature deviates from the normal range the thermostats should be removed and checked.

**Radiator**

When the coolant leaves the engine, it is quite hot-often well over 200°F (93.3°C). If it were to be immediately pumped back into the engine, it would start to boil and would be ineffective as a coolant. Therefore, before the water can be reused, it must be cooled by circulation of water and air.

Cooling is accomplished by passing the water, as it leaves the engine, into the top or side tank of a radiator.

From the top tank, it flows down through tiny metal (copper or aluminum) tubes. The tubes have thin copper fins soldered over their entire length. As the water makes its way down through the tubes, it gives off heat to the tubes and fins. Since these metals are an excellent conductor, the tubes give off their heat, via the fins, to the air passing around the tubes.

By the time the water reaches the bottom tank, it is cool enough to reuse.

**Water Pump**

The pump housing is cast either of iron or aluminum. The impeller shaft is supported on double row ball bearings, usually of the sealed type or bushings. A special seal is used to prevent water leakage. A hub is fastened to the front of the impeller shaft. A pulley and a fan are bolted to this hub.

Some pumps place the impeller in the water jacket of the engine, while others keep the impeller enclosed in the pump housing. Figure 2-26 illustrates a typical water pump. The water pump is usually secured to the front of the engine by bolts.

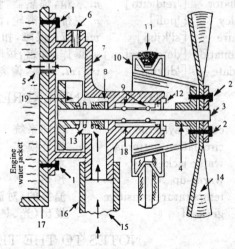

Figure 2-26 Typical water pump

1-Bolts-pump to block.   2-Bolts-fan and pulley.   3-Pump shaft.
4-Hub.   5-Water outlet.  6-Bypass.   7-Pump housing.
8-Seal.   9-Ball bearings.   10-Pulley.   11-V-belt.
12-Dust seal.   13-Seal spring.   14-Fan.   15-Water inlet.
16-Hose.   17-Block.   18-Bearing race.   19-Impeller.

## NEW WORDS

| | | |
|---|---|---|
| soar | [sɔ:l] | vi. ;n. ;vt. 高飞,暴涨;高飞范围;飞达 |
| circulate | ['sə:kjuleit] | vi. ;vt. 循环,环流;使环流 |
| dilute | [dai'lju:t] | vt. ;adj. 冲淡,稀释;稀释的,淡的 |
| misture | ['mɔistʃə] | n. 潮气,水气 |
| sludge | [slʌdʒ] | n. 油泥,软泥,泥状沉积物,酸碱 |
| foul | [fəul] | adj. ;vt. ;vi. 污秽的;污蚀,弄脏;腐烂 |
| individual | ['individjuəl] | adj. ;n. 个别的,独特的;个体,个人 |
| sensitive | ['sensitiv] | adj. 敏感的,感觉性的,感光的,极为微妙的 |
| essential | [i'senʃən] | adj. ;n. 本质的,必需的;本质,实质 |
| radiator | ['reidieitə] | n. 水箱,辐热器,辐射体,辐射源 |
| pulley | ['puli] | n. 皮带轮,滑轮,滑车 |
| secure | [si'kjuə] | vt. ;adj. 保障,扣紧;安心的,可靠的 |
| detonation | [detəu'neiʃən] | n. 爆炸,爆燃,爆鸣 |
| deviate | ['di:vieit] | vi. ;vt. 背离,偏离;使背离,使偏离 |

## PHRASES AND EXPRESSIONS

| | |
|---|---|
| cooling systems | 冷却系统 |
| circulation patterns | 循环模式 |
| water jackets | 水套 |
| warm-up | 预热 |
| temperature-sensitive | 温控的,对温度敏感的 |
| give off | 发出(光、热)等,释放 |

## NOTES TO THE TEXT

1. The air absorbs heat from the coolant, so that the coolant can

go back into the engine and absorb more heat.

空气将吸收冷却液中的热量以便冷却液能够返回到发动机中而重新吸收发动机的热量。

so that 以至于…，引导目的状语从句，the air 是主句中的主语，from the coolant 是介词短语做状语。

2. The two patterns are controlled by the thermostat, which is a temperature-sensitive valve that opens and closes a passage between the engine and the radiator.

这两种方式由节温器控制，节温器是一个温度敏感阀，它放在发动机和散热器之间并能开能关。

which 引导非限制定语从句，修饰 thermostat；主句是被动语态，by the… 是方式状语；在非限制性定语从句中，还包含一个由 that 引导的限制性定语从句，修饰 valve。

### 2.3.2 Lubrication Systems

**Lubrication Principles**

Engine oils are the lifeblood of the internal combustion engine. The quality and performance are often taken for granted, without full appreciation of the severe service conditions under which the engine oil must function. Lubrication must be accomplished despite highly oxidizing conditions, very high temperatures, and the presence of large amounts of contaminants. The high output of today's engines, coupled with extended drain intervals, has increased the severity under which the oil must perform.

Extensive research and in-service field testing are required to develop oils meeting the increasing severity demanded by today's engines.

Engine oils are formulated from selected lube basestocks and fortified with the right additives to provide the performance level required (Figure 2-27).

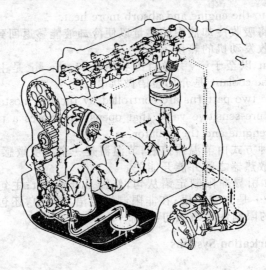

Figure 2-27  Cutaway showing oil flow through a four-cylinder engine

**Engine Oil Functions**

The engine oil must perform many direct functions, while not causing any debits in other areas of engine performance.

**Lubrication**

The oils must provide a fluid film between all moving engine parts to reduce friction, heat, and wear. Friction and wear are caused by metal-to-metal contact of the moving parts. Wear is also caused by acidic corrosion, rusting, and the abrasion from the contaminants carried in the oil.

**Sealing**

High combustion pressures are encountered. Piston rings require an oil film between ring and liner and between ring and piston groove to seal against these high pressures and to prevent blowby.

**Cooling**

The engine oil is largely responsible for piston cooling. This is done by direct heat transfer through the oil film to the cylinder walls and on to the cooling system. Heat is also carried by the oil from the undercrown and skirt to the crankcase. Thermally stable oils are required to withstand the high temperatures encountered.

**Deposit Control**

Rings must remain free to function properly and to maintain a good seal. Deposit buildup in the ring grooves and on piston lands must therefore be controlled.

**Varnish Control**

Engine parts, particularly the piston, must be kept free of varnish to ensure performance and proper cooling.

**Sludge Control**

High and low-temperature sludge-forming contaminants must be held in suspension and not allowed to drop out and accumulate. The larger particles are removed by the filter. Sludge and abrasives are removed with the oil when drained.

**Bearing Protection**

Oil breakdown and corrosive products of combustion can cause bearing corrosion. The additives in the oil counteract this action by minimizing breakdown, neutralizing blowby products, and helping to form a protective film.

**Rust Control**

Engine components including valve lifters, valve stems, rings, cylinder wall, etc., are subjected to severe rust-promoting conditions, particularly in winter stop-and-go driving. Rusting is controlled by oil formulation.

**Wear Control**

Wear occurs through metal-to-metal contact, acidic corrosion, rusting, and abrasive action of the oil's contaminant load. Metal-to-metal contact is controlled by proper viscosity selection and use of film-forming compounds. Acidic corrosion and rusting are controlled by formulation of the oil while the abrasive wear is controlled by air and oil filtration and oil drain intervals.

### Scuff Protection

High-peak pressures occur in such areas as valve train mechanisms, particularly the camshaft lobes. Antiweld-or antiseize-type additives are required to minimize this type of wear.

### Control of Combustion Chamber Deposits

Deposits, including oil-derived, accumulate in the combustion chamber, increasing the compression ratio and creating hot spots.

Combustion chamber deposits increase exhaust emissions. Oils must be formulated to reduce such deposits.

### Control of Valve Deposits

Some higher ash oils tend to create deposits on exhaust valves in some severe type services. This tendency must be minimized.

How successful the lubrication system is in performing all these functions depends on a number of factors and conditions. There must be an adequate supply of good-quality lubricant delivered to all moving engine parts under sufficient pressure to provide hydrodynamic lubrication for rotating parts and oil adhesion to surfaces subject to sliding friction.

1. The oil and filter must be changed at regular intervals.
2. The enigne must operate at its most efficient temperature.
3. Engine oil temperatures must not be excessively hot or cold.

### Oil Pumps

There are four principal types of oil pumps that have been used on engines. They are the gear, rotary, vane, and plunger pumps. The two most widely used are the gear and the rotary types.

### Gear Pump

The gear pump uses a driving and a driven spur gear as the

moving force to pump oil. These gears are placed in a compact housing. The driven gear revolves on a short shaft, while the driving gear is fastened to a longer shaft that is turned by a spiral gear meshed with a similar gear on the camshaft.

The teeth of the two gears must mesh with a minimum amount of clearance. The housing just clears the top, bottom, and sides of both gears.

An inlet pipe allows oil to be drawn in by the whirling gear teeth. Each tooth catches what is will hold and carries it around. When the oil reaches the opposite side, it cannot come back through the center of the gears as they are closely meshed.

As each tooth carries a load of oil around and deposits it on the outlet sides, the oil has nowhere to go but through the outlet to the oil channels. The gear pump is efficient and produces oil pressure needed.

A somewhat different adaptation of the gear pump is pictured in Figure 2-28. The driving gear (center) and driven gear (outer) teeth carry oil around to the outlet area. As the teeth mesh, the oil is compressed and forced through the outlet.

## Plunger Pump

The plunger type pump is used in many small one cylinder engines to maintain the oil level in the dipper trays.

It utilizes a cylinder, plunger, and check valves. It is usually driven by a cam on the camshaft.

As the cam releases the plunger, it is pushed upward by a strong spiral spring. The inlet check valve opens and oil is drawn in. As the cam continues to rotate, it will press the plunger down. This closes the inlet valve and opens the outlet. The process is repeated over and over, producing a steady stream of oil (Figure 2-29).

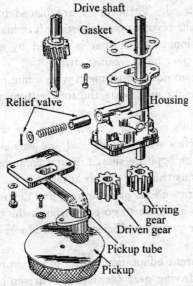

Figure 2-28  Exploded view of a gear type oil pump

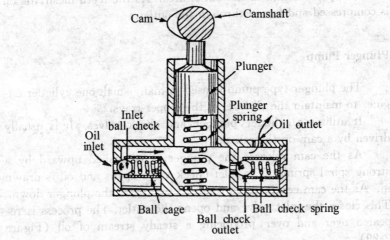

Figure 2-29  Plunger oil pump

## Rotary Pump

A rotary pump uses a housing, an inner rotor, and an outer rotor. The outer rotor is cut away in the form of a star with rounded points (Figure 2-30).

The inner rotor is shaped in the form of a cross with rounded points that fit in the outer rotor star. The inner rotor is much smaller. It is driven by a shaft turned by the camshaft.

The inner rotor is mounted off center so that when it turns, the rounded points "walk" around in the star-shaped outer rotor. This causes the outer rotor to revolve also. As the inner rotor "walk" the outer rotor around, the outer rotor openings pick up oil at the inlet pipe and pull it around until it lines up with outlet. It is then forced out as the inner and outer rotor points close together. The oil cannot make a circuit around, as the inner rotor fist snugly against the outer rotor one spot.

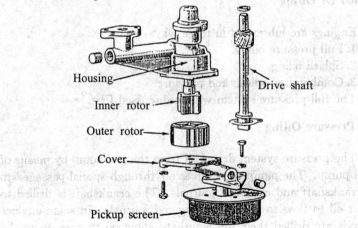

Figure 2-30  Exploded view of a rotor type oil pump

**Vane Pump**

This pump uses a round housing with a round rotor placed off center. This rotor contains two or more vanes, or rotor blades, that fit into slots in the rotor. The vanes are held out against the round housing by springs between the vanes. Some designs feed oil, under pressure, to the inner vane ends. This pressure along with centrifugal force, helps hold the vanes in firm contact with the housing wall.

As the shaft turns, the vanes are forced in and out to keep contact with the housing. As they swing out, they pick up a charge of oil and carry it around. As the vane is forced in, this places a squeeze on the oil and it is pushed out of the pump. As a steady stream of charges are picked up, carried around, and squeezed out, the pump produces a good stream of oil.

**Method Of Oiling**

Engines are lubricated in three ways:
1. Full pressure oiling
2. Splash oiling
3. Combination splash and pressure.
The full pressure system will be discussed first.

**Full Pressure Oiling**

The pressure system draws oil from the pan sump by means of an oil pump. The pump then forces oil, through special passages, to the crankshaft and camshaft journals. The crankshaft is drilled to permit oil to flow to the connecting rod journals. In some engines the rods are drilled their full length to allow oil to pass up to the wrist pin bushings. Bearing throw-off may be helped, by spurt holes in the rod, to lubricate the cylinder walls. Timing gears, lifters, and rocker arms, where used, are also oiled. In the pressure system, all bearings are oiled by either pumping oil into the bearings, or squirting or dripping it on (Figure 2-31).

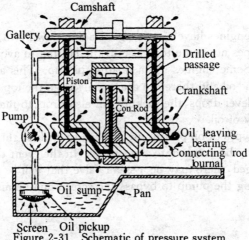

Figure 2-31  Schematic of pressure system

## Splash System

The splash system supplies oil to moving parts by attaching dippers to the bottom of the connecting rods. These dippers can either dip into the sump itself, or they can dip into shallow trays. The whirling dippers splash oil over the inside of the engine. The dipper is usually drilled so that oil is forced into the conneting rod bearings.

An oil pump may be used to keep oil trays full at all times. The splash system is used primarily on small one cylinder engines.

The pressure system best meets the needs of the modern car engine and is therefore in almost universal use. This chapter will deal primarily with the pressure system.

## Combination Splash and Pressure

This system uses dippers and trays. An oil pump supplies oil to the camshaft and crankshaft bearings. On overhead engines, oil is pumped to the rocker arms and valves.

## Oil Pickup

Some engines have a rigid pipe leading down into the oil in the sump. It does not come too close to the bottom to avoid picking up sediment. Some engines use a floating pickup. This actually floats on top of the oil and therefore draws only from the top of the sump. As the oil level drops, the pickup will also drop, to maintain a constant supply of oil.

Both types of oil pickup use screens to exclude the larger particles that may be drawn into the system. In the event the screen becomes clogged, there may be a small valve that will be drawn open, thus allowing the pump to bypass the screen and obtain oil.

## Sump

Oil is poured into the engine and flows down into the pan. One end of the pan is lower and forms a reservoir called a sump. Baffle plates are sometimes used to prevent the oil from sloshing around. The drain plug is placed in the bottom of the sump.

## NEW WORDS

| | | |
|---|---|---|
| oxidize | ['ɔksaidaiz] | vi. ;vt. 使氧化,使生锈；氧化 |
| formulate | ['fɔ:mjuleit] | vt. 公式化,简述,制定…的配方 |
| fortify | ['fɔ:tifai] | vt. 筑垒于,加强,使…坚强 |
| sludge | [slʌdʒ] | n. 软泥,淤泥,酸渣,碱渣 |
| abrasive | [əb'reisiv] | adj. ;n. 腐蚀的；腐蚀剂,研磨料 |
| viscosity | [vis'kɔsiti] | n. 粘性,粘度,粘滞性 |
| adhension | [əd'hi:dʒən] | n. 粘附,粘附力,附着力 |
| spiral | ['spaiərəl] | adj. ;n. ;vi. ;vt. 盘旋的；螺线；盘旋；使成螺旋形 |
| mesh | [meʃ] | n. 网眼,网孔,筛眼 |
| blade | [bleid] | n. 叶片,刀片,草片,浆片 |
| sump | [sʌmp] | n. 槽池,贮槽,油盘,曲柄箱 |
| sediment | ['sedimənt] | n. 沉积物,沉积,沉淀,渣滓 |

## PHRASES AND EXPRESSIONS

| | |
|---|---|
| full pressure oiling | 压力润滑 |
| splash oiling | 飞溅润滑 |
| lubrication principles | 润滑原理 |
| metallic detergents | 金属洗涤剂 |
| plunger pump | 柱塞泵 |
| drop out | 掉落,掉出 |
| tend to | 趋向,趋势 |
| cut away | 切掉,砍掉 |

## NOTES TO THE TEXT

1. The quality and performance are often taken for granted, without full appreciation of the severe service conditions under which the engine oil must function.

它的质量和特性是常被考虑的,要求发动机必须在恶劣的不能完全满意的环境下运转。

take for granted 考虑,被动语态形式,在句中做谓语;without full appreciation of…function 是状语,指明被考虑的情况;在状语中有 under which 引导的限制性定语从句,修饰 conditions。

2. The driven gear revolves on a short shaft that is turned by a spiral gear meshed with a similar gear on the camshaft。

被动齿轮绕一短轴旋转,而主动齿轮绕一长轴旋转,此长轴端有一斜轮与凸轮轴上的斜齿轮啮合。

整个句子是由 while 引导的两个并列分句构成的,while 表示转折的意思;that 引导的是限制性定语从句修饰 shaft,定语从句为被动语态;by 是介词短语做方式状语,而 meshed with … camshaft 为过去分词短语做后置定语,修饰 gear。

## EXERCISES

Ⅰ. Answer the following questions according to the text:

1. What are the three jobs that the cooling system must perform?

2. Can you give six reasons why an engine must not run too cool?

3. Water pumps are generally of the gear type. True or False?

4. A radiator is generally made of copper and brass to aid in cooling. True or False?

5. What is the purpose of the thermostat?

6. How do thermostats work?

7. What is meant by the heat range of a thermostat?

8. A good engine oil has four tasks. What are they?

9. Can you name the major ways of lubricating a engine?

10. How are two-stroke cycle engine lubricated?

11. How do you determine how much oil there is in the oil sump?

Ⅱ. Fill in the blank in each sentence with one of the four words or phrases which correctly complete the sentence:

1. The heated gases must ____ heat to the cylinder walls.
A. give up     B. give in     C. get back     D. take from

2. Water flowing in the water jackets ____ heat ____ the metal shell that forms the upper part of the combustion chamber.
A. transfers…to…         B. obtains…with…
C. removes…from…       D. reduces…into…

3. The coolant contained in the cooling jacket ____ heat produced in the engine cylinder.
A. gives off         B. leaks out
C. lets go of        D. picks up

4. The degree of cooling is adjusted ____.
A. by the engine         B. by a thermostat
C. through a lever       D. with a blower

5. For heating the cab, the cooling system is additionally ____ a hot water heater.
A. provided with         B. provided for
C. protected from        D. prevented against

6. When the coolant temperature drops below 80℃, the slide valve is forced by the return spring ____ oil and the fan stops.
A. to seal in            B. to seal off

C. to release the    D. to send out

7. The aim of lubrication is ___ metal-to-metal contact.
A. to affect    B. to expand the
C. to reduce    D. for the purpose of

8. The duty of engine oil is also ___ a considerable amount of heat from the piston.
A. to centralize    B. to decentralize
C. in building up    D. to carry away

9. The oil pump serves to create the required ___ in the lubricating system.
A. lubricant    B. pressure
C. amount of oil    D. temperature

10. The engine lubricating system provides a flow of lubricating oil ___ in the engine.
A. with elements    B. for working parts
C. to all moving parts    D. against cylinder walls

11. The engine oil, as it passes trough the engine, ___ heat and carries it back to the oil pan.
A. gives up    B. picks up
C. makes up    D. bears off

Ⅲ. Choose a phrase from the list for each space in the passage below:

1. are made of            2. consists of
3. is soldered to         4. owing to
5. a series of            6. is dissipated into
7. is equipped with       8. are connected to
9. by means of            10. is filled with

The purpose of the radiator is to cool the water that enters it from the water jacket of the engine. The radiator of the engine cooling system ___ a header (upper) and a collector (lower) tank, a core, and mounting components. For better conduction of heat, the tanks and the core, which ___ the tanks, ___ brass.

The radiator core, or matrix, comprises ___ thin horizontal fins through which pass numerous vertical tubes of flattened oval section, the fins and the tubes being solder bonded together. The heated water entering the radiator ____ a large number of fine streams through its core. With such a core structure, the water is cooled more intensively, ____ the increased contact surface area between the water and the tube walls.

The header and collector tanks ____ the engine cooling jacket ____ suitable pipe connections and hoses. The collector tank ____ a drain cock to drain water from the radiator. Screwed in the cylinder block in its lower part is a similar cock to enable the engine jacket to be drained.

The cooling system ____ water through a filler neck provided on the header tank. The neck is closed by a cap.

Ⅳ. Translate the following sentences into Chinese:

  1. Not only will this water tend to form sludge when whipped with the oil by the rotating crankshaft, but also the water will cause rusting of the engine parts.

  2. The outside of the water jacket dissipates some of the heat to the air surrounding it, but most of the heat is carried by the cooling water to the radiator for dissipation to the surrounding air.

  3. It is important, therefore, for the engine to be brought to operating temperature as quickly as possible after first starting, and then maintained at that temperature throughout the operation of the engine.

  4. The oil lines consist of brass or rubberized pipes inter-connecting individual sections of the lubricating systems, and of passages drilled in the cylinder block, crankshaft, connecting rods, rocker fulcrums, rockers, filter bodies, etc.

  5. In addition, the oil forms a seal between the piston rings and the cylinder wall, and washes the working surfaces free of chemical deposits to protect from corrosion.

  6. The simplest method of lubricating an engine is to mix the oil with the petrol, as is done in two-stroke engine.

  7. Rigidly fixed to the rotor spindle of this filter is the oil swirler insert having oil ducts tangent to its circumference.

Ⅴ. Translate the following passage into Chinese:

  Motor oil has five major jobs in an engine: reducing friction, cooling, cleaning, sealing, and absorbing shock. Additives mixed with the oil help it to do these jobs. Two oil rating systems are generally used: the API service classification and the SAE viscosity rating. The API number rates an oil's performance in a laboratory engine, and the SAE viscosity number rates the oil's thickness. An oil may have one or more API ratings. An oil's service classification and viscosity rating must be matched to an engine's requirements for best performance, economy, and emission control.

An engine lubrication system includes the pan, filter, pump, oil galleries or oil lines (or both), dipstick, and pressure warning lamp or pressure gauge. The oil is stored in the oil pan. The pump takes it from the pan, pressurizes it, and sends it through the oil galleries or oil lines to lubricate the moving parts of the engine. The filter traps dirt and other particles that the oil holds in suspension, so the oil and filter must be changed periodically. A dipstick is used to measure the oil level in the pan when the engine is not running, and a pressure warning lamp (for low oil pressure) or a pressure gauge (for continuous pressure reading) is used when the engine is running.

The main purpose of engine lubrication is control of mechanical wear. Excessive wear will hurt performance, economy, and emission control. The use of the proper oil, and regular oil and filter changes, will keep engine wear to a minimum.

## 2.4 Gasoline Fuel Injection Systems

### 2.4.1 Electronic Control Systems

To meet stringent emission control requirements in the early 1970s, automotive engineers began to apply electronic control to basic automotive systems. The use of electronics was first applied to ignition timing and later to fuel metering. Electronic control introduced a degree of precision that electromechanical and vacuum-operated systems could not achieve in matching fuel delivery and ignition timing with engine load and speed requirements. With electronic control came a significant decrease in emission levels, major improvements in driveability, and increased reliability of the systems.

Electronic ignitions appeared first, followed a few years later by electronic fuel metering systems which were quickly integrated with the electronic ignitions to form the early engine management systems. By the early 1980s, many automotive systems were controlled by an onboard computer.

### Parts of A Computer

We have dealt with the functions, logic, and software used by a computer. The software consists of the programs and logic functions stored in the computer's circuitry. The hardware is the mechanical and electronic parts of the computer.

### Central Processing Unit (CPU)

As mentioned earlier, the microprocessor is the central processing unit, or CPU of a computer. Since it does the essential mathematical operations and logic decisions that make up its processing function, the CPU can be considered the heart of a computer. Some computers use more than one microprocessor, called a coprocessor.

### Computer Memory

The computer storage or memory function is provided by other integrated circuit (IC) devices. These simply store the computer operating program, system sensor input data, and system actuator output data for use by the CPU. Automobile computers use three different types of memory for their storage functions (Figure 2-32).

    1. Read-only memory (ROM) or programmable read-only memory (PROM)
    2. Random-access memory (RAM)
    3. Keep-alive memory (KAM)

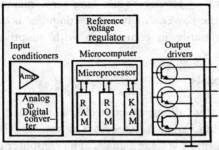

Figure 2-32  Three different types of memory are used by an engine control computer

Permanent memory is called read-only memory (ROM) because the central computer can read the contents of the memory but cannot change the information contained within it. Data stored in ROM is retained even when power to the computer is turned off. The computer control program and specific vehicle data are stored in ROM so they will not be lost when power to the computer is interrupted. ROM containing the control program is built into the computer. The specific vehicle data is located in a separate ROM chip called a programmable read only memory (PROM). The PROM is used to individualize a single computer for use in various models.

Temporary memory is called random-access memory (RAM) because the central computer can both read information from it and write new information into it as dictated by the computer program. However, data contained in RAM is lost whenever power to the computer is interrupted. Depending upon the computer design, RAM can provide both short-or long-term memory. Short-term memory is lost every time the ignition switch is turned off; long-term memory is retained until the computer power supply is completely disconnected. System trouble codes and diagnostic test results are common items stored in RAM.

Keep-alive memory (KAM) shares characteristics of ROM and RAM. Like RAM, data can be written into keep alive memory. It also can be read and erased, but like ROM, it is not lost when the ignition is turned off. However, like long-term memory, KAM is erased whenever the power supply to the computer is disconnected. KAM is used primarily in conjunction with adaptive strategies, which we will study.

**Common Components**

As we have seen, all engine control systems use a computer, a series of sensors, and various actuators. The sensors feed data to the computer in the form of voltage signals. The computer processes the sensor data according to its internal program and then signals the actuators to exercise the desired control over the subsystems that require adjustment.

**System Sensors**

As we learned a sensor is an input device used to change temperature, motion, light, pressure, and other forms of energy into voltage signals that a computer can read. Input sensors tell the computer what is happening in several areas of vehicle operation at any given moment. For our purposes here, a quick review of their outstanding characteristics should refresh your memory before we look at specific sensor applications.

1. Switch the simplest form of sensor, it signals an on or off condition.

2. Timer used to delay a signal for a predetermined length of time to prevent the computer from compensating for momentary conditions that do not significantly affect engine operation.

3. Resistive sensors may be potentiometers, thermistors, or piezoresistive devices.

4. Transformer contains a movable core that varies its position between input and output windings to produce a voltage signal.

5. Generator may be a magnetic pulse generator, a Hall-effect switch, or a galvanic battery. These sensors do not require a reference voltage but generate their own signal voltage.

## Characteristics And Features

Automotive sensors function in a severe environment. For this reason, they must be designed for long-term, dependable operation while providing reliable signals. A sensor must have certain characteristics, or operating features, for it to operate properly. These characteristics affect the selection of a particular sensor for a given function, and establish the specifications for troubleshooting and service. The important characteristics are:

1. Repeatability the sensor must function consistently. For example, a temperature switch must open and close at the design points thousands of times without deviation. If the sensor produces a voltage in proportion to the condition being measured, it must do so throughout its operating range.

2. Accuracy the sensor must work within the tolerances or limits designed into it. Our temperature switch may close at $195°\pm1°$, or it may close at $195°\pm10°$. The tolerances depend on how the sensor is used, but once established, the sensor must work consistently. These tolerances are used to design sensor test specifications for troubleshooting.

3. Operating range an operating or dynamic range within which it must function is established for the sensor. A digital sensor has only one or two switching points. Since the operating range of an analog sensor is wider, it must be proportional. Signals outside the operating range are ignored by the computer.

4. Linearity this refers to sensor accuracy throughout its dynamic range. Within this range, an analog sensor must be as consistently proportional as possible to the measured value. While sensor linearity is most accurate near the center of its dynamic range, no sensor has perfect linearity and computer programs rely on memory data to compensate for this.

## Airflow Sensors

Some fuel injection systems use a vane-type airflow sensor

(Figure 2-33), positioned between the air filter and the intake manifold. The airflow sensor monitors the volume of air entering the intake manifold. A thermistor is used to sense air temperature and is part of the vane. Since the angular position of the vane is proportional to airflow, a potentiometer connected to the vane sends a voltage signal proportional to intake air volume to the computer.

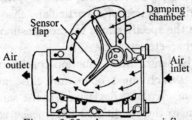

Figure 2-33  A vane-type airflow sensor

**Manifold pressure, vacuum, and barometric pressure sensors**

These sensors keep the computer informed about air volume and engine load, allowing it to adjust fuel metering accordingly. Their in-put also is used by the computer to adjust timing and EGR flow relative to load. They may be a piezoresistive device, a transformer, or a potentiometer operated by an aneroid bellows or vacuum diaphragm.

**Temperature sensors**

Two types of temperature sensors are used: engine coolant and air charge temperature (ACT). If the computer is only interested in whether coolant or air temperature is above a stated point, a simple bimetal switch is used. However, when the computer requires information about a temperature range, a thermistor is used.

The thermistor-type sensor used to track coolant temperature is threaded into a passage where its sensing bulb is immersed in engine coolant.

An air charge temperature sensor is similar in construction to the coolant temperature sensor, but provides a faster response time to air temperature changes. It may be located in the air cleaner (Figure 2-34), to measure only air temperature, or in the intake manifold where it measures the air-fuel mixture temperature.

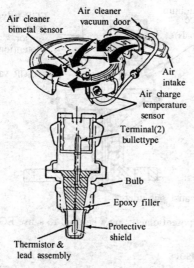

Figure 2-34   An air charge temperature (ACT) sensor may be installed in the air cleaner or intake manifold

**Vehicle speed sensors**

Vehicle speed information necessary to control torque converter lockup is provided to the computer by a pulse generator or optical sensor. The most common type now in use has a reflective blade attached to the speedometer assembly. As the blade spins, it passes through a light emitting diode (LED) beam. Each time the blade cuts through the LED beam, it reflects light back to a phototransistor. This creates a low-power signal which is amplified and sent to the ECM.

**EGR sensors**

A sliding-contact potentiometer may be connected to the top of the EGR valve stem to inform the computer of EGR flow rate (Figure 2-35). This information is used by the computer to control timing, fuel metering and EGR valve operation.

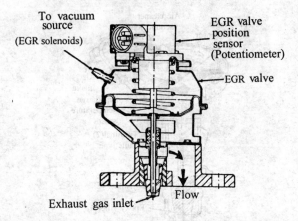

Figure 2-35  A potentiometer may be used to sense EGR flow

## Air Conditioning Sensors

An air conditioning compressor adds to the engine load when the compressor clutch is engaged. To allow the computer to make the necessary adjustments to compensate for the increased load, a simple on/off switch is used to tell the computer whether the compressor clutch is engaged or disengaged.

## Detonation sensors

Detonation sensors generally use a piezoresistive crystal which changes resistance whenever pressure is applied to it . A reference voltage from the computer is applied to one terminal. The return signal voltage from the other terminal remains at its programmed value as long as there is no detonation and as long as pressure on the crystal is uniform. However, if detonation occurs, the unequal pressure on the crystal changes the sensor's resistance and the return voltage signal changes.

## Throttle position sensors

A throttle position sensor (TPS) may be a simple on/off switch, used to indicate wide-open throttle or idle position with a high or low voltage. The carburetor switch used on some Chrysler carburetors is an example of this type of TPS.

A potentiometer also can be used to indicate the exact position and speed of throttle movement. The TPS may be a rotary or a linear potentiometer, depending upon its application. A rotary throttle position sensor is used on fuel injection assemblies. A linear TPS generally is used with carburetors. The two types differ primarily in how they work, but both send the computer an analog signal proportional to the angle of the throttle plate opening. The rotary potentiometer moves on an axis with the throttle shaft; the linear potentiometer uses a plunger that rides on a throttle shaft cam.

**Ignition timing, crankshaft position, and engine speed sensors**

These sensors send analog and digital signals which the computer uses to control timing, fuel metering, and EGR. A Hall-effect switch is mounted on or in the engine block. A timing disc mounted on the harmonic balancer or cast as part of the crankshaft, passes through the Hall-effect switch field. This is used as a signal to inform the computer of cylinder position and firing order.

**Exhaust Gas Oxygen Sensors and Fuel Metering Control**

The exhaust gas oxygen (EGO) sensor is one of the most important sensors on a car. It is usually installed in the exhaust manifold, although in some vehicles it may be located downstream from the manifold in the head-pipe (but before the catalytic converter). This places it directly in the path of the exhaust gas stream where it can monitor both the exhaust gas and ambient air. The sensor tip contains a thimble made of zirconium dioxide ($Z_rO_2$), an electrically conductive material capable of an generating a small voltage in the presence of oxygen.

Exhaust gases from the engine pass through the end of the sensor installed in the manifold where they contact the outer side of the thimble. Atmospheric air enters through the other end of the sensor and contacts the inner side of the thimble (Figure 2-36). The inner and outer surfaces of the thimble are plated with platinum. The inner surface is a negative electrode; the outer surface is a positive electrode.

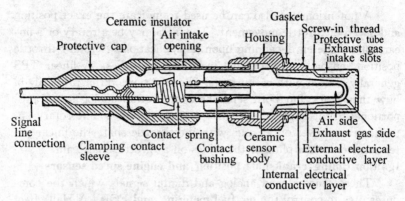

Figure 2-36  The components of a typical EGO sensor

The atmosphere contains a relatively constant 21 percent oxygen. Rich exhaust gases contain virtually no oxygen. Exhaust from a lean mixture combustion, or from a misfire, contains more uncombined oxygen (still far less than the atmosphere, however).

Negatively charged oxygen ions are drawn to the thimble, where they collect on both the inner and outer surfaces. Because the oxygen present in the atmosphere exceeds that in exhaust gases, the air side of the thimble draws more negative oxygen ions than the exhaust side. The difference between the two sides creates an electrical potential. When the concentration of oxygen on the exhaust gas side of the thimble is low, a high voltage (0.60 to 1.00 volt) is generated between the electrodes. As the oxygen concentration on the exhaust side increases, the voltage generated drops (0.00 to 0.40 volt).

This voltage signal is sent to the computer, where it passes through the input conditioner for amplification. The computer interprets the high-voltage signal as a rich air-fuel ratio, and a low-voltage signal as a lean air-fuel ratio. Based on the EGO signal, the computer will either lean or enrich the mixture as required to maintain as close to a 14.7 air-fuel ratio as possible. The EGO sensor is therefore the key sensor of an electronically controlled fuel-metering system.

An EGO sensor does not send a voltage signal until its tip reaches a temperature of about 572℉ (300℃). EGO sensors provide their fastest response to mixture changes at about 1,472℉ (800℃). This is the primary reason for open-loop fuel control on a cold engine.

Unlike resistive sensors, an EGO sensor (as well as any other generator sensor) does not require a reference voltage. The computer, however, uses an internal reference voltage as a comparison for the sensor signal. Because the EGO sensor signal ranges from 0.1 to 0.3 volt (100 to 300 millivolts) with a lean mixture to 0.6 or 0.9 volt (600 to 900 millivolts) with a rich signal, the computer uses an internal reference of 0.45 volt (450 millivolts) as a reference. The internal reference voltage also is the basis for fuel-metering signals during open-loop operation.

To make the system more responsive, carmakers went first to the concept of installing a separate EGO sensor in each manifold of a V-type engine. While this arrangement is still used, the heated exhaust gas oxygen (HEGO) sensor (Figure 2-37) is the most recent development.

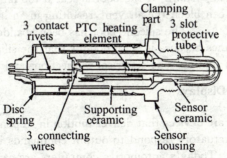

Figure 2-37 The components of a typical HEGO sensor

A HEGO sensor is constructed and operates the same as an EGO sensor, but contains a built-in heater powered by the vehicle battery whenever the ignition is in the run position. A third wire to the sensor delivers battery current(1 ampere or less)to the sensor electrode. This helps warm the sensor to operating temperature more quickly and permits the sensor to operate at a lower exhaust gas temperature(approximately 392℉ or 200℃). The heating element also keeps the sensor from cooling off when exhaust temperature drops,such as during prolonged idling in cold weather. HEGO sensors often are used on turbocharged engines where the sensor is installed sownstream from the turbocharger,which absorbs much of the heat in the exhaust.

All EGO sensors work on the principles just discussed,but they are not all built the same. They may have one,two,or three wires that connect to the vehicle wiring harness. Early model sensors had two wires and were grounded through the computer or to some point on the chassis or engine. Later sensors have a single wire and ground through their outer shell to the exhaust pipe or manifold. Single-and double-wire EGO sensors are not interchangeable (the three-wire sensor is an HEGO).

Some sensors have a silicone boot to protect the sensor and to provide a vent for ambient air circulation. The positioning of a boot (when used)is important. If the boot is seated too far down on the sensor body,it can block the air vent,resulting in an inaccurate signal to the computer. The silicone boot has been abandoned on some late-model engines because it was thought that the silicone material gives off fumes that corrode electrical connections and terminals.

**Actuators and Displays**

Actuators are devices that deliver motion in response to an electrical signal. Actuators respond to output commands issued by the microcomputer. Today's automotive computers are capable of issuing up to 600 000 commands per second. Automotive actuators include solenoids,relays,and motors.

The most common actuator is a valve powered by a solenoid. By energizing and de-energizing the solenoid coil,the movable core of the solenoid can be made to open or close valves. The valve,in turn, controls vacuum, fuel vapor, air, oil, or water flow. Both normally open and normally closed solenoid valves are used. A normally open solenoid valve remains open when no voltage is applied. A normally closed solenoid valve remains closed when no voltage is applied.

A fuel injector (Figure 2-38) is a small, normally closed precision solenoid valve. When the microcomputer outputs an injection signal to the injector, the coil built into the injector pulls the needle's valve back, and fuel is injected through the nozzle. The amount of fuel injected is controlled by the injection pulse duration, or the length of time that the coil remains energized.

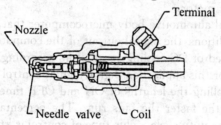

Figure 2-38  Fuel injector solenoid valve

The microprocessor relays digital voltage signals to an output driver (usually a power transistor), which, in turn, controls an actuator. Battery voltage (B+) is supplied from the battery to the actuator. Ground for the actuator is provided through the microprocessor, via the output driver transistor. The control signal from the microprocessor causes the output driver transistor to open or close the ground circuit of the actuator, thus controlling its operation.

The output driver circuit from the microcomputer is sometimes used to operate a relay, which, in turn, controls some secondary automotive actuator. This application is often used for heavy current loads that normally draw too much current to be operated directly by the output driver's transistor. Some manufacturers refer to this type of circuit as an enabler circuit. The computer grounds an enabler relay to control the output device. One common automotive example is the electric cooling fan motor. To turn the cooling fan motor ON, the microcomputer turns ON the appropriate driver transistor with a signal from the microprocessor. The transistor then completes the relay coil circuit path to ground to energize the relay coil and develop a magnetic field in the core. The magnetic field causes the relay switch contacts to close, completing the relay power circuit from the battery to the cooling fan motor, and the motor runs.

When electric motors are used as actuators, there are usually two types used: the permanent magnet direct current (DC) motor and the stepper motor.

In a typical automotive body microcomputer that controls environmental conditions, the digital output of the computer can be used to vary the speed of DC cooling fan motors according to cooling requirements. For this application digital signals control the DC motor speed by controlling the lengths of ON and OFF times. The longer the ON time, the faster the fans run. The percentage of the ON time is called the duty cycle. This type of control is known as pulsewidth modulation. Compared with conventional rheostat control, it offers a much higher degree of accuracy and control with a minimum of wasted energy.

Another type of motor that lends itself to digital control operation is the DC stepper motor. A typical stepper motor is constructed with a permanent magnet armature called a toothed rotor and two field coils. The motor is designed so that applying a single pulse of voltage from the microcomputer causes the motor shaft to turn a specific number of degrees. Another pulse results in another equal displacement, or step. The computer can apply a series of pulses in order to move the controlled device (usually a valve) to whatever position is desired. In this way, the stepper motor provides precise positional control of movement. By keeping count of the pulses applied, it knows in exactly what position it is without use of a feedback signal. Stepper motors utilizing position control have been used to control air/fuel mixture and idle speed. Stepper motors can also be used to drive mechanical odometers. In this case, the motor operates from digital pulses generated by the vehicle speed sensor to operate mechanical gear-driven numbers similar to the traditional odometer.

## Control System Development

Engine computer control systems have developed considerably since they first appeared a decade ago. Today's systems, however, are undergoing even more rapid development into a highly sophisticated electronic network composed of many microprocessors (computers) that eventually will manage all operational and customer convenience systems in a vehicle. The body computer module (BCM) concept which appeared on some 1986 GM luxury cars is the first generation of these "total control" systems, and their development should be more rapid than the progress. We've seen with engine control systems.

The early full-function control systems had one or more of the following characteristics; late-model systems have all of them.

1. The computer controls timing electronically instead of relying on distributor vacuum and centrifugal advance mechanisms.

2. The computer controls air-fuel ratio as close as possible to the stoichiometric value (14.7) through an EGO sensor and a 3-way catalytic converter.

3. The computer controls fuel metering by operating a carburetor mixture control solenoid or by pulsing fuel injectors according to data received from various sensors.

4. Engine operation is divided into open-and closed-loop operational modes. A separate "limp-in mode", or "limited operational strategy", is provided when a serious system malfunction occurs, allowing the vehicle to be driven in for service.

5. The computer can set a number of trouble codes and may have a self-diagnostic capability.

# NEW WORDS

| | | |
|---|---|---|
| stringent | ['strindʒnt] | *adj.* 严格的,严厉的,紧的,有说服力的 |
| individualize | [ˌindividjuəlaiz] | *vt.* 使个体化,使具有个性,列举,分别定述 |
| magnetic | [mægnetik] | *adj.* 磁性的,磁的,有吸引的,有魅力的 |
| galvanic | [gæl'vænik] | *adj.* 电流的,触电似的,突然而勉强的 |
| deviation | [diːvi'eiʃən] | *n.* 偏向,偏差,背离 |
| proportional | [prə'pɔːʃənl] | *adj.* 比例的,均衡的,相称的 |
| compensate | ['kɔmpenseit] | *v.* 赔偿,补偿,酬劳 |
| thermistor | [θəː'mistə] | *n.* 热敏电阻,热变阻器 |
| potentiometer | [pəˌtenʃi'ɔmitə] | *n.* 电位计,电势计,分压器 |
| aneroid | ['ænərɔid] | *adj.* ;*n.* 无液的;空盒气压表 |
| bulb | [bʌlb] | *n.* ;*vi.* 电灯泡,水银球;生球茎 |
| amplify | ['æmplifai] | *vt.* 放大,增强,扩大 |
| catalytic | [ˌkætə'litik] | *adj.* ;*n.* 催化的;(石油)催化裂化器 |
| ambient | ['æmbiənt] | *adj.* 周围的,包围着的 |
| thimble | ['θimbl] | *n.* 套筒,套管,顶针,嵌环 |
| platinum | ['plætinəm] | *n.* [化]铂,白金 |
| amplification | ['æmplifi'keiʃən] | *n.* 扩大,放大,扩充,详述 |
| inaccurate | [in'ækjurit] | *adj.* 不精密的,不准确的,错误的 |
| corrode | [kə'rəud] | *vt.* ;*vi.* 腐蚀,侵蚀,起腐蚀作用 |
| sophisticate | [sə'fistikeit] | *vt.* ;*vi* 窜改,曲解,使腐化;诡辩 |
| convenience | [kən'viːnjəns] | *n.* ;*vt.* 便利,方便,设施;为…提供方便 |
| centrifugal | [sen'trifjugəl] | *adj.* ;*n.* 离心的,利用离心的,输出的;离心机 |
| stoichiometric | [stɔikiə'metrik] | *adj.* 化学计算的 |
| solenoid | ['səulinɔid] | *n.* 螺线管,圆筒形线圈 |
| diagnostic | [daiəg'nɔstik] | *adj.* ;*n.* 诊断的,特征的;症状,特征 |
| actuator | ['æktjueitə] | *n.* 促动器,调节器,传动机构,螺线 |

| | | 管 |
|---|---|---|
| modulation | [ˌmɔdjuˈleiʃən] | n. 调整,调节,转调,调制 |
| rheostat | [ˈriːəstæt] | n. 变阻器,电阻箱 |
| odometer | [ɔˈdɔmitə] | n. 里程表,路码表,自动计程仪 |

## PHRASES AND EXPRESSIONS

| | |
|---|---|
| electronic fuel injection system | 电子燃油喷射系统 |
| electronic control system | 电控系统 |
| airflow sensor | 气流传感器 |
| temperature sensor | 温度传感器 |
| vehicle speed sensor | 车速传感器 |
| detonation sensor | 爆震传感器 |
| throttle position sensor | 节气门位置传感器 |
| deal with | 对付,应付,处理 |

## NOTES TO THE TEXT

1. Electronic ignitions appeared first, followed a few years later by electronic fuel metering systems which were quickly integrated with the electronic ignitions to form the early engine management systems.

电子点火刚出现不久,紧接着几年后产生与电子点火相结合的电子燃油计量系统从而形成早期的发动机控制系统。

which 引导限制性定语从句,修饰 metering systems;electronic ignitions 做为主句的主语,appear 为谓语;followed…为过去分词短语做定语,修饰主句中的主语。

2. Compared with conventional rheostat control, it offers a much higher degree of accuracy and control with a minimum of wasted energy.

与传统的变阻控制式相比较,它(脉宽调整型)能提高到较高的精度控制耗电。

Compared 是过去分词短语状语从句,由于它的逻辑主语 it 与谓语是动宾关系,因此用过去分词引导。

## 2.4.2 Fuel Injection

A carburetor is a mechanical device that is neither totally accurate nor particularly fast in responding to changing engine requirements. Adding electronic feedback mixture control im-proves a carburetor's fuel metering capabilities under some circumstances, but most of the work is still done mechanically by the many jets, passages, and air bleeds. Adding feedback controls and other emission-related devices in recent years has resulted in very complex carburetors that are extremely expensive to repair or replace.

The intake manifold also is a mechanical device that, when teamed with a carburetor, results in less than ideal air-fuel control. Because of a carburetor's limitations, the manifold must locate it centrally over (V-engines), or next to (inline engines), the intake ports while remaining within the space limitations under the hood. The manifold runners have to be kept as short as possible to minimize fuel delivery lag, and there cannot be any low points where fuel might puddle. These restrictions severely limit the amount of manifold tuning possible, and even the best designs still have problems with fuel condensing on cold manifold walls.

The solution to the problems posed by a carbureted fuel system is electronic fuel injection (EFI). EFI provides precise mixture control over all speed ranges and under all operating conditions. Its fuel delivery components are simpler and often less expensive than a feed-back carburetor. Some designs allow a wider range of manifold designs. Equally important is that EFI offers the potential of highly reliable electronic control (Figure 2-39).

We will discuss:
1. The advantages of fuel injection over carburetion
2. The differences among various fuel injection systems
3. The fundamentals of electronic fuel injection
4. The subsystems and components of typical fuel injection systems now in use.

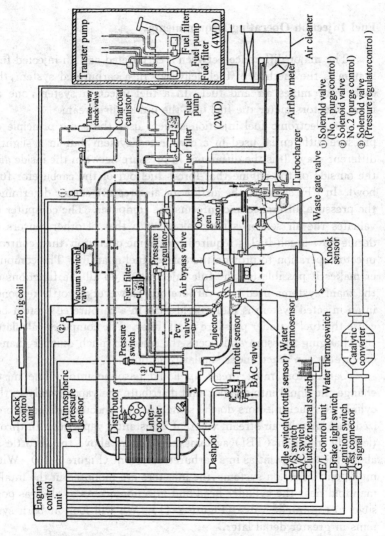

Figure 2-39  One type of gasoline fuel injection system that uses a turbocharger with an intercooler

## Fuel Injection Operating Requirements

The major difference between a carbureted and an injected fuel system is the method of fuel delivery. In a carbureted system, the carburetor mixes air and fuel. In a fuel injection system, one or more injectors meter the fuel into the intake air stream.

An electronic fuel injection system uses the same principle of pressure differential used in a carbureted system, but in a slightly different way. It is the difference in pressure between the inside and the outside of the engine that forces fuel out of the carburetor fuel bowl. In EFI systems, the airflow or air pressure sensor determines the pressure difference and informs the computer. The computer evaluates the air sensor's input along with that of other sensors to decide how much fuel is required for engine operation, then controls injector operation to provide the correct fuel quantity. The computer makes it possible for the fule injectors to do all the functions of the main systems used in a carburetor. However, throttle response in an injected system is more rapid than in a carbureted system because the fuel is under pressure at all times. The computer calculates the changing pressure and opens the injector much quicker than a carburetor can react under similar conditions.

Carburetors must break up liquid gasoline into a fine mist, change the liquid into a vapor, and distribute the vapor evenly to the cylinders. Fuel injectors do the same. A fule injector delivers atomized fuel into the air stream where it is instantly vaporized. In throttle body injection (TBI) systems, this occurs above the throttle at about the same point as in a carbureted system (Figure 2-40). With multipoint injection systems, the injectors are mounted in the intake manifold near the cylinder head and injection occurs as close as possible to the intake valve (Figure 2-41). We will look at both systems in greater detail later.

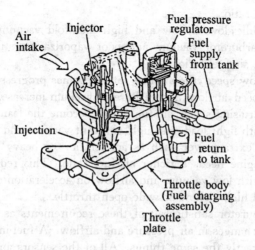

Figure 2-40 Air and fuel combine in a TBI unit at about the same point as in a carburetor

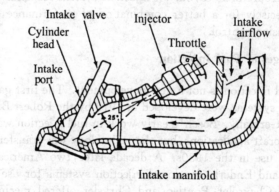

Figure 2-41 In a multipoint system, the air and fuel combine at the intake valve

To review basic engine air-fuel requirements:

1. When an engine starts, low airflow and manifold vacuum, combined with a cold engine and poor fuel vaporization, require a

rich air-fuel ratio.

2. At idle, low airflow and high manifold vacuum, combined with low carburetor vacuum and poor vaporization, still require a slightly rich air-fuel ratio.

3. At low speed, the air-fuel ratio becomes progressively leaner as engine speed, airflow, and carburetor vacuum increase.

4. At cruising speed, air-fuel ratios become the leanest for best economy with light load and high, constant vacuum and airflow.

5. For extra power such as acceleration or heavy load operation, the engine needs a richer air-fuel ratio. This requirement is combined with low vacuum and airflow on acceleration or with low vacuum and high airflow at wide-open throttle.

A carburetor satisfies all of these requirements as its systems respond to changes in air pressure and airflow. A fuel injection system does exactly the same things. All of the sensors and other devices in an injection system respond to the same operating conditions that a carburetor does, but an injection system responds faster and more precisely for a better combination of performance, economy, and emission control.

**Advantages of Fuel Injection**

Fuel injection is not a new development. The first gasoline fuel injection systems were developed in 1912 by the Robert Bosch Company in Germany. Bosch's early work in fuel injection was restricted to aircraft applications, but the technology was transferred to automotive use in the 1930s. A decade later, two Americans named Hilborn and Enderle developed injection systems for use on racing engines. Chevrolet, Pontiac, and Chrysler offered mechanical fuel injection systems during the late 1950s and early 1960s. Some imported vehicles have had fuel injection since 1968. Among domestic manufacturers, Cadillac made electronic fuel injection standard on its 1976 Seville model, and other automakers soon followed suit.

What really made fuel injection a practical alternative to the carburetor was the development of reliable solid-state components during the 1970s. Automakers were quick to apply these advances in electronics to fule injection. The result was a more efficient and dependable system of fuel delivery.

Electronic fuel injection systems offer several major advantages over carburetors:

1. Injectors can precisely match fuel delivery to engine requirements under all load and speed conditions. This reduces fuel consumption with no loss of engine performance.

2. Since intake air and fule are mixed at the engine port, keeping a uniform mixture temperature is not as difficult with multipoint fuel injection systems as it is with carburetors. There is no need for manifold heat valves.

3. The manifold in a multipoint injection system carries only air, so there is no problem of the air and fuel separating.

4. Exhaust emissions are lowered by maintaining a precise air-fuel ratio according to engine requirements. The improved air-fuel flow in an injection system also helps to reduce emissions.

5. Continuing improvements in electronic fuel injection design have allowed some automakers to eliminate other emission control systems such as heated intake air and air pumps.

**Types of Fuel Injection Systems**

There are three general ways to categorize modern fuel injection systems:

1. Mechanical or electronic injection
2. Throttle body or multipoint (port or manifold) injection
3. Continuous or intermittent injection.

However, the distinctions between the various types of fuel injection systems are not simple and clear-cut. All mechanical systems make use of some electronic components, and electronic systems may share some of the features of multipoint and TBI in a single system. One example is Chrysler's continuous-flow TBI system introduced in 1981 and used exclusively on V-8 engines in the Imperial. Although a technological dead end, this system breaks the rules of operation we're about to discuss. It has two injectors, mounted in the throttle body, which respond to varying pressure from a control pump and deliver fuel continuously. A unique airflow sensor in the air cleaner inlet measures the volume of air passing into the system. The entire operation is controlled electronically.

## Mechanical or Electronic Injection

A mechanical fuel injection system delivers gasoline by using its pressure to open the injector valve. Mechanical injection systems generally are continuously operating. In other words, they inject fuel constantly while the engine is operating. The Bosch K-Jetronic is a typical example of a mechanical injection system (Figure 2-42).

An electronic fuel injection EFI system generally uses one or more solenoid-operated injectors to spray fuel in timed pulses, either into the intake manifold or near the intake port. EFI systems are operated intermittently. All domestic manufacturers use some form of EFI.

## Throttle Body or Multipoint Injection

The most common type of EFI system is throttle body injection (TBI). This design is something of a halfway measure between feedback carburetion and multipoint injection. It generally is classified as a single-point, pulse-time, modulated injection system. TBI injection, as its name implies, has one or two injectors in a carburetor-like TBI assembly that mounts on a traditional intake manifold. Fuel is kept at a constant pressure by a regulator built into the throttle body.

The computer controls injector pulsing in one of two ways: synchronized or nonsynchronized. If the system uses a synchronized mode, the injector pulses once for each distributor reference pulse. When dual injectors are used in a synchronized system, the injectors pulse alternately. In a nonsynchronized system, the injectors are pulsed once during a given period (which varies according to calibration) completely independent of distributor reference pulses.

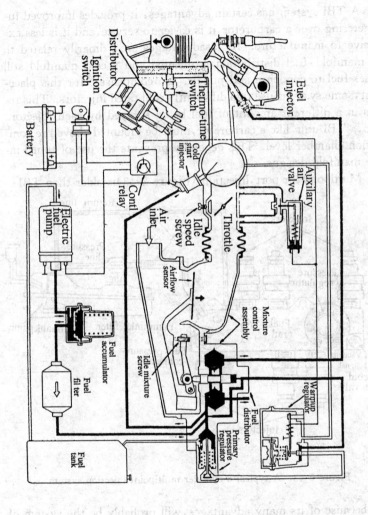

Figure 2-42 The Bosch K-Jetronic is a mechanical continuous injection system

A TBI system has certain advantages: it provides improved fuel metering over a carburetor, it is easier to service, and it is less expensive to manufacture. Its disadvantages are primarily related to the manifold: fuel distribution is unequal and a cold manifold still causes fuel to condense and puddle. To compensate for this placement, some systems use two differently calibrated injectors. This results in a different amount of fuel being sprayed by each injector. Also, a TBI unit, like a carburetor, must be mounted above the combustion chamber level. This generally prevents the use of tuned intake manifold designs.

Multipoint, or port, injection (Figure 2-43) is older than TBI

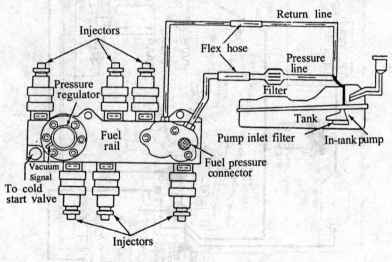

Figure 2-43  A typical 6-cylinder multipoint injection system

and because of its many advantages, will probably be the system of choice for all but ecomomy-class vehicles in the future. Multipoint systems have one injector for each engine cylinder. The injectors are mounted in the intake manifold near the cylinder head where they can inject fuel as close as possible to the intake valve.

The advantages of this design also are related to characteristics of intake manifolds:

1. Fuel distribution is equal to all cylinders because each cylinder has its own injector (Figure 2-44).

2. The fuel is injected almost directly into the combustion chamber, so there is no chance for it to condense on the walls of a cold intake manifold.

3. Because the manifold does not have to carry fuel or properly position a carburetor or TBI unit, it can be shaped and sized to tune the in-take airflow to achieve specific engine performance characteristics.

The primary disadvantage of multipoint injection is the higher cost of individual injectors and other parts, as well as the computer software to control their operation.

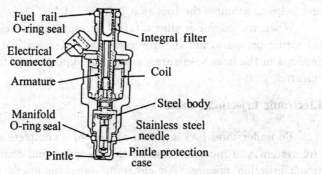

Figure 2-44 A multipoint (port) electronic fuel injector

**Continuous or Intermittent Injection**

A continuous injection system constantly injects fuel whenever the engine is running. The most common example used on production vehicles is the Bosch K-Jetronic mechanical con-tinuous injection system. (Many carmakers refer to K-Jetronic simply as CIS.)

The individual injectors operate on the opposing forces of fuel pressure and the spring-loaded valve in the injector tip. When inlet fuel pressure reaches about 45 psi (310 kpa), it overcomes spring pressure and forces the injector open. Each injector then delivers fuel continuously to the port near the intake valve. Fuel collects or "waits" at the valve to mix with incoming air. When the intake valve opens, the air-fuel moisture enters the cylinder.

In the K-Jetronic system, fuel pressure controls injector opening and the amount of fuel that is injected. Fuel pressure varies continually during different engine operating conditions. Under heavy load, for example, fuel pressure may reach 70 psi (483 kpa). This forces the injector farther open to admit more fuel.

The main fuel distributor and regulator controls fuel pressure in response to airflow and preset regulator pressure. Injector spring force and fuel pressure cause the injector valve to vibrate. This constantly varies the amount of fuel in relation to engine requirements and helps to atomize the fuel as it is injected.

When the engine is shut off, fuel pressure drops below injector tip spring pressure, and the injectors close. Residualfuel pressure is retained in the lines to ensure a ready fuel supply when the engine is restartel.

### Electronic Injection Nozzle

To understand fuel injection as part of a complete engine control system, you must understand the operation and control of electronic injection nozzles. An elecrtonic injection nozzle is simply a specialized solenoid (Figure 2-45). It has an armature and a needle or ball valve. A spring holds the needle or ball closed against the valve seat, and the armature opens the valve when it receives a current pulse from the system computer. When the solenoid is energized, it unseats the valve to inject fuel.

The injector always opens the same distance, and the fuel pressure is maintained at a constant value by the pressure regulator. The amount of fuel delivered by the injector depends on the amount of time that the nozzle is open. This is the injector pulse width: the time in milliseconds that the nozzle is open.

The system computer varies pulse width to supply the amount of fuel that an engine needs at a specific moment. A long pulse width delivers more fuel; a short pulse width delivers less fuel.

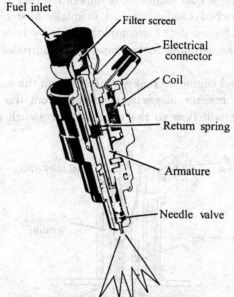

Figure 2-45  Solenoid actions intermittently open the EFI nozzles

Injector pulse width relates to another important concept that you will use to test injection systems. This is the injector duty cycle. The duty cycle relates to any intermittently operating device. Ignition dwell, for example, is really the ignition duty cycle. The complete operating cycle of any solenoid-operated device is the entire time from on to off to back on again. The duty cycle is the percentage of on-time to total cycle time.

A solenoid can operate at any number of cycles per second: 10, 20, 30, 60, or whatever the engineer chooses to design. Each complete cycle lasts the same amount of time, but duty cycle can vary as a percentage of each cycle. Pulse width varies along with the duty cycle because it is the actual time that the solenoid is energized.

**Cold Start Valve**

When starting a cold engine, it is imperative that the mixture be somewhat enriched (adding of fuel to intake airstream). The cold start valve (Figure 2-46) accomplishes this by injecting extra fuel into the intake manifold for a temperature controlled period of time.

When the cold engine is cranked, current from the starter is fed to the cold start injector magnetic winding. From the cold start windings, current will flow to the thermal time switch and on to ground.

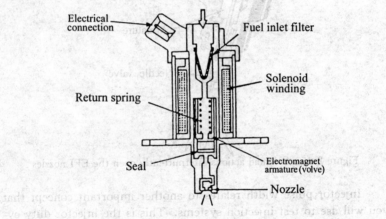

Figure 2-46  One type of cold start valve (injector)

Current will flow for a maximum of 12 seconds when engine temperature is below -5 ℉ (-21 ℃). At temperatures exceeding this level, the amount of time current is passed to the winding will gradually decrease until an engine temperature of 95 ℉ (35 ℃) is reached.

Above this point, the cold start will not be actuated. None; Regardless of temperature, current flow will stop when the starter switch is released.

Current passing through the winding will form a magnetic field and draw the armature up, which allows seal to be drawn off of its seat. The fuel will flow through the unit and spray out at the injector nozzle.

Cold-start injector duration is regulated by a thermal-time switch in the thermostat housing. This switch grounds the cold-start injector circuit when the engine is cranked at a coolant temperature below a specified value. A heating element inside the switch also is activated during cranking and starts to heat a bimetallic strip in the ground circuit. Once the bimetallic strip reaches the specified temperature, it opens the ground circuit and shuts off power to the cold-start injector.

## NEW WORDS

| | | |
|---|---|---|
| lag | [læg] | v. 走得慢,延迟,滞后 |
| puddle | ['pʌdl] | vt. ;vi. ;n. 搅拌;搅泥浆;水坑,胶土 |
| condense | [kən'dens] | vt. ;vi. 压缩,浓缩;凝结,(气体)变成液体(固体) |
| evaluate | [i'væljueit] | vt. 求…的值,以数目表示,评价 |
| cruise | [kru:z] | vi. ;vt. ;n. 巡游,徘徊;巡航于 |
| alternative | [ɔ:l'tənətiv] | adj. ;n. 两者挑一的,选择的;取舍 |
| consumption | [kən'sʌmpʃən] | n. 消费,消耗,肺结核,结核病 |
| eliminate | [i'limineit] | vt. 排除,消除,消灭,消去 |
| intermnttent 的 | ['intə:'mitənt] | adj. 间歇的,断断续续的,周期性 |
| distinction | [dis'tiŋkʃən] | n. 区分,区别,差别,个性 |
| exclusively | [iks'klu:sivli] | adv. 除外地,排外地,专有地 |
| imperial | [im'piəriəl] | n. ;adj. 特大品,特等品;特大的 |
| modulate | [mɔdjuleit] | vt. 调整,调节,调制 |
| regulator | ['rægjuleitə] | n. 调节器,标准器,调节剂,标准钟 |

| | | |
|---|---|---|
| synchronize | ['siŋkrənaiz] | vi. ;vt. 同时发生,同步;使同步 |
| calibration | [,kæli'breiʃən] | n. 标准,标定,刻度,测量口腔 |
| vibrate | [vai'breit] | vt. ;vi. 使振动,使摆;摆动 |
| imperative | [im'perətiv] | adj. ;n. 绝对,必要的;命令,规则 |

## PHRASES AND EXPRESSIONS

| | |
|---|---|
| manifold runner | 歧管通道 |
| break up | 打碎,拆散,破碎 |
| fuel injector | 燃油喷射器 |
| multipoint injection | 多点喷射 |
| combine with… | 使结合,使联合 |
| fuel rail o-ring seal | 油道 O 型密封圈 |
| electronic injection nozzle | 电子喷油嘴 |
| ignition devell | 停止点火 |
| bimetallic strip | 双金属片 |

## NOTES TO THE TEXT

1. The solution to the problems posed by a carbureted fuel system is electronic fuel injection(EFI).

这个由化油器供油方式产生的问题的解决办法由电子燃油喷射来完成,即 EFI 系统。

The solution 是句子的主语,后接后置定语 to the problems…systems,在后置定语中,又由 pose 的过去分词短语做定语,修饰 problems。

2. What really made fuel injection a practical alternative to the carburetor was the development of reliable solid-state components during the 1970s.

真正使燃油喷射系统有效地替换化油器的的应用是在 19 世纪 70 年代中可依靠的固态硬件的发展。

整个句子的主语是由 what 引导的主语从句,what 为主语,made 为谓语,fuel injection 为宾语;主句的谓语是 was,the development 为表语,of…components 是 development 的定语,during 为整句的状语。

# EXERCISES

I. Answer the following questions according to the text:
1. Can you explain how an automotive microprocessor processes information?
2. What is the purpose of the various input sensors as part of an automotive microcomputer-based control system?
3. In what way is ROM different from RAM?
4. Generally, in what two ways do input sensors convert non-electrical parameters into electrical signals?
5. Can you define actuator as if applies to a microcomputer-based control system?
6. Why is a return fuel line used in a fuel injection system?
7. How is the ON and OFF operation of an injector controlled?
8. Can you list four types of fuel injection systems?
9. Under what engine temperature condition do most engine microcomputer control systems operate in open loop?

II. Fill in the blank in each sentence with the word or phrase from the list that correctly completes the meaning:
1. compression    2. matched    3. mixed    4. rated
5. is sensitive to    6. provides with    7. provides for

1. During the short period of time, the air and fuel are _____ within the combustion chamber.
2. Dr. Rudoph Diesel is considered to be the father of the workable _____ ignition engine.
3. The fuel delivery delay device also _____ altitude compensation and air density.
4. This device _____ intake manifold(boost)air pressure.
5. The _____ top speed of an engine is an important factor affecting exhaust emissions.
6. The shape of the combustion chamber must be _____ with the injection spray pattern.

III. Completing the sentences: The sentences below are incomplete. After each sentence there are four words or phrases, only one of which will correctly complete the sentence, selecting the proper word or phrase to complete it correctly:

1. Fuel injection systems can lower emissions ____.
   A. by matching the air-fuel ratio to engine requirements
   B. only at high speeds
   C. by using the intake manifold to vaporize fuel
   D. by matching engine speed to load conditions

2. All of the following are common kinds of gasoline fuel injection system except ____.
   A. multipoint injection        B. throttle body injection
   C. direct cylinder injection   D. continuous injection

3. Mechanical fuel injectors are operated ____.
   A. continuously by fuel pressure
   B. intermittently by the computer
   C. alternately by air pressure
   D. sequentially by firing order

4. Modern fuel injection systems are based on work begun by ____.
   A. Rochester Products Division of GM
   B. Ford Motor Company
   C. Hitachi
   D. Robert Bosch GmbH

5. A cold-start injector is a ____.
   A. temperature-controlled detonation device
   B. solenoid-operated auxiliary injector
   C. mechanical intermittent injector
   D. none of the above

6. Multec injectors used in a multipoint injection system differ from those produced by Robert Bosch in that they use a ____.
   A. pintle valve
   B. swirl nozzle
   C. pin and spring
   D. ball-seat valve with director plate

7. All of the following are filter locations in a fuel injection system except ____.

    A. in the pressure regulator
    B. at the fuel pump
    C. in the fuel line
    D. in the fuel injectors
8. A hot-wire, or heated-film, air mass sensor measures ____.
    A. airflow velocity entering the engine
    B. barometric absolute pressure
    C. air temperature in a turbocharged system
    D. molecular mass of air entering the engine

Ⅳ. Translate the following sentences into Chinese:

    1. All computers must perform four basic functions: input, processing, storage, and output. Engine control computers use various sensors to receive input data, the computer output takes the form of voltage signals to its actuators.

    2. Computer-controlled engine systems began as a way of managing fuel metering for better mileage and emission control, manufactures used electronic ignitions with the fuel metering systems to form the basis for an engine management system.

    3. The most recent systems, such as GM's CCC and Ford's EEC-IV systems, have self-diagnostic capabilities, control many more functions, and are far more efficient and powerful than their predecessors.

    4. A computer-controlled fuel injection system which gives precise mixture control and almost instant response to all operating conditions at all speed ranges.

    5. A fuel injection system in which one or two injectors are installed in a carburetor-like throttle body mounted on a conventional intake manifold, fuel is sprayed at a constant pressure above the throttle plate to mix the incoming air charge.

    6. The fuel delivery system consists of an electric fuel pump, a filter, a pressure regulator, one or more injectors, and the necessary connecting fuel distribution lines.

    7. Multipoint injection systems that use mass airflow for fuel adjustment have a movable plate or vane called an airflow sensor which is deflected by intake airflow.

V. Translate the following passage into Chinese:

Fuel injection systems must do the same tasks as carburetors. However, they do so in a slightly different way. Two types of injection systems are used: throttle body injection (TBI) or multipoint (port) injection.

The TBI system uses a carburetor-like throttle body containing one or two injectors. This throttle body is mounted on the intake manifold in the same position as a carburetor. Fuel is injected above the throttle plate and mixed with incoming air.

In a multipoint system, individual injectors are installed in the intake manifold at a point close to the intake valve where they inject the fuel to mix with the air as the valve opens. Intake air passes through an air intake throttle body containing a butterfly valve or throttle plate and travels through the intake manifold where it meets the incoming fuel charge at the intake valve. The difference in injector location permits more advance manifold designs in multipoint systems to aid in fuel distribution.

Fuel injection has numerous advantages over carburetion. It can match fuel delivery to engine requirements under all load and speed conditions, maintain an even mixture temperature, provide more efficient fuel distribution, and reduce emissions while improving driveability.

## 2.5 Emission Control Systems

Approximately 99.9 percent of the exhaust from the average car engine (gasoline powered) consists mostly of water, nitrogen, carbon dioxide, and carbon monoxide. About 0.1 percent (one tenth of one percent) of the exhaust is made up of hydrocarbons (unburned gasoline).

Some of these emissions, such as water, oxygen, nitrogen, and carbon dioxide, are of little concern. Others, such as hydrocarbons (HC), oxides of nitrogen ($NO_x$), and carbon monoxide (CO), can pose a health problem for the nation if uncontrolled.

Hydrocarbon emission into the atmosphere, where it reacts with the sunlight, tends to produce what may be called photochemical (sunlight causing chemical reactions or change) smog.

Excellent progress has been made in the development of a number of emission control devices. These units, when properly installed, serviced and maintained, do an excellent job of reducing harmful emissions. Ongoing research and development in this vital area will undoubtedly bring about further reductions.

**Emission Control**

Early researchers dealing with automotive pollution and smog began work with the idea that all pollutants were carried into the atmosphere by the car's exhaust pipe. But auto manufacturers doing their own research soon discovered that pollutants were also given off from the fuel tank and the engine crankcase. The total automotive emission system contains three different types of controls. This picture illustrates that the emission controls on a modern automobile are not a separate system, but part of an engine's fuel, ignition, and exhaust systems.

Automotive emission controls can be grouped into major families, as follows:

1. **Crankcase emission controls** Positive crankcase ventilation (PCV) systems control HC emissions from the engine crankcase.

2. **Evaporative emission controls** Evaporative emission control (EEC or EVAP) systems control the evaporation of HC vapors from the fuel tank, pump, and carburetor or fuel injection system.

3. **Exhaust emission controls** Various systems and devices are used to control HC, CO, and $NO_x$ emissions from the engine exhaust. These controls can be subdivided into the following general groups:

1. **Air injection systems** These systems provide additional air to the exhaust system to help burn up HC and CO in the exhaust and to aid catalytic conversion.

2. **Engine modifications** Various changes have been made in the design of engines and in the operation of fuel and ignition system components to help eliminate all three major pollutants.

3. **Spark timing controls** Automakers have used various systems to delay or retard ignition spark timing to control HC and $NO_x$ emissions. Most of these systems modify the distributor vacuum advance; however, latemodel cars with electronic engine control systems have eliminated the need for mechanical or vacuum timing devices.

4. **Exhaust gas recirculation** An effective way to control $NO_x$ emissions is to recirculate a small amount of exhaust gas back to the intake manifold to dilute the incoming airfuel mixture. Exhaust gas recirculation(EGR)systems will be described.

5. **Catalytic converters** The first catalytic converters installed in the exhaust systems of 1975-76 cars helped the chemical oxidation or burning of HC and CO in the exhaust. Later catalytic converters, which began to appear on 1977-78 cars, also promoted the chemical reduction of $NO_x$ emissions.

**Exhaust Gas Recirculation(EGR)**

When peak combustion temperature exceeds 2 500℉, (1 372℃), the nitrogen in the air mixes with the oxygen to produce oxides of nitrogen($NO_x$).

By introducing a metered portion of the hot exhaust gases into the intake manifold, the incoming fuel charge will be diluted and flame temperatures lowered. This, in turn, reduces the level of $NO_x$ emissions. Figure 2-47 shows one method that has been used to admit exhaust gas into the intake manifold. Note how gas flows through floor jets.

The amount of exhaust gas that is recirculated can be controlled by an EGR valve. Such valves are widely used as they can be designed to admit carefully controlled amounts of exhaust gases into the intake air stream. The exact amount will very according to engine speed and loading.

EGR valves are of three basic types, vacuum modulated (ported), back pressure modulated, and electronic-vacuum modulated.

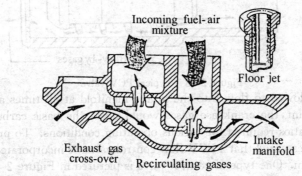

Figure 2-47  One method that has been used to circulate a portion of exhaust gases

## Positive Crankcase Ventilation (PCV)

The combustion process produces many gases, some very corrosive. A great deal of water (almost a gallon of water for each gallon of gasoline) is also formed.

The high pressure in the cylinder during the firing stroke forces some of these gases by the piston rings into the crankcase area. To prevent acid, etc., dilution of the oil, these blow-by gases must be removed.

For many years a simple road draft tube pulled the gases out into the atmosphere. This created significant amounts of air pollutants. The closed positive crankcase ventilation system removes the gases without discharging them into the atmosphere.

By connecting a hose between the engine interior and the intake manifold, engine vacuum will draw the crankcase fumes out of the engine and into the cylinders where the gases will be burned along with the regular fuel charge. A schematic illustrating a typical PCV system is shown in Figure 2-48.

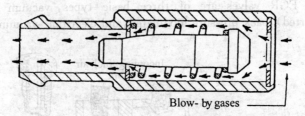

Figure 2-48  Typical PCV valve

If allowed to flow into the intake manifold at all times and in any amount, the crankcase gases would upset the basic carburetor air-fuel ratios required for various operating conditions. To prevent this, it is essential that a PCV flow control valve be incorporated into the system. One type of control valve is pictured in Figure 2-49.

When the engine is stopped, no intake manifold vacuum exists and the PCV valve is held closed by spring action.

During periods of idle or deceleration, vacuum is high. The tapered valve plunger is drawn into the metering opening. This reduces the size of the passageway allowing only a small flow of crankcase gases to the intake manifold.

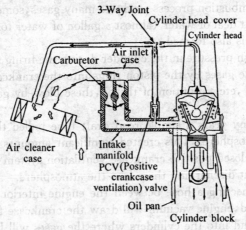

Figure 2-49  Schematic illustrating positive crankcase ventilation system

When the vehicle is operating at a normal load, the vacuum

drops off somewhat. This allows the spring to push the plunger partway out of the opening. This increases the opening and gas flow is reasonably heavy.

Acceleration or heavy loading causes manifold vacuum to drop greatly. The spring instantly pushes the plunger further out of the opening. Crankcase gas flow is now at its heaviest.

In the event of a "backfire" in the manifold, the reverse pressure allows the spring to fully close the valve, to prevent the flame from traveling into the crankcase. This prevents a possible explosion in the crankcase area.

### Evaporation Control System (ECS)

The evaporation control system (also called evaporative emission control system) is designed to prevent the release of either liquid gasoline or gasoline vapor into the atmosphere.

Although setups vary, a typical system is composed basically of a special pressure-vacuum filler cap, a nonvented (closed to atmosphere) fuel tank, a tank fill limiter, vapor separator, vent line, a charcoal canister, purge valve, and an excess fuel and vapor return line to the tank. A roll-over valve may also be used to prevent fuel leakage from tank in the event the vehicle is rolled and lands upside down.

The fuel tank is sealed with a pressure-vacuum cap. This is a special cap, using both a pressure and a vacuum relief valve, that prevents excessive pressure or vacuum in the tank in the event of system failure. The valves remain closed under normal operating conditions. When pressure exceeds around 0.8 psi (5.52 kpa) or a vacuum forms in excess of 0.1 Hg (0.69 kpa) the valves are activated.

The fuel tank "breathes" through the vent tube as fuel is consumed or when it expands or contracts from heating and cooling.

The tank is designed so that when it is filled to capacity, there is sufficient air dome above the fuel to permit thermal expansion without forcing liquid gasoline into the vent lines. When filling the tank, the small orifice (hole) in the vent restricter slows down the venting of the tank while filling so that an air dome is present thus limiting fill capacity.

Any vapors in the tank travel through the fuel tank vent tube to the charcoal canister. The carburetor float bowl is also vented to the canister so that bowl vapors generated by "engine off heat soak" (heat from engine transferred to carburetor after engine is stopped), will be forced into the canister.

Study the system portrayed in Figure 2-50. Note that the bowl vent line is conneced to a bowl vent valve. An idle purge and off-idle purge port are provided for the idle purge line.

The system is in the engine OFF mode. The bowl vent valve spring has forced the vent valve to the OPEN position. Vapors from the float bowl are moving through the bowl vent line and are entering the canister. Vapors from the fuel tank are also entering the canister.

The canister is filled with highly activated charcoal granules (small particles). When the vapors touch the charcoal, the granules absorb and store the vapors.

As long as the engine remains off, the vapors will be retained by the canister.

Upon starting the engine, vacuum will be formed in the carburetor-intake manifold assembly. This vacuum, working on the bowl vent valve diaphragm, pulls the vent valve up against spring pressure and closes the bowl vent valve.

At the same time, vacuum under the throttle valve will work on the idle purge port and draw fresh air through the charcoal bed. As the air passes over the charcoal, it will pick up the stored vapors and draw them into the carburetor where they will be mixed with fuel charge for burning.

As the throttle valve is opened wider, the off-idle purge port will be uncovered and the flow of air through the canister will be increased somewhat. As the engine continues to run, the canister will be purged (cleaned) of vapors.

When the engine is stopped, the canister bowl vent diaphragm will release the valve and the spring will force it open, permitting bowl vapors to once again enter the canister (See Figure 2-50).

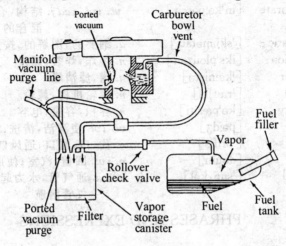

Figure 2-50  Study parts of an evaporation control system

**Dual Flow Air Injection System**

One air injection system applies full pump air flow to the exhaust valve area only during the warmup period. When a specific engine temperature is reached, a vacuum operated air-switching valve diverts a large percentage (not all) of the air to a point further along the exhaust system. This helps the EGR system to function effectively in reducing $NO_x$ emissions on this specific installation.

## NEW WORDS

| | | |
|---|---|---|
| hydrocarbons | ['haidrəu'kaːbən] | n. 烃,碳氢化合物 |
| evaporation | [iˌvæpə'reiʃən] | n. 蒸发,发散 |
| modification | [ˌmɔdifi'keiʃən] | n. 缓和,减轻,限制,修改 |
| recirculate | [ri'səkjuleit] | v. 再循环 |
| dilution | [dai'ljuːʃən] | n. 冲淡,稀释,冲淡物,稀度 |

| | | |
|---|---|---|
| ventilation | [ˌventiˈleiʃən] | n. 通风,流通空气 |
| fume | [fjuːm] | n. ;vt. 烟,气;熏,冒(烟) |
| incorporate | [inˈkɔːpəreit] | vt. ;vi. ;adj. 结构,合并;混合;混合的 |
| schematic | [ˈskiːmətaiz] | a. 纲要的,图解的,按照图示的 |
| explosion | [iksˈplouʒən] | n. 爆炸,炸裂,爆发 |
| canister | [ˈkænistə] | n. 罐,滤清罐 |
| ratchet | [ˈrætʃit] | n. 棘轮机构,棘轮 |
| capacity | [kəˈpæsiti] | n. 容积,容量,电容 |
| purge | [pəːdʒ] | vt. ;vi. 使清洁,清洗;清除 |
| ovifice | [ˈɔrifis] | n. 孔,口,洞口,通风口 |
| dome | [dəum] | n. ;vt. 圆盖,汽室;使成圆顶 |
| snorkel | [ˈsnɔːkəl] | n. ;vi. 通气管,水力起重;用通气管潜航 |

## PHRASES AND EXPRESSIONS

| | |
|---|---|
| carbon dioxide | 二氧化碳 |
| carbon monoxide | 一氧化碳 |
| photochemical smog | 光化学烟雾 |
| subdivide into | 把…细分,再分 |
| catalytic converters | 催化转化器 |
| intake manifold | 进气岐管 |
| vapor separator | 蒸气分离器 |
| charcoal canister | 碳罐 |
| activated charcoal granules | 活性碳颗粒 |
| vent tube | 通风管 |

## NOTES TO THE TEXT

1. But auto manufacturers doing their own research soon discovered that pollutants were also given off from the fuel tank and the engine crankcase.

但是自行探索的汽车制造商很快发现污染物的另外来源是油箱和发动机曲轴箱。

主句的主语是 auto manufactures,谓语是 discovered,主语后

有后置定语,由 do 的现在分词引导;that 引导宾语从句,在宾语从句中,pollutants 为主语,谓语是 give 的被动语态形式,from…crankcase 为状语。

2. By connecting a hose between the engine interior and the intake manifold, engine vacuum will draw the crankcase fumes out of the engine and into the cylinders where the gases will be burned along with the regular fuel charge.

在发动机内部与进气歧管之间连一个软管,发动机的真空度就会将曲轴箱内的烟气抽出,进入气缸后按照规则的供油而燃烧。

engine vacuum 为主语,谓语是 draw 的将来时,crankcase fumes 是宾语,out of…and into… 为状语,修饰 draw,而 where 引导定语从句,修饰 cylinders,而 by connecting… 为动词的现在分词引导的状语从句。

## EXERCISES

Ⅰ. Answer the following questions according to the text:

1. What are the three major exhaust pollutants?
2. What are the three general types of emission controls?
3. Crankcase gases are allowed to flow heavily into the intake manifold during engine idle. True or False?
4. Vapor control canisters only store engine crankcase vapor. True or False?
5. What is the function of the exhaust gas recirculation(EGR) system?
6. In what way is engine performance affected by the EGR system?
7. The EGR valve admits exhaust gas to the intake manifold at all times. True or False?
8. What is the purpose of an evaporative emission-control system?
9. What is the function of the early fuel evaporation(EFE)system?

Ⅱ. In each case, choose one of the four words that best matches the definition given below:

1. A black, porous carbonaceous material, produced by the destructive distillation of wood and used as fuel, filter, and ab-sorbent.

   A. coal     B. petroleum     C. charcoal     D. strainer

2. process of changing from a liquid to evapor.

   A. evaporation     B. expansion
   C. evaporator     D. petrol burning

3. A leakage or loss of pressure, of ten used with reference to leakage of compression past piston ring between piston and cylinder.

   A. pressure drop     B. blow by
   C. blow down     D. pressure loss

4. A common, nonmetallic element that is an excellent con-ductor of electricity.

   A. carbon     B. carbon dioxide
   C. canister     D. carburetor

5. Reservoir of evaporative emission control system, usually containing activated charcoal granules for absorbing fuel vapors.

   A. muffler     B. air cleaner
   C. canister     D. oil filter

6. Container or holder in which things may be put away safely or out of sight.

   A. breather     B. storehouse
   C. toolbox     D. receptacle

7. products of combustion that are discharged through exhaust system of vehicle.

   A. exhaust gas     B. exhaust emission
   C. combustible material     D. explosive mixture

8. A substance or thing that contaminates air, soil, or water.

   A. contamination     B. pollution
   C. polluter     D. pollutant

Ⅲ. Fill in the blanks with the phrases or words given below:

1. When the engine is operating, some fuel and exhaust fumes _____ the piston rings, down the cylinders, and into the crankcase.

   A. are pushing     B. are forced past
   C. enter into     D. are circling around

2. If the rate of airflow is too rapid, it may pull oil ____ the crankcase.
   A. into      B. apart     C. over      D. out of

3. If severe, such a drop in the oil level could ____ engine failure unless noticed by the operator.
   A. result from          B. result in
   C. get rid of           D. get down with

4. If there is no vacuum or if there is a positive pressure, there is a ____ in the PCV system.
   A. malfunction          B. multifunction
   C. manifold pressure    D. mutual overtaking

5. The filter element and road-draft-ventilation systems should ____ at regular intervals.
   A. be instructed        B. be inspected
   C. be trouble-free      D. exchange

6. Exhaust emission controls are designed to reduce or eliminate pollutants before they leave the ____ system.
   A. fuel     B. cooling    C. ignition    D. exhaust

7. The only major type of pollutant that comes from a vehicle source other than the exhaust is ____.
   A. HC                   B. CO
   C. $CO_2$               D. $NO_x$

8. The three major pollutants automobile exhaust are ____.
   A. sulfates, particulates, carbon dioxide
   B. sulfates, carbon monoxide, nitrous oxide
   C. carbon monoxide, oxides of nitrogen, hydrocarbons
   D. hydrocarbons, carbon dioxide, nitrous oxide

IV. choose a phrase from the list for each space in the passage below:

   1. is accomplished by      4. is calibrated for
   2. improving               5. are equipped with
   3. have been developed     6. is included to

Several different types of engine emission control system ____ to reduce or eliminate carbon monoxide and hydrocarbon emissions at their source before they reach the exhaust system. These include

General Motors' controlled combustion system (CCS), Ford's improved exhaust emission control system (IMCO), and chrysler's cleaner air systems.

Engine emission-control systems reduce carbon monoxide and hydrocarbon emissions at their source in the engine combustion chamber by ＿＿ combustion efficiency. This ＿＿ using specially calibrated carburetors and distributors, higher operating temperatures, and modified engines.

The carburetor ＿＿ a cleaner air-fuel mixture at idle and part-throttle to reduce emissions. In some carburetors, an idle speed solenoid ＿＿ close the throttle plates more completely after the ignition is shut off. This eliminates the "after-run" or "dieseling" that frequently occurs in gasoline engines with high idle speeds. The carburetors used with engine emission-control systems ＿＿ limiters to make it impossible to increase the richness of the idle air-fuel mixture beyond a predetermined point.

V. Translate the following sentences into Chinese:

1. Approximately 15 percent of the vehicle emission that contribute to atmospheric pollution are in the form of vapors that escape from the fuel tank and carburetor float bowl.

2. These pressure differences draw in fresh air to ventilate the crankcase and suck the fuel and exhaust fumes into the air cleaner or intake manifold.

3. A vacuum switch, which is sensitive to engine temperature, closes the valve and forces the hot exhaust gases through the crossover passage in the intake manifold.

4. By maintaining the air at these warmer temperatures, the carburetor can be calibrated to reduce hydrocarbon emissions, minimize carburetor icing, and improve engine warm-up characteristics.

5. Rapid acceleration will cause a drop of vacuum in the system to a point that allows the diaphragm spring to overcome the vacuum and close the damper door, thereby opening the ambient air passage through the snorkel tube.

6. Because intake-manifold vacuum is used to operate the PCV system, the PCV flow into the intake manifold must be regulated so

that it varies in proportion to the regular air-fuel ratio being drawn into the intake manifold through the carburetor.

Ⅵ. Translate the following passage into Chinese:

The automobile is a major source of air pollution resulting from the gasoline burned in the engine and the vapors escaping from the crankcase, the fuel tank, and the rest of the fuel sys-tem. The major pollutants are unburned hydrocarbons (HC), carbon monoxide (CO), and oxides of nitrogen ($NO_x$). The most visible and irritating form of air pollution is photochemical smog, which is formed when HC and $NO_x$ emissions combine in the presence of sunlight. The use of emission controls in the past two decades has reduced automotive pollutants by 65 to 98 percent.

Emission controls began as separate "add-on" components and systems, but are now completely integrated into engine and vehicle design. The major emission control systems used are PCV systems, evaporative control systems, air injection, spark timing controls, exhaust gas recirculation, catalytic converters, and electronic engine control systems.

California introduced the first emission control legislation, and the Federal government followed. The Federal Environmental Protection Agency and California's Air Resources Board establish and enforce pollution control standards for automobiles. Increasingly stringent emission standards combined with the CAFE regulations imposed during the late 1970's have reshaped the domestic automotive industry. The end result has been smaller, more fuelefficient vehicles that produce much less pollution than those of two decades ago.

## 2.6 Electrical System

### 2.6.1 Charging System

The charging system operates only when the engine is running. It changes some of the engine's mechanical energy into electrical energy to operate the vehicle's electrical and electronic systems (Figure2-51). Some of the basic functions performed by the charging system by the charging system include the following:

1. Recharging the battery
2. Supplying all the vehicle's electrical energy when the engine is running
3. Providing a voltage output that is slightly higher than the battery voltage
4. Changing its output to meet different engine speed and electrical load conditions.

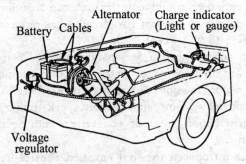

Figure 2-51 The major components of an automotive charging system.

The fundamental components of a charging system include the following:

**Alternator** The altermator is an alternating current (AC) generator driven by engine power to produce electricity A set of diodes in the recifier allows the generated alternating current to pass in only one direction, thus converting the AC current to DC (which the vehicle uses).

**Voltage regulator** The voltage regulator keeps the alter-nator voltage constant over the entire engine-speed range and under varying load conditions. Without a regulator, the alternator would exceed safe voltage levels (about 15.5V). This would damage certain components and overcharge the battery.

**Alternator drive belt** The alternator drive belt spins the rotor shaft in the alternator by coupling the engine crankshaft pulley with the alternator pulley to drive the alternator.

**Charge indicator**  The charging indicator device most commonly used is a simple on/off warning lamp. It is normally off and can be designed to come on when the alternator is not satisfying electrical load requirements, not charging at all, or if voltage is either too high or too low. It also lights when the ignition is turned on, before the engine starts for a check of the lamp circuit. An ammeter or voltmeter is used on some vehicles instead of the warning light to inform the driver of the state of the charging system output.

**Battery**  The battery supplies current to initially energize the magnetic field of the alternator. During charging, the battery changes electrical energy from the alternator into chemical energy to maintain its state of charge. It also provides electricity when the load is too heavy for the alternator to handle alone. The battery also acts as a "shock absorber" to stabilize alternator voltage output.

**Ignition switch**  The ignition switch is turned on to supply power to operate the indicator light and energize the alternator.

**Fusible link**  A fusible link is used in the charging circuit to protect the wiring harness and alternator from damage that can be caused by overloads or short circuits.

## Indicators

A charging system indicator lets the driver check on the charging system. It can be :

1. A warning lamp that lights when the alternator is not supplying voltage greater than battery voltage.

2. An ammeter that shows current flow into and out of the battery

3. A voltmeter that shows the battery or electrical system voltage.

## Battery

A battery is an electrochemical device. It contains positive and negative plates that are connected in such a way as to produce three or six groups or cells. The plates are covered with electrolyte.

A charged battery will amass (gather a great quantity) a surplus of electrons at the negative post. When the battery is placed in a completed circuit, the electrons will flow from the negative post, through the circuit, and on to the positive post.

The battery must be kept charged by passing electricity through it in a reverse direction to that of battery current flow.

The battery is checked for charge by using a hydrometer to determine the specific gravity of the electrolyte.

Batteries can explode and should never be exposed to sparks or open flame.

The battery is used to supply current for starting the car. Upon starting, the generator will recharge the battery.

Car batteries are of the 12V type.

Be careful of battery electrolyte it is dangerous!

**Generator (Alternator)**

The primary job of the generator is to supply the necessary current for the electrical needs of the car and to keep the battery charged (Figure 2-52).

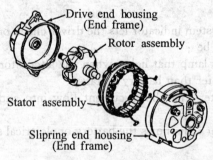

Figure 2-52    The alternator housing encloses the rotor and stator

The generator functions by spinning an armature in a strong

magnetic field produced by field coils. As the armature loops spin in the magnetic field, current is induced in the loops. A commutator at one end of the armature is contacted by carbon brushes. The insulated brush picks up the voltage generated by the whirling armature and conducts it to the rest of the electrical system. Both alternating current (most common) and direct current generators are in use.

**Generator Regulator**

It is necessary to control the maximum voltage and current output developed by the generator. This is done by using the generator regulator.

The dc generator regulator contains a cutout relay, voltage and current controls. The acgenerator (alternator) regulator does not need a cutout relay.

When either current or voltage output attempts to exceed that for which the generator is designed, an electromagnet breaks a set of contact points, and inserts a resistance in the generator field circuit. With a resistance in the field, voltage and current will lower.

The voltage regulator and the current regulator both operate points in a vibrating manner. As the points vibrate, they produce a smooth, controlled generator output. Either unit can work, but they will not function together.

## NEW WORDS

| | | |
|---|---|---|
| alternator | ['ɔːltəc(ː)neitə] | n. 交流发电机 |
| diode | ['daiəud] | n. 二极管 |
| rectifier | ['rektifiə] | n. 整流器,整流管,矫正器 |
| regulator | ['regjuleitə] | n. 调节器,校准器,调整者 |
| pulley | ['puli] | n. 皮带轮,滑轮 |
| indicator | ['indikeitə] | n. 指示器,示功器,指示者 |
| voltmeter | ['vəultˌmiːtə] | n. 伏特计,电压表 |
| magnetic | [mæg'netik] | adj. 磁的,有磁性的,有吸引力的 |
| stabilize | ['steibilaiz] | vt. 稳定,安定,给装稳定器 |

| switch | [switʃ] | n. ;vt. 开关,电键;接通…的电流 |
| --- | --- | --- |
| energize | ['enədʒaiz] | vt. 给予…能量,加强,给与…电压 |
| fusible | ['fjuːzəbl] | adj. 易熔的,可熔化的 |
| ammeter | ['æmitə] | n. 电流计,安培计 |
| postive | ['pɔzətiv] | adj. ;n. 正的,阳性的;明确,阳板 |
| cell | [sel] | n. 电池,电荷 |
| electrolyte | [i'lektrəulait] | n. 电解质,电离质,电解液 |
| circuit | ['səːkit] | n. ;vt. 电路,回路,线路;结…环行 |
| hydrometer | [hai'drɔmitə] | n. 比重计 |
| explode | [iks'pləud] | vt. ;adj. 使爆破,使破裂;爆炸了的 |
| armature | ['aːmətjuə] | n. 电枢,转子,电容器板,衔铁 |
| loop | [luːp] | n. ;v. 圈,环,环状物;把…连成回路 |
| commutator | [kə'mjuːteitə] | n. 交换器 |

## PHRASES AND EXPRESSIONS

| charging system | 充电系统 |
| --- | --- |
| alteranating current | 交流电 |
| voltage regulator | 电压调节器 |
| alternator drive belt | 传动带 |
| charge indicator | 充电指示器 |
| ignition swich | 点火开关 |
| such…as to | 像…这样的,诸如…之类的 |
| carbon brush | 炭刷 |
| pick up | 拾起,捡起,搭乘 |
| in use | 在使用着 |
| generator regulator | 交流发电机调节器 |
| cutout relay | 截流继电器 |
| either…or | 或者…或者…,不论…还是 |

## NOTES TO THE TEXT

1. Some of the basic functions performed by the charging system include the following:

充电系的基本作用如下：
Some of the basic functions 为主语；performed by the charging system 做 basic functions 的定语。

2. The battery also act as a "shock absorber" to stabilize voltage output.
蓄电池还起"减震器"作用，使发电机的输出电压稳定。
act as 起作用，在句中做谓语；to stabilize voltage output 做目的状语。

3. The dc generator regulator contains a cutout relay voltage and current controls.
直流发电机中包括断电（截流）继电器，电压和电流调节器。句中"dc"为直流一词的缩写，下句的"ac"为交流一词的缩写。

## 2.6.2 Starting System

The vehicle's starting system is designed to turn or "crank" the engine over until it can operate under its own power. To do this, the starter motor receives electrical power form the storage battery. The starter motor then converts this energy into mechanical energy, which it transmits through the drive mechanism to the engine's flywheel.

A typical starting system has five basic components and two distinct electrical circuits. The components are

1. Battery
2. Key switch (of staring switch)
3. Battery cables
4. Magnetic switch
5. Starter motor

The starter motor draws a great deal of electrical current from the battery. A large starter motor might require 300 to 400 amperes of current. This current flows through the heavy-gauge cables that connect the battery to the starter.

The driver controls the flow of this current using the starting switch. However, if the cables were routed from the battery to the starting switch and then on to the starter motor, the voltage drop caused by resistance in the cables would be too great. To avoid this problem, the system is designed with two connected circuits: the starter circuit and the control circuit.

The starter circuit carries the high current flow within the system and supplies power for the actual engine cranking. Components of the starting circuit are the battery, battery cables, magnetic switch or solenoid, and the starter motor.

**Starting Safety Switch**

The starting safety switch is also called a neutral start switch. It is a normally open switch that prevents the starting system from operating when the automobile's transmission is in gear. If the car has no starting safety switch, it is possible to spin the engine with the transmission in gear. This will make the car lurch forward or backward which could be dangerous. Safety switches or interlock devices are used with all automatic transmissions and on many late-model cars with manual transmissions. The safety switch can be an electrical switch that opens the control circuit if the car is in gear. It can also be a mechanical interlock device that will not let the ignition switch turn to start if the car is in gear.

**Magnetic Switch (Relays and Solenoids)**

A magnetic switch in the starting system allows the control circuit to open and close the starter circuit. The switch can be a:
1. Relay which uses the electromagnetic field of a coil to attract an armature and close the contact points.
2. Solenoid which uses the electromagnetic field of a coil to pull a plunger into the coil and close the contact points. The plunger's movement can also be used to do a mechanical job, such as shifting the starter motor gear in a solenoid-actuated drive.

## Starter Motor

The starter motor converts electrical energy from the battery into mechanical energy to turn the engine. It does this through the interaction of magnetic fields. When current flows through a conductor, a magnetic field is formed around the conductor. If the conductor is placed in another magnetic field, the two fields will be weakened at one side and strengthened at the other side, position A. The conductor will tend to move from the strong field into the weak field, position B. Positions C and D show how a simple motor can use this movement to make the conductors rotate. An automotive starter motor has many conductors and uses a lot of current to create enough rotational force to crank the engine.

Figure 2-53 shows a cutaway view of a starter motor. The armature is the collection of conductors that will spin to crank the engine. The starter drive gear is mounted on the armature shaft. The

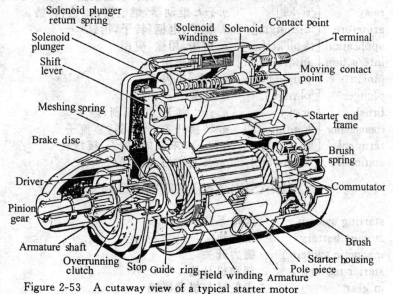

Figure 2-53   A cutaway view of a typical starter motor

pole pieces are the stationary magnetic fields. The motor housing encloses the armature and pole pieces, holds the bearings that support the armature shaft, and provides the terminals for connecting the motor to the rest of the starting system.

## NEW WORDS

| | | |
|---|---|---|
| crank | [kræŋk] | n. ;vt. ;adj. 曲柄;把…弯成曲柄状;不正常的 |
| flywheel | [flai'wi:l] | n. 飞轮 |
| component | [kəm'pəunənt] | n. ;adj. 组成部分,部件;组成的 |
| distinct | [dis'tiŋkt] | adj. 独特的,明显的 |
| cable | ['keibl] | n. 电缆,钢丝缆 |
| ampere | ['æmpɛə] | n. 安培 |
| spin | [spin] | v. ;n. 使旋转;旋转,自旋 |
| lurch | [lə:tʃ] | vi. ;n. 突然倾斜;倾侧 |
| interlock | [,intə:'lɔk] | vi. ;n. (使)联锁,联锁装置 |
| relay | ['ri:lei] | n. ;vt. 继动器,继电器;传达,转播 |
| armature | ['a:mətjuə] | n. 盔甲,电枢,转子,衔铁 |
| application | [,æpli'keiʃən] | n. 用法,用途,应用 |
| interaction | [,intər'ækʃən] | n. 相互作用 |
| pinion | ['pinjən] | n. [机]小齿轮 |
| plunger | ['plʌngə] | n. 柱塞 |
| brush | [brʌʃ] | n. ;vt. 刷子,电刷;刷,擦 |
| commutator | ['kɔmjuteitə] | n. 转换开关,转换器,整流子 |
| terminal | ['tə:minl] | adj. ;n. 末端的;端子,接线柱 |
| stationary | ['steiʃənəri] | adj. 不动的,静止的 |

## PHRASES AND EXPRESSIONS

| | |
|---|---|
| starting system | 起动系统 |
| storage battery | 蓄电池 |
| magnetic switch | 磁力开关 |
| starter motor | 起动机马达 |
| in gear | 齿轮已与机器联接 |
| starter solenoid | 电磁起动机线圈 |

| | |
|---|---|
| solenoid plunger | 电磁线圈柱塞 |
| shift mechanism | 换档机构 |
| electromagnetic field | 电磁场 |
| meshing spring | 网状弹簧 |
| pole piece | 磁极片 |

## NOTES TO THE TEXT

1. The startor motor then converts this energy into mechanical energy, which it transmits through the drive mechannism to the engine's flywheel.

起动马达从蓄电池得到电能,再将这部分电能转化成机械能通过驱动机构传到发动机上的飞轮。

which 修饰前句中的 energy,同时引导非限制性定语从句,在从句中做 transmits 的宾语。

2. If the conductor is placed in another magnetic field, the two fields will be weakened at one side and strenghthened at the other side.

当这样的导体被放置到另一个电磁场中时,这两个磁场将有一测被加强而另一侧被减弱。

if 引导的为假设条件状语从句,本句的主语是 conductor, is placed 为被动语态,做谓语; the two fields 为主句的主语,主句是由二个并列句来充当,be weakened 为被动语态,与 strengthened 为并列谓语。

### 2.6.3 Igniting System

The purpose of the ignition system is to provide an electric spark to the correct cylinder at the correct time to ignite the air/fuel mixture. This provides energy, which is used to force the piston down and turn the engine crankshaft. The spark consists of an electric arc produced by applying a high voltage across the electrodes of a spark plug. This spark must occur near the end of the compression stroke, as the piston approaches top dead center (TDC). The cylinders must fire in the proper order and at a precise instant, depending on engine speed, load and temperature conditions.

A spark plug consists of a pair of electrodes, called the center and ground electrodes, separated by a gap (Figure 2-54). The gap size (in inches or millimeters) is important and is specified for each engine on vehicle specification data sheets. The center electrode must be insulated from the ground electrode and the metallic shell assembly. The ground electrode is grounded through the engine block and frame. A spark is produced by applying a high voltage (from approximately 6 kV to 40 kV) between the center electrode and ground. The actual voltage required to start the arc varies with the size of the gap, the compression ratio, and the air/fuel ratio. Once the arc is started, a much lower voltage is required to sustain the arc because the gas mixture near the gap ionizes to lower the resistance to ground. The arc is sustained long enough to ignite the air/fuel mixture.

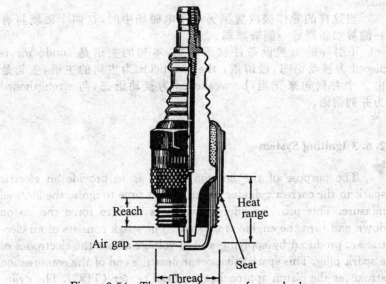

Figure 2-54  The design features of a spark plug

## Primary and Secondary Circuits of The Ignition

The ignition system is divided into two circuits: the primary and the secondary. The primary circuit is the low-voltage side of the system and controls the secondary circuit, which is the high-voltage side of the system.

The following are the basic parts of the primary ignition circuit:

1. **Battery and/or alternator**  Supplies the low voltage (14 V) used to operate the primary circuit.

2. **Ignition switch**  Key-operated switch used to feed battery voltage to the primary circuit.

3. **Primary wires**  Low-voltage wires used to connect the electrical components of the primary circuit.

4. **Ignition coil primary winding**  Current flow through the coil produces an electromagnetic field, which is used to induce a high voltage in the secondary coil.

5. **Electronic control unit**  Contains a switching transistor controlled by a speed sensor and is used to open and close the primary circuit.

6. **Speed sensor, or pickup**  Produces a pulsating voltage that signals the generation of an ignition spark.

**The following are the basic parts of a secondary ignition circuit:**

1. **Ignition coil secondary winding**  Has a high voltage (40 000 V or more) induced in it each time the primary magnetic field collapses.

2. **Coil wire**  Heavily insulated wire that feeds high voltage from the ignition coil to distributor cap.

3. **Distributor rotor**  Operates in conjunction with the distributor cap to distribute the high voltage from the ignition coil to the individual spark plug wires in the firing order.

4. **Distributor cap**  Insulated cap that transfers high voltage from the distributor rotor to spark plug wires.

5. **Spark plug wire**  Heavily insulated wire that carries high voltage from the distributor to the spark plugs; also referred to as high-tension, or secondary ignition, cables.

6. **Spark plug**  Provides the air gap within the combustion chamber for the high voltage to arc across, thus igniting the air/fuel mixtue.

The basic operation of the ignition system with the ignition switch closed and the engine started, is as follows:

1. The trigger wheel rotates with engine RPMs and causes the speed sensor, or pickup coil, to produce triggering voltage pulses that correspond to engine speed and piston position.

2. The electronic control unit allows current to flow through the ignition coil primary winding until it senses a triggering voltage pulse from the speed sensor, or pickup coil.

3. Each triggering voltage pulse actuates the electronic control module to open the circuit to the ignition coil primary winding, causing the magnetic field to collapse quickly and induce a high voltage in the secondary winding.

4. The high secondary voltage travels from the coil wire to the distributor rotor and cap and then on to fire the spark plug of the cylinder that is on the proper stroke for igniting the air/fuel mixture.

**Distributor Ignition Systems**

All ignition systems operate in a similar manner; current flow in the coil's primary circuit is interrupted to produce high voltage in the coil's secondary circuit, which fires the spark plug. The difference is how the ignition systems control the current in the primary circuit and how the secondary high voltage is distributed to the spark plugs.

**Electrical Breakerpoint Ignition Systems**

For the most part, automobiles designed in the 1960s and before use mechanical breaker points as the primary circuit switch device. Figure 2-55 illustrates how an electrical point-type ignition system works. The distributor contains the ignition points, condenser(capacitor), and distributor cam. As the destributor cam rotates, the points open and close the primary ignition circuit. With the points closed, current flows through the primary circuit, building up the magnetic field. As the distributor cam lobe opens the points, the current stops flowing in the primary circuit, causing the magnetic field to collapse and the high secondary voltage to be induced. The condenser(capacitor) is connected across the points to prevent arcing of the points when they are opened. The primary resistor (resistance wire or ballast resistor) is used to limit the current in the primary to prevent overheating the coil at low engine speeds. Mechanical centrifugal-or vacuum-advance units located in the distributor are used to control ignition timing. The spark dwell is determined by the breaker point's gap.

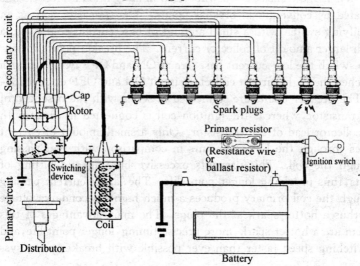

Figure 2-55  The ignition system is divid into the primary circuit and the secondary circuit

Point-type ignition systems have drawbacks. The breaker points wear out both mechanically and electrically (increased resistance). Spring tension, gap, alignment, and wear on the cam-lobe follower are critical to efficient operation. In addition, they are susceptible to damage from water, electrical and mechanical load, improper adjustment, and improper service.

**Solid-State (Electronic) Ignition Systems**

Solid-state (also called) ignition systems were introduced in the mid-1970s. These ignition systems were introduced primarily due to their ability to help meet stringent mileage and emission-control standards. The first electronic ignition systems were separate systems, independent of the engine-control system. Current systems function as a part of the engine's computer-control system.

When the transistor was first used in an ignition system, it was operated by conventional breaker points. The transistor acts as an amplifying switch with a small amount of base current controlling a much larger amount of collector current. The breaker points act only to switch the low-current base circuit ON and OFF, which in turn switches the high-current collector circuit ON and OFF electronically. The breaker points are connected in series with the base lead of the transistor, whereas the ignition coil is connected in series with the collector lead of the transistor. Only a small amount of current passes through the breaker points in comparison with that passing through the coil. This prevents excessive burning and pitting of points, thus providing longer point life. The larger current passing through the coil primary produces a much higher secondary voltage and thus a hotter spark at the plugs. The main advantages of this system are a hotter spark, more precise timing, longer point life, and a switching speed faster than ever possible with breaker point systems.

The problem with the breaker-controlled transistorized ignition system is that it does not totally eliminate the use of breaker points, nor does it eliminate entirely their wear and need for frequent replacement. In a fully electronic ignition system, the timing is controlled by a triggering device (often located in the distributor), whereas the coil current is controlled by a transistor located in the ignition module.

## Spark Advance

There are two basic factors that govern ignition timing: engine speed and load. All changes in timing are related to these two factors:

Timing must increase, or advance, as engine speed increases; it must decrease, or retard, as engine speed decreases.

Timing must decrease, or retard, as load increases; it must increase, or advance, as load decreases.

Optimum ignition timing under any given combination of these basic factors will result in maximum cylinder pressure. In turn, this delivers maximum power with a minimum of exhaust emissions and the best possible fuel economy.

When ignition takes place too early, the combustion pressure slows down the piston. If timing is too far advanced, the increased combustion pressure will cause an engine knock. When ignition takes place too late, the piston is too far down on its power stroke to benefit from the combustion pressure, resulting in a power loss.

Before the introduction of computer-controlled timing, most automotive distributors had two spark advance mechanisms to react to engine operating changes and alter ignition timing:

1. The centrifugal advance changes ignition timing to match engine speed by altering the position of the distributor cam or trigger wheel on the desdributor shaft.

2. The vacuum advance changes ignition timing to match engine load by altering the position of the breaker points or the magnetic pickup coil (electronic sensor).

These changes in position alter the time, relative to crankshaft position, at which the primary circuit is opened.

### Centrifugal Advance—Speed

The centrifugal, or mechanical, advance mechanism consists of two weights connected to the distributor drive shaft by two springs. The distributor cam, or electronic trigger wheel, and the destributor rotor are mounted on another shaft. The second shaft fits over the drive shaft like a sleeve. Drive shaft motion is transmitted to the second shaft through the centrifugal advance weights. When the weights move, the relative position of the drive shaft and the second shaft is changed.

As engine speed increased, distributor shaft rotation speed increases. The advance weights move outward because of centrifugal force. The outward movement of the weights shifts the second shaft and the cam of the trigger wheel. The primary circuit opens earlier in the compression stroke, and the spark occurs earlier.

Each advance weight is connected it the distributor drive shaft by a control spring. These springs are selected to allow the correct amount of weight movement and ignition advance for a particular engine.

At low engine speeds, spring tension holds the weights in, so that initial timing is maintained. As engine speed increases, centrifugal force overcomes spring tension and the weights move outward. The advance is not a large, rapid change, but rather a slow, gradual shift. The advance curve can be changed by changing the tension of the control springs. Remember that centrifugal advance responds to engine speed.

In most distributors, the centrifugal advance mechanism is mounted below the cam and breaker points, or below the trigger wheel and pickup coil.

### Vacuum Advance-Load

The vacuum advance mechanism allows efficient engine performance within a range of air-fuel ratios. These ratios are important, since there are limits to how rich or how lean they can be and still remain fully combustible. The air-fuel ratio with which an engine can operate efficiently ranges from 8 to 18. 5 to 1 by weight (Figure 2-56).

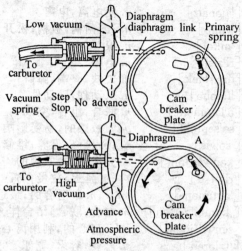

Figure 2-56　Vacuum advance mechanism

These ratios are generally stated as eight parts of air combined with one part of gasoline (8 : 1), which is the richest mixture that an engine can tolerate and still fire regularly. A ratio of 18. 5 parts of air mixed with one part of gasoline (18. 5 : 1) is the leanest mixture that an engine can tolerate without misfiring.

An average air-fuel ratio is about 15 : 1. This mixture takes about 3 milliseconds to burn. A lean mixture (one with more air and less fuel) will require more time to burn. The ignition timing must be advanced to provide maximum combustion pressure at the correct piston position. A rich mixture (one with more fuel and less air) will burn more quickly and emit more exhaust pollutants. Ignition timing should be retarded for complete combustion and emission control.

# NEW WORDS

| | | |
|---|---|---|
| ionize | ['aiənaiz] | v. 使电离,电离 |
| trigger | ['trigə] | n. ;v. 闸柄,板柄;松开 |
| nickel | ['nikəl] | n. 镍 |
| resistor | [ri'zistə] | n. 电阻 |
| drawback | [drɔ:bæk] | n. 欠缺,弊端,障碍 |
| follower | ['fɔləuə] | n. 从动件,随动件 |
| alignment | [ə'lainmənt] | n. 联合,组合,空线 |
| susceptible | [sə'septəbl] | adj. 敏感的,易受影响的 |
| service | ['sə:vis] | n. ;v. 检修,保养;维修 |
| conventional | [kən'venʃnl] | adj. 惯例的,常规的 |
| —retard | [ri'ta:d] | v. ;n. 延迟,放慢;妨碍 |
| optimum | ['ɔptiməm] | adj. ;n. 最适合的;最适条件 |
| combination | [ˌkɔmbi'neiʃən] | n. 结合,联合,结合体 |
| centrifugal | [sen'trifjugəl] | adj. 离心的,利用离心的 |
| tolerate | ['tɔləreit] | v. 忍受,容忍,宽恕 |
| misfiring | ['mis'fairiŋ] | adj. 不发火的,不奏效的 |
| diaphragm | ['daiəfræm] | n. 隔板,隔膜,膜片 |

## PHRASES AND EXPRESSIONS

| | |
|---|---|
| electric arc | 电弧 |
| in the proper order | 按正常顺序 |
| spark plug | 火花塞 |
| correspond to … | 符合,一致 |
| triggering voltage pulse | 触发电压脉冲 |
| center electrode | 中心(央)电极 |
| side electrode | 侧电极 |
| distributor ignition system | 分电器点火系统 |
| transistorized ignition system | 晶体管点火系统 |
| triggering device | 触发器 |
| spark advance | 点火提前 |
| refer to… | 把…归类,谈到,涉及 |

## NOTES TO THE TEXT

1. The ignition system is divided into two circuits: the primary and secondary.

点火系统分为两个回路:初级和次级回路。

句中 primary 和 secondary 分别表示点火系中的初级和次级回路。

2. The arc is sustained long enough to ignite the air/fuel mixture.

电弧被保持足够长的时间点燃混合气。

将 sustained 译作"保持"是根据点燃 air/fuel 混合气需足够的能量,所以取这个词义。

3. Current flow in the coil's primary circuit is interrupted to produce high voltage in the secondary circuit, which fires the spark plug.

初级线圈中的电流被切断,次级线圈中产生出高电压,这个电压使火花塞产生火花。

to produced high voltage 是结果状语,which 引导的非限定性定语从句修饰 high voltage;produce 有"产生"之意,此处指由于电磁感应而产生高电压。

## EXERCISES

Ⅰ. Answer the following questions according to the text:

1. Can you outline four basic functions performed by the charging system?

2. What is the purpose of each of the following components of a typical charging system? (a) Alternator (b) Voltage regulator (c) Alternator drive belt (d) Charge indicator (e) Battery (f) Ignition switch

3. What type of distributor ignition systems use mechanical centrifugal-and vacuum-advance units?

4. Can you describe the basic operating principle of a typical destributor centrifugal-advance mechanism?

5. What is the purpose of the starting system?

6. The power required to operate the starting system is supplied by the battery. This is the most difficult task the battery must perform. Why?

7. Do you explain the basic principle of operation of a motor?

8. How must the spark timing be adjusted for different engine load conditions to prevent the air/fuel mixture from burning too muck on the compression stroke?

9. What opens and closes the breaker points?

Ⅱ. Fill in the blank in each sentence with the word or phrase from the list that correctly completes the meaning:

    A. depends upon    B. in series    C. due to    D. provided    E. ignited    F. eliminated    G. produced

1. The high-voltage surges necessary to produce the sparks at the spark plugs are ____ by the ignition system components.

2. The compressed air-fuel mixture in the engine cylinders is ____ by the sparks.

3. The magnetic saturation of the secondary coil ____ the amount of voltage applied to the primary coil.

4. At high speeds, the current flow to the primary coil has only a few milliseconds to flow ____ the rapid opening and closing of the contact points.

5. The resister is ____ between the battery and the primary coil windings in order to keep primary circuit voltage at a desired level.

6. The magnetic field ____ by the primary coil windings must completely saturate the secondary windings.

Ⅲ. Fill the blank in each sentence with one of the four words or phrases which correctly completes the sentence:

1. The correct ratio of water to sulfuric acid in battery electrolyte is approximately ____.

    A. 80 percent water to 20 percent sulfuric acid
    B. 60 percent water to 40 percent sulfuric acid
    C. 40 percent water to 60 percent sulfuric acid
    B. 20 percent water to 80 percent sulfuric acid

2. Batteries are rated in terms of ____.

    A. ampere-hours    B. reserve capacity

C. cranking performance at 0℉   D. any of the above

3. The electrolyte in a fully charged battery will generally not freeze until the temperature drops to ____.
   A. 32℉(0℃)                    B. 0℉(-18℃)
   C. -20° to -30℉ (-29°to -34℃)  D. below -60℉(-51℃)

4. Alternating current in an alternator is rectified by ____.
   A. brushes              B. diodes
   C. sliprings            D. transistors

5. During cranking, all electrical energy for the automobile system is supplied by the ____.
   A. alternator     B. battery
   C. generator      D. none of the above

6. ____ convert mechanical energy to eletrical energy.
   A. battery        B. alternator
   C. generator      D. Voltage regulator

7. ____ is not part of the starter control circuit.
   A. the ignition switcth       B. the starting safety switch
   C. the starter relay          D. the starter motor

8. The distributor rotates at ____ the speed of the crankshift.
   A. one-half       B. the same speed as
   C. twice          D. none of the above

Ⅳ. Translate the following sentences into Chinese:

1. In the case of diesel and dual-fuel engines, the cylinder charge, after being compressed, must be hot enough to ignite the oil fuel when it is injected at the top center.

2. Many engines using an electric starting system are also provided with means for hand starting in case the storage battery or the starter motor should fail.

3. After the engine starts, the pinion should be immediately disengaged from the flywheel ring gear, otherwise the latter will spin the drive pinion with a high speed and the armature winding turns may fly out of the slots under the effect of the centrifugal force.

4. The secondary ignition circuit not only transforms the 6 or 12 volts of the battery to a voltage high enough to cause an arc at the spark plug but also delivers this high-voltage surge to the spark

plugs.

5. It also has a mechanism that controls the point at which the breaker points open, thereby advancing or retarding the spark in accordance with engine requirements.

6. With the ignition switch on, and ignition distributor contacts closed; current will flow from the battery, through the primary winding of the ignition coil, to the distributor contact points, to the ground connection and back to the battery.

V. Translate the following passage into Chinese:

The basic problems with the starter motor are as follows: the starter motor fails to crank; the starter motor cranks slowly; the drive pinion clashes and grinds when being meshed with the flywheel ring gear.

When you turn the ignition key to start and nothing happens, the first thing you probably think about is a dead battery. You might be right, but before you check the battery, turn on the headlights or dome light and try cranking. If the lights do not come on, either the battery is dead or a connection is bad. Check the connections at the battery, at the starter motor solenoid switch, and at the starter switch or relay. If the lights go out as you try to crank, there may be a bad connection at the battery. The bad connection lets only a small current through-enough for the lights to go on. But when you try to start, all the current goes to the starter motor because the motor has much less resistance than the lights. Therefore, the lights go out. Try wiggling the battery connections to see if this helps. If the lights dim only slightly, the trouble probably is in the starter motor.

If the starter motor cranks slowly and the engine does not start, the trouble is probably due to a discharged battery. The battery does not have enough power to crank the engine fast enough for starting.

# Chapter 3　Chassis System

## 3.1 Clutch

The clutch in a heavy-duty truck provides a means of connecting and disconnecting the engine from the transmission. It must transfer engine torque to the transmission gradually to minimize torsional shock on the drivetrain. After engagement, the clutch must continue to transmit all the engine torque to the transmission without slippage. The clutch must also provide the means of disconnecting the engine from the drivetrain whenever the gears in the transmission are being shifted from one gear ratio to another.

The transmission of power through the clutch is accomplished by gradually bringing one or more rotating drive members connected to the engine crankshaft into contact with one or more driven members connected to the transmission input shaft. The driven members, prior to engagement with the driving members, can be either stationary or rotating at a speed that is slower or faster than the driving members. Contact between the members is established and maintained by spring pressure. The pressure exerted by the springs on the driven members is controlled by the driver through the clutch pedal and linkage. The positive engagement of the driving and driven members is made possible by the friction between the surfaces of the members. When full spring pressure is applied, the speed of the driving and driven members should be the same. At this point, the clutch is a direct connection between the engine and the transmission.

The flywheel may either be flat of countersunk—a "pot-type" flywheel. The surface of the flywheel that mates with the driven discs is machined smooth. For the clutch to work properly, the flywheel must be perpendicular to the crank-shaft with very little allowable runout (as little as 0.005 inch).

The clutch cover assembly contains the pressure plate, springs, and-depending on the design of the clutch—a variety of levers, sleeves, adjusting rings, and retainers. The cover is bolted to the flywheel and rotates with it at crankshaft speed.

Between the cover and the pressure plate are springs. Depending on the design of the clutch, any number of coil springs might be used to force the plate against the driven discs, or the clutch might utilize a single diaphragm spring. In some clutches, coil springs are positioned perpendicular to the pressure plate and are equally spaced around the perimeter of the cover. Other clutches use fewer coil springs and angle them between the cover and a retainer (Figure 3-1). Connected to the retainer are several layers that, when forced forward by the retainer, multiply the force of the springs. Pivot points on the levers press the pressure plate against the driven discs.

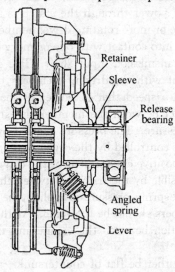

Figure 3-1   The coil springs in this clutch are angled between the cover and a retainer

Clutches with a diaphragm spring also use a retainer and lever arrangement to exert pressure on the pressure plate.

The pressure plate is machined smooth on the side facing the engine and driven disc (or discs) and is itself driven by pins or lugs on the clutch cover. The plate is free to slide back and forth on the pins or lugs, and when spring pressure is applied to the plate it meshes with the driven friction plates sand-wiched between it and the flywheel.

Some two plate clutches utilize an adapter ring when the clutch is installed on a flat flywheel. The adapter ring is bolted between the clutch cover and the flywheel. It is sized to provide the needed depth to accommodate the second clutch disc (Figure 3-2) and the intermediate plate.

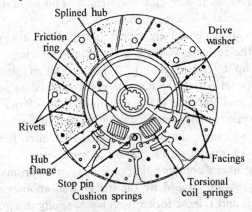

Figure 3-2 One type of clutch disc

If the clutch has two driven discs, an intermediate, or center, plate will separate the discs. The plate is machined smooth on both sides since it is pressed between two friction surfaces. An intermediate plate increases the torque capacity of the clutch by increasing the friction area, giving more area for the transmission of torque. Some intermediate plates have slots in their edge. These slots mate with and are driven by pins in the flywheel housing. Other intermediate plates have four or more tabs that fit into and are driven by slots in the clutch cover or adapter ring.

Some clutches with heavy-duty intermediate plates require antirattle springs. These reduce wear between the intermediate plate and the drive pin, and improve clutch release. Without the springs, the drive slots in the plate would wear excessively, resulting in poor clutch release. Three or four antirattle springs are positioned between the edge of the plate and the inside wall of the "pot-type" flywheel. These are spaced equal distances apart (three springs-120 degrees apart; four springs-90 degrees apart).

Most clutches on heavy-duty trucks are controlled by a mechanical linkage between the clutch pedal and the release bearing. Some trucks have hydraulic clutch controls. The linkage connects the clutch pedal to the fork, or yoke.

With the clutch pedal fully raised, there should always be free play between the fork, or yoke, and the release bearing. This free play is taken up by the first 1 to 1-1/2 inches of pedal travel. Then, as the pedal is depressed farther, the fork bears against the release bearing and forces it along the input shaft of the transmission. On pull-type clutches with a clutch brake. the last inch or two of pedal travel will force the bearing against the clutch brake.

There are two types of mechanical linkages used in heavy-duty trucks: one that uses a combina-tion of levers and fulcrums to multiply the pedal pressure applied by the driver, and another that links the clutch pedal and release fork through a specially designed clutch control cable.

Figure 3-3 shows the components of a typical hydraulic clutch control system. The clutch is controlled and operated by hydraulic fluid pressure and is assisted by an air servo cylinder. This clutch con-sists of a master cylinder, hydraulicfluid reservoir, and an air-assisted servo cylinder. These are all connected by metal and flexible hydraulic lines.

When the truck driver presses down on the clutch pedal, the plunger forces the piston in the master cylinder to move forward.

This closes off the reservoir and carses the hydraulic fluid to move down the line to a reaction plunger and pilot valve in the servo cylinder.

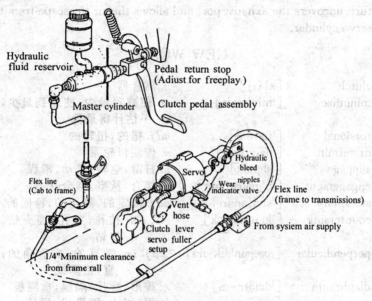

Figure 3-3  Overall view of hydraulic controls

As the hydraulic pressure increases, it forces the reaction plunger to move forward to close off an exhaust port and to seat the pilot valve. When the plunger is moved farther, it unseats the pilot valve, which allows air to enter the servo cylinder, exerting which allows air to enter the servo cylinder, cxerting pressure onto the rear side of the air piston. The movement of the air piston assists in clutch pedal application.

As the clutch pedal pressure increases, the air piston is moved farther forward and the air pressure overcomes the hydraulic pressure in the reaction plunger. This causes the pilot valve to reseat, preventing any more air from reaching the air piston. The pilot valve and reaction plunger will remain in this position until there is a change in the pressure.

When the hydraulic pressure decreases, the return spring returns the reaction plunger and the pilot valve seats itself, which in turn uncovers the exhaust port and allows the air to escape from the servo cylinder.

## NEW WORDS

| | | |
|---|---|---|
| clutch | [klʌtʃ] | n. 离合器 |
| minimize | ['minimaiz] | vt. 使减到最少,使缩到最少,把…估计得最低 |
| torsional | ['tɔːʃənl] | adj. 扭的,扭转的 |
| drivetrain | ['daivtrein] | n. 传动齿轮系 |
| slippage | ['slipidʒ] | n. 打滑,空转,滑动,滑程 |
| engagement | [in'geidʒmənt] | n. 接合,从事,啮合状态 |
| stationary | ['steiʃənəri] | adj. 固定的,静止的,稳固的 |
| countersink | ['kauntəsiŋk] | vt. ;n. 钻孔,穿孔;埋头钻,锥口钻 |
| perpendicular | [ˌpəːpən'dikjulə] | adj. ;n. 垂直的,成直角的;垂直,铅垂线 |
| diaphragm | ['daiəfræm] | n. 碟形,膜片,隔膜,横隔板 |
| perimeter | [pə'rimitə] | n. 周,周边,周界线,周长 |
| retainer | [ri'teinə] | n. 导圈,护圈,档板,(滚动轴承)保持架 |
| multiply | ['mʌltiplai] | v. 扩大,增加,增多 |
| pivot | ['paivət] | n. vi. ;vt. 枢,枢轴;在枢轴上转动;装枢轴子 |
| lug | [lʌg] | vt. ;vi. 拖,拉,硬扯,拖拉 |
| intermediate | [ˌintəː'miːdjət] | adj. ;n. 中间的;中间体,中间人 |
| capacity | [kə'pæsiti] | n. 容量,容器,能力,能量 |
| adapter | [ə'dæptə] | n. 接合器,接头 |
| slot | [slɔt] | n. ;vt. 狭孔,缝,槽,狭槽;开槽于 |
| release | [ri'liːs] | vi. 释放,减轻,下降 |
| antirattle | [ænti'rætl] | adj. 减振的;减声的 |

| | | |
|---|---|---|
| linkage | ['liŋkeidʒ] | n. 连接,联动装置;联锁 |
| fulcrum | ['fʌlkrəm] | n. 支点,支轴,支架 |
| component | [kəm'pəunənt] | n. 构件,部件,组成 |
| servo | ['sə:vəu] | n. 伺服,伺服系统,随动系统 |
| reservoir | ['rezəvwa:] | n. 贮液器,水库,贮液囊,储蓄器 |
| plunger | ['plʌndʒə] | n. 活塞,(轮胎)气门嘴柱塞 |
| flexible | ['fleksəbl] | adj. 柔韧的,易弯曲的,挠性的 |

## PHRASES AND EXPRESSIONS

| | |
|---|---|
| prior to | 在先,在前,比…重要 |
| pressure plate | 压盘 |
| antirattle springs | 减振弹簧 |
| release bearing | 分离轴承 |
| clutch pedal | 离合器踏板 |
| be free to | 不受…的约束 |
| diaphragm spring | 膜片弹簧,碟形弹簧 |
| take up | 由…来实现,承担,装载(货物) |
| torsional coil spring | 扭转螺旋弹簧 |
| pedal travel | 踏板行程 |
| relay lever | 摆杆 |
| hydraulic fluid reservoir | 贮液室 |
| clutch fork | 分离拨叉 |
| release lever | 分离杠杆 |
| master cylinder | (制动)主油缸 |

## NOTES TO THE TEXT

1. The transmission of power through the clutch is accomplished by gradually bringing one or more rotating drive members connected to the engine crankshaft into contact with one or more driven members connected to the transmission input shaft.

经过离合器的动力输出主要是由与发动曲轴相联的一个或多个驱动元件与一个或多个动力输入轴相联的被驱动元件相接触形成的。

bringing 为动名词短语做介词 by 的宾语;rotating 现在分词

短语作定语；driven 过去分词做定语修饰 members；connected to…过去分词做定语修饰 members。

2. An intermediate plate increases the torque capacity of the clutch by increasing the friction area, giving more area for the transmission of torque.

中间的压盘通过增加摩擦面积而提高扭矩传递能力,以有更多的面积传递扭矩。

giving… 是现在分词短语做目的状语；increasing 是动名词短语做 by 的宾语。

3. As the hydraulic pressure increases, it forces the reaction plunger to move forward to close off an exhaust port and to seat the pilot valve.

当液压上升时,它迫使反应柱塞向前移动以关闭排放口,并使阀回位。

force sth to do 强制,迫使…做…,是谓语；to close …, to seat … 是动词不定式短语在句中做目的状语。

## EXERCISES

I. Answer the following questions according to the text:

1. Define the word clutch what are the three main uses of the clutch?

2. Name the major parts that make up the clutch. what is the clutch disc?

3. Of what use is the pressure plate? By what driven is the pressure plate?

4. What part does the flywheel play in the clutch?

5. What is clutch pedal free travel? How is free travel adjusted?

6. What kind of release levers are used in the diaphragm clutch?

7. What is meant by riding the clutch?

8. What two parts of the clutch and transmission are splined together?

9. From what type material is the facing used on the clutch disc made?

Ⅱ. Choose the one word or phrase that best complete the sentence:

1. To drive the wheels of the automobile the power devel-oped by the engine must ____ to them.
   A. transmit          B. be transmitted
   C. be attached       D. be engaged

2. A clutch is used to ____ the drive from the engine to the gear-box as the required gear is being selected.
   A. disengage         B. pass
   C. engage            D. connect

3. The clutch ____ the two duties of disengagement and sub-sequent re-engagement smoothly progressively.
   A. brings about      B. carries over
   C. takes up          D. makes up

4. The clutch should be made ____ so that engine takes hold gradually and the inertia of the vehicle is over come.
   A. by the way        B. in the way
   C. in a manner       D. in such a way

5. The clutch is usually ____ the engine flywheel.
   A. concerned with    B. attached directly to
   C. related to        D. operated by

6. The spring pressure must be sufficient for preventing ____ when the clutch is fully engaged.
   A. applying more force  B. vibration
   C. slippage             D. jolt

7. The spring pressure of the clutch is mainly ____ maintain-ing the force of friction.
   A. responsible for   B. coupled with
   C. to do away with   D. to get rid of

8. In order to carry the load, the contact surfaces must be of ____ material as to provide sufficient friction.
   A. a such            B. such a
   C. similar           D. those

Ⅲ. Chose the best answer for each of the following questions:

1. Which of the following clutch components is a driven member?

  A. clutch cover     B. clutch disc
  C. intermediate plate   D. pressure plate
 2. Which of the following is not a part of the clutch cover assembly?
  A. pressure spring    B. release lever
  C. pressure plate     D. adapter ring
 3. Which of the following clutch components is splined to the input shaft of the transmission?
  A. clutch disc      B. pressure plate
  C. release bearing    D. flywheel
 4. Which of the following is used to stop the rotation of the input shaft when upshifting into higher gears?
  A. conventional clutch brake
  B. torque limiting clutch brake
  C. clutch pedal
  D. none of the above
 5. Which of the following driving procedures will result in clutch damage?
  A. driving with foot on the clutch pedal
  B. using the clutch as a brake to hold the truck on a hill and incline
  C. coasting downhill with the transmission in gear and the clutch disengaged
  D. all of the above
 6. Which of the following could be a cause of poor clutch release?
  A. worn friction facings on the clutch discs
  B. worn clutch linkage
  C. worn release bearing
  D. all of the above
 7. On which of the following types of flywheels would the center intermediate plate be driven by drive pins?
  A. flat flywheel     B. pot flywheel
  C. torque converter   D. all of the above
 8. When installing a 15-1/2-inch clutch, which of the following

components should be installed in the clutch cover before installing the clutch on the vehicle?

  A. release bearing    B. front clutch disc

  C. intermediate plate   D. clutch brake

Ⅳ. Translate the following sentence into Chinese:

  1. In early cars the clutch was often of the cone type, the rim of the flywheel being tapered internally, and the driven member, also tapered to fit, was pressed into it by a single heavy spring.

  2. The material used for facing the clutch disc is similiar to that used for lining brakes, being composed of woven asbestos bonded with phenol resin, and sometimes enclosing metal wire mesh to strengthen it.

  3. The pressure plate is pressed to the disk by the springs so that the torque is transmitted owing to friction forces from the engine to the input shaft of the transmission.

  4. The springs spaced around the circumference between the pressure plate and the clutch cover clamp the driven disk between the pressure plate and the flywheel.

  5. As engine speed increases, the rollers wedge themselves between the pressure plate and cover so that the faster the clutch rotates, the greater the pressure exerted on the pressure plate and disk.

  6. As distinct from the conventional clutch, the clutch pedal system operates through the release bearing direct on to the central portion of the plate.

Ⅴ. Translate the following passage into Chinese:

  In the transmission system of a motor vehicle, different components concerned with the transmitting of engine power to the road wheels are the clutch and gearbox or automatic transmission, universal joints, the propeller shaft and the final drive gearing and the axles as well as bearings for the driving wheels and half shafts.

  The characteristics of an internal combustion engine is to develop small power or torque at slow rotational speed. Moreover, in order to start cin engine from rest more power is required as compared to the one already in motion requiring to keep it in motion. For this purpose, it is necessary for the engine to attain increased speed of rotation before putting the automobile, truck in motion. On the other hand, a sudden shock is resulted if a sudden connection of the rapidly rotating engine is made to the propelling means of the stationary vehicle. To provide reasonable and comfortable start to the vehicle, gragual application of the load along with some slowing of the engine speed is necessary. A large number of connecting coupling means have been used between the engine and the driving wheels. These devices known as clutches may be of mechanical, electrical and hydraulic types. In simple words, a clutch is a mechanism which connects or disconnects the transmission of power from one working part to another. It is generally fitted to the flywheel at the rear end of the crankshaft or between the flywheel and the gearbox.

## 3.2 Manual Transmission

During normal operating conditions, power from the engine is transferred through the engaged clutch to the input shaft of the transmission. Gears in the transmission housing alter the torque and speed of this power input before passing it on to the transmissions output shaft. The rotating output shaft then drives the propeller shaft. drive axle shafts, and finally the road wheels.

The various size gears in a standard transmission work to give the truck's engine a mechanical advantage over the vehicle's driving wheels. Without this mechanical advantage, an engine can generate only limited torque at low speeds. And without sufficient torque. moving a heavily loaded vehicle from a standing start is impossible.

In any engine, the crankshaft always rotates in the same direction. If the engine transmitted its power directly to the drive axles, the wheels could be driven only in one direction. Instead, the transmission provides the gearing to reverse power drive direction so the vehicle can be driven backward.

The standard or manual transmission installed in heavy-duty

trucks commonly has between five to twenty separate speed ranges. This enables the driver to operate the vehicle at top engine efficiency under a variety of loads and road conditions. The low speed/high torque gear ratios needed for start-up and climbing steep grades can also be used to provide engine braking on severe downgrades.

Transmissions having a limited number of gear ranges often have a single set of gears contained in a single housing. This main gearing is used to generate all gear ranges. Such a transmission can be a single or twin countershaft design.

Many heavy-duty truck transmissions consist of two distinct sets of gearing. One is the main or front gearing. The second is the auxiliary gearing located directly on the rear of the main gearing. The main and auxiliary gearing may be contained in a separate housing, with the auxiliary housing bolted directly onto the main or front housing. However, in some transmissions, both the main and auxiliary gearing are contained in a single housing.

The major advantage of this gearing setup is the large number of gearing combinations. The main section normally contains gearing for five forward speeds plus reverse. The auxiliary housing contains gearing for two or three speeds. Two-speed auxiliary gearing creates high and low speed ranges. Three-speed auxiliary gearing adds an overdrive gearing. When combined with the power flows generated in the main sections, the auxiliary gearing can be used to create 9-, 13-, 15-, 18-, and 20-speed transmissions.

A transmission is a speed and power changing device installed at some point between the engine and driving wheels of the vehicle. It provides a means for changing the ratio between engine rpm (revolutions per minute) and driving wheels rpm to best meet each particular driving situation.

Given a level road, an automobile without a trans-mission could be made to move by accelerating the engine and engaging the clutch. However, a start under these conditions would be slow, noisy and uncomfortable. In addition, it would place a tremendous strain on the engine and driving parts of the automobile.

So in order to get smooth starts and have power to pass and

climb hills, a power ratio must be provided to multiply the torque and turning effort of the engine. Also required is a speed ratio to avoid the need for extremely high engine rpm at high road speeds. The transmission is geared to perform these functions.

The transmission is designed for changing the torque transmitted from the engine crankshaft to the propeller shaft, reversing the vehicle movement and disengaging the engine from the drive line for a long time at parking or coasting A higher torque should be applied to the wheels to set an automobile in motion or move uphill with a full load than to keep it rolling after it gets under way on level stretches of the road, when inertia is high and tractive resistance is low. To meet these variable torque requirements, special gear boxes are used. Such gear boxes are called fixed-ratio transmissions.

In a gear train consisting of a driving gear and a driven gear, the torque at the driven gear will increase as many times as the number of teeth of the driven gear is larger than that of the driving gear.

The figure obtained by dividing the number of driven gear teeth by that of the driving gear is called gear ratio. If a train consists of several pairs of gears, the overall ratio is the product of the gear ratios of all the gear pairs in the train.

To provide the different torques required under the varying operating conditions of a vehicle, the transmission incorporates several pairs of gears with different gear ratios.

If an intermediate gear is introduced between the driving gear and the driven gear, the rotation of the driven gear will be reversed.

The transmission consists of a housing, an input shaft and gear, an output and gear, an idler shaft, a reverse gear, a cluster of gears and a gear shift mechanism (Figure 3-4).

The cast iron housing has upper and side covers and bores for the installation of shafts. The bottom and side walls are provided with holes for filling and draining oil.

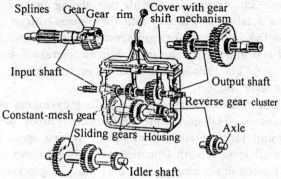
Figure 3-4  Manual automobile transmission

The input shaft is made of steel integral with the driving gear and the rim. The front end of the input shaft is installed on the bearing in the bore of the crankshaft, while the rear end rotates in the bore of the front wall of the housing. The input shaft is arranged so that only the driving gear and the rim are accommodated inside the housing while the splined portion of the shaft protruding from the transmission carries the hub of the clutch driven disk. The output shaft is splined and rests with its front end on a roller bearing installed in the bore of the input shaft. The other end of the output shaft rotates in a ball bearing in the transmission housing wall. The output shaft splines carry the sliding gears. The output shaft is coaxial with the input shaft.

The idler shaft carries a cluster of gears of different sizes. The cluster is mounted in the roller bearings on an axle or, together with the shaft, on bearings in the housing wall bores. The idler shaft constantly rotates with the input shaft because their gears are in constant mesh. The reverse gear (a single gear or a two-gear cluster) rotates on an axle secured in the holes of the housing walls.

The gear shift mechanism is designed for engaging gears, setting them neutral and engaging the reverse speed. The speeds are changed by shifting the gears or sleeves along the output shaft. The transmission type depends on the number of the sliding gears or sleeves. The transmission with two sliding gears or synchronizer sleeves is called two-range, with three gears, threer-ange. Depending on the number of forward speeds there are three, four and five-speed transmissions. The gear shift mechanism is mounted on the top cover. The shift lever is arranged on the cover or on the bracket of the lever support.

The transmission gears are shifted by means of a gear shift mechanism. The gear shift mechanism consists of a lever, shift rails, shift forks, retainers, locks and a reverse speed safety device. The shift lever mounted on the transmission cover has a spherical bulb housed in a socket in the cover boss. A pin keeps the lever against rotation. The cover drillings accommodate shift rails which carry the shift forks and shift blocks with slots. The lower end of the lever enters the slots of the shift blocks. The forks fit into the grooves of the sliding gears and synchronizer sleeves. To change a speed, the upper end of the lever is slid to a certain position, the lower end of the lever moves the shift block and the latter pushes the shift rail with the fork and gear until the required speed is engaged. Retainers keep the gears in the engaged or neutral positions.

The retainer consists of a ball and a spring accommodated in a channel drilled in the transmission cover. The shift rail has slots whose number is equal to that of speeds engaged by the given shift, plus one slot for neutral.

When the transmission is in gear or in neutral, the ball is forced into the slot to lock the shift rail. To move the shift rail when changing gear, the force applied to it must be sufficient to push the ball out of the slot.

During a gear change, the lower end of the lever may stop between two shift blocks and move two shift rails simultaneously, thereby engaging two speeds at once. As the output shaft cannot rorate at two different speeds simultaneously, this will result in breaking the gear teeth. Simultaneous engagement of two gears is prevented by locks. The locks are made in the form of balls or bars located in a horizontal channel between the shift rails. The shift rails have recesses which align with the channel of the locks when the shift rails are in the neutral position. The length of the lock bar plus the diameters of two balls is equal to the distance between the shift rails plus one recess. It is impossible to move any of the shift rails before a part of the ball or the end of the bar snaps into the recess of the other shift rail thus locking the latter.

## NEW WORDS

| | | |
|---|---|---|
| means | [mi:nz] | n. 方法,手段,工具 |
| particular | [pə'tikjulə] | adj. 特殊的,特别的,个别的 |
| situation | [sitju'eiʃən] | n. 形势,情况,环境 |
| uncomfortable | ['ʌn'kʌmfətəbl] | adj. 不舒适的,不方便 |
| tremendous | [tri'mendəs] | adj. 巨大的,非常的,惊人的 |
| strain | [strein] | vt.;n. 拉紧,紧张,应变,变形 |
| extremely | [iks'tri:mli] | adv. 极端,极其,非常 |
| coasting | ['koustiŋ] | n. 滑行,惯性运转,滑行距离 |
| stretch | [stretʃ] | n. 一段路程,距离,路段 |
| variable | ['vɛəriəbl] | adj. 易变的,反复不定的,不同的 |
| intermediate | [ˌintə(:)'mi:djət] | adj. 中间的,中等的,居中的 |
| installation | [instɔː'leiʃən] | n. 安装,装配,设备,设置 |
| drain | [drein] | v. 排出,排水,排放 |
| coaxial | [kəu'æksəl] | adj. 共轴的,共心的,同轴的 |
| retainer | [ri'teinə] | n. 导圈,(滚动轴承)保持架,夹持;挡板 |
| simultaneously | [siməl'teinjəsli] | adv. 同时地,一齐地,同时发生地 |
| align | [ə'lain] | v. 使成一行,排成一行,成一线 |
| snap | [snæp] | v. 咬住,抓住,卡断 |

## PHRASES AND EXPRESSIONS

| | |
|---|---|
| propeller shaft | 传动轴,方向节轴 |
| be applied to | 施加于,应用于 |
| tractive resistance | 牵引阻力 |
| gear train | 齿轮传动等 |
| as many times as | 是…许多倍 |
| idler shaft | 惰轮轴 |

a cluster of gears　　　　　齿轮组
synchronizer sleeves　　　　同步器啮合套
gear shift mechanism　　　　换档机构

## NOTES TO THE TEXT

1. During normal operating conditions, power from the engine is transferred through the engaged clutch to the input shaft of the transmission.

正常的操纵情况下,发动机的动力通过接合的离合器传递到变速器的输入轴。

is transferred 是被动语态,在全句中做谓语;from the engine 是介词短语做 power 的后置定语;through…transmission 是整个句子的状语。

2. Without this mechanical advantage, an engine can generate only limitted torque at low speeds.

若没有这个机械优点,发动机只能在低的速度下输出有限的扭矩。

Without this mechanical advantage 是 without 引导的状语从句;limitted 是 limit 的过去分词做定语,修饰 torque。

## EXERCISES

Ⅰ. Answer the following questions according to the text:

1. Of what value is a transmission?
2. How does a transmission multiply torque?
3. Can you name the various gears that are available in a manual transmission?
4. What are the approximate ratios of these gears?
5. How are these shafts turned or driven?
6. What is a synchromesh unit? How does synchromesh work?
7. What lubricates a transmission? What is a constant mesh gear?
8. How is the end play in the reverse idler gear and cluster gear controlled?
9. Can you list the gear ratios for a typical six-speed transmis-

sion?

10. Six-speed transmissions can provide an overdrive feature when in sixth gear. True or False?

Ⅱ. Choose the best answer for each of the following questions:

1. Which of the following gear ratios shows an overdrive condition?
  A. 2.15:1    B. 1:1
  C. 0.85:1    D. none of the above

2. Which type of gear develops the problem of gear whine at higher speeds?
  A. spur gear    B. helical gear
  C. worm gear    D. all of the above

3. When sliding gearshift mechanisms are used, which gears do they control?
  A. high and low gears in the auxiliary section
  B. first and reverse gears in the main section
  C. all forward gears except first in the main section
  D. direct and overdrive gears in the auxiliary section

4. Which of the following is the most widely used manual transmission gear train arrangement in heavy-duty trucks?
  A. single countershaft  B. twin countershaft
  C. triple countershaft  D. none of the above

5. In a range shift air control system, which component distributes inlet air pressure to both the low and high range air hoses running to the range cylinder?
  A. slave valve    B. splitter valve
  C. air regulator    D. air compressor

6. To provide for overdrive gearing in the high and low auxiliary transmission ranges, which of the following comp-onents is added to the basic range shift air control system?
  A. splitter
  B. button actuated shift tower valve
  C. additional slave valve
  D. both A and B

Ⅲ. Choose the one word or phrase that best complete the sentence:

1. Some automobiles ____ a dual high transmission.
   A. provided with      B. provide for
   C. are equipped with  D. are used to
2. Noiseless shifting of gears is achieved ____ a synchroniz-er.
   A. by means of        B. by all means
   C. to adapt for       D. to the extent of
3. These speed and power changing devices are known as ____.
   A. speed governor     B. transmission
   C. distributor        D. speed indicator
4. The transmission drive gear shaft is made ____ transmis-sion drive gear and tooth rim.
   A. separate from      B. up for
   C. through with       D. integral with
5. The reverse idler gear ____ in the form of a twin-gear cluster.
   A. fabricated         B. is made
   C. operates           D. is supported
6. The cluster gear is moved forward to mesh ____ the countershaft second gear.
   A. with               B. to
   C. on                 D. around
7. The number of gear teeth per unit measurement of the gear's pitch diameter(such as teeth/in. )is known as gear ____.
   A. ratio              B. pitch
   C. size               D. load
8. When an idler gear is placed between the driving and driven gear, the driven gear ____.
   A. rotates in the same direction as the driving gear
   B. rotates in the opposite direction of the driving gear
   C. remains stationary
   D. none of the above
9. The part used to ensure that the main shaft and the main shaft gear to be locked to it are rotating at the same speed is known as a ____.
   A. synchronizer       B. sliding clutch

C. transfer case　　　　　D. PTO unit
　　10. An auxiliary drive for truck accessories that is used with the transmission is called ___.
　　　A. a transfer case　　　　B. a power take off unit
　　　C. an auxiliary transmission　D. a synchronizer
Ⅳ. Translate the following sentence into Chinese:
　　1. A higher torque is required to drive a heavily-loaded truck up a hill than that required to drive an empty truck on a flatroad.
　　2. The engine torque is applied at the input shaft of the gearbox and is transmitted to the countershaft by means of a smaller gearwheel on the input shaft and a larger gearwheel on the countershaft.
　　3. The required gear ratio is selected by means of the gear lever, which moves a sliding sleeve on the output shaft so that the appropriate gearwheels will mesh with the corresponding gearwheels on the countershaft.
　　4. A higher torque should be applied to the wheels to set an automobile in motion or move uphill with a full load than to keep it rolling after it gets under way on level stretches of the road, when inertia is high and tractive resistance is low.
　　5. The input shaft is arranged so that only the driving gear and the rim are accommodated inside the housing while the splined portion of the shaft protruding from the transmission carries the hub of the clutch driven disk.
Ⅴ. Translate the following passage into Chinese:
　　The transmission is a sort of speed and power changing device needed between the engine of the automobile and its driving wheels. It provides means of varying the gear ratio between the engine and rear wheels. Much more power is required to set an automobile in motion as compared to power required for keeping it rolling after starting. This means that at the start the automobile requires much more power while the engine may be developing very little power. A transmission system helps to turn the engine crankshaft to four, eight or twelve time approximately for each wheel revolution. For backing the car, a reverse gear is also provided.

A transmission system includes whole of the mechanism required to transfer torque from the engine flywheel to rear road wheel, i. e. the clutch, gear box, propeller shaft, final drive, differential and axle shafts.

## 3.3 Automatic Transmissions

Automatic transmissions upshift and downshift with no direct assistance from the driver. Factors such as road speed, throttle position, and governed engine speed control and trigger shifting between gears.

The majority of automatic transmissions rely on planetary gear sets to transfer power and generate torque from the engine to the drive line. Planetary gear sets are quite different from the cluster gear arrangements used in manual shift gearboxes. The shifting of planetary gears is actuated by the use of hydraulic force. An intricate system of valves is used to control and direct pressurized fluid in the colsed system. The force generated by this fluid is used to apply and release the various clutches and brakes that control planetary gear operation. Many systems now use electronic controls to obtain optimum operating performance.

A second type of automatic transmission does not use planetary gears controlled by a hydraulic system. Instead, it uses advanced electronics to automatically shift a cluster gear arrangement similar to the manual units. It uses a twin countershaft design having both main and auxiliary sections. The manually controlled clutch has been replaced with a torque converter. The torque converter uses automatic transmission fluid to transfer power from the flywheel to the main section input shaft, but this is the only use of hydraulics in the transmission. The shifting of main and auxiliary gearing is done through the movement of components activated by compressed air. Both the torque converter and air control systems are electronically managed and controlled.

Finally, semiautomatic transmissions offer automatic shifting in the cruise range above 40 to 45 mph. Computer logic controls the shift point and the shift is performed through air actuation of a splitter gear. These transmissions offer optimum fuel economy within a narrow operating range. All other gears, except the top two cruise range gears are manually selected.

The transmission operating range is programmed by the manual control at the steering column or on-the-floor console selector. The selector quadrant has six positions, in the following order: P-R-N-D-2-1

- **P** **Park** The gear train is in neutral and the output shaft is mechanically locked to the case by an internal locking pawl and parking gear; an engine start is provided.
- **R** **Reverse** A single reduction ratio provides the transmission with a reverse mode.
- **N** **Neutral** The gear train is in neutral and the output shaft is not locked; an engine start is provided.
- **D** **Drive** This is the normal driving range for economy. A first-gear start is provided with automatic shifts to intermediate (second) and high (direct) determined by road speed and throttle opening. Forced downshifts 3-2, 3-1, and 2-1 are available at wot kickdown, depending on the vehicle speed and engine crankshaft torque reserve. A 3-2 part-throttle downshift provides for controlled acceleration at lower speeds. At closed throttle, the transmission downshifts 3-1 at about 10 mph (16 km/h), except the C-3 sequence, which is 3-2 at about 15 mph (24 km/h) and 2-1 at about 7 mph (11 km/h).
- **2** **Manual second gear** This operating range has second gear only, no first-gear start. Early C-4/C-6 units shifted 2-3.
- **1** **Manual low gear** The transmission is locked in low gear; no upshifts. If the range selector is moved from D to 1 at excessive speed, the transmission will shift to intermediate until the vehicle slows to a safe speed. Once low gear is engaged, the transmission cannot upshift.

### 3.3.1 Hydraulic Control Systems

The hydraulic control system is responsible for a variety of major activities that involve pressure and performance circuits that determine the clutch/band combinations for the select action of the planetary gear train. Although the design of the system appears to be complex, it is made up of basic interrelated components and subsystems that are easy to understand. The hydraulic control system typically consists of the following:

1. A pump to provide a steady supply of regulated mainline oil to meet the hydraulic demands of the transmission.

2. A regulator valve to control the variable mainline pressure requirements and the feed oil to the converter-cooling-lubrication circuits.

3. A control valve assembly that allows for manual or automatic control of the gear ratio clutch/band combinations.

4. A governor to produce a regulated vehicle speed sensing hydraulic pressure. It is used primarily as one of two pressures to control the shift schedule. In some systems it may be used to modify the mainline pressure; it causes a pressure drop.

5. A throttle or modulator valve to produce an engine torque sensing hydraulic pressure. It is used primarily as one of two pressures to control the shift schedule. It has the added job of always modifying the mainline pressure; it causes a pressure increase.

There is always a support cast of auxiliary valves and check balls to augment the primary components of the hydraulic control system, and these do vary between transmission products. To simplify the discussion, these product variances will be avoided and the main concentration directed at the basic working of the primary controls in the hydraulic system. Of course, this includes the fundamentals of automatic shifting. Complete hydraulic system features of product specifics can always be found in the manufacturer's service or training manuals. We reemphasize that domestic and import systems typically have similar components in function, construction, and operation.

## Pump and Pressure Regulation System

The transmission hydraulic operation is keyed to a hydraulic pump that is engine driven through the converter. The pump must essentially deliver a steady supply of oil under controlled pressure to meet the demands of the transmission circuits. It provides the basic fluid supply and operating pressure. The pump output is sensitized by a pressure regulator valve that controls the pressure head.

## Shift System

The shift system provides both automatic and nonautomatic gear selection. The nonautomatic selections are provided by the manual valve and typically include neutral, reverse, and forward range plus the operating ranges used for engine braking. Automatic gear selection provides for gear ratio changes that are compatible to the vehicle speed and available performance desired by the driver. In a three-speed system, the shift schedule is programmed for a 1-2 and a 2-3 shift in the fully automatic drive range.

The shift system can be viewed as a hydraulic computer. Through driver selection, the manual valve is properly indexed in the valve body and programs the transmission for the desired operating range. In fully automatic drive range, the two shift valve arrangements digest a hydraulic road speed signal and a hydraulic torque signal. The shift valves evaluate the information and automatically trigger clutch/band circuits ON or OFF to provide the best gear ratio for the driving load.

The essential hydraulic support systems for transmission operation have already been discussed: the pressure supply system, converter-cooling-lube system, throttle and modulator systems, and the governor system. Add to these the manual valve servos and bands, clutches, and accumulators and you are ready to tie it all together with the shift system operation. A gradual buildup of a three-speed hydraulic control system shows how a seemingly complex subject is made up of a number of simple circuits and assorted devices that are easy to understand. Our control system uses the standardized range selection P-R-N-D-2-1 as it relates to a typical Simpson planetary gear train.

**Servo and Clutch Assemblies**

The use of hydraulic power to apply the bands and clutches is confined to a single device, the hydraulic piston. The pistons are housed in cylinder units known as servo and clutch assemblies. The function of the piston is to convert the force of fluid into a mechanical force capable of handling large loads. Hydraulic pressure applied to the piston strokes the piston in the cylinder and applies its load. During the power stroke, a mechanical spring or springs are compressed to provide a means of returning the piston to its original position. The springs also determine when the apply pressure build-up will stroke the piston. This is critical to clutch/band life and shift quality.

**Servo Assembly**

A servo unit provides the method of application and disengagement of the bands. A band is energized hydraulically by the piston force acting on one end of the band while the other end is anchored to the transmission case and absorbs the reaction force of the gear ratio. The servo unit consists of a piston in a cylinder and a piston return spring. It may be a separate cylinder assembly bolted to the transmission case, or the cylinder can be designed as an integral part of the case. Through suitable linkage and lever action, the servo is connected to the band it operates. The servo force acts directly on the ent of the band with an apply pin or through a lever arrangement that provides a multiplying force.

The servo unit band application must rigidly hold and ground a planetary gear member to the transmission case for forward or reverse reduction. To assist the hydraulic and mechanical apply forces, the servo and band anchor are po-sitioned in the transmission to take advantage of the drum rotation. In Figure 3-5 the drum rotational effort is in the counterclockwise direction. When the band is applied, it becomes self-energized and wraps itself around the drum in the same direction as drum rotation. This self-energizing effect reduces the force that the servo must produce to hold the band. The principle is the same one used to describe the action of self-energized drum brakes.

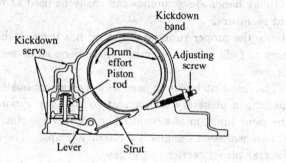

Figure 3-5  Servo unit lever arrangement; self-energizing

To release the servo apply action on the band, the servo apply oil is exhausted from the circuit or a servo release oil is introduced on the servo piston that opposes the apply oil (Figure 3-6). The servo piston in Figure 3-6 is shown in the apply position. When servo release oil is introduced on a 2-3 shift, the hydraulic mainline pressure acting on the top side of the piston plus the servo return spring will overcome the servo apply oil and move the piston downward.

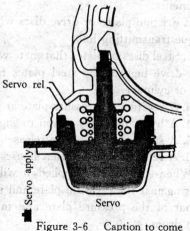

Figure 3-6  Caption to come

• 207 •

## Clutch Assembly

The multiple-disc clutch is the favored clutch unit used in automatic transmissions. It offers the following features:

1. Multiple discs give the clutch a sufficient area of frictional or torque-holding capacity in an overall small-diameter drum. The number of contacting surfaces is a factor in determining holding torque.

2. Unlike bands, disc clutches can easily be used as rolating engagement members.

3. Once the proper running clearance has been established during factory or field service assembly, there is no adjustment requirement for wear.

4. The disc clutch can be used as a reaction or holding member by connecting a planetary component to the case ground. It performs the same function as a band. The low-reverse clutch used in a variety of transmission designs is a classic example. The clutch connects the rear planet carrier to the case.

A typical rotating clutch drive unit is made up of the following components.

1. Friction plates or drive discs with internal splines that fit on a torque transmitting hub

2. Steel discs or plates that mate with the friction plates; the external drive lugs of the steel plates fit into a torque-transmitting drum or cylinder

3. A reaction or pressure plate at the end of the clutch pack

4. A hydraulic apply piston to engage the clutch pack

5. A spring-loaded piston release

6. A retainer or drum that houses the complete assembly.

When the piston is applied, it will squeeze the clutch pack together against the pressure plate and snap ring. The snap ring fits in front of the pressure plate and into a snapping groove in the clutch drum.

In Figure 3-7 a pair of multiple-disc clutch assemblies show a more exact relationship to a transmission power flow. Both clutches are oil-applied and spring-released. With both clutches off, there is no power to the gear set, whereas a front clutch apply drives the

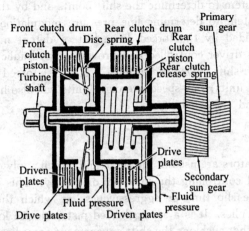

Figure 3-7  Front and rear disc clutch assemblies controlling power input to planetary gear train

primary sun gear and a rear clutch apply drives the secondary sun gear. This is how power enters the gear set for forward speeds and reverse. In high gear, the front and rear clutches are applied and drive both sun gears together.

**Valve Body Assembly**

The valve body assembly is the heart of the hydraulic control system. It is an intricate network of interrelated passages, precision valves, springs, check balls, and orifices. The assembly normally contains the manual valve, the throttle and forced-downshift valves, shift valves, and sometimes the pressure regulator valve. In response to external messages and driver demands, the valve body controls the hydraulic circuits to the clutch/band combinations for the planetary gear ratios.

The valve body, or brain, works like a computer. It is programmed for the operating range by the manual valve and monitors two gydraulic signals, one from the throttle system and another from the governor system. These signals are evaluated by the automatic shift system to determine the shift points and by the pressure regulation system to determine line pressure modulation. A third signal is provided by the forced-downshift or detent mechanism. The system is driver controlled and provides a hydraulic command to overrule the shift valves for either a 3-2 or 3-1 forced downshift in three-speed units; four-speed overdrive units will also have an additional 4-3 and 4-2 capability.

**Accumulator**

Accumulators are used in the servo and clutch apply circuits for the purpose of controlling the shift feel or quality. This is done by controlling the slip time or aggressiveness at which the band or clutch fully applies. It is a spring-loaded piston device located in a cylinder bore that cushions the shift engagement according to engine torque output.

It does this by absorbing a certain amount of fluid flow in the circuit during a band or clutch application. Accumulators were traditionally employed only in automatic shift circuits; however, it is not unusual to find that they may be integrated into the manually controlled forward and reverse circuits in the newer transmissions. The garage shift from N to D or N to R can hardly be felt, and harsh engagements from fast engine idle rpm are eliminated.

A series of illustrations will show how a typical accumulator system works. First, let's look at a simple clutch circuit without provisions to cushion the automatic shift. With this arrangement, the clutch engagement is sudden and the car jerks forward. The shift sensation is similar in effect to "popping" the clutch pedal on a manual transmission. The driver gets a kick and a jerk in the back.

It is common practice to build-in an accumulator action with the servo unit. A servo piston in the apply position for intermediate gear operation is shown in Figure 3-8. On the 2-3 shift, direct clutch apply oil is routed into the servo-release side of the piston. The release oil plus the release springs overcome the servo apply force and the piston strokes downward. This action releases the band while the clutch is being applied. Note that the servo release, or downward piston movement, provides an accumulator action for the direct clutch. The intermediate band adjustment is therefore critical to the accumulator action because it controls the servo release spring load. A loose band adjustment, for example, will result in a longer piston apply stroke. The band apply is not affected on a 1-2 shift because of the transition from a holding one-way clutch, but the release spring load is increased. Therefore, during direct clutch apply, the servo is released too early and the accumulator acction occurs too early. The end result is an engine flare-up on the 2-3 shift.

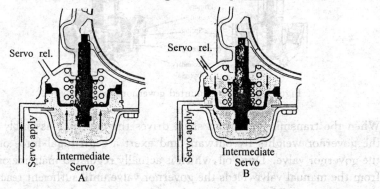

Figure 3-8. Caption to come

## Governor System

The governor is a hydraulic speedometer that is driven by the output shaft of the transmission. It receives fluid from the mainline pressure and produces a regulated governor pressure signal that is proportional to vehicle speed. It is used primarily for scheduling the transmission shifts along with throttle or modulator pressures. It is also used as a pressure signal for auxiliary or supporting control valves in the valve body. In some transmissions, the governor oil acts to reduce the line pressure with increasing vehicle speed. We concentrate on its use for shift scheduling, in which capacity it opens the shift valve and causes the shift to happen. There are several types of governor valve assembly designs in current use, but they all rely on the centrifugal effort of a rotating mass (weights).

Illustrated in Figure 3-9 is a case-mounted governor assembly.

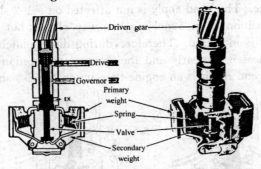

Figure 3-9   Case-mounted governor assembly

When the transmission output shaft drives the governor assembly, the governor weights fly outward and exert a centrifugal force on the governor valve. Drive oil, which is actually regulated mainline oil from the manual valve, feeds the governor valve until sufficient reaction pressure buildup on top of the valve balances the centrifugal force of the weights. The greater the vehicle speed, the greater the centrifugal force of the weights, and hence the greater the governor pressure necessary to balance the centrifugal force. Eventually, vehicle speed reaches a point at which the governor valve cannot balance itself against the centrifugal force of the weights. When this happens, the governor valve is permanently in the open position and governor pressure equals the mainline supply pressure.

The governor weight assembly is made up of two sets of weights, primary and secondary, plus two springs. These parts are combined to produce a two-stage output curve. The primary (heavy) and secondary (light) weights have their own independent action; however, the primary weights are arranged to work together initially with the secondary weights; the springs hold the secondary weights against the primary weights. The weights are arranged so that the lighter secondary weights act directly on the regulating valve.

At low speeds the heavy mass is needed to generate a regulated governor oil for the 1-2 shift. The weights move in and out together as the governor valve regulates. Since the centrifugal force of a rotating mass increases by the square of the speed, it becomes difficult to schedule a 2-3 shift with good spacing (doubling the rpm increases the centrifugal force by four times, etc.). It therefore becomes necessary to arrange for a cutback in the rate of centrifugal advance. At approximately 20 mph (16km/h), the centrifugal force of the primary heavy weight exceeds the spring force and permanently stays moved out against a stop. The primary weights are now separated from the secondary (light) weights and are ineffective. The governor valve now balances against the centrifugal force of the secondary weights plus the spring force. The two-stage governor action results in a more even governor output distribution with increases in vehicle speed.

## NEW WORDS

| | | |
|---|---|---|
| cluster | ['klʌstə] | n. 一串,一束,一组 |
| quadrant | ['kwɔdrənt] | n. 扇形体,四分之一圆周 |
| performance | [pə'fɔːməns] | n. 性能,特性,执行,完成 |
| augment | [ɔːg'mənt] | vt. 扩大,增加,增长 |
| concentration | [kɔnsen'treiʃən] | n. 集中,专心,浓缩 |
| feature | ['fiːtʃə] | n. ;vt. 手册,特征,特色;是…的特色,起…作用 |
| regulation | [ˌregju'leiʃən] | n. 调节,校准,稳压 |
| digest | [di'dʒest] | n. ;vt. 文摘,摘要;整理,领悟,消化 |
| evaluate | [i'væljueit] | vt. ;n. 评价,把…定值;估价,评价 |

| | | |
|---|---|---|
| accumulator | [ə'kju:mjuleitə] | n. 储蓄器,蓄能器 |
| confine | [kən'fain] | v. ;n. 限制,禁闭;边缘,范围 |
| drum | [drʌm] | n. 鼓轮,滚筒,鼓状物 |
| multiple | ['mʌltipl] | adj. ;n. 多重的,复合的;倍数 |
| sufficient | [sə'fiʃənt] | adj. ;n. 足够的,充分的;足够 |
| clearance | ['kliərəns] | n. 清除,间隙,出空,许可 |
| belleville | ['beləvil] | n. 碟形,膜片式 |
| intricate | ['intrikit] | adj. 复杂的,错综的 |
| network | ['netwə;k] | n. ;adj;vt. 电路,网络;广播的;使成网状 |
| interrelate | [ˌintə(:)ri'leit] | vt. 使…相互联系 |
| orifice | ['ɔrifis] | n. 节流口,通气口,孔,口 |

## PHRASES AND EXPRESSIONS

| | |
|---|---|
| automatic transmission | 自动变速器 |
| rely on | 依靠,依赖 |
| hydraulic control systems | 液力控制系统 |
| pressure supply system | 压力供给系统 |
| servo assembly | 伺服系统 |
| return spring | 回位弹簧 |
| multiple-disc clutch | 多片离合器 |
| valve body assembly | 阀体 |
| governor system | 调解系统 |

## NOTES TO THE TEXT

1. The majority of automatic transmissions rely on planetary gear sets to transfer power and generate torque from the engine to the drive line.

大多数自动变速装置依赖行星齿轮机构传递来自发动机的动力和产生扭矩到驱动系。

rely on 依靠,依赖,在句中做谓语;to transfer power… 做目的状语;from the engine to … 做状语,修饰 transfer。

2. There is always a support cast of auxiliary valves and checkballs to augment the primary components of the hydraulic control

system, and these do vary between transmission products.

一般地,总有辅助阀和控制球这样的零件来增强主要部件在液压控制系统中的效能,这些在变速器生产中也是多样化的。

There is… 是固定句型,有…;to augment the primary… 做定语,修饰 valves and balls。

3. The servo unit band application must rigidly hold and ground a planetary gear member to the transmission case for forward or reverse reduction.

应用伺服机构必须有刚性支承,并在行星齿轮部件的基础上安装在变速器壳体上,以实现前减速或后减速。

forward or reverse reduction 向前或向后驱动;application 在句中做主语;for 引导的是目的状语。

4. Since the centrifugal force of a rotating mass increase by the square of the speed, it becomes difficult to schedule a 2-3 shift with good spacing (doubling the rpm increases the cen-trifugal force by four times, etc).

由于重物的离心力是以车速的平方增加,这就使为 2-3 档安排出合适的间隙变得困难多了(增加转速二倍就使离心力提高四倍)。

it 是形式主语,to schedule … becomes difficult 的真正主语;the square of the speed 指速度的平方;increase …by… 以…速度率增长,做谓语。

### 3.3.2 Torque Converters

The torque converter operates through hydraulic force provided by automatic transmission fluid often simply called transmission oil. The torque converter changes or multiplies the twisting motion of the engine crankshaft. It then directs it through the transmission to give an infinite number of speeds suitable for the particular load and speed of the vehicle.

The torque converter automatically engages and disengages power transfer from the engine to the transmission in relation to engine rpm. With the engine running at the correct idle speed, there is not enough fluid flow for power transfer through the torque converter. As the engine speed is increased, the added fluid flow creates sufficient force to transmit engine power through the torque converter assembly.

**T/C Exterior**   The exterior of the torque converter shell is shaped like two bowls standing on end, facing each other and welded or bolted together (Figure 3-10). To support the weight of the torque converter, a short stubby shaft projects forward from the front of the torque converter shell located in a socket at the rear of the crankshaft. This forms the frontal support for the torque converter assembly. At the rear of the torque converter shell is a hollow shaft with notches or flats at one end, ground 180 degrees apart. This shaft is called the pump drive hub; the notches or flats drive the transmission pump assembly. At the front of the transmission within the pump housing is a pump bushing supporting the pump drive hub and providing rear support for the torque converter assembly.

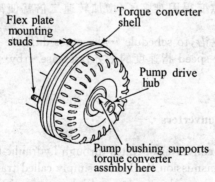

Figure 3-10   External view of a typical torque converter. In this view the front pilot is hidden by the torque converter

**T/C Interior**   The pump or impeller forms one section of the torque converter shell (Figure 3-11). The impeller has numerous curved blades that rotate as a unit with the shell. The impeller turns at engine speed, acting like a pump to start the transmission oil circulating within the torque converter shell.

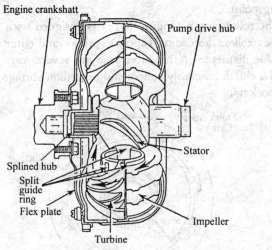

Figure 3-11   An interior view of a typical torque converter showing the pump/ impeller, turbine, and stator

While the impeller is positioned with its back facing the transmission housing, the turbine is positioned with its back to the engine. The curved blades of the turbine face the impeller assembly. The hub of the turbine is splined so the turbine can connect to and drive the turbine shaft. The turbine shaft transfers power flow to the main shaft of the transmission.

The turbine blades have a greater curve than the impeller blades. This helps eliminate oil turbulence between the turbine and impeller blades that would slow impeller speed and reduce the converter's efficiency.

**Overrunning Clutch**

An overrunning clutch Keeps the stator assembly from rotating when driven in one direction and permits overrunning (rotation) when turned in the opposite direction. Rotating stators generally use a roller type overrunning clutch that allows the stator to freewheel (rotate) when the speed of the turbine and impeller reach the coupling point.

The roller clutch (Figure 3-12) is designed with a movable inner race, rollers, accordion (apply) springs, and outer race. Around the inside diameter of the outer race are several cam-shaped pockets. The clutch assembly rollers and accordion springs are located in these pockets.

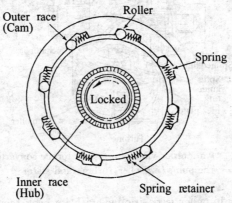

Figure 3-12  Roller-type overrunning clutch

As the vehicle begins to move the stator stays in its stationary or locked position because of the wide difference between the impeller and turbine speeds. This locking mode takes place when the inner race rotates counterclockwise. The accordion springs force the rollers down the ramps of the cam pockets into a wedging contact with the inner and outer races. With the outer race grounded to the automatic transmission housing, the stationary part connected to the inner race will be held stationary.

As vehicle road speed increases, turbine speed increases until it approaches impeller speed. Oil exiting the turbine vanes strikes the back face of the stator, causing the stator to rotate in the same direction as the turbine and impeller. At this higher speed, clearance exists between the inner stator race and hub. The rollers in each slot of the stator are pulled around the stator hub. The stator freewheels or turns as a unit.

If the vehicle slows, engine speed also slows along with turbine speed. This decrease in turbine speed allows the oil flow to change direction. It now strikes the front face of the stator vanes, halting the turning stator and attempting to rotate it in the opposite direction.

As this happens, the rollers jam between the inner race and hub, locking the stator in position. In a stationary position, the stator now redirects the oil exiting the turbine so that torque is again multiplied.

## Split Guide Rings

Power only can flow through the converter when the pump/impeller is turning faster than the turbine. When the impeller is turning at speeds much greater than the turbine, a great deal of oil turbulence can occur. Fast moving oil exits the impeller blades, striking the turbine blades with a great deal of force. It then has a tendency to bounce back toward the center sections of both impeller and turbine.

To control this bounce and the turbulence it creates, a split guide ring is located in both the impeller and turbine sections of the T/C. The guide ring suppresses bounce back and turbulence, allowing for more efficient operation.

## Stator

The stator mounts through its splined center hub to mating stator shaft, often called a ground sleeve. The ground sleeve is solidly connected to the transmission housing and therefore does not move. The stator can, however, freewheel when the impeller and turbine reach the coupling stage.

A stator is either a rotatinge velocity or kinetic energy given to the transmission oil by the impeller's rotation plus the velocity of the oil that is directed back to the impeller by the stator action. During operation, the oil gives up part of its kinetic energy as it strikes the turbine vanes. The stator then redirects the fluid flow so the oil reenters the impeller moving in the same direction the impeller is turning. This allows the kinetic energy remaining in the oil to help rotate the impeller even faster, multiplying the torque produced by the converter.

**Fluid Coupling**

Because the fluid coupling is the simplest form of fluid drive unit, the principles of fluid coupling operation serve as an ideal introduction to how a fluid force can put a solid object into motion. Some of these working principles will apply later to our discussion of the fluid converter-coupling operation. The construction of a fluid coupling is very simple. It consists of impeller and turbine members of identical structure contained in a housing filled with oil. The coupling members face one another closely, with the impeller driven by the engine and the turbine driving the wheels through the transmission and axle.

The following describes what happens inside a fluid coupling when starting the car or when accelerating under heavy load. As the engine drives the impeller, it sets the fluid mass into motion, creating a fluid force. The path of the fluid force strikes on a solid object, the turbine. The impact of the fluid jet stream against the turbine blades sets the turbine in motion. An energy cycle has been completed: mechanical to fluid and back to mechanical.

The fluid action that takes place between the impeller and turbine is an interesting science. When the impeller spins up, two separate forces are generated in the fluid. One is rotary flow, which is the rotational effort or inertia of the impeller rotation. The other is vortex flow, which circulates the fluid between the coupling members and is caused by the centrifugal pumping action of the rotating impeller (Figure 3-13). The vortex flow is the fluid exist velocity from the impeller.

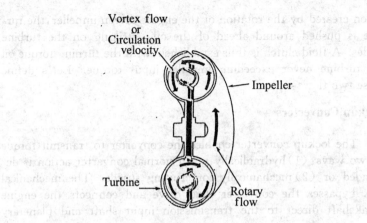

Figure 3-13   Rotary and vortex flow shown

The rotary and vortex flows can also be explained by using a bucket of water as an example. Any time there is a spinning mass, the mass (in the case of a transmission, the oil) follows the rotational movement, but it also creates a centrifugal force. This dual effect is illustrated by swinging a bucket of water in a circle. As the bucket is swinging, the water is following the circular path of the bucket. At the same time it is developing a centrifugal force that keeps the water in the bucket as it passes through the overhead position. The water is confined by the solid side and bottom of the bucket and cannot discharge (fly) outward, so it is forced to follow the bucket rotation only.

In a fluid coupling, however, the centrifugal force of the oil is not confined. The oil at the center of the spinning impeller follows the curved shell and is discharged along the outer diameter and into the turbine to establish a circular path between the impeller and the turbine. The combination of rotary and vortex flow causes an oil motion that follows the course of a rotating corkscrew. It is like watching the blade tips of a rotating pinwheel at the end of a stick, with the stick itself turning about a center. With the corkscrew oil action created by the rotation of the engine-driven impeller, the turbine is pushed around ahead of the oil , striking on the turbine blades. A fluid clutch is thus established, with the turning torque on the turbine never exceeding impeller input torque. Let's define these two flows:

**Lockup Converters**

The lockup converter enables the converter to transmit torque in two ways: (1) hydraulically when normal converter action is demanded or (2) mechanically for cruising speeds. The mechanical lock bypasses the converter fluid drive and connects the engine crankshaft direct to the transmission input shaft and planetary gearset.

Normal slippage that occurs between the converter impeller and turbine during coupling phase is eliminated. The improved efficiency in crankshaft torque transmission boosts fuel economy.

There are a number of lockup converter designs using their own unique control circuitry that automatically dictates the unlock and lockup modes of the converter. The control circuitry may be pure hydraulic or mechanical, or a combination electro/hydraulic using either a computer-or non-computer-controlled electrical circuit. The objective at this time is to limit the lockup story to a "look-see" at the various converter internal design configurations. Lockup control circuitry is featured.

All the lockup converters are still three-element/single-stage units. For lockup, however, they may feature (1) a hydraulically applied clutch piston, (2) a centrifugal locking clutch, (3) a planetary splitter, or (4) a direct mechanical shaft connection.

**Converter/Engine Match**

In operation on the road, the converter provides effortless driving characteristics.

1. At engine idle, the converter acts as an automatic clutch and permits the engine to run and the car to stand still.

2. The converter automatically adjusts its torque output to driveshaft torque requirements within its design limits. It acts as a fluid coupling for level-road, constant-speed conditions, but when performance is needed for acceleration or hill climbing, it responds with the necessary extra torque dictated by the slowdown of the turbine from increased driveshaft torque.

3. As the converter is a fluid unit, it acts as a natural shock absorber during gear ratio changes and adds to shift smoothness. The fluid also absorbs the torsional vibrations from the engine crankshaft.

4. The converter permits continuous shock-free acceleration, extending the life of drivetrain components-especially important for stop-and-go driving.

The torque converter must be engineered to balance its performance with the engine rpm and vehicle load. For a particular converter torque output and vehicle load, the engine throttle opening and rpm should be producing an optimum crankshaft torque for the drive load. The converter acts like a variable dynamometer load on the end of the engine. The converter and engine are matched when the wot stall rpm meets engineered specifications. This is basically achieved by a choice of conveter diameter sizing and internal blade angularity of the converter elements.

If the converter size is too small or has too high a stall speed for a particular application, the engine will operate at higher rpms and lower torque efficiency for the drive load. In the situation where too large a converter or one that has a low stall speed is used, the engine would lug and starve the torque output to meet the vehicle loads. Both converter extremes result in undesirable overspeed or underspeed conditions that downgrade engine performance and efficiency. It should be apparent to the field technician that the engineered converter-to-engine match should not be altered. A mismatch is almost guaranteed to cause a drive ability complaint and worse yet, turn on the "check engine" light.

## NEW WORDS

| | | |
|---|---|---|
| hydraulic | [hai'drɔːlik] | adj. 水力的,液力的 |
| fluid | ['fluːid] | adj. 流动的,流体的,液体的 |
| twist | [twist] | vt. 捻搓拈,使扭转,拧扭转 |
| disengage | ['disin'geidʒ] | vt. 解开,解脱,使脱离 |
| impeller | [im'pelə] | n. 推动者,推动器,叶轮,泵轮 |
| exterior | [eks'tiəriə] | adj.;n. 外表的,外面的;外观,外部 |
| bow | [bəu] | n.;v. 弓,弓形物;使弯成弓形,拉弓 |
| stubby | ['stʌbi] | adj. 粗短的,矮胖的 |
| hub | ['hʌb] | n. 轮毂,(兴趣、活动)中心 |
| notch | [nɔtʃ] | n.;v. (V 字型)槽口,凹口;在…上开槽 |
| interior | [in'tiəriə] | adj.;n. 内部的,内心的;内部,内地 |
| stator | ['steitə] | n. (发动机,汽轮机)定子,导轮 |
| ramp | [ræmp] | n. 斜面,斜度,坡道 |
| wedge | [wedʒ] | vt. 楔入,劈开,分裂,挤入 |
| turbulence | ['təːbjuləns] | n. 骚动,汹涌,湍流 |
| jam | [dʒæm] | vt. 把…楔进,塞进 |
| suppress | [sə'prəs] | vt.;n. 镇压,压制;抑制器,消除器 |
| vortex | ['vɔːteks] | n. 旋涡,旋风 |
| coupling | ['kʌpliŋ] | n. 联结,连接器,联轴节 |
| velocity | [vi'lɔsiti] | n. 速度,速率,周转率 |
| kinetic | [kai'netik] | adj. 动力的,运动的, |
| bucket | ['bʌkit] | n. 破旧的大汽车,水桶,吊桶 |
| corkscrew | ['kɔːkskruː] | n.;adj.;vi. 开塞钻;螺旋状的;使盘旋前进 |
| lockup | ['lɔkʌp] | n. 闭,锁住,锁 |
| planetary | ['plænitəri] | adj. 行星的,由于行星作用的 |
| slippage | ['slipidʒ] | n. 滑动,滑程,滑动量,动力传递,损耗 |

configuration [kənˌfigju'reiʃən] n. 构造,结构,形状,外形
optimum ['ɔptiməm] n. ;adj. 最适条件,最适的
dynamometer [ˌdainə'mɔmitə] n. 测力计,功率计
angularity [ˌæŋgju'læriti] n. 成角度,棱角,斜度
undersirable ['ʌndi'zaiərəbl] adj. ;n. 不合需要的,不受欢迎的;不良分子

## PHRASES AND EXPRESSIONS

torque converter 液力变矩器
overrunning clutch 超速离合器
planetary gearset 行星齿轮传动装置
torsional vibration 扭转摆动
fluid coupling 液力偶合器
three element converter 三元件转化器
converter's efficiency 转换效率
coupling point 偶合点
bounce back 反冲,反射

## NOTES TO THE TEXT

1. It then directs it through the transmission to give an infinite number of speeds suitable for the particular load and speeds of the vehicle.

液力变矩器就可以直接通过传动系产生适合不同载荷和车速的发动机转速值。

第一个 it 指液力变矩器,第二个 it 指扭矩;through the transmission 做状语;to give an…speeds 做目的状语。

2. The exterior of the torque converter shell is shaped like two bowls is standing on end, facing each other and welded or bolted together.

变矩器的外壳就象两张弓面对面而立,通过楔子或螺栓固定在一起。

facing 是现在分词修饰 torque converter shell 做状语。

3. An overrunning clutch keeps the stator assembly from rotating when driven in one direction and permits overrunning (rotation)

when turned in the opposite direction.

超速离合器保持导轮在沿一个方向驱动时静止,及允许在沿相反方向转动时的超速。

这里说明的是 overrunning clutch 的 stator 的单向传动性; when 引导时间状语从句;overrunning 现在分词短语做定语。

4. The torque converter must be engineered to balance its performance with the engine rpm and vehicle load.

液力变矩器的设计必须使它的特性与发动机转速和车辆载荷相平衡。

its 指 torque converter,这里说明的是液力变矩器与发动机转速和车辆载荷相匹配的性质;must be engineered 是含有情态动词的被动语态。

### 3.3.3 Planetary Gear Systems

The simple planetary gear set acts as a minitransmission. Under proper operating conditions it provides overdrive, reverse, forward reduction, neutral, and direct drive. The simple planetary gear set can also supply fast and slow speeds for each operating condition with the exception of neutral and direct drive.

A simple planetary gear set consists of three parts: a sun gear, a carrier with planetary pinions mounted to it, and an internally toothed ring gear or annulus. The sun gear is located in the center of the assembly (Figure 3-14). It is the smallest gear in the assembly and exerts the least leverage on the center of the axis. The sun gear can be either a spur or helical gear design. It meshes with the teeth of the Planetary pinion gears. Planetary pinion gears are small gears fitted into a framework called the planetary carrier. The planetary carrier can be made of cast iron, aluminum, or steel plate and is designed with a shaft for each of the planetary pinion gears (For simplicity, planetary pinion gears will be simply called planetary pinions).

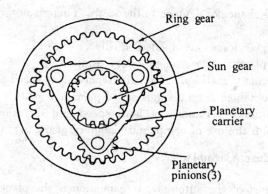

Figure 3-14 Planetary gear configuration is similar to the solar system, with the sun gear surrounded by the planetary pinion gears. The ring gear surrounds the complete gear set

Planetary pinions rotate on needle bearings positioned between the planetary carrier shaft and the planetary pinions. The number of planetary pinions in a carrier depends on the load the gear set is required to carry. Passenger vehicle automatics might have three planetary pinions in the planetary carrier. Heavy-duty highway trucks can have as many as five planetary pinions in a planetary carrier. The carrier and pinions are considered one unit the mid-size gear member.

The planetary pinions surround the sun gear's center axis and they themselves are surrounded by the annulus or ring gear, which is the largest part of the simple gear set. The ring gears act like a band to hold the entire gear set together and provide great strength to the unit. The ring gear is located the greatest distance from the center of the axis and therefore exerts the most leverage on the center of the axis. To help remember the design of a simple planetary gear set, use the solar system as an example. The sun is the center of the solar system with the planets rotating around it. Hence the name planetary gear set.

Some advantages of the simple planetary gear set include:
1. Constantly meshed gears. With the gears constantly in mesh

there is little chance of damage to the teeth. There is no grinding or missed shifts.

2. The gear forces are divided equally.

3. The planetary gear sets are very compact.

4. Extreme versatility. Seven combinations of speed and direction can be obtained from a single set of planetary gears.

5. Additional variations of both speed and direction can be added through the use of compound planetary gears.

**Planetary Gear Assembly**

The heart of the automatic transmission is the planetary gear system. It is therefore essential to review the basic construction of a simple planetary gearset as an introduction to how planetary gears operate. A simple planetary gearset (Figs. 3-15 and 3-16) consists

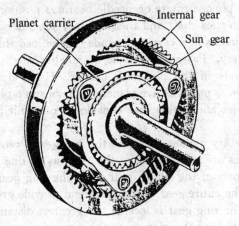

Figure 3-15 Simple planetary gear assembly

of a sun gear or center gear that is surrounded and in constant mesh with the planet or pinion gears. The pinion gears are mounted and free to rotate on their support shafts, which are pinned to a planet carrier. The internal gear, also referred to as the ring or annulus gear, is in constant mesh with the planetary pinions and surrounds the entire assembly. It should be noted that the sun gear, planet carrier, and internal gear rotate on a common center, while the planet pinion gears rotate on their own independent centers. For clarification, the planet pinion gears are considered to be part of the planet carrier.

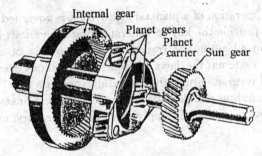

Figure 3-16    Planetary gear assembly-exploded view

The planetary gearset gets its name from the action of the planet pinion gears. As can be observed in later discussion, they have the ability to turn on their own centers and at the same time revolve around the sun gear. This is similar to the earth turning on its axis and rotating around the sun.

**Advantages**

1. All members of the planetary gearset share a common axis, which results in a structure of compact size.
2. Planetary gears are always in full and constant mesh, eliminating the possibility of gear tooth damage from gear clash or partial engagement. The full and constant mesh feature also permits automatic and quick gear ratio changes without power flow interruption.
3. Planetary gears are strong and sturdy and can handle larger torque loads for their compact size, compared to other gear combinations in manual transmissions. This is because the torque load as it passes through the planetary set is distributed over the several plan-

et pinion gears, which in effect allows more tooth contact area to handle the power transmission.

4. The location of the planetary members makes it relatively easy to hold the members or lock them together for ratio changes.

## Laws of Planetary Gear Operation

The operation of a planetary gear train is governed by five basic laws that provide the key to understanding the various gearing power flows in all automatic transmissions, regardless of differences in planetary systems: the laws of neutral, reduction, overdrive, direct drive, and reverse. Study them carefully, one at a time. As an assist in understanding the powerflow in each of the planetary operating modes, several rules will apply governing planetary member rotation.

1. When the internal gear and carrier pinions are free to rotate at the same time, the pinions will always follow the same direction as the internal gear.

2. The sun gear always rotates opposite carrier pinion gear rotation.

3. When the planet carrier is the output, it always follows the direction of the input gear.

4. When the planet carrier is the input, the output gear member always follows carrier direction.

## Simpson Planetary System

The Torque Flite transmission combines a three-element torque converter with a fully automatic controlled Simpson planetary system widely used in many three-speed transmission applications worldwide. Chrysler has used this gear train in the Torque Flite family from 1960 to current models in their RWD and FWD applications.

The transmission power train consists of the follwoing:
1. A three-element fluid torque converter

2. Two multiple-disc driving clutches, referred to as the front and rear clutches

3. Two holding bands with hydraulic servos, referred to as the kickdown(front)and low and reverse (rear)bands

4. A holding one-way roller clutch for breakaway first gear

5. A compound planetary system made up of two single planetary sets, front and rear in series, integrated by a common sun gear shaft and output shaft.

The Simpson system is used for most three-speed automatic transmissions (Figure 3-17). For a fourth-gear overdrive, look for a single overdrive planetary incorporated into either the input or output side of the three-speed planetary.

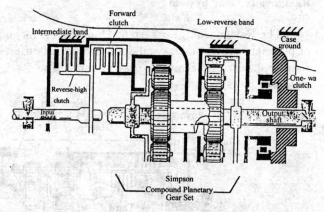

Figure 3-17 Typical Simpson planetary system

For planetary control it features forward and direct driving clutches complemented by two holding bands and a holding one-way clutch. The two planetaries share a sun gear and output shaft. The sharing or integration of common planetary elements gives an additional classification of the arrangement, referred to as a compound planetary. Another identifying mark of the unit is the drive shell or bell-shaped housing that couples the sun gear to the direct clutch drum.

The Simpson design in its basic configuration will produce the following power flows:
1. Neutral
2. Reduction (first and second gears)
3. Direct drive
4. Reverse

Simpson geartrains remain the standard in heavy-duty units and many passenger car automatics. The Simpson geartrain combines two simple planetary gear sets so that load can be spread over a greater number of teeth for strength and also to obtain the largest number of gear ratios possible in a compact area.

**Ravigneaux Gear System**

The Ravigneaux gear system (Figure 3-18) is another example of planetary compounding and does have major differences in design compared with the Simpson gear system. The Ravigneaux design includes:

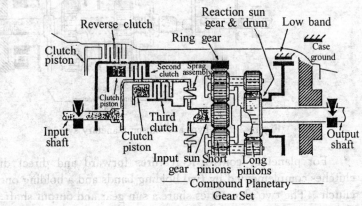

Figure 3-18    Ravigneaux planetary set

1. One carrier with three sets of dual pinions. Each dual pinion

set is made up of one short and one long pinion

2. Two independent sun gears that mesh with the carrier dual pinions

3. One holding band

4. A driving one-way sprag clutch

5. A Ravigneaux planetary design with the planet carrier as the output member (see the simplified Ravigneaux schematic arrangement).

The planetary operation provides neutral, three forward gear ratios, and reverse. The manual range selector has six positions (P-R-N-D-2-1), with the operating characteristics typical of General Motors three-speed automatic transmissions with the exception of manual low (1). Should manual low be selected with the vehicle on the move, the transmission will shift to first gear immediately. It is important, therefore, to avoid engaging manual low at vehicle speeds that exceed the manufacturer's recommendation.

### Planetary Gear Operation

Each member of a planetary gear set-the sun gear, pinion gear carrier, and ring gear—can spin (revolve) or be held at rest. Power transmission through a planetary gear set is only possible when one of the members is held at rest, or if two of the members are locked together.

Any one of the three member—sun gear, pinion gear carrier, or ring gear—can be used as the driving or input member. At the same time, another member might be kept from rotating and thus becomes the held or stationary member. The third member then becomes the driven or output member. Depending on which member is the driver, which is held, and which is driven, either a torque increase or a speed increase is produced by the planetary gear set. Output direction can also be reversed through various combinations.

**Maximum Forward Reduction** With the ring gear stationary and the sun gear turning clock wise, the external sun gar will rotate the planetary pinions counterclockwise on their shafts (Figure

3-19). The inside diameter of each planetary pinion pushes against its shaft, moving the planetary carrier clockwise. The small sun gear (driving) will rotate several times, driving the middle size planetary carrier one complete revolution, resulting in an underdrive. This combination represents the most gear reduction or the maximum torque multiplication that can be achieved in one planetary gear set. Input speed will be high, but output speed will be low.

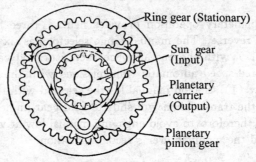

Figure 3-19  Maximum forward reduction (greatest torque, lowest speed) is produced with the sun gear as input, ring gear stationary, and carrier as the output

**Minimum Forward Reduction**  In this combination the sun gear is stationary and the ring gear rotates clockwise. The ring gear drives the planetary pinions clockwise and walks around the stationary sun gear. The planetary pinions drive the planetary carrier in the same direction as the ring gear-forward. This results in more than one turn of the input as compared to one complete revolution of the output. The result is torque multiplication. But since a large gear is driving a small gear, the amount of reduction is not as great as in combination. The planetary gear set is operating in a forward reduction with the large ring gear driving the small planetary carrier. Therefore, the combination produces minimum forward reduction.

**Maximum Overdrive**  With the ring gear stationary and the planetary carrier rotating clockwise (Figure 3-20). The three planetary pinion shafts push against the inside diameter of the planetary pinions. The pinions are forced to walk around the inside of the ring gear, driving the sun gear clockwise. The carrier is rotating less than one turn input compared to one turn output, resulting in an overdrive condition. In this combination, the middle size planetary

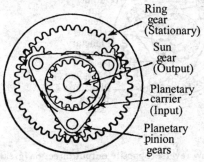

Figure 3-20   Maximum overdrive (lowest torque, greatest speed) is produced with the carrier as input, ring gear stationary, and sun gear as output

carrier is rotating less than one turn and driving the smaller sun gear at a speed greater than the input speed. The result is a fast overdrive with maximum speed increase.

**Slow Overdrive**   In this combination, the sun gear is stationary and the carrier rotates clockwise. As the carrier rotates the pinion shafts push against the inside diameter of the pinions and they are forced to walk around the held sun gear. This drives the ring gear faster and the speed increases. The carrier turning less than one turn causes the pinions to drive the ring gear one complete revolution in the same direction as the planetary carrier. As in combination, an overdrive condition exists, but the middle size carrier is now driving the larger size ring gear so only slow overdrive occurs.

**Slow Reverse**   Here the sun gear is driving the ring gear with the planetary carrier held stationary (Figure 3-21). The planetary pinions, driven by the external sun gear, rotate counterclockwise on their shafts. The external planetary pinions drive the internal ring gear in the same direction. While the sun gear is driving, the planetary pinions are used as idler gears to drive the ring gear counterclockwise. This means the input and output shafts are operating in

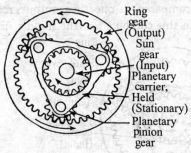

Figure 3-21  Slow reverse (opposite output direction, greatest torque, lowest speed) is produced with the sun gear as input, planetary carrier stationary, and the ring gear as output

the opposite or reverse direction to provide a reverse power flow. Since the driving sun gear is small and the driven ring gear is large, the result is slow reverse.

**Fast Reverse**  For fast reverse, the carrier is still held as in slow reverse, but the sun gear and ring gear reverse roles, with the ring gear now being the driving member and the sun gear driven. As the ring gear rotates counterclockwise, the pinions rotate counterclockwise as well, while the sun gear turns clockwise. In this combination, the input ring gear uses the planetary pinions to drive the output sun gear. The sun gear rotates in reverse to the input ring gear. In this operational combination, the large ring gear rotating counterclockwise drives the small sun gear clockwise, providing fast reverse.

**Direct Drive**  In the direct drive combination, both the ring gear and the sun gear are input members (Figure 3-22). They turn clockwise at the same speed. The internal teeth of the clockwise turning ring gear will try to rotate the planetary pinions clockwise as well. But the sun gear, an external gear rotating clockwise, will try to drive the planetary pinions counterclockwise. These opposing forces lock the planetary pinions against rotation so that the entire

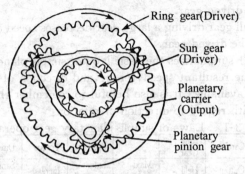

Figure 3-22  Direct drive is produced if any two gear set members are locked together

planetary gear set rotates as one complete unit. This ties together the input and output members and provides a direct drive. For direct drive, both input members must rotate at the same speed.

**Neutral Operation**  Combinations 1 through 7 all produce an output drive of various speeds, torques, and direction. In each case, one member of the planetary gear set is held or two members are locked for the output to take place. When no member is held stationary or locked, there will be input into the gear set, but no output. The result is a neutral condition.

The following are helpful tips in remembering the basics of simple planetary gear set operation.

1. When the planetary carrier is the drive (input) member, the gear set produces an overdrive condition. Speed increases, torque decreases.

2. When the planetary carrier is the driven (output) member, the gear set produces a forward reduction. Speed decreases, torque increases.

3. When the planetary carrier is held, the gear set will produce a reverse.

To determine if the speed produced is fast or slow, remember the rules regarding large and small gears.

1. A large gear driving a small gear increases speed and reduces torque of the driven gear.

2. A small gear driving a large gear decreases speed and increases torque of the driven gear.

Table 3-1 summarizes the basic laws of simple planetary gears. It indicates the resultant speed, torque, and direction of the various combinations available. It is also helpful to remember the following two points with regard to direction of rotation:

Table 3-1　Laws of simple planetary gear operation

| Sun Gear | Carrier | Ring Gear | | Speed | Torque | Direction |
|---|---|---|---|---|---|---|
| 1. Input | Output | Held | Maximum | reduction | Increase | Same as input |
| 2. Held | Output | Input | Minimum | reduction | Increase | Same as input |
| 3. Output | Input | Held | Maximum | increase | Reduction | Same as input |
| 4. Held | Input | Output | Minimum | increase | Reduction | Same as input |
| 5. Input | Held | Output | Reduction | | Increase | Reverse of input |
| 6. Output | Held | Input | Increase | | Reduction | Reverse of input |
| 7. When any two members are held together, speed and direction are the same as input. Direct 1:1 drive occurs. | | | | | | |
| 8. When no member is held or locked together, output cannot occur. The result is a neutral condition. | | | | | | |

## NEW WORDS

| | | |
|---|---|---|
| reverse | [ri'və:s] | vt. ;n. 使倒转;使回动;回动装置 |
| neutral | ['nju:trəl] | adj. ;n. 中立的;空档,中立者 |
| helical | ['helikəl] | adj. 螺旋形的,螺旋线的 |
| mesh | [meʃ] | vi. 紧密配合,相啮合 |
| axis | ['æksis] | n. 轴,轴线,中心线 |
| annulus | ['ænjuləs] | n. 环状物,气室环,横沟 |

| | | |
|---|---|---|
| grind | [graind] | vt.;vi.磨(碎),磨光,磨,碾 |
| revolve | [ri'vɔlv] | vt.;vi.使旋转,细想;旋转 |
| versatility | [ˌvə:sə'tiliti] | n.(才能,用途等的)多面性 |
| clarification | [ˌklæri'keiʃən] | n.澄清,阐明 |
| sturdy | ['stə:di] | adj.强健的,坚固的,稳定的,茁壮的 |
| servo | ['sə:vəu] | n.伺服,伺服机构 |
| spin | [spin] | vt.;n.旋转;自旋 |
| interruption | [ˌintə'rʌpʃən] | n.中断,打断,障碍物 |
| identify | [ai'dentifai] | vt.;vi.使等同于,让出,识别;一致,和…打成一片 |
| clockwise | [klɔk'wais] | adj.;adv.顺时针方向的(地) |

## PHRASES AND EXPRESSIONS

| | |
|---|---|
| planetary gear | 行星机构 |
| in sequence | 按次序 |
| planetary pinions | 行星轮 |
| ring gear | 环形齿轮 |
| Simpson planetary system | 辛普森行星机构 |
| reverse clutch | 倒档离合器 |
| external gear | 外齿轮 |
| with regard to | 关于 |
| direct drive | 直接档 |
| neutral operation | 空档位置 |
| regardless of | 不顾,不管 |
| multiple-disc clutch | 增力盘离合器 |

## NOTES TO THE TEXT

1. The simple planetary gear set acts as a minitransmission. Under proper operating conditions it provides overdrive, reverse, forward reduction, neutral and direct drive.

简单的行星齿轮装置象小变速器一样工作。在适当的工作条件下提供超速、倒行驶、前减速、空转和直接驱动。

这是两个独立的分句;第一个分句的主语是 set,第二个句子的主语是 it；act as 象…一样工作，as 引导方式状语。

2. A simple planetary gear set consists of three parts：a sun gear, a carrier with planetary pinions mounted to it, and an internally toothed ring gear or annulus.

简单的行星齿轮装置由三部分构成：太阳轮、带行星齿轮的行星架、内齿圈。

a sun gear…ring gear or annulus 是 three parts 的同位语，同作 consists of 的宾语；mounted to it 过去分词短语做定语。

3. The Torque Flite transmission combines a three-element torque converter with a fully automatic controlled Simpson planetary system widely used in many three-speed transmission applications worldwide.

扭矩转换变速器由带有全自动控制的辛普森行星系统的三元件液力变扭器组成，被广泛地用于世界上许多三档变速器上。

Simpson：人名，发明了辛普森行星系统；controlled … 过去分词短语做定语。

4. Power transmission through a planetary gear set is only possible when one of the members is held at rest, or if two of the members are locked together.

当三元件中的一个固定，或其中的两个连在一起，通过行星齿轮机构只有一种可能的动力转变。

two of the members are locked together 三元件中的两个元件联接在一起传动(此时为直接档，传动比为 1)；when 引导时间状语从句；If 引导条件状语从句。

## EXERCISES

Ⅰ. Answer the following questions according to the text.

1. What is a planetary gearset? Name the parts in a planetary gearset?

2. What is a fluid coupling? How does a fluid coupling work?

3. What is the principal difference between a fluid coupling and a torque converter?

4. Of what value is the split ring in the fluid coupling and torque converter?

5. What is a stator? How does a stator work?

6. The stator can revolve in one direction only. What stops its rotation in one direction?

7. Why are torque converter vanes curved?

8. What is a servo and what does it do?

9. What value is there in the use of an accumulator piston?

10. What lubricates an automatic transmission?

Ⅱ. Choose the best answer for each of the following questions:

1. Which of the major torque converter parts is the driving member, receiving power from the engine crankshaft?
 A. pump /impeller     B. stator
 C. turbine        D. lockup clutch

2. Which torque converter component is splined to a shaft that connects to the forward clutch of the transmission?
 A. stator         B. turbine
 C. pump/impeller     D. flex plate(disc)

3. What is used to transfer energy through the torque converter components?
 A. engine oil       B. transmission fluid(oil)
 C. distilled water     D. brake fluid

4. Which type of fluid flow must occur for torque multiplication to take place?
 A. rotary         B. vortex
 C. primary        D. secondary

5. Which is the largest member of a simple planetary gear set?
 A. sun gear       B. carrier
 C. ring gear       D. pinions

6. Which of the following components are added to a manual gearbox to produce automatic shifting?
 A. a torque converter
 B. a shift sled and autoshift finger
 C. a power synchronizer
 D. all of the above

7. Which type of hydraulic retarder is located between the torque converter and the transmission gearing?

A. input retarder      B. output retarder
C. torque retarder     D. none of the above

8. Which type of hydraulic retarder applies a friction clutch while the unit is charging with hydraulic fluid?

A. input retarder      B. torque retarder
C. output retarder     D. all of the above

Ⅲ. Choose the one word or phrases that best complete the sentence:

1. A ____ is used to mount the torque converter to the crankshaft.

A. lockup clutch      B. stator
C. flex plate (disc)    D. turbine

2. The stator is located ____ .

A. between the flex plate and pump/impeller housing
B. between the pump/impeller and turbine
C. between the turbine and the first clutch of the transmission
D. on the crankshaft

3. In a torque converter, ____ fluid flow is the flow or fluid from the pump/impeller to the turbine and back to the pump by way of the stator.

A. rotary        B. vortex
C. primary      D. secondary

4. The vanes of the torque converter are fitted with ____ to reduce fluid turbulence that can interfere with the power transfer through the unit.

A. splash guards      B. overruning clutch
C. Split guide ring    D. variable pitch stator

5. In order for torque multiplication to take place, the ____ .

A. pump/impeller must turn faster than the turbine
B. turbine must turn faster than the pump/impeller
C. stator must freewheel
D. lockup clutch must be engaged

6. When any two members of a simple planetary gear set are locked together or held stationary, ____ .

A. there is a reverse in rotation direction at the output member
B. direct 1:1 drive occurs

C. an overdrive situation results

D. an underdrive situation results

7. In a closs ratio transmissions all power flows must pass through the ____ before reaching the output shaft.

A. front planetary gear set

B. rear planetary gear set

C. low planetary gear set

D. center sun gear shaft

8. The ____ assists governor pressure in moving any shift signal shafts during an upshift.

A. priority valve          B. modulator valve
C. trimmer valve           D. inhibitor valve

Ⅳ. Translate the following sentences into Chinese:

1. The automatic transmission eliminates the clutch pedal and, instead of a solid type conventional clutch, it utilizes a fluid coupling between the engine and transmission.

2. It is important to remember that the only difference between the five-speed transmissions and the four-speed units is that an additional low clutch and low planetary gear set are added to the back of the transmission behind the existing front, center, and rear gear sets.

3. The Simpson geartrain combines two simple planetary gear sets so that load can be spread over a greater number of teeth for strength and also to obtain the largest number of gear ratios possible in a compact area.

4. Typically, for an automatic transmission application the powertrain system includes a flex or drive plate, fluid torque converter, transmission, U-joints and driveshaft, final drive/differential, and the drive axles and wheels.

5. To provide the automatic gear ratio changes, fluid energy from a hydraulic pump is routed through a valve control system to apply the band and clutch combinations that work the planetary gear set.

6. Transmission oil is the power transmitting medium in the torque converter. It's velocity drives the converter turbine and its

flow cools and lubricates the transmission. its pressure operates the various control valves and applies the clutches.

V. Translate the following passage into Chinese:

In modern passenger cars, the torque converter has gradually taken over as the prime fluid drive unit. The fluid coupling has not been used in American automatic transmissions since 1965. When using the term torque converter in connection with automatic transmissions, it is understood that it has a dual function. It must act as a torque multiplier with infinitely variable ratios from its maximum engineered torque output to unity (1:1), where it acts as a fluid coupling.

The converter offers several desirable operating features. It is a simple, rugged unit that operates as a clutch in a constant oil bath that gives unlimited life and requires no maintenance, in contrast to the foot-operated friction clutch that it elminated. Because it is a fluid unit, it provides a silky-smooth attachment of the engine power to the vehicle that eliminates any sudden engagement shock to the powertrain components and results in their longer life and reduced repair costs. Another dividend is the excellent dampening of engine torsional vibration that is taken up by the fluid before it extends into the transmission and driveline. The converter can be likened to a cushion that protects the powertrain from shocks and vibrations and prevents lugging or stalling of the engine.

Although a variety of fluid torque converter designs have been used in automatic transmissions, the simple three-element unit (impeller, turbine, and stator) is currently used. The discussion of converter operation concentrates on this unit.

## 3.4 Drive Axles

### 3.4.1 Axles

There are basically three types of axies: driving axle, steering axle, and trailer axle. By far the most complex is the driving axle. Not only are driving axles available in various configurations but they contain complex gearing components that are not installed in the other two types. A typical driving axle contains the axle shafts and a differential carrier assembly. The differential contains the gearing to vary the wheel speed when turning corners as well as to transfer power to the gripping wheel when the truck is operated in mud or on uneven road conditions. Driving axles are usually employed as rear axle assemblies on heavy-duty trucks because of the differential and are often referred to as rear live (driving) axles.

Steering and trailer axles are similar to the driving axle but do not feature the differential carrier assembly. They are mainly used to carry and support the weight of the vehicle placed on them and provide a mounting surface for their respective suspension systems.

In the early days of motoring, the driving, or powered, wheels of a vehicle were rigidly fixed to the ends of a continuous, one-piece axle shaft. Therefore, as the axle was turned by engine power, the wheels at each end of the axle turned together and at the same speed.

This was an effective way to move the vehicle. But wheels tended to scrub or scuff on the road surface whenever the vehicle traveled in any direction but straight or when the powered wheels were of mismatched diameters.

That was tolerable as long as speeds were slow, loads were light and distances traveled were short. But as technology improved, vehicle speeds, cargo loads, and journey lengths increased. Scrubbing of tires become more and more expensive and inefficient.

Engineers searched diligently for ways to allow each driving wheel to operate at its own speed. Many ideas were tried with mixed results before the basic design for the present-day, standard differential was finally developed. The successful idea that is still used in principle today was to divide the engine power by dividing the axle in two-attaching each driving wheel separately to its own half-axle and placing in between, an ingenious, free-rotating pinion and gear arrangement. The arrangement was called the differential because it differentiates between the actual speed needs of each wheel and splits the power from the engine into equal driving force to each wheel.

On/off road vehicles and other trucks required to haul heavy loads are sometimes equipped with double reduction axles. A double reduction axle uses two gear sets for greater overall gear reduction and peak torque development. This design is favored for severe-service applications, such as dump trucks, cement mixers, and other heavy haulers.

The double reduction axle uses a heavy-duty spiral bevel or hypoid pinion and ring gear combination for the first reduction. The second reduction is accomplished with a wide-faced helical spur pinion and gear set. The drive pinion and ring gear function just as in a single reduction axle. However, the differential case is not bolted to the ring gear. Instead, the spur pinion is keyed to and driven by the ring gear. The spur pinion is in turn constantly meshed with the helical spur gear to which the differential case is bolted.

Many heavy duty trucks are equipped with two rear drive axles. These tandem axle trucks require a special gear arrangement to deliver power to both the forward and rearward rear driving axles. This gearing must also be capable of allowing for speed differences between the axles.

Two axle hub arrangements are available to provide support between the axle hub and the truck's wheels: the semi-floating type axle and the fully floating type axle. Of the two, the semi-floating is the simplest, cheapest design to incorporate, but the fully floating axle is more popular in heavy-duty trucks.

In the semi-floating type axle, drive power from the differential is taken by each axle half-shaft and transferred directly to the wheels. A single bearing assembly, located at the outer end of the axle, is used to support the axle half-shaft. The part of the axle extending beyond the bearing assembly is either splined or tapered to a wheel hub and brake drum assembly. The main disadvantage of this type of axle is that the outer end of each axle shaft must carry and support the weight of the truck that is placed on the wheels. If an axle half-shaft should break, the truck's wheel will fall off.

## Differential

Drive axle operation is controlled by the differential carrier assembly. A differential carrier assembly consists of a number of major components. These include:
1. Input shaft and pinion gear
2. Ring gear
3. Differential with two differential case halves, a differential spider (or cross), four pinion gears, and two side gears with washers.

Figure 3-23 shows an exploded view of the differential. This

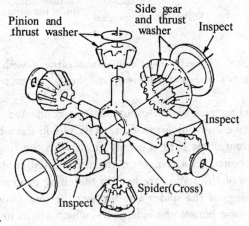

Figure 3-23  Components of a typical differential

differential assembly fits between the axle shafts, with the shafts being splined to the differential side gears. Figure 3-24 shows an exploded view of the complete carrier assembly. The parts of the differential carrier are held in position by a number of bearings and thrust washers.

· 247 ·

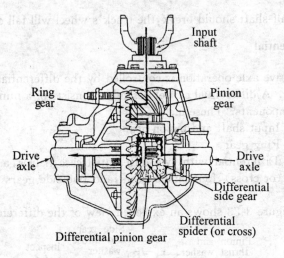

Figure 3-24  Cutaway view of a differential carrier assembly showing the major components and the path of power flow through the unit

The leading end of the input shaft is connected to the drive shaft by a yoke and universal joint. The pinion gear on the other end of the input shaft is in constant mesh with the ring gear. The ring gear is bolted to a flange on the differential case. Insied the case, the legs of the spider are held in matching grooves in the case halves. The legs of the spider also support the four pinion gears. In addition, the case houses the side gears, which are in mesh with the pinions and are splined to the axle shafts.

When the drive shaft torque is applied to the input shaft and drive pinion, the input shaft and pinion rotate in a direction that is perpendicular to the truck's drive axles. The drive pinion is beveled at 45 degrees and engages the ring gear, which is also beveled at 45 degrees, causing the ring gear to revolve at 90 degrees to the drive shaft. This means the torque flow changes direction and becomes parallel to the axles and wheels.

As the ring gear revolves, the differential case revolves with it since the ring gear and case are bolted together. The spider or cross mounted in the grooves in the casing halves must also rotate with the case and the ring gear.

The differential pinions mounted on the legs of the spider revolve around the center axis of the spider as the differential case rotates.

These four pinions act as bridges between the side gears. They drag the side gears along as they turn. As the side gears rotate, they transfer torque to the drive axles, which in turn transfer it to the wheels. As long as the truck is moving in a straight line, the ring gear, differential gears, and drive axles turn together without variation of speed.

## NEW WORDS

| | | |
|---|---|---|
| available | [ə'veiləbl] | adj. 可用的,通用的,有效的 |
| configuration | [kənˌfigju'reiʃən] | n. 外形形状,轮廓 |
| install | [in'stɔːl] | vt. 安装,安置,设置 |
| gripe | [graip] | v. ;n. 握紧,紧握;柄把手 |
| uneven | [ʌn'iːvən] | adj. 不规则的,不平坦的,不稳定的 |
| trailer | [treilə] | n. 拖车,挂车,拖曳物 |
| rigid | ['ridʒid] | adj. 坚硬的,刚硬的,不易弯的 |
| scuff | [skʌf] | v. (探测时)用脚去戳,磨损 |
| scrab | [skrʌb] | vt. ;n. 擦洗,擦掉,磨擦;矮树,灌木 |
| ingenious | [in'dʒiːnjəs] | adj. 灵巧的,巧妙的,精巧制成的 |
| haul | ['hɔːl] | vt. 拖曳,用力拖,拖运 |
| tandem | ['tændəm] | n. ;adj. 载重拖车;前后直排(的),串联(的) |
| incorporate | [in'kɔːpəreit] | vt. 结合,合并,使具体化 |
| spider | ['spaidə] | n. 星形轮,十字叉,三脚架 |
| groove | [gruːv] | n. 槽,排屑槽,螺槽 |
| perpendicular | [ˌpəːpan'dikjulə] | adj. 垂直的,正交的 |
| bevel | [bevəl] | vt. 使成斜角,斜切 |

| | | | |
|---|---|---|---|
| parallel | ['pærəlel] | adj. ;n. | 平行的,并行的;平行线,并联,垫片 |
| bolt | [bəut] | n. | 螺栓 |

## PHPASES AND EXPRESSIONS

cutaway view　　　　　　　剖视图
by far　　　　　　　　　　非常,最…
two axle hub arrangements　两轴衬套装置
semi-floating type axle　　　半浮动轴
thrust washer　　　　　　　止推环
input shaft　　　　　　　　输入轴

## NOTES TO THE TEXT

1. There are basically three types of axles:driving axle,steering axle,and trailer axle. By far the most complex is the driving axle.
轴分为三种形式:驱动轴、转向轴、拖动轴,其中最复杂的轴是驱动轴。
　　by far …非常,更加…得多,后接形容词最高级,后面的句子倒装;the driving axle 是主语;by far…complex 是表语。

2. The differential contains the gearing to vary the wheel speed when turning corners as well as to transfer power to the gripping wheel when the truck is operated in mud or on uneven road conditions.
差速器包括转弯时改变车轮速度的传动装置,该装置在车辆运行于泥泞地不平滑路面时,会将功率传给附着轮。
　　as well as 又,也;to vary… 是动词不定式短语做后置定语,修饰 gearing。

3. As the ring gear revolves,the differential case revolves with it since the ring gear and case are bolted together.
因为齿圈与差速器壳体用螺栓固定在一起,所以当齿圈转动时,差速器壳体也会随之而转动。
　　As 引导的从句做时间状语;since 引导原因状语从句。

## 3.4.2 Drive Shafts

Drive shafts — or propeller shafts, as they are sometimes called—have one basic function: transferring power or torque from one drive line component to another in a smooth, continuous fashion. In a heavy-duty truck, that means transmitting engine torque from the output shaft of the transmission to a rear axle or to an auxiliary transmission. Drive shafts are also used to connect forward and rear axles on $4 \times 6$ tractors.

In most cases, a drive shaft must transfer torque at an angle to the centerlines of the drive line components it is fastened to. Because the rear axle is not connected to the rigid rails of the truck frame but is mounted to the rear suspension system, the drive shaft must also be able to change angles as the rear suspension jounces and rebounds.

The drive shaft must also be able to change in length while transmitting torque. As the rear axle reacts to road surface changes, torque reactions and braking forces, it tends to rotate forward or backward, requiring a corresponding change in the length of the drive shaft.

The drive shaft is able to contract, expand, and change operating angles while transmitting torque through the use of universal joints and slip joints. Figure 3-25 shows the various components of

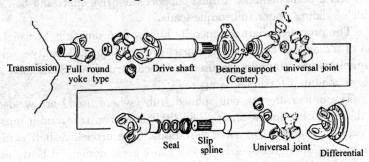

Figure 3-25  Exploded view of a heavy-duty drive shaft

· 251 ·

a typical heavy duty truck drive shaft.

In order to transmit engine torque to the rear axles, the drive shaft must be durable and strong. An engine producing 1 000 pound—feet of torque, when multiplied by a 12 to 1 gear ration in the transmission, will deliver 12 000 pound-feet breakaway torque to the drive shaft. The shaft must be strong enough to deliver this twisting force to a loaded axle without deforming or cracking under the strain.

Drive shafts are constructed of high-strength steel tubing to provide maximum strength with minimum weight. The diameter of the shaft and wall thickness of the tubing is determined by several factors: maximum torque and vehicle payload, type of operation, road conditions. and the brake torque that might be encountered. One-piece, two-piece, and three-piece drive shafts are used, depending on the length of the drive line.

Each end of the drive shaft has a yoke used to connect the shaft to other drive line components. The yoke might be rigidly welded to the shaft tube or it might be a spline, or slip yoke. The tube yokes are connected through universal joints to end yokes on the output and input shafts of the transmission and axle.

A typical slip joint consists of a hardened, ground splined shaft welded to the drive shaft tube that is inserted into a slip yoke that has matching internal splines. The sliding splines between a slib joint and a permanent joint must support the drive shaft and be capable of sliding under full torque loads.

The propeller shaft is generally hollow to promote light weight and of a diameter sufficient to impart great strength. Quality steel, aluminum, and graphite are used in its construction. Some have a rubber mounted torsional damper.

The universal yoke and splined stub (where used) are welded to the ends of a hollow shaft. The shaft must run true, and it must be carefully balanced to avoid vibrations. The propeller shaft is often turning at engine speeds. It can cause great damage if bent, unbalanced or if there is wear in the universal joints.

As the rear axle moves up and down, it swings on an arc that is different from that of the drive line. As a result, the distance between transmission and rear axle will change to some extent.

When the propeller shaft turns the differential, the axles and wheels are driven forward. The driving force developed between the tires and the road is first transferred to the rear axle housing. From the axle housing, it is transmitted to the frame or body in one of three ways:

1. Through leaf springs that are bolted to the housing and shackled to the frame.

2. Through control or torque arms shackled (bolted, but free to swivel) to both frame and axle housing.

3. Through a torque tube that surrounds the propeller shaft, which is bolted to the axle housing and pivoted to the transmission by means of a large ball socket (sometimes referred to as a torque ball).

**Universal Joint**

It is clear that a solid drive line would be bent and finally broken as the angle of drive changes. To allow the drive line, or propeller shaft, to move without breaking, a flexible joint is used. This is called a universal joint.

By using a universal joint, torque can be transmitted constantly even though the rear axle is moving up and down.

Another type of universal, called the ball and trunnion, is sometimes used. This universal, in addition to allowing the drive line to bend, also allows fore and aft (forward and backward) movement of the propeller shaft.

A ball and trunnion joint is illustrated in Figure 3-26. The cross pin is inserted in the hole in the ball on the end of the propeller shaft. The ball and roller assembly mounts on the ends of the cross pins. The round ball slides back and forth in a round hole in the center of the joint body. The rollers also slide and tip in grooves in the outer body.

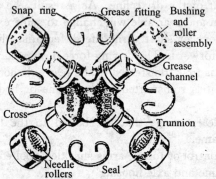

Figure 3-26  Universal joint cross with bushing and roller assemblies

The cross and roller, sometimes called cardan, is in common use. It consists of a center cross, often referred to as a spider, and two yokes, frequently called kuncles. The yokes surround a needle roller.

## NEW WORDS

| | | |
|---|---|---|
| propeller | [prə'pelə] | n. 螺旋桨,推进器,推进者 |
| auxiliary | [ɔːg'ziljəri] | adj. 辅助的,补助的,附属的,从属的 |
| rebound | [ri'baund] | vi. ;n. 回跳,回弹;返回,跃起 |
| twist | [twist] | u. 拧,扭,绞,盘旋,旋转,螺旋运动 |
| deform | [di'fɔːm] | v. 使变形,损坏…的形状 |
| yoke | [jəuk] | n. 架,横档,夹板,圈座,偏转线圈 |
| graphite | ['græfait] | n. 石墨 |
| damper | ['dæmpə] | n. 阻尼器,减震器,阻尼线圈,气闸 |
| stub | [stʌb] | n. 树桩,短柱,焊条头,短管,管接头 |
| swing | [swiŋ] | v. 摆动,悬挂,回转,旋转 |
| pivot | ['pivət] | n. 轴尖,仪表枢轴,支点,回转运动,中枢 |
| trunnion | ['trʌnjən] | n. 耳轴,枢轴,耳筒 |
| spider | ['spaidə] | n. 星形轮,星形接头,三脚架 |
| cardan | ['kaːdən] | n. 万向接头,万向节 |
| knuckle | ['nʌkl] | n. 指(关)节,肘节,铰链接合,万向接头 |

## PHRASES AND EXPRESSIONS

drive axles　　　　　驱动轴
torsional damper　　　扭力减振器
universal joint　　　　万向节
a flexible joint　　　　弹性连轴器
propeller shaft　　　　传动轴

## NOTES TO THE TEXT

1. Drive shaft—or propeller shaft, as they are sometimes called—have one basic function: transferring power or torque from one drive line component to another in a smooth, continuous fashion.

驱动轴或传动轴，有一个基本功用：将功率或扭矩由传动线上的一个零件传动另一个零件，既平顺又连续。

as they are…called 正如…所称，引导方式状语从句；in a smooth, continuous fashion 以光滑连续的方式，in 表示方式，是介词短语做状语。

2. As the rear axle reacts to road surface changes, torque reactions, and braking forces, it tends to rotate forward or backward, requiring a corresponding change in the length of the drive shaft.

当后轴随路面的改变，扭矩的改变，刹车力而产生相应变化时，会趋向于向前或向后旋转，因此就需要驱动轴的长度能相应改变。

As 引导的从句做时间状语；it 是主语，代表前 the rear axle；tends to 趋向于，做谓语。

3. Drive shafts are constructed of high-strength steel tubing to provide maximum strength with minimum weight.

驱动轴由高强度钢管制成，以最小的自重提供最大的强度。

to 引导的从句做目的状语；constructed 动词的过去分词形式做表语。

4. A typical slip joint consists of a hardened, ground splined shaft welded to the drive shaft tube that is inserted into a slip yoke that has matching internal splines.

典型的滑动连接包括一个焊在驱动轴上的光滑坚硬的花键

轴,它插进一个内有相配合的花键的滑动轭形物里。

welded 为过去分词做定语,修饰 shaft;that is 也就是,that 代替 welded to…tube;that has matching…splines 是 that 引导的定语从句,修饰 yoke。

# EXERCISES

Ⅰ. Answer the following questions according to the text:

1. Can you list seven functions of the rear axle assembly?

2. The rear axle assembly can be broken into three basic units of sections, Can you name?

3. What are the two types of housing? Which one is more often used?

4. Why is a differential necessary? Name the parts that make up the differential assembly.

5. Can you describe the action of the differential in straight line driving?

6. What is the name of the unit that connects the tran-smission output shaft to the differential pinion gear shaft?

7. What are two common types of drive?

8. Most propeller shafts are solid. true or false? Name two types of universal joints.

9. What advantage is there in making the propeller shaft in two pieces?

Ⅱ. Choose the best answer for each of the following questions:

1. Which of the following is a function of a rear drive axle?

A. provides gear reduction necessary to power the truck.

B. redirects the torque from the drive shaft to the drive wheels.

C. carries and supports the weight of the truck or load placed on it.

D. all of the above.

2. Which of the following type of axle is designed to allow a difference in the speed of the truck's wheels?

A. steering axle   B. drive axle

C. trailer axle    D. all of the above

3. Which of the following axle configurations do not allow for a second gear reduction to increase drive torque?
   A. single reduction axles    B. double reduction axles
   C. two-speed axles    D. dual range axles

4. Which of the following gear combinations allows for a speed differentiation between wheels on the opposite ends of an axle?
   A. drive pinion gear and ring gear
   B. differential gears and side gear
   C. idler pinions and sun gear
   D. all of the above

5. Which of the following actions permits the drive wheels on either end of an axle to turn at different speeds?
   A. rotation of the ring gear
   B. rotation of differential pinion gears
   C. rotation of the sun gears
   D. rotation of the differential case

6. Which of the following axles would be equipped with a pneumatic shifting device?
   A. two-speed differential
   B. tandem axle power divider
   C. no-spin locking differential
   D. all of the above

7. In which of the following differentials would you find friction plates alternately splined to a driver and tanged to the gear support case?
   A. controlled tracction differentials
   B. no-spin locking differentials
   C. two-speed tandex axles
   D. all of the above

8. Which of the following will not affect the drive shaft balance?
   A. missing balance weights    B. U-joint lubrication
   C. foreign material    D. dents

Ⅲ. Fill the blank in each sentence with one of the four words or phrases which correctly completes the sentence:

1. U-joint failures, center bearing failures, and vibrations are caused by ____.
   A. loose end yokes      B. bent shafts
   C. missing balance weights      D. all of the above

2. If, while lubricating a U-joint, fresh lubricant appears at the bearing seals, ____.
   A. the bearings are worn and should be replaced
   B. the seals are worn and should be replaced
   C. the trunnions are worn and the U-joint should be replaced
   D. the U-joint has been properly purged

3. A drive shaft is in phase when ____.
   A. the shaft is in line with the output shaft of the transmission
   B. the slip yoke and tube yoke lugs are aligned with each other
   C. when the shaft is balanced
   D. all of the above

4. The working angle on most heavy-duty truck applications should not exceed ____.
   A. 3 degrees      B. 5 degrees
   C. 8 degrees      D. 10 degrees

5. The drive shaft size rating is determined by ____.
   A. shaft length      B. working angle
   C. rpm      D. all of the above

6. Grooves worn into the trunnions by the bearings are called ____.
   A. brinelling      B. galling
   C. spalling      D. pitting

Ⅳ. Translate the following sentence into Chinese:

1. It is essentially a double-hinged joint through which the driving shaft can transmit power to the driven shaft, even though the two shafts are somewhat out of line with each other.

2. The engine crankshaft being arranged at right angles to the rear axle, it follows that at the back axle some form of gearing must be provided to transmit the power to each of the rear wheels, and at right angles to the propeller shaft.

3. In the case of the bevel gear, which consists merely of two

toothed cones meshing together, their axles meeting in a point, a smaller bevel gear attached to the rear end of the propeller shaft or its flexible coupling, meshes with a larger bevel wheel, known as the differential gear, driving the two rear wheels.

4. The friction of the wheels against the road, and the friction of the differential gears, make the pinion shafts resist turning so that the driving force causes the pinion shaft ramps to slide against the differential case ramps, pushing the pinion shafts apart slightly.

5. As the pinion shafts move outward, two of the pinions on one of pinion shafts bear against one of pinion thrust members, and two pinions on the other pinion shaft bear against the other thrust member.

V. Translate the following passage into Chinese:

Corrosive wear is attributed to the action of corrosive media (acids, alkalis, oxygen) on the part surface.

Fatigue wear is caused by multiple alternating loads. Most automobile parts are subject to several types of wear simultaneously.

The mating parts have definite clearances established during the design and manufacture of mechanisms and units. As the parts wear, the clearances increase, the parts reach the limit of size at which they continue to operate normally and then additional loads imposed by excessive wear disrupt normal functioning. The clearance grows progressively which may finally lead to breakage of the parts and ruining of the entire unit or mechanism. Besides, excessive wear of parts of the steering system, brakes, power line may cause a traffic accident.

Deviation of the technical condition of an automobile (trailer) or its units from the established norms is called defect.

Disabling of an automobile resulting in the interrupted haulage is called failure.

## 3.5 Suspension Systems

The primary purpose of the suspension system is to support the weight of that truck. Additional requirements placed upon the suspension system include: the ability to stabilize the truck when traveling over normal terrain as well as over rough ground; be capable of absorbing or cushioning the truck chassis from road shocks while simultaneously allowing the driver/operator to steer the truck; maintain the proper axle spacing and alignment; and be efficient over a wide range of speed and load conditions. Any attempts to overload or exceed the maximum suspension load rating will damage not only the suspension system itself but also the truck's frame, axles, and tires.

There are four types of suspension systems:
1. Spring
2. Equalizing beam
3. Torsion bar
4. Air bag (or spring).

The systems employed are used not only on heavy-duty trucks (for example, the tractor) but also on the accompanying trailers that they might be pulling. Each type of suspension system will be discussed from system description of components to the servicing of those components.

### Spring-Type Suspensions

Three types of spring suspension systems are constant rate, progressive or vari-rate, and auxiliary (Figure 3-27).

Constant rate springs are leaf-type spring assemblies that have a constant rate of deflection. For example, if 500 pounds deflect the spring assembly 1 inch, 1000 pounds would deflect the same spring assembly 2 inches.

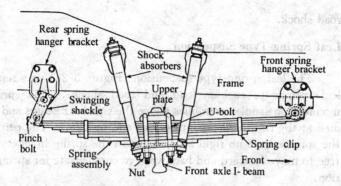

Figure 3-27  Spring suspension with torque rods

Constant rate sprins are mounted to the axle with U-bolts, nuts, and lock washers. The front end of the spring is mounted to a stationary brucket. The rear end of the spring is mounted to a spring shackle. The shackle allows for variations in spring length during compression and rebound. The spring leaves are held together by a long bolt that passes through the spring center. The spring suspension system is secured to the axle housing by U-bolts. Leaf alignment is maintained by spring clips that are typically located at the two ends of the spring leaves.

**Equalizing Beam Suspension**

Tandem drive axles require a special suspension that permits flexibility between the axles but still withstands rugged usage with long service life. The equalizing beam-type suspension system described in these paragraphs embodies these required characteristics. The types of equalizing beam suspensions used on heavy-duty trucks are the leaf spring type and the rubber load cushion type.

The equalizing beam suspension system is designed to lower the center of gravity of the axle load. This is accomplished by placing the beam below the axle centerline. This design provides additional leverage to work with the torque rods in absorbing axle torque and road shock.

## Leaf Spring-Type Suspension

The leaf spring-type suspension (Figure 3-28) uses semielliptic leaf springs to cushion load and road shocks. The springs are mounted on saddle assemblies above the equalizer beams and are pivoted at the front end on spring pins and brackets. The rear ends of the springs have no rigid attachment to the spring brackets, but are free to move forward and backward to compensate for spring deflection.

The equalizing beams utilize the "lever" principle to distribute the load equally between axles and to reduce the effect of bumps and road irregularities. The torque rods permit complete absorption of torque, which is the tendency of the axles to turn backward or forward on their axis due to starting or stopping inertia. The cross tube connecting the equalizing beams assures correct alignment of the tandem and prevents damaging load transfer.

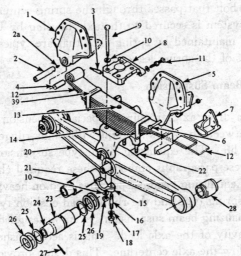

Figure 3-28   Leaf spring type suspension system

1 Spring bracket
2 Spring pin
2a Zerk fitting
3 Draw key
4 Bushing
5 Spring bracket
6 Rebound bolt with spacer
7 Spring bracket
8 Top pad
9 Top pad bolt
10 Washer
11 Setscrew
12 Leaf spring assembly
13 Center bolt
14 Saddle assembly
15 Saddle cap
16 Stud
17 Washer
18 Nut
19 Nut
20 Equalizer beam
21 Center bushing
22 Cross tube
23 Center bushing bronze
24 Sleeve
25 Seals
26 Washer
27 Zerk fitting
28 End bushing
29 Part number

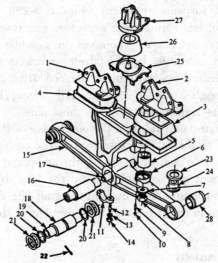

Figure 3-29   Rubber cushion type suspension system

1 Frame hanger
2 Frame hanger
3 Rubber cushion
4 Saddle assembly
17 Cross shaft
18 Center bushing bronze
19 Sleeve
20 Seal

· 263 ·

5 Drive pin bushing
6 Bushing retainer cap
7 Rebound washer
8 Drive pin nut
9 Stud
10 Nut
11 Saddle cap
12 Stud
13 Washer
14 Nut
15 Equalizer beam
16 Center bushing
21 Thrust washer
22 Zerk fitting
23 Rebound bumper
24 Stop nut
25 Plate
26 Rubber cushion
27 Frame hanger
28 End bushing

## Rubber Cushion-Type Suspension

This type of suspension system (Figure 3-29) uses rubber cushions in place of leaf springs to absorb load and road shock. On these units, rubber cushions are mounted on a saddle assembly at each side. Positive mounting between frame brackets and the suspension unit is secured by four rubber-bushed drive pins, each of which passes through a rubber cushion. All driving, braking, and cornering torces are transmitted through these pins.

Without load, the unit rides on the outer edge of the load cushions. As the load increases, the cross bars of the cushions are progressively brought into contact to absorb the additional load. Cushioning and alignment are accomplished by the four drive pins encased in rubber bushings. The bushings permit the drive pins to move up and down in direct relation to movement of the load cushions.

## Torsion Bar Suspensions

This type of suspension system utilizes torsion bars in lieu of the commonly used steel leaf spring arrangements. The typical torsion bar suspension consists of a torsion bar, front crank, and rear crank with associated brackets, a shackle pin, and assorted bushings and seals. Axle torque and truck loading are supported and taken on by two hardened steel bushings located at the end of each crank assembly. End thrusts are normally absorbed by a center-threaded bushing and a center-threaded area shackle pin. When the central area of the shackle pin is located within the mating threaded bushing, the axles can be aligned correctly. Seals are used at the bushing ends and at the shacckle links to inhibit water seepage and highway debris.

Typical torsion bar suspensions utilize prestressed bars that acquire a permanent right-hand or left-hand twist. Normal manufacturing practice is to stamp the bars with an R or L to indicate on which side of the truck the bars are to be installed.

**Air Bag (Spring) Suspensions**

Many heavy-duty trucks are equipped with air spring suspension systems from the steering axle to the trailer suspension. The air bag or air spring suspension system is the ultimate in smooth, shock-and vibration-free riding with a preset constant frame height. The air springs on the suspension system take the place of the normally used mechanical leaf-type springs. This design, therefore, overcomes interleaf friction and helps to minimize road shock from being transferred to the truck frame, cargo, and the driver/operator. The air spring suspension system adjusts to load conditions automatically, providing a low rate suspension with light or no loads, and a high rate suspension with heavier loads.

Advantages of the air spring suspension include the following:

1. Front pivotal bushing controls truck roll and axle alignment, yet allows easy up and down travel.

2. Structural frame brackets attach by welding or bolting.

3. Trailing arms are steel box beams.

4. The axle connection is a seat assembly, which is welded as part of the beam and U-bolted for double safe operation.

5. Usually incorporates a preset check valve to prevent any leaks in the suspension system from affecting the truck's air brake system.

The major components of an air spring suspension system, whether installed on a single axle or on tandem alxes, are as follows: a height control valve, air lines, tapered leaf springs, shock absorbers, torque rods, and wear pads.

The brain of the air spring suspension system is the height control valve. The valve is sensitive to height variations and when properly adjusted it will automatically provide and maintain truck riding height. The height control valve is usually mounted at the rear of the trucl frame. The valve has a lever connected to the rear axle assembly through a linkage. This height control lever is sensitive to frame height and will provide automatic filling or exhausting of the air springs to maintain the truck's level. The lever arm also has a neutral position that serves to automatically return the valve to a closed position.

**Independent Front Suspension**

With independent suspension, each front wheel is free to move up and down with a minimum (least attainable) effect on the other wheel. There is also far less twisting motion imposed on the frame.

This effect is achieved by using two arms at each side of the frame. The upper arm is considerably shorter than the lower, giving rise to the term long and short arm suspension.

The inner ends of both arms are pivoted to the frame via threaded bushings (same principle as threaded U-shackle). Or, as currently in wide usage, rubber bushings. The outer ends are attached to the steering knuckle by threaded bushings or a ball joint.

When one wheel strikes a bump, it is deflected upward. This allows it to travel up or down without affecting the other wheel.

By calculating the positioning and lengths of both upper and lower arms, it is possible for the wheel assembly to move up or down with a minimum of tip ping (change in camber angle, which will be described later). Figure 3-30 shows inner pivot points 1 and 2, on typical long and short arm suspension. Note the different arcs transcribed by each arm.

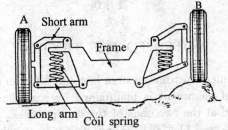

Figure 3-30　Action of individual front wheel suspension system

## NEW WORDS

| | | |
|---|---|---|
| torsion | ['tɔːʃən] | n. 扭转,扭矩,挠曲 |
| suspension | [səs'penʃən] | n. 悬,吊,悬挂物 |
| stabilize | ['steibilaiz] | v. 稳定,安定,(使)坚固 |
| terrain | ['terein] | n. 地面,地势,地带,地形 |
| cushion | ['kuʃən] | n. ;vt. 软垫,垫层,缓冲器,缓冲 |
| chassis | ['ʃæsiz] | n. 底盘,机架,底架 |
| simultaneously | [ˌsiməl'teinjəsli] | adv. 同时发生地,同时地,一齐地 |
| shackle | ['ʃækl] | n. 束缚装置,钩环,绝缘器 |
| secure | [si'kjuə] | adj. ;vt. 安心的;使安全,掩护 |
| rugged | ['rʌgid] | adj. 不平的,粗壮的,强健的 |
| usage | ['juːzidʒ] | n. 使用,用法,利用 |
| leverage | ['liːvəridʒ] | n. 杠杆作用,杠杆 |
| compensate | ['kɔmpenseit] | vt. 补偿,赔偿,补整 |
| inertia | [i'nəːʃjə] | n. 惯性,惯量 |
| prestress | ['priː'stres] | vt. 对…预加应力 |
| oscillation | [ˌɔsi'leiʃən] | n. 摆动,振动,动摇 |
| pivotal | ['pivətl] | adj. 枢轴的,中枢的 |

## PHRASES AND EXPRESSIONS

| | |
|---|---|
| suspension system | 悬架系统 |
| shock absorber | 减震器 |
| hang bracket | 悬架 |
| spring clip | 弹簧卡圈,弹簧夹 |

spring assembly　　　　　簧片组
in lieu of　　　　　　　　作为…替代

## NOTES TO THE TEXT

1. The spring suspension system is secured to the axle housing by U-bolts. leaf alignment is maintained by spring clips that are Typically located at the two ends of the spring leaves.

弹簧悬架系统靠 U 型螺栓安全地固定在轴上。叶片式组合的维护和保养借助于那些特有的安装在弹簧叶片两端的弹簧垫圈。

that 指 spring clips 引导定语从句,修饰 clips；谓语用 secure 的过去分词短语构成被动语态。

2. This type of suspension system utilizes torsion bars in lieu of the commonly used steel leaf spring arrangements.

这类(扭矩杆悬架)悬架系统使用扭矩杆替代了普遍使用的钢板弹簧装置。

in lieu of 做为…的替代；used 是 use 的过去分词短语做定语,修饰 arrangement。

3. Many heavy-duty trucks are equipped with air spring suspension systems-from the steering axle to the trailer suspension.

很多重型卡车在转向轴到拖车之间配置空气弹簧悬架系统。

air spring 空气弹簧；equip 的过去分词构成被动语态做谓语；from…to… 做状语,修饰 equip。

4. With independent suspension, each front wheel is free to move up and down with a minimum (least attainable) effect on the other wheel.

利用独立悬架,每个前轮对其他车轮几乎无影响地自由上下运动。

independent suspension 独立悬架；with independent suspension 是介词短语做状语；with a minimum effect on the other wheel 是介词短语做方式状语。

## EXERCISES

Ⅰ. Answer the following questions according to the text：
　　1. What is the basic job of the suspension system?

2. Describe a coil spring. How are coil springs mounted?
3. How does the torsion bar spring differ from the coil spring?
4. What is the principle of the air spring?
5. What unit provides air for the air spring system?
6. Can you explain the difference between sprung and unsprung weight?
7. Is it possible to use torsion bar springs at both front and rear?
8. How does the shock absorber control spring oscillation?
9. Can you describe the action of the independent front wheel suspension system?
10. What is one the great advantages of the independent from wheel suspension system?

II. In each case, choose one of the four words or phrases which will correctly complete the sentence to complete the following sentences:

1. Generaly the different parts are ____ the basic structure by means of spring suspension system.

  A. provided with    B. attached to
  C. opposite to    D. esential for

2. The occupants of the vehicle will feel uncomfortable ____ on the road surface.

  A. due to jerky motion    B. for running fast
  C. during motion    D. when it is moving

3. The suspension system provides ____ and minimises these shocks from being experienced by the occupants.

  A. proper connection    B. correct support
  C. cushioning effect    D. balancing effect

4. Suspension system maintains the stability of the vehicle in ____ during motion.

  A. going or stopping    B. staying or moving
  C. advancing or retarding    D. pitching or rolling

5. The frame of a car, which supports the engine, body, and running gears, ____ two hollow boxlide sections of steel.

  A. is mounted on    B. is equipped with
  C. is made up of    D. are located at

6. Crossmembers or braces, ____ the frame ____ twisting when the car strikes a bump in the road.
   A. turn…into          B. translate…into
   C. protect…against    D. keep…from

7. Most shock absorbers are tubular ____, and have one end fastened to the car frame and the other to the wheel support.
   A. in shape           B. as a whole
   C. in diameter        D. at first appearance

8. The rear shock absorbers are straddle-mounted ____ body sway on curves.
   A. to increase        B. for controlling
   C. to minimize        D. so as to transmit

9. The car frame is connected to the axles ____ which absorb road shock.
   A. by using torsion bars   B. by springs
   C. via levers              D. by means of washers

10. Torsion bars are used ____ front springs in some applications.
    A. making place for       B. for allowing room for
    C. to leave room for      D. in place of

Ⅲ. Fill the blank in each sentence with one of the four words or phrases with correctly completes the sentence:

1. Loose U-bolts on a suspension system can cause ____.
   A. hard steering          B. leaf spring breakage
   C. abnormal tire wear     D. all of the above

2. Torque arms are used on a suspension system to ____.
   A. retain axle alignment       B. control axle torque
   C. both A and B                D. neither A nor B

3. A device that is used to reduce road shocks and transfer loads through the suspension components to the frame of the trailer ____.
   A. is an equalizer bracket     B. is a torque rod
   C. are springs                 D. is a frame hanger

4. A leaf-type spring suspension system is usually mounted on top of the truck rear spring assemblies and is only used when a truck

is under a heavy load?
   A. progressive spring suspension
   B. constant spring suspension
   C. auxiliary spring suspension
   D. air spring suspension
   5. ____ is used to absorb energy and prevent suspension oscillations.
   A. equalizer bracket　　　　B. torque rod
   C. springs　　　　　　　　　D. shock absorber
   6. The brain of the air spring suspension system is the ____.
   A. leveling valve　　　　　B. air spring
   C. hydraulic shock absorber
   D. quick release valve or height control valve
   7. An equalizing beam suspension ____.
   A. distributes the load equally between the axles
   B. reduces wheel hop
   C. utilizes the lever principle for its basic operation
   D. all of the above
   8. ____ of spring suspension system is usually mounted on top of the truck rear spring assemblies and is only used when a truck is under a heavy load.
   A. progressive spring suspension
   B. constant spring suspension
   C. auxiliary spring suspension
   D. air springs suspension

Ⅳ. Translate the following sentence into Chinese:
   1. Each front wheel is independently mounted so that either one may move up or down without affecting the other, which reduces body movement to a considerable degree.
   2. To the lower body plate, suspension system is attached which transmits the weight of the body and other components to the axles and wheels.
   3. An extremely flexible spring, or too soft, would allow too much movement, while a stiff or hard spring would give too rough a ride.

4. Another popular system is that which employs the swinging arm and the wheel, hub, and so on are mounted on one end of a carrier arm which carries the steering swivel pin, the latter acting as a pivot for the whole assembly.

5. The main leaf has an eye rolled in each end through which the bolts are inserted to attach the spring ends to the frame of the car.

6. One end of the main spring leaf is attached to the car frame by means of a hanger, the other by means of a shackle.

V. Translate the following passage into Chinese:

The telescopic or direct action shock absorber is found on both front and rear suspension systems. On the present day automobiles, it consists of a cylinder in which a piston is moved up and down by a rod. The piston rod is attached to the chassis and the base of the cylinder to the axle. Surrounding the cylinder is a reservoir and the upper portion of the unit is surrounded by a dust cover. The dust cover is larger in diameter than the reservoir and moves up and down around the reservoir.

On a rebound stroke, the piston in the cylinder is drawn upward. The fluid above the piston passes through the holes to the lower part of the cylinder. There is not enough fluid above the piston to fill the space below the piston due to the volume occupied by piston rod. The lower part of the cylinder is thus slightly vacuumized and additional fluid enters the cylinder from the reservoir.

On a compression stroke, the piston is forced downward in the cylinder. The fluid below the piston passes through to the upper part of the cylinder by opening piston intake compression relief valve. The piston rod displaces its own volume as it enters the cylinder. The fluid thus displaced, is forced out of the cylinder through check valve located between the bottom of the cylinder and the reservoir. The air above the fluid level is slightly compressed which does not play any part in the operation of shock absorber.

## 3.6 Steering Systems

The steering system (Figure 3-31) must deliver precise directional control. And it must do so requiring little driver effort at the steering wheel. Truck steering systems are either manual or power assisted, with power assist units using either hydraulic or air assist setups to make steering effort easier.

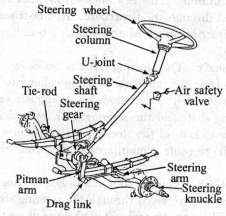

Figure 3-31  Parts of manual steering system

In addition to its vital role in vehicle control, the steering system is closely related to front suspension, axle, and wheel/tire components. Improper steering adjustment can lead to alignment and tire wear problems. Suspension, axle, and wheel problems can affect steering and handling.

The key components that make up the steering system are the steering wheel, steering column, steering shaft, steering gear, pitman arm, drag link, steering arm, ball joints, and tie-rod assembly.

**1. Steering Wheel**  This is the driver's link to the entire system. The wheel is formed of a strong steel rod shaped into a wheel. Spokes extend from the wheel to the wheel hub, which is fastened securely at the top of the steering column. The wheel assembly is covered with rubber or plastic. The steering column transfers driver input to the steering gear. In other words, driver effort applied to the steering wheel at the rim becomes torque in the steering shaft. The larger the steering wheel. diameter, the more torque is generated from the same amount of drive effort. Most steering wheels on heavy-duty trucks are 22 inches in diameter.

    2. **Steering Column**  This is a hollow tube that extends from the steering wheel through the floorboard. It is fastened to the cab at or under the instrument panel and contains bearings to support the steering shaft.

    3. **Steering Shaft**  The steering shaft is basically a rod, usually jointed, that runs from the top of the steering column to the steering gear. U-joints in the shaft accommodate any angular variations between the steering shaft and the steering gear input shaft. Usually found at one or both ends of the steering shaft, U-joints may also be used in the middle to route a multipiece shaft around the engine or accessories.

    4. **Steering Gear**  This gearbox multiplies steering torque and changes its direction as received through the steering shaft from the steering wheel. There are two widely used types of gears: worm and roller, and recirculating ball. These are explanied later in this chapter.

    5. **Pitman Arm**  The pitman arm is a steel arm clamped to the output shaft of the steering gear. The outer end of the pitman arm moves through an arc in order to change the rotary motion of the steering gear output shaft into linear motion. The length of the pitman arm affects steering quickness. A longer pitman arm will generate more steering motion at the front wheels for a given amount of steering wheel movement.

    6. **Drag Link**  This forged rod connects the pitman arm to the steering arm. The drag link can be a one or two-piece component. The two-piece design is adjustable in length, a fact that makes it easy to center the steering gear with the wheels straight ahead. One-piece drag links are used in systems with very close tolerances.

Other components are used to make adjustments to the system when a one-piece drag link is used. The drag link is connected at each end by ball joints. These ball joints isolate the steering gear and pitman arm from axle motion.

7. **Steering Arm**   Sometimes called a steering lever, this forged steel component connects the drag link to the top portion of the driver's side steering knuckle and spindle. As the steering arm moves, it changes the angle of the steering knuckle and thus alters the direction in which the steering knuckle spindle is spointing.

8. **Ball Joints**   This ball-and-socket assembly consists of a forged steel ball with a threaded stud attached to it. A socket shell grips the ball. The ball stud moves around to provide the freedom of movement needed for various steering links to accommodate relative motion between the axle and the frame rail when the front axle springs flex. A ball stud is mounted in the end of each steering arm and provides the link between the drag link and the steering arm.

9. Tie-Rod Assembly   The steering arm or lever controls the movement of the driver's side steering knuckle. There must be some method of transferring this steering motion to the opposite, passenger side steering knuckle. This is done through the use of a tie-rod assembly that links the two steering knuckles together and forces them to act in unison. The tie-rod assembly is also called a cross tube.

## NEW WORDS

| | | |
|---|---|---|
| precise | ['prisais] | adj. 正确的,准确的,明确的 |
| vital | ['vaitl] | adj. 重要的,生机的,有生命的 |
| alignment | [ə'lainmənt] | n. 调准,准线,组合,直线对准 |
| pitman | ['pitmən] | n. 连杆,联接杆,摇杆 |
| spoke | [spəuk] | n.;vt.(轮)辐;给…装上辐,用煞车煞住车(车轮) |
| rim | [rim] | n.;vt. 轮辋,缘;形成边状 |
| extend | [iks'tend] | vt. 延长,伸出,扩充 |
| accomodate | [ə'kɔmədeit] | v. 容纳,提供,供应 |

| multipiece | ['mʌltipiːs] | n. 多块 |
| accessory | [æk'sesəri] | n. 附件,附属的 |
| linear | ['liniə] | adj. 线的,直线的,长度的 |
| forge | [fɔːdʒ] | v. ;n. 锻造,伪造;锻工,锻件 |
| tolerance | ['tɔlərəns] | n. 忍受,容忍,忍耐力 |
| isolate | ['aisəleit] | vt. 隔离,分离,孤立,使脱离 |
| spindle | ['spindl] | n. 轴,芯轴,纺锭,锭子 |
| stud | [stʌd] | n. 中介轴销,双头螺栓 |
| grip | [grip] | n. ;vt. 紧握;握,支配,控制,夹具 |
| knuckle | ['nʌkl] | n. 关节,节,钩爪 |

## PHRASES AND EXPRESSIONS

| steering system | 转向系统 |
| air assist setups | 空气助力机构 |
| steering wheel | 转向盘 |
| steering column | 转向轴 |
| pitman arm | 转向臂 |
| drag link | 直拉杆 |
| steering arm | 转向节臂 |
| ball joint | 球形节销 |
| instrument panel | 仪表板 |

## NOTES TO THE TEXT

1. The ball stud moves around to provide the freedom of movement needed for various steering links to accommodate relative motion between the axle and the frame rail when the front axle springs flex.

球头销座通过转动提供各种转向所需的运动自由度,当前轮轴减振弹簧屈曲时来调整轮轴与车架之间的有关运动。

between the axle and…rail 介词短语做状语;when the… 是时间状语从句。

### 3.6.1 Manual Steering Gears

As was mentioned earlier in this chapter, there are basically two types of manual steering gears. They are the worm and roller type and the recirculating ball and worm type.

**Worm and Roller Gears**

In this type of gear (Figure 3-32) an hourglass-shaped worm gear is attached to the input shaft. The threads of the worm gear are meshed with the threads of a sector gear, commonly called a roller. The sector gear transfers the rotary motion of the worm gear input shaft to the output shaft. The output shaft is splined to the pitman arm, which translates the rotary motion of the shaft to linear motion. Movement in the pitman arm is transmitted through a drag link to the steering arm and knuckle and thus to the wheels.

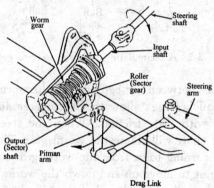

Figure 3-32  An hourglass-shaped worm gear and the sector roller manual steering gear

**Recirculating Ball Gears**

The input shaft of this type of steering gear (Figure 3-33) is also connected to a worm gear, but the worm gear in a recirculating ball type unit is straight. Mounted on the worm gear is a ball nut. The ball nut has interior spiral grooves that mate with the threads of the worm gear. The ball nut also has exterior gear teeth on one side. These teeth mesh with teeth on a sector gear and shfat.

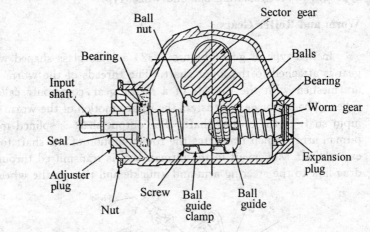

Figure 3-33 A recirculating ball type steering gear

In the grooves between the ball nut and the worm gear are ball bearings. The ball bearings allow the worm gear and ball nut to mesh and move with little friction. When the steering wheel is turned, the input shaft will rotate the worm gear. The ball bearing will transmit the turning force from the worm gear to the ball nut, causing the ball nut to move up and down the worm gear. Ball return guides are connected to each end of the ball nut grooves. These allow the ball bearing to circulate in a continuous loop.

As the ball nut moves up or down on the worm gear, it causes the sector gear to rotate which, in turn, causes the pitman arm to swivel back and forth. This motion is transferred to the steering arm and knuckle to turn the wheel.

## Power Steering

Power steering is designed to reduce the steering wheel turning effort by utilizing hydraulic pressure to bolster (strengthen) the normal torque developed by the steering gearbox. It should ease steering wheel manipulation and, at the same time, offer some resistance so that the driver can retain some "road feel".

Road feel is the feeling imparted to the steering wheel by the wheels of a car in motion. This feeling is very important to the driver in sensing and predetermining vehicle steering response. A good driver can tell when the front wheels are approaching the walk (slipping sideways) point or if more or less turning effort is required to stabilize the car body on turns, in winds, etc. Complete and effortless power steering would rob the driver of this valuable road feel.

To maintain road feel, power steering systems require some wheel effort, approximately 1 to 3 lbs, pull on the steering wheel rim.

Power steering systems are of two general types. One type controls and utilizes the hydraulic pressure directly within the steering gearbox housing. The other type uses a hydraulic cylinder and control valve attached to the linkage system. This second type uses a conventional standard gearbox. Both systems use a hydraulic pump, generally belt driven by the engine, to produce the necessary hydraulic pressure.

In both the self-contained and linkage types, a control valve is actuated by driver steering effort. This valve admits oil, under heavy pressure, to one side or the other of a hydraulic piston. The pressure the oil creates against the piston is transferred to either the pitman shaft, or to a direct connection to the steering linkage, which assists the driver in manipulating the front wheels.

## Stearing Knuckle

The steering knuckle mounts to the front axle through the use of a heavy steel pin known as a kingpin or knuckle. The steering knuckle includes the spindle on which the wheel bearings and wheel hubs are mounted, a flange to which the brake's back plate is bolted, and an upper and lower knuckle to which the steering arm and tie-rod arm (also called a cross tube arm or an Ack erman arm) are attached.

The kingpin can be either tapered or straight. Tapered pins are drawn into the axle center and secured by tightening a nut at the upper pin end. Straight kingpins are secured to the axle with tapered draw keys that bear against flats on the pin. Tapered pins are usually sealed and do not require periodic lubricating. Straight pins have a cap on either end in which grease fittings are mounted. A heavy-duty, multipurpose lithium base (#2 grade) grease is typically specified for use in the steering knuckle.

The steering arm is fastened to the upper knuckle of the steering knuckle with a key and nut. The tie-rod arm is fastened to the lower knuckle in the same way.

## NEW WORDS

| worm | [wə:m] | n. 蜗杆,螺杆,螺纹 |
| hourglass | ['auəgla:s] | n. 沙漏,水漏 |
| sector | ['sektə] | n. 扇形,扇形门,部分,部门 |
| recirculating | [ri'sə:kjuleitiŋ] | n. 再循环 |
| thread | [θred] | n. ;vt. 螺纹;加工螺纹 |
| linear | ['liniə] | adj. 线的,直线的,长条的 |
| mate | [meit] | n. ;vt. 配对物;使配对 |
| spiral | ['spaiərəl] | adj. ;n. 螺线的,盘旋;螺线,螺旋形的东西 |
| interior | [in'tiəriə] | adj. 内部的,国内的 |
| exterior | ['eks'tiəriə] | adj. ;n. 外部的;外部 |
| guide | [gaid] | n. ;vt. ;vi. 导轨,管理,操纵;可导的 |
| swivel | ['swivl] | n. ;vt. 转节,转环;使旋转 |
| bolster | ['bəulstə] | n. 软垫,垫木,车架,悬梁 |

| mainipulation | ['meinipjuːleiʃən] | n. 操作,控制,执行 |
| impart | [im'paːt] | vt. 传递,给予 |
| stabilize | ['steibilaiz] | vt. ;vi. 稳定,安定;稳定 |
| conventional | [kən'venʃənl] | adj. 常规的,普通的 |
| linkage | ['liŋkidʒ] | n. 链等,联动装置 |
| kingpin | [kiŋpin] | n. 中心立轴,转向主销 |
| periodic | [ˌpiəri'ɔdik] | adj. 间歇的,定期的,循环的 |
| grease | [griːs] | n. 润滑脂,润滑油 |
| taper | ['teipə] | n. ;vt. 拔销;使逐步形成 |
| multipurpose | ['mʌlti'pəːpəs] | adj. 多种用途的 |
| lithium | ['liθiəm] | n. 锂 |

## PHRASES AND EXPRESSIONS

| manual steering gear | 手动转向器 |
| worm and roller gear | 蜗杆滚轮转向器 |
| recirculation ball gear | 循环球转向器 |
| mesh with | 与…相啮合,紧密配合 |
| attach to | 与…相联 |
| in motion | 在移动中 |
| be connected to | 与…相接 |
| spiral groove | 螺旋槽 |
| mate with | 与…紧密配合 |
| power steering | 动力转向 |
| steering knuckle | 转向节 |
| in the same way | 以同样方式 |
| be fastened to | 紧固于 |

## NOTES TO THE TEXT

1. The input shaft of this type of steering gear is also connected to a worm gear, but the worm gear in a recirculating ball type unit is straight.

这种型式转向器的输入轴也与蜗杆相连接,但在循环球式转向器中的蜗杆是直的。

worm gear 蜗杆装置,在循环球中的蜗杆是直的,而在蜗杆滚轮式转向器中蜗杆是球面形的；but 但是，并列连词，连接两个并列句；is connected to 被动语态做谓语。

2. Power steering is designed to reduce the steering wheel turning effort by utilizing hydraulic pressure to bolster (strengthen) the normal torque developed by the steering gear box.

动力转向是通过利用液力作用而使转向器的扭矩增大；降低转向盘的作用力而设计的。

developed 过去分词做状语；by utilizing … 介词短语做方式状语，to reduce … 动词不定式短语做目的状语。

### 3.6.2 Fornt-End Alignment

The components of a truck's front axle, steering system, and suspension are carefully aligned by the vehicle manufacturer to balance all the forces created by friction, gravity, centrifugal force, and momentum while the vehicle is in motion. When properly aligned, the wheels of a loaded vehicle will contact the road correctly, allowing the wheels to roll without scuffing, dragging, or slipping on the road. A front end that is properly aligned will result in:

1. Easier steering
2. Longer tire life
3. Directional stability
4. Less wear on front-end parts
5. Better fuel economy
6. Increased safety.

The primary alignment angles are toe, caster, and camber. Kingpin inclination, turning angle. Ackerman geometry, and axle alignment will also affect tire wear and steering characteristics. Frontend alignment should be checked at regular intervals and particularly after the front suspension has been subjected to extremely heavy service or severe impact loads. Before checking and adjusting alignment, components such as wheel bearings, tie-rods, steering gear, shock absorbers, and tire inflation should be inspected and corrected where where necessary.

## Toe In

Toe-in is accomplished by placing the front of the wheels closer together than the back, when viewed from the top.

When a wheel is cambered, the tire engages the road at an angle. Since the tire will adapt itself to the road, the rolling edge of the tire will not be at right angles to the centerline of the wheel. This will cause it to roll as though it were cone shaped, tending to roll outward while moving forward.

To compensate for this roll out (as well as toe-out tendencies produced when steering axis intersects road inside CL of wheel), the wheels must be adjusted for toe-in.

## Caster

By tilting the top of the kingpin (or, in case of ball joint, top of steering knuckle) toward the rear of the car, the centerline of the swivel, or steering point, will be in front of the point at which the tire encounters the road. As this places the point of resistance to forward motion behind the steering centerline, the wheel is forced to track behind, automatically lining up with the moving car. This is referred to as positive caster.

Positive caster tends to force the wheels to travel in a straight ahead position. It also assists in recovery (wheels turning back to straight ahead position after making a turn). On late model cars, there is often little or no positive caster. Positive caster makes it more difficult to turn the wheels from the straight ahead. Position than when no caster angle is present. Another effect of positive caster is a mild tipping effect when cornering. When making a right-hand turn, the right-hand wheel will cause the steering knuckle to raise slightly, while the left-hand wheel will allow the knuckle to lower. This creates a tipping effect, and it is obvious that raising the side of the car on the inside of the turn will have an adverse effect on its cornering ability. When the wheels are turned to the left, the left side raises and the right side drops.

To ease turning, many cars employ a negative caster angle (tipping top of steering knuckle to front of car). This will ease steering and cause a mild banking effect when cornering (side of car on inside of turn will drop and outside will raise). Proper tracking is still provided by kingpin or steering knuckle inclination (to be discussed later).

**Camber**

Positive front wheel camber is provided by tipping the tops of the wheels out. When viewing the car from the front, the top of the wheels are farther apart than the bottom. In short, the centerline (CL) of the wheel is on longer in a vertical plane (straight up and down)(Figure 3-34).

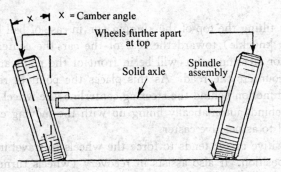

Figure 3-34   Positive camber.

If the tops of the wheels are closer together than the bottoms, the camber is considered negative.

Positive camber places the centerline of the wheel closer to the centerline of the kingpin, or steering axis, where both intersect the road. This assists in reducing the tendency of the front wheels to toe-out (spread apart at front) and materially lessens road shock to the steering system. Most cars use a small amount of positive camber (less than one degree).

## Kingpin or Steering Axis Incination

The top ball joints of the steering knuckles are closer together at the top than the bottom. The steering axis (view from front of car) places the centerline of the steering ball joints nearer to the centerline of the wheel.

When the center line of the wheel is to the outside of the center line of the steering axis (where they intersect road), the wheels tend to toe-out. This is caused by the road-tire resistance pushing back on the spindle, causing it to swivel backward on the ball joints.

When the centerline of the wheel intersects the road at a point inside the intersection of the steering axis centerline, the wheels tend to toe-in (fronts of tires are closer together than backs).

Steering axis inclination (Figure 3-35) helps to bring the centerline of the wheel and the steering axis centerline closer together where they intersect the road surface. This also causes suspension shocks to be transmitted to and absorbed by the heavy inner spindle and knuckle assembly.

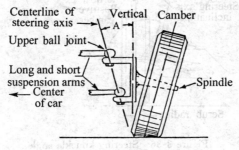

Figure 3-35 Steering axis inclination

Steering axis inclination also helps the car wheels follow the straight ahead position. This tracking effect is caused by the fact that whenever the wheels are turned from the straight ahead position, the car is actually lifted up. Remember that the wheel spindle, when turned, is moved about the steering axis. As the axis is tilted, the spindle will move in a downward direction. Since a downward movement of the spindle is impossible (it is supported by wheel assembly), the steering knuckle is forced upward. This will raise the car a small amount. The effect is similar on both sides.

The weight of the car will tend to force the spindles to swivel back, returning the wheels to the straight ahead position.

**Steering Knuckle Angle**

The steering knuckle angle is determined by the arc formed between the steering axis and the centerline of the spindle. Figure 3-36 illustrates the steeringg knuckle angle, as well as positive camber and the steering axis. You will notice that the steering axis inclination angle, and the camber angle, are directly dependent upon each other.

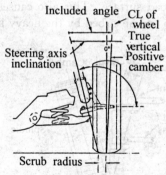

Figure 3-36　Steering knuckle angle

## NEW WORDS

| | | |
|---|---|---|
| align | [ə'lain] | vt. 使成一线,使密切合作 |
| momentum | [məu'mentəm] | n. 动量,(总)冲量 |
| scuff | [skʌf] | v. ;n. 磨损,使磨损;磨损处 |
| toe | [təu] | n. ;vt. 轴踵,球棒尖;用脚趾踢(或触) |

| caster | [ˈkɑːstə] | n. 主销后倾, 小脚轮, 自位轮 |
| camber | [kæmbə] | n. ; vt. 上挠度, 反挠度; 造成弧形 |
| inclination | [ˌinkliˈneiʃən] | n. 倾斜, 倾角 |
| geometry | [dʒiˈɔmitri] | n. 几何学, 几何形状 |
| adapt | [əˈdæpt] | n. ; vt. 接合器, 接头; 使适应, 调整 |
| cone | [kəun] | n. 锥形, 锥体 |
| adverse | [ˈædvəːs] | adj. 相反的, 有害的, 不利的 |
| bank | [bæŋk] | v. ; n. 倾斜, 倾斜行驶; 银行 |
| track | [træk] | v. 形成车辙, 跟踪 |
| intersect | [ˈintəsekt] | n. 相交, 交叉 |
| lessen | [ˈlesn] | vt. ; vi. 减少, 贬低; 变少, 变小 |
| encounter | [inˈkauntə] | vt. ; n. 遇到; 遭遇 |
| resistance | [reˈzistəns] | n. 抵抗, 抵制 |
| negative | [ˈnegətiv] | adj. 否定的, 负的 |
| tilt | [tilt] | vt. ; vi. ; n. 使倾斜; 倾斜; 斜度 |
| tendency | [ˈtendənsi] | n. 趋向, 趋势 |

## PHRASES AND EXPRESSIONS

| kingpin inclination | 主销倾斜角 |
| axle alignment | 轴的调整 |
| steering characteristics | 操纵特性 |
| tire inflation | 轮胎充气压力 |
| toe-in | [车轮]前束, 车轮内向 |
| toe-out | [车轮]后束, 车轮外向 |
| in short | 简言之 |
| refer to sb (sth) as | 称某人(某物)为, 把某人(某物)叫做 |
| tend to | 趋向, 倾向, 引起, 造成 |

## NOTES TO THE TEXT

1. The components of a truck's front axle, steering system, and suspension are carefully aligned by the vehicle manufacturer to balance all the forces created by friction, gravity, centrifugal force, and momentum while the vehicle is in motion.

卡车前轮轴零件, 转向系统和悬架必须由制造厂仔细调整, 以平衡由于车轮运动所产生的摩擦力、地球引力,离小力及冲力。

the components of a trucks front axle, steering system and suspension 三个并列的短语做主语;are aligned 构成被动语态;to balance… 做目的状语。

# EXERCISES

Ⅰ. Answer the following questions according to the text:

1. Define the meaning of camber. What effect does camber have on the system?

2. What is toe-in? Of what particular use is toe-in?

3. How is toe-out on corners produced?

4. What is caster? Why is it used?

5. Kingpin, or steering axis inclination, affects the steering in what way?

6. The term steering geometry refers to what? what is slip angle?

7. When turning a corner, one side of the car raises while the other lowers. What is the reason for this?

8. Can you explain the actions involved in a typical power steering unit for straight ahead position, left turn, right turn?

9. What is road feel and how is it maintained in the power steering systems?

Ⅱ. Choose the best answer for each of the following questions:

1. Which of the following components uses universal joints?

　A. steering wheel　　B. steering shaft
　C. pitman arm　　　D. tie-rod assembly

2. Which of the following components contains ball joints?

　A. steering gear　　B. pitman arm
　C. steering knuckle　D. tie-rod end

3. Which of the following components connects the pitman arm to the steering arm?

　A. drag link　　　B. tie-rod assembly
　C. cross tube　　　D. steering column

4. Which of the following alignment angles has the potential to

cause the most tire wear?
  A. incorrect toe     B. incorrect camber
  C. incorrect caster  D. insufficient turning angle

5. Which of the following is defined as the forward or rearward tilt of the kingpin centerline when viewed from the side of the vehicle?
  A. camber  B. caster
  C. toe     D. kingpin inclination

6. Which of the following can be defined as the inward or outward tilt of the top of the tires when viewed from the front of the vehicle?
  A. turning radius  B. Ackerman geometry
  C. camber          D. toe

7. Which of the following alignment angles can be corrected using shims?
  A. toe     B. caster
  C. camber  D. none of the above

8. Which of the following alignment angles should be corrected by bending the axle?
  A. caster             B. camber
  C. kingpin inclination D. none of the above

Ⅲ. Choose the one word or phrase that best complete the sentence:

1. A shaft having an extremely coarse thread which is designed to operate in engagement with a toothed wheel, as a pair of gear, is known as ____.
  A. steering wheel   B. worm gear
  C. toothed sector   D. globoil gear

2. The steering gear ____ transmission oil.
  A. is lubricated with  B. is lubricating the
  C. is provided with    D. can be driven by the

3. The leakage of oil from the steering box is _____ a. lip-type seal, a felt ring, and sealing gaskets.
  A. protected against  B. replenished by
  C. flowing to         D. prevented by

4. The difference in angles between the two front wheels when

they are making a turn ____ the turning radius.

A. uses  B. has
C. is referred to as  D. has something to do with

5. The sharper the turning angle, ____ toe-out results.

A. the more  B. the more quickly
C. the better  D. a great deal

6. The ends of the steering connecting rod and steering knuckle tie rod ____ ball joints.

A. are fitted with  B. has
C. depends on  D. are used as

7. Steering gear is a device for ____ the rotary motion of the driver's steering wheel ____ the angular turning of the front wheels.

A. transmitting…to  B. deriving…from
C. engaging…with  D. converting…into

8. Three piece steering linkage is a typical modern steering linkage ____ independent suspension system.

A. by means of  B. through
C. used with  D. served as

9. The centre-arm steering linkage ____ a traverse drag link.

A. consists of  B. is made of
C. is connected with  D. connects with

10. In the direct cross type linkage, the steering arms ____ the outer ends of the tie rods.

A. are separated from  B. are related to
C. are connected to  D. contact with

Ⅳ. Translate the following sentence into Chinese:

1. For the personal safety of the driver and the passengers of the car, steering gear plays a vital part.

2. The design and layout of the steering gear should be such as to handle the car easily and quickly without any fatigue on the driver for safe and accident free travel.

3. The steering linkage is so designed as to prevent side-slip of all automobile wheels in cornering, thus ensuring ease of steering and minimizing wear of tires.

4. The rack having ball joints at each end for allowing the rise and fall of the wheels is engaged with the pinion mounted on the end of the steering shaft.

5. Some automobiles are equipped with a hydraulic power steering system intended to decrease the efforts spent by the driver to turn the wheels and to damp the road jolts transmitted to the steering wheel.

6. For light saloon and sports cars, the rack and pinion steering provides a sufficiently low gear reduction, it can also be made suitable for heavier motor vehicles by power assisting.

Ⅴ. Translate the following passage into Chinese:

The condition of the steering system has a profound effect not only on the performance of the automobile, but also on road and operation safety.

It is prohibited to operate an automobile suffering from the following steering troubles: hard steering, excessive play in the steering system, excessive wear of steering system components, loose joints and fasteners, and damaged cotter pins.

Even a slight binding of the steering gear or linkage may result in an accident, for this condition is very tiring to the driver. Hard steering in conditions of heavy traffic and high running speeds is conducive to collisions and runovers. If hard steering occurs just after the steering system has been worked on, the trouble is probably due to excessively tight adjustments in the steering gear or linkage. If it occurs at other times, hard steering could be due to excessive friction in the steering gear or linkage or at the ball joints, bent steering rods, or damaged steering worm bearings.

## 3.7 Brake Systems

Hydraulic brake systems utilize liquid to transfer force from the driver's foot to the brake shoes. Depressing the brake pedal creates a mechanical force that is transmitted through a pushrod to a piston in the master cylinder (Figure 3-37). The piston, in turn, pushes the brake fluid through the brake lines to pistons in a caliper or a cylinder on each wheel. The pressure acting on these pistons pushes brake shoes against a rotating disc or drum, This friction, generated by the contacting brake shoes and rotating disc/drum, slows and eventually stops the wheels. Releasing the brake pedal causes this action to reverse-with brake fluid returning to the master cylinder. Hydraulic brake systems can be found on light-and medium-duty trucks. Usually, they will be equipped with disc brakes on the front wheels and drum brakes on the rear wheels.

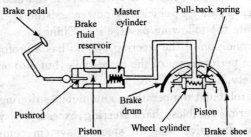

Figure 3-37   A typical hydraulic braking system

The second type of system—the air brake system—utilizes compressed air as a source of force to stop the truck. Air braking systems have been popular on heavy-duty trucks for a long time for the following reasons:

1. Without much physical effort the driver/operator can apply a powerful braking force.

2. For most heavy-duty applications, air brakes provide the safest method of stopping the truck. Air brakes remain effective even at reduced capacity.

3. Since the system is air powered. there is no shortage of energy.

4. A pneumatic system allows the tractor and trailer brake systems to be quickly disconnected and reconnected.

5. Also if air pressure fails, the brakes are automatically applied by the spring brakes.

Air braking systems first appeared on heavy-duty trucks in the 1920s. Since then, truck design has changed and federal safety standards and new technology have improved the entire air braking system. These changes have also made the systems much more complex.

### 3.7.1 Air Brake System

An air brake system is shown in Figure 3-38. A complete air brake system includes the following:

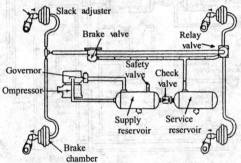

Figure 3-38  A basic air brake system

1. **Foundation Brakes**  This is the S-cam, wedge or disc brake mechanism itself, linings or pads, and related pads such as brake chamber, slack adjuster and parking brake.

2. **Air System**  This starts with the compressor and includes reservoirs, air lines, application valves, drain valves, tractor protection valves, brake valves, and governors.

3. **Optional Brake Equipment**  These can range from air dryers, automatic drain valves, and bobtail proportioning valves to antilock brake systems.

### Single Circuit Brake Systems

Basically, there are two types of air brake systems: the single circuit braking system and the dual circuit braking system. A single

· 293 ·

circuit braking system(Figure 3-39), as one might expect, has a single source of air pressure that is supplied to both front and rear axle braking, as well as to the trailer/tanker system. This system was quite common until the Federal Motor Vehicle Standard No. 121 was passed in 1975. After 1975, all newly manufactured vehicles were required to use the dual circuit system. The following sequence shows the basic single cirauit operation:

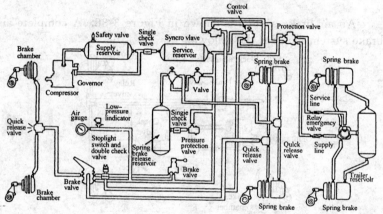

Figure 3-39 A single circuit air brake system

1. Through a belt, coupling, or drive gear, the vehicle's engine powers the air compressor. In most cases the engine provides cooling and lubrication for the compressor.

2. The compressor builds and maintains the system's air pressure. The amount of air produced by the compressor depends on the level of air energy necessary to operate the air brake and air auxiliary systems.

3. Since the compressor runs continuously while the vehicle's engine runs, the governor and compressor unloading mechanism start and stop the compression cycles, maintaining safe air pressure

levels.

4. During compression, the compressor unloading device remains closed. Compressed air constantly flows into the supply reservoir.

5. Once air pressure reaches the supply reservoir's maximum, the governor activates the compressor's unloader mechanism. Air compression stops. The inlet valve draws in and exhausts out air.

6. When air pressure falls below the minimum in the supply reservoir, the governor deactivates the unloader mechanism and the compression cycle starts again.

7. Installed in the supply reservoir, a safety valve releases excess pressure if the governor or compressor unloading mechanism fails. The safety valve usually acts at 150 psi, although other pressure settings are possible.

8. From the supply reservoir, air flows through a one-way check valve to the service reservoir.

9. From the service reservoir, compressed air flows to the brake valve. The foot pedal controls the brake valve. Depressing the pedal sends air from the brake valve (or service reservoir) to the brake chamber.

10. Once inside the brake chamber, compressed air forces the diaphragm against the push plate. Push plates are attached to slack adjusters. The slack adjusters transfer energy from the brake chambers to the foundation brakes (discs, pads, or calipers).

11. When the foundation brakes are applied, the wheels are slowed to a gradual stop.

The significant factor in this system is the single service reservoir; hence, the name of the system.

**Drum Brake**

Drum brakes can be classified as either cam actuated or wedge actuated. Wedge brakes are an earlier design and new trucks are usually equipped with cam or disc brakes. Cam-actuated brakes use a flat cam, or the much more common "S"-type cam to apply the vehicle's brakes. The wedge-actuated brakes use (as the name implies) a wedge to apply the brakes. Most often, both the cam brake and wedge brake systems use the same air brake valves and components, up to the brake chambers. The differences are in how they convert the system air pressure into mechanical brake pressure.

Cam-actuated brakes are furnished in a variety of designs. The cam may be flat or "S"-shaped.

Automatic slack adjusters perform the same function as the manual units (Figure 3-40), except that they automatically adjust for lining wear. Some of the benefits of the automatic slack adjusters are as follows:

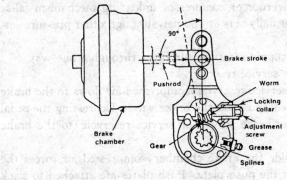

Figure 3-40 Manual slack adjuster

1. Automatic brake adjustment
2. Reduced downtime and maintenance costs
3. Improved brake balance
4. Reduced chamber travel and less air consumption
5. Reliable spring brake engagement.

One design of an automatic slack adjuster is a mechanism designed to take the brake chamber stroke and convert it to torque to turn the "S"-cam camshaft and apply the brakes, and automatically adjust the lining-to-drum clearance when the brake linings wear.

The brake drum bolts to the wheel hub between the hub and

the wheel. It completely surrounds the brake shoe assembly and comes very close to the backing plate so that water and dust will be excluded.

The primary (forward or leading) brake shoe is the shoe that faces toward the front of the car. It often has different lining than the other shoe.

The seconday (reverse of trailing) brake shoe is the shoe that faces the rear of the car.

Brake lining is generally made from asbestos fibers impregnated with special compounds which bind them together. At present, the most widely used lining is molded (asbestos fibers ground up and pressed into shape). Current developments in lining, however, incorporate the use of synthetic fibers, iron powders, steel fibers, ceramic and metallic powders, etc. For heavy-duty braking, special metallic lining, very resistant to brake fade is offered.

Most wheel brake assemblies use two brake shoes. These shoes are of stamped steel and have brake linings either riveted or bonded (glued) to the outer surface.

## Disc Brake

An air disc brake has an air chamber (as opposed to hydraulic chambers for hydraulic disc brakes) that rotates an input shaft. This rotational movement is then converted into axial movement by a power screw or helical ramps inside a caliper assembly. The axial or outward movement is then transferred to a piston or power nut, which, in turn, presses the inner lining against the rotor. Most air disc brake systems are of the sliding or floating caliper type. This means that when pressure is exerted on the inner lining it also pulls the caliper toward the piston, forcing the outer lining to contact the rotor with equal pressure.

1. **Weight and Expense**   They are usually lighter than the standard heavy-duty drum brakes. They also generally are less expensive.

2. **Maintenance**   In most cases, air disc brakes can be checked

by a lining wear indicator.

3. **Directional Stability**   Disc brakes do not depend on the servo action or wrap-up effect of the drum brake shoes to increase brake power as do drum brake systems.

4. **Improved Braking Efficiency**   The clamping effect of disc brakes generates more braking power than do drum brakes. Water and contaminants are thrown off the brake surface of the rotor, thereby increasing braking power during inclement weather.

Disc brakes provide friction by squeezing brake pads against the inside and outside edge of a rotor. The rotor is mounted inboard of the vehicle wheel and rotates with the wheel. The pads are attached on the inboard side to a piston and on the outboard side to a caliper housing.

The basic caliper used on most vehicles has the following parts, in addition to those just mentioned. There is a dust boot to keep contamination out of the piston chamber. Caliper pins or rails allow the caliper housing to slide and also attach the caliper housing to the anchor plate. Wear indicators on the outer pad and lining assembly emit a noise when the brake pads are worn. Certain rotors are cast with fins between the outer plates; these fins channel air, through the rotors to dissipate heat more rapidly.

The piston has a special seal that performs several functions. It seals pressure in the cylinder and functions as a return spring for the piston. The seal distorts to allow the piston to be pushed out to bring the pad into contact with the rotor. When air pressure is diminished, the seal functions as a return spring to retract the piston. In addition, as the disc brake pads wear, the seals allow the piston to move further out, to adjust automatically for the wear.

When air pressure is applied to the disc brakes, the piston forces the pad against the rotor surface. The air pressure also pushes the caliper housing away from the piston; this brings the outboard pad against the outer side of the rotor. The lining then grip the rotor, stopping the vehicle.

## NEW WORDS

| | | |
|---|---|---|
| caliper | ['kælipə] | n. 长箍,长钳,两脚规,制动钳 |
| pneumatic | [nju:mætik] | adj. 气动的,充空气的,装有气胎的 |
| trailer | ['treilə] | n. ;vt. 拖车,挂车;用拖车运 |
| foundation | [fəun'deiʃən] | n. 基础,基本,基本原则 |
| pad | [pæd] | n. ;vi. 缓冲器,把手柄,衬垫;走路 |
| slack | [slæk] | adj. ;n. 松驰的;间隙,空隙 |
| drain | [drein] | v. 排水,放…(水、液、油、气) |
| governor | ['gʌvənə] | n. 控制器,调节器,节速器 |
| optional | ['ɔpʃnəl] | adj. 可任意选择的,非强制的 |
| bobtail | ['bɔbteil] | adj. ;n. 截尾的,截短的;拖车头 |
| ompressor | ['ʌmpresə] | n. 压力控制器,调压器 |
| deactivate | [di:'æktiveit] | vt. 使不活动,使无效 |
| diaphragm | ['daiəfræm] | n. 隔板,隔膜 |
| significant | [sig'nifikənt] | adj. 有意义的,重大的,有效的 |
| actuate | ['æktjueit] | vt. 开动(机器),激励,驱使 |
| asbestos | [æz'bestɔs] | n. 石棉 |
| impregnate | ['impregneit] | vt. ;n. 浸透;浸渗,浸透 |
| synthetic | [sin'θetik] | adj. 合成的,人造的 |
| ceramic | [si'ræmik] | adj. ;n. 陶瓷的;陶瓷制品 |
| fade | [feid] | vi. ;n. 衰弱,消失,渐弱,调节器 |
| inclement | [in'klemənt] | adj. 险恶的,严酷的 |
| squeeze | [skwi:z] | v. 压,榨,挤 |
| housing | ['hauziŋ] | n. 套壳,遮蔽物 |
| fin | [fin] | n. 散热片,(铸件)周缘翅片 |
| ramp | [ræmp] | n. ;vt. 斜面,斜坡;使有斜面 |

## PHRASES AND EXPRESSIONS

| | |
|---|---|
| hydraulic brake system | 液力制动系统 |
| act on | 对…起作用,按照…行动 |
| brake fluid reservoir | 贮液室 |
| pull-back spring | 回位弹簧 |
| slack adjuster | 调隙机构 |

| | |
|---|---|
| relay valve | 加速阀,中继阀,继动阀 |
| supply reservoir | 贮气筒 |
| synchro valve | 分路开关(同步阀) |
| pressur protection valve | 压力安全阀 |
| low pressure indicator | 低压压力表 |
| air gauge | 气压表 |
| cam actuated brake | 凸轮驱动制动器 |
| wedge actuated brake | 楔驱动胀式制动器 |

## NOTES TO THE TEXT

1. Depressing the brake pedal creates a mechanical force that is transmitted through a pushrod to a piston in the mastor cylinder.
压踏板产生的机械力通过推杆传递到主缸的活塞上。
depressing 现在分词引导的从句做主语;that is … 引导定语从句,修饰 force.

2. The amount of air produced by the compressor depends on the level of air energy necessary to operate the air brake and air auxiliary systems.
空压机产生的空气量决定于可制动和气压辅助系统所需要的气压能量的级别。
produced 过去分词做后置定语,修饰 air;depends on 取决于,做谓语;necessary 是形容词做 energy 的宾语补足语。

3. One design of an automatic slack adjuster is a mechanism designed to take the brake chamber stroke and convert it to torque to turn the "S"-cam camshaft and apply the brakes, and automatically adjust the lining-to-drum clearence when the brake linings wear.
自动调隙机构有一种机械式的,通过转变制动气室的力矩来调节 S 型齿轮的凸轮轴位置,当磨擦衬片磨损时,来调整摩擦衬片与轮毂之间的间隙。
designed 过去分词做定语,修饰 mechanism；to take the brake … 是目的状语。

### 3.7.2 Hydraulic Brake System

The modern car uses hydraulic brakes as a stopping medium.

A special fluid (hydraulic brake fluid), confined in rubber flex hose and steel tubing lines, is used to transmit both motion and pressure from the brake pedal to the wheels.

Air confined under pressure will compress, thereby reducing its volume.

A liquid, under confinement, can be used to : transmit pressure; increase or decrease pressure; transmit motion.

Basically, the car hydraulic system consists of a master cylinder (containing piston A), rubber hose and steel tubing to form connecting lines, and one or two wheel cylinders (containing pistons B), for each wheel.

When the driver depresses the brake pedal and exerts a force on the master cylinder piston, this force is transmitted, undiminished, to each wheel cylinder. The wheel cylinder pistons transfer this force (increased or decreased, depending on piston area) to the brake shoes.

When the master cylinder piston A moves, the wheel cylinder pistons will move until the brake shoes engage the revolving brake drum. Further movement is impossible. Any attempt to depress the master cylinder piston beyond this point will transmit pressure, not motion.

Hydraulic brake fluid is used to transmit motion and pressure to the wheel cylinders and disc brake caliper pistons.

Some of the more important characteristics of a quality brake fluid are:

1. Maintains even viscosity (thickness) throughout a wide temperature variation and does not freeze at coldest possible temperature vehicle system may encounter.

2. Boiling point of the brake fluid must be above the highest operating temperature of the brake system parts.

3. Fluid should be hygroscopic (ability to absorb and retain moisture) to prevent internal freezing of parts.

4. Should act as a lubricant for pistons, seals, cups, etc., to aid in reducing internal wear and friction.

5. Fluid must not corrode the metal parts of the system. It

must not deteriorate the rubber parts.

A recent development is silicone brake fluid. It is believed that this fluid will offer extended service life and top performance under a wide range of operating conditions.

Never mix different fluids. Do not install silicone fluid in a glycol-based (standard brake fluid) system without first removing all of the old fluid.

**Master Cylinder**

The master cylinder is the central unit in which hydraulic pressure is developed. Pressure of the driver's foot on the brake pedal is transmitted, via various linkage arrangements, to the master cylinder piston. As the piston is forced forward in the cylinder, it pushes brake fluid ahead of it. Since the brake lines and wheel cylinders are filled with brake fluid, the piston is acting upon a solid column of fluid.

When the wheel cylinder pistons have pressed the brake shoes against the drums, fluid movement ceases and pressure rises according to the force on the master cylinder piston.

Figure 3-41 illustrates brake pedal linkage, master cylinder, lines, and brake assemblies. Four systems are shown in one schematic.

Most master cylinders are manufactured of cast iron or aluminum and contain brackets with holes for mounting.

Modern practice leans heavily upon fire wall mounting (metal wall between driver and engine compartment). With the master cylinder in this location, it can be inspected and serviced easily, and it is less apt to become contaminated by water and dirt. It is operated by a suspended pedal.

The master cylinder generally has an integral reservoir, or reservoirs in double-piston (dual) master cylinders, for brake fluid. This will provide additional fluid, when needed, to compensate for minute leaks, lining wear requiring more fluid movement, etc. The reservoir cover is vented (has an air hole in it) to allow expansion and contraction of the fluid without forming pressure or vacuum. A rubber diaphragm contacts the fluid and follows the level up and down. The diaphragm excludes dust, moisture, etc.

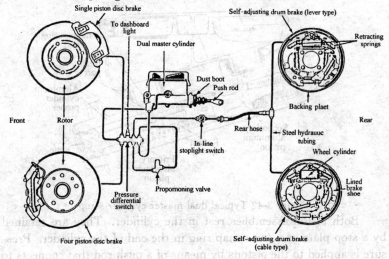

Figure 3-41 Schematic of hydraulic brake system.

A cylinder with a very smooth wall is provided in the master cylinder. This cylinder contains two aluminum pistons. The cylinder is connected to each reservoir by two ports (holes), the compensating port and intake or breather port (Figure 3-42).

Two close fitting aluminum pistons are placed in the cylinder. The inner face of the piston presses against a rubber primary cup. This cup prevents leakage past the piston. The outer piston end has a rubber secondary cup to prevent fluid from leaving the master cylinder. The inner piston head has several small bleeder ports that pass through the head to the base of the rubber primary cup.

• 303 •

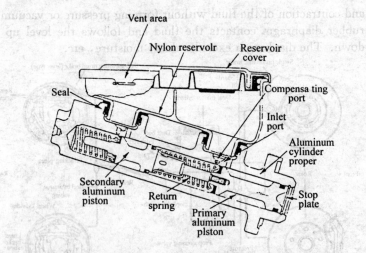

Figure 3-42 Typical dual master cylinder setup

Both piston assemblies rest in the cylinder. They are retained by a stop plate and/or a snap ring in the end of the cylinder. Pressure is applied to the pistons by means of a push rod that connects to the brake linkage.

**Retarders**

A vehicle retarder is an optional type of braking device that has been developed and successfully used over the years to supplement or assist the service brakes on heavy-duty trucks. These trucks are usually equipped with a vehicle retarder or engine brake for one or more of the following reasons:

1. **Less Wear On Service Brakes** The typical vehicle retarder starts to slow down the vehicle once the driver/operator removes his/her foot off the throttle. The vehicle retarder will then reduce the vehicle's speed without having to touch the service brakes. This leaves the service brakes cool, in good, working order, and ready for any emergency. The less the service brakes are used, the longer they will last.

2. **Less Wear on Tires**   Every application of the service brakes leaves a deposit of tire rubber on the highway. The vehicle retarder, however, will slow down the vehicle in an even, smooth process, preventing tire flat spots and wheel hop.

3. **Longer Clutch Life**   There will be less clutch slippage when using a vehicle retarder especially when attempting a high-speed downshift.

4. **Better Fuel Economy**

5. **Less Cargo Damage**   (through gradual braking)

6. **Better Straight Line Braking on Wet or Icy Roads**

7. **Safety**   A vehicle retarder coupled with efficient service brakes provides greater control over the vehicle's speed, thereby, contributing to highway safety standards.

There are basically four types of vehicle retarders in use today:
1. Hydraulic retarders
2. Electric retarders
3. Engine exhaust brakes
4. Exhaust brakes.

Hydraulic retarders are normally built into the vehicle's automatic transmission. The electric retarder, operating independently of the vehicle's engine, transmission, or exhaust system, is used to provide a drag force to the drive shaft. Engine brakes are the most popular type of vehicle retarder used on heavy-duty trucks. By releasing compression as each piston reaches the top of its compression stroke, the engine brake removes force that world have pushed the piston down. In effect, this turns the engine into a retarder. The exhaust brake depends on exhaust back pressure for its retarding power. Each type of system—description, operation and maintenance—will be discussed.

Several manufacturers offer hydraulic retarders as built-in braking devices with automatic transmissions. All hydraulic retarders operate on the same basic concept, regardless of whether they are installed in on-highway or off-highway automatic transmissions. Typically, a hydraulic retarder is mounted between the transmission torque converter and the range gear housing assembly.

There is only one moving part associated with a hydraulic retarder. This moving part is called a rotor, which rotates within a vaned stator housing. The rotor is installed as an integral part of the output shaft on the torque converter. A vaned stator housing is used to enclose the rotor. The fixed stator vanes are part of the housing casting. The use of this design affords minimal wear on the components and no service adjustments.

A foot pedal/switch or a hand valve (ordinarily used on off-highway vehicles) in the vehicle cab activates the hydraulic retarder. Operation of the control pedal/switch is very similar to the operation of an air brake pedal—the degree of braking is proportional to how far the pedal is depressed. During operation, the housing is filled with transmission oil. However, when not in use, no oil is present in the housing and does not interfere with the normal transfer of power to the driving wheels of the vehicle.

## NEW WORDS

| | | |
|---|---|---|
| medium | ['miːdjəm] | n. 媒质,媒介物,手段,工具 |
| flex | [fleks] | n. ;vt. 屈曲,折曲;屈曲(四肢) |
| hygroscopic | [ˌhaigrə'skɔpik] | adj. 吸湿的,湿度器的 |
| silicone | ['silikɔn] | n. 硅酮,聚烃硅氧 |
| bracket | ['brækit] | n. 托架,括号 |
| contaminate | [kən'tæmineit] | vt. 弄脏,污染,毒害 |
| integral | ['intigrəl] | adj. 构成整体所必要的,组成的 |
| expansion | [iks'pænʃən] | n. 张开,扩张,膨胀 |
| contraction | [kən'trækʃən] | n. 收缩,缩短,招致 |
| moisture | ['mɔistʃə] | n. 潮气,水分,湿度 |
| exclude | [iks'kluːd] | vt. 把…排除在外,排斥,逐出 |
| leakage | ['liːkidʒ] | n. 漏,漏出,泄漏,漏出物 |
| bleeder | ['bliːdə] | n. 放气装置,分压器 |
| linkage | ['linkidʒ] | n. 联系,连锁,联动 |
| retarder | [ri'taːdə] | n. 减速器,延时期 |
| optional | ['ɔpʃnəl] | adj. 可任意选择的,非强制的 |
| emergency | [i'məːdʒənsi] | n. 紧急情况,突然事件 |

| | | |
|---|---|---|
| deposit | [dɪˈpɔzɪt] | vt. ;vi. 存放,储蓄;沉淀,淤积 |
| slippage | [ˈslɪpɪdʒ] | n. (机)滑动,滑程,滑程量,动力传递 |
| description | [dɪsˈkrɪpʃən] | n. 种类,描写,描述,形容 |
| maintenance | [ˈmeɪnˈteɪnəns] | n. 保护,维修 |
| mount | [maʊnt] | vt. 安装,将…置于,放置 |

## PHRASES AND EXPRESSIONS

| | |
|---|---|
| hydraulic brake system | 液力制动系统 |
| master cylinder | 主液压缸,制动总泵 |
| cast iron | 铸铁 |
| compensate for | 补偿,赔偿 |
| by means of | 通过…方式 |
| brake shoes | 制动蹄 |
| bleeder screw | 放气螺塞 |
| couple with | 连接,接合 |

## NOTES TO THE TEXT

1. It is believed that this fluid will offer extended service life and top performance under a wide range of operating conditions.

据说,这种制动液能延长使用寿命,并能在各种工况条件下运做。

It is believed that 据说,that 引导从句做主语;在主语从句里,this fluid 做主语,will offer … and top … 做谓语,under…conditions 做状语。

2. This will provide additional fluid, when needed, to compensate for minute leaks, lining wear requiring more fluid movement.

当必要时,它将提供额外的液体,以补偿微量的泄漏,以及管路磨损所需要更多的液体移动。

when needed 过去分词做状语; to compensate for 为目的状语

3. Brake return or retracting spring are used to pull the shoes together when hydraulic pressure is released.

当液压力下降时,制动回位弹簧或压缩弹簧就用于将制动蹄回位。

retracting 为现在分词短语做定语；when 引导时间状语从句；brake return or … spring 作主语；are used 是被动语态做谓语。

4. A vehicle retarder is an optional type of braking device that has been developed and successfully used over the years to supplement or assist the service brakes on heavy-duty trucks.

汽车辅助制动器是一种可选装的制动装置，多年来已经被成功地用来增加或辅助完成重型卡车的行车制动作用。

that 引导的从句修饰 braking device，that 在从句中代替 braking。

## EXERCISES

Ⅰ. Answer the following questions according to the text：

1. What is the purpose of a master cylinder?
2. Can you explain how a master cylinder works in the released position, in the applied position, quick release, and final release positions?
3. The reservoir cover must be vented. True or False? Why must a reservoir be provided?
4. Of what use is the master cylinder check valve?
5. Wheel cylinders are generally fastened to the brake drum. True or False?
6. Of what use is flexible high pressure brake hose?
7. Why are some wheel cylinders of stepped construction?
8. How does the shape of the rubber pistons in the master cylinder and wheel cylinders help them to seal?
9. A small amount of air in the brake system is permissible. True of False?
10. Can you explain what happens in the wheel assembly when the master cylinder builds up pressure in the brake lines?

Ⅱ. Fill in the blanks with the words or expressions：

1. That part of the air brake system that converts air pressure energy into mechanical force is known as a _____.
2. A single circuit brake system supplies air pressure to the _____.

3. In an air brake system, the air dryer is installed on the _____.
4. Air compressor cyclic operation is controlled by a _____.
5. That part of the air brake system that converts linear motion into rotary motion is known as a _____.
6. A braking system that provides friction by squeezing brake pads against the inside and outside edges of a rotor is known as a _____.
7. Brake lines must be made of _____.
8. Brake lines, where connections are made, must have a _____ flare.

Ⅲ. Choose the best answer for each of the following questions:

1. Which of the following characteristics does not describe a dual circuit brake system?
   A. it has three independent braking systems that operate together.
   B. front and rear axle circuits have separate air reservoirs
   C. it has a dual brake valve
   D. it operates from a sole air service reservoir.

2. Which of the following is not truly classified as an air dryer?
   A. alcohol evaporator      B. moisture drain valves
   C. aftercooler             D. desiccant in-line filtration unit

3. Typical air dryers utilize which one of the following to trap and remove contaminants and moisture from the air system?
   A. alcohol vapors          B. desiccant material
   C. condensed air           D. check valves

4. Excessive oil and water is present in the air brake system. which of these could be the cause?
   A. excessive oil (flooding) in the compressor crankcase
   B. compressed air strainer restricted
   C. reservoirs not being drained frequently
   D. all of the above

5. Which valve prevents air backflow from the reservoir tanks in the event of a break in the air compressor line?
   A. check valve             B. tractor protection valve

  C. relay valve      D. ratio valve

  6. After starting his truck, a driver notices that the air pressure will not rise to normal. Which of these is the most likely cause?

  A. frozen glad hand coupling
  B. slipping compressor drive belt
  C. excessive condensation in the air supply line
  D. unloading mechanism stuck in the closed position

  7. What types of valves are used to prevent the back flow of compressed air through the brake system?

  A. safety      B. check
  C. operational-control    D. all of the above

Ⅳ. Fill the blank in each sentence with one of the four words of phrases which correctly completes the sentences:

  1. The check valve is completely ____ its seat by back pressure from the pipe line.

  A. left out      B. lift off
  C. sprung from     D. held onto

  2. Brake drums are the thin cylindrical members ____ cast iron, cast iron and steel; steel and chromenickel iron.

  A. made of      B. consist of
  C. made up of     D. connecting with

  3. The hydraulic pressure ____ to operate the system is produced by the master cylinder.

  A. developed     B. recirculating
  C. required      D. releasing

  4. The brake shoe return springs ____ the shoes free of the drum to compress the wheel cylinder piston.

  A. push      B. repel
  C. pull       D. reject

  5. By means of an anchor pin, the other end of the brake shoe ____ the brake backing plate.

  A. rotates with     B. separates from
  C. is related to     D. is attached to

  6. Hand brake is situated close to the gear change lever usually ____ the seats in case of cars having two bucket seats.

    A. above           B. far from
    C. between         D. within easy distance of

7. In modern cars having straight across front seats, hand brake lever is ____ the lower part of the dashboard.
    A. located on        B. used as
    C. independent of    D. known as

8. When foot pedal is depressed, the rear mechanical brakes are usually actuated ____ cable action.
    A. by     B. with     C. on     D. against

9. The transmission brake is one of the widely ____ brakes on motor vehicles.
    A. employing      B. employed
    C. demanding      D. requirement

10. For making closer contact with the drum, the shoes are ____ by turning the star wheel of the screw.
    A. moved farther apart   B. removed
    C. taken away         D. dismounted

Ⅴ. Translate the following sentence into Chinese:

1. As the brake pedal is allowed to come up, the hydraulic fluid returns to its original position, the pistons retract, and a spring attached to each brake shoe returns it also to its original position.

2. However, fading is unlikely to occur except after the brakes have been used repeatedly in slowing the car from a high speed or after braking continuously down a steep hill.

3. Moreover, when the brake pedal is depressed, very little movement of the wheel cylinder pistons and shoes is resulted by this large leverage or mechanical advantage of the system.

4. When the brake pedal is quickly released, a rough vacuum is created in the brake master cylinder which makes the fluid from the space behind the piston through the holes in it and around the piston cup into the cylinder space before the piston thus preventing ingress of the ambient air.

5. The greater is the force, the higher is the pressure of air applied to the diaphragm of the hydrovacuum unit, hence the higher is the pressure of the fluid in the wheel cylinders.

6. The system's automatic self-adjuster operates in conjunction with the actuator over the full lining thickness-maintaining correct lining-to-rotor clearance at all times.

Ⅵ. Translate the following passage into Chinese:

For parking purposes as well as during an emergency, different types of brakes operated by different means are used. In passenger cars, mechanical brakes operated by a hand or foot lever are used for the purpose. Depending upon whether these act either on the rear wheels or are attached to the transmission or to the propeller shaft, they are known as the rear wheel type parking brake or transmission or propeller shaft parking brake. In this brake system, the brake lever is usually mounted in the driver's compartment, under the instrument panel to the left. A ratchet locks in the brake lever when the brake is applied. For releasing of brakes, different methods are used. In certain designs of hand brake, lever and control finger are squeezed together while the others are released by turning the lever and pushing it down. Special release levers are used for releasing the foot pedal type brakes.

# Chapter 4　Automobile Body

## 4.1 Body Construction

An automobile body is generally divided into four sections—the front, the upper or top, rear and the underbody. These sections are further divided into small units, called assemblies, which in turn are divided into even smaller units, called parts.

The front section is composed of a number of assemblies, such as the grille, the hood, the right and left fender, and the cowl assembly.

The cowl assembly, one of the largest of all assemblies, is composed of the shroud upper panel, shroud vent panel, windshield glass support, instrument panel, front body hinge pillar to rocker panel, and the dash panel.

The roof panel is usually the largest of all body panels and is supported by the upper inner windshield frame, the front body hinge pillars, the logitudinal roof bows on its sides, and the inner back window panel at the rear. The center of the roof panel is reinforced by the roof bow.

The quarter-panel assemblies are located in the rear section of the automobile and are composed of the lower inner rear quarter panel, wheelhouse panel, and outer rear quarter side panel.

The automobile body (Figure 4-1) is divided into three distinctly separate compartments and these are serviced by the following assemblies. Doors provide easy access to the body compartment, hoods to the engine compartment, and the deck lids to the luggage compartment. They are all similar in design and construction in that each is made with an outer panel whose flanged edges are not only folded over but are also spot-welded to a box-type frame or inner construction, thus giving them a great deal of strength. All are mounted on hinges and equipped with locks for easy opening and closing.

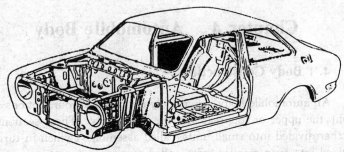

Figure 4-1 Integral body and frame construction

Rocker panels are rust-proofed assemblies of box-type construction and are composed of the outer door-opening rocker panel, the rear outer rocker panel reinforcement, and the front outer-rocker panel reinforcement. They are located directly below the doors and are not only spotwelded to the sides of the floor pans, thereby greatly reinforcing the underbody section, but also to the cowl assembly in front and the rear quarter-panel assembly at the rear.

The front and rear bumpers not only provide a certain amount of protection to the automobile but also enhance its appearance. The bumpers are held in position by means of brackets, shock absorbers or insulators that are bolted to each end of the frame side rails, commonly called frame horns.

## NEW WORDS

| | | |
|---|---|---|
| grille | [gril] | n. 格栅,格子窗,铁格子 |
| hood | [hud] | n. ;vt. 车盖,车篷;加车盖,加罩于 |
| fender | ['fendə] | n. 护板,保护栅,档泥板 |
| cowl | [kəul] | n. 外壳,盖,发动机罩 |
| panel | ['pænl] | n. 板,控制板,操纵盘 |
| shroud | [ʃraud] | n. 遮蔽物,侧板,罩 |
| vent | [vent] | n. ;vt. 通风孔,排气道;通风 |
| hinge | [hindʒ] | n. ;vt. 绞链,折叶;绞接 |
| pillar | ['pilə] | n. ;vt. 支柱,柱状物;用柱支持 |

| rocker | ['rɔkə] | n. 摇臂,摇轴,摇摆器 |
| dash | [dæʃ] | n. ;vt. 挡泥板,控制板;撞击,冲撞 |
| roof | [ruːf] | n. 车顶,机顶,顶部 |
| frame | [freim] | n. 框架,车架,构造,组织 |
| reinforce | [ˌriːin'fɔːs] | vt. ;n. 加强;加固物,钢筋 |
| distinctly | [dis'tiŋktli] | adv. 性质不同地,显然地 |
| quarter | ['kwɔːtə] | n. 弦,四分之一,四等分 |
| flange | [flændʒ] | n. 凸缘,边缘 |
| compartment | [kəm'paːtmənt] | n. 间,室,箱,舱 |
| bumper | [bʌmpə] | n. 缓冲器,保险杆 |
| enhance | [in'haːns] | vt. 提高,加强,增涨 |
| bracket | ['brækit] | n. 支架,托架,夹子,筋条 |
| insulant | ['insjuleit] | n. 绝缘材料,绝热材料 |
| rail | [reil] | n. 横杆,栏杆,铁轨 |

## PHRASES AND EXPRESSIONS

| instrument panel | 仪表板 |
| be divided into | 被分为… |
| windshield glass | 风挡玻璃 |
| dash panel | 挡泥板 |
| at the rear | 在后部 |
| wheel-house | 轮箱 |
| be composed of | 由…组成 |
| not only…but also | 不仅…而且 |

## NOTES TO THE TEXT

1. The front section is composed of a number of assemblies, such as the grille, the hood, the right and left fender, and the cowl assembly.

前部由很多组件组成,如格栅、车盖、左右护格板和外壳系统。

The front section 做主语;the grille, the hood… 由 such as 连接的短语做 a number of assemblies 的同位语。

2. They are all similar in design and construction in that each is made with an outer panel whose flanged edges are not folded over

but are also spot-welded to a box-type frame or inner construction, thus giving them a great deal of strength.

它们在设计和结构上相似,每个都制造成外部板扳合边,不仅折合且点焊成箱形框架或箱形内部结构,这样就提供了足够的强度。

这是一个主从复合句,两个定语从句 that…,whose flanged …; giving them … 现在分词短语做目的状语。

3. The automobile body is divided into three distinctly separate compartments and these are serviced by the following assemblies.

车身可分为三个直接独立的部分,而各部分又由以下装置服务。

be divided into 被分为…; distinctly 副词修饰 separate,而 separate 又做为定语修饰 compartments; following 是现在分词做定语。

## 4.2 Frame

The frame is a load-carrying beam structure consisting of two side rails, and several cross members (Figure 4-2). The frame is a base to which all main parts and units are fastened. The channel side rails and cross members are steel stampings. The cross section

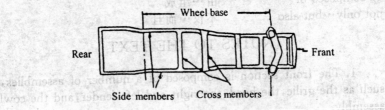

Figure 4-2　Simple frame

of the side rails varies lengthwise, the most heavily loaded middle section being thicker than the ends. The side rails and cross members are interconnected by rivets and are stiffened by gussets and angles. The frame also includes brackets for mounting the fenders, footboards, fuel tank, springs, front bumper, two hooks and a pintle hook at the rear.

The frame of an automobile provides the support for the engine, body and transmission members. The frame transmits the load through suspension system and axles to the wheels. It withstands the static and dynamic loads within permissible deflection. It should be stiff and strong to resist the severe twisting and bending forces to which it is subjected during motion of the vehicle on the road.

The frame is a fabrication of box, tubular, channel, I, angle, sections etc. The members of suitable cross section are selected and jointed either by welding or by riveting. The cross members reinforce the frame and also provide support for the engine and wheels. The frame and also provide support for the engine and wheels. The frame is up swept at the front and rear and it may be having a lower height in the centre for lowering the centre of gravity of the vehicle. The frame is made narrow at the front end to have a better steering lock. The wider frame at the rear end provides more space for body etc.

The engine is attached to the frame at three or four places. To prevent the noise and vibrations of the engine through the frame rubber pads or washers are placed in between the engine and the frame.

Some of the modern cars use the body itself as a frame (Figure 4-3) i. e. no separate frame is provided on which the body is to be placed. The lower plate of the body is a steel pressing and reinforced with suitable member. To the lower body plate, suspension system is attached which transmits the weight of the body and other components to the axles and wheels.

The frame of the vehicle is attached to the rear and front wheel and axles with the help of spring and shock absorbers. In some cases torsion bar is also used. Leaf springs and helical coil springs are generally used. Springs, torsion bar and other components necessary for jointing purposes are called the members of the suspension system.

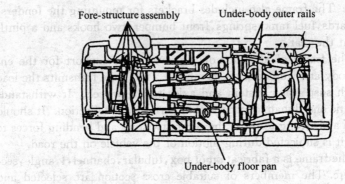

Figure 4-3 One type of unit body construction

The function of the suspension system is to absorb the road shocks and to prevent them from being transmitted to the other components of the vehicle. They protect the components from impact and dynamic load. Due to this provision, other components become safe during working and their life is increased. The occupants of the vehicle are not subjected to the jerks due to the presence of the suspension system and their journey becomes much smoother and less tiring. The suspension system maintains the stability of the vehicle during pitching or rolling while in motion.

## NEW WORDS

| beam | [biːm] | n. 梁,杆,横杆 |
| channel | ['tʃænl] | n. 槽钢,槽铁,槽,通道 |
| stamp | [stæmp] | vt. 冲压,用印模冲压 |
| lengthwise | ['leŋθwaiz] | adv. 纵长地,纵向方向 |
| interconnect | ['intə(ː)kə'nekt] | vt. 互连,互相结合 |
| rivet | ['rivit] | vt. ;n. 铆接,钉牢;铆钉 |
| stiffen | ['stifn] | vt. 粘接,使胶粘 |
| gusset | ['gʌsit] | n. 加力片,角铁,角板 |
| hook | [huk] | n. ;vt 钩,挂钩;钩住 |
| pintle | ['pintl] | n. 枢轴,针栓 |

| | | |
|---|---|---|
| withstand | [wiˈstænd] | vt. 耐心,经受住,反抗 |
| static | [ˈstætik] | adj. 静止的,静电的,平静的 |
| dynamic | [daiˈnæmik] | adj.;n. 动态的,动力的;动力,动态 |
| deflection | [diˈflekʃən] | n. 挠度,偏差,挠曲 |
| stiff | [stif] | adj. 刚性的,硬的,非弹性的 |
| severe | [siˈviə] | adj. 剧烈的,严重的 |
| subject | [ˈsʌbdʒikt] | adj. 易受…的,常遭…的 |
| fabrication | [ˌfæbriˈkeiʃən] | n. 构造,生产,制配,伪造 |
| tubular | [ˈtjuːbjulə] | adj. 管状的,有管的,管声的 |
| section | [ˈsekʃən] | n. 载面,断面,剖面 |
| pad | [pæd] | n. 衬垫,垫片,垫料 |
| washer | [ˈwɔʃə] | n. 垫圈,垫片,衬垫 |
| helical | [ˈhelikəl] | adj. 螺旋形的,螺旋的 |
| impact | [ˈimpækt] | vt. 冲击,影响,冲量,动能 |
| occupant | [ˈɔkjupənt] | n. 占有人,居住者,任职者 |

## PHRASES AND EXPRESSIONS

| | |
|---|---|
| load-carrying beam | 承载梁 |
| attach to | 与…联系在一起,系在一起 |
| cross section | 横剖面 |
| use …as | 把…用作… |
| dynamic load | 动载 |
| prevent …from doing | 阻止…做… |
| leaf springs | 钢板弹簧 |
| due …to | 归咎于,由于 |
| helical coil spring | 圆柱螺旋冷拔弹簧 |
| torsion bar | 扭力杆 |

## NOTES TO THE TEXT

1. The cross section of the side rails varies lengthwise, the most heavily loaded middle section being thicker than the ends.
　　边轨的支架部分纵向方向变化,中间的承受最重负载的部分比末端厚。
　　the most heavily loaded…than the ends 是带逻辑主语的现在

分语短语,称为独立结构做状语;the most … 是付词最高级,loaded 为过去分词做定语。

2. It should be stiff and strong to resist the severe twisting and bending forces to which it is subjected during motion of the vehicle on the road.

车架应有足够的刚度和坚固性,以克服车辆在路面上运动时所承受到的剧烈的扭转和弯曲应力。

to resist … 是由不定式引导目的状语;which it is subjected 是由 which 引导的定语从句;twisting 与 bending 是现在分词短语做定语。

3. The function of the suspension system is to absorb the road shocks and to prevent them from being transmitted to the other components of the vehicle.

悬挂系统的作用是吸收路面振动、防止振动传递到车辆其他构件上,保护这些构件不受冲击和动载的作用。

prevent…from doing 防止…做…;该句由两个并列的动词不定式短语 to absorb…和 to prevent…from…做表语。

## EXERCISES

Ⅰ. Answer the following questions according to the text:

1. What are the four sections of an automobile body?
2. What's the cowl assembly composed of?
3. What's the construction of doors and deck?
4. What's the rocker panels composed of?
5. What's the function of the front and rear bumpers?
6. What's the frame consisted of?
7. Why the middle section of the cross section of the side rails is thicker than the ends?
8. What'sthe use of the frame?
9. How to prevent the noise and vibrations of the engine?
10. Why do modern cars use frameless construction?
11. What's the function of the suspension system?

Ⅱ. Find one word from the four which matches the definition given above them:

1. framework of a vehicle without a body and finders.
   A. mounting        B. chassis
   C. driver's cabin  D. wagon
2. portion of body between engine compartment and driver, which ordinarily contains instruments used by operator.
   A. cowl    B. cab    C. carriage    D. coach
3. A connection for transmitting power from a driving to a driven shaft through an angle.
   A. clutch            B. differential
   C. universal joint   D. release mechanism
4. the pieces of apparatus fixed to the wheels of a car, motorcycle, etc., to lessen the effect of rough road surfaces.
   A. springs    B. rubber    C. washer    D. suspension
5. shaft or shafts of a vehicle upon which wheels are mounted.
   A. bolts    B. support    C. axle    D. frame
6. A strong beam, usually of iron or steel, which supports the smaller beams.
   A. bracing    B. girder    C. channel bar    D. panel
7. the force which tries to stop one surface sliding over another.
   A. fiction    B. friction    C. wear    D. resistance
8. a substance which is able to make parts that move next to each other, as in a machine, move more easily.
   A. coolant    B. sealing agent    C. lubricant    D. hydraulic oil
9. any of a group of chemicals unchanged by heat and cold, and used in making types of rubber, oil and resin
   A. silicon    B. silicone    C. carbonite    D. carbon fibre
10. causing the wearing away of a surface
   A. abrasive    B. scratch    C. brush    D. bump

Ⅲ. Choose the words or a phrase from the list for each space in the passage below:

1. in operation       2. takes place
3. is attached        4. are made form
5. is accommodated    6. instead of

7. acts as          8. so that

Leaf springs ____ flat strips of spring steel. Each strip is called a leaf. Several strips are placed one on the other. They are jointed together by clamps (rebound clips) and a central bolt. The length of each leaf decreases ____ the spring assembly ____ a flexible beam and is of uniform strength. The longest strip is called main leaf spring or master leaf spring. The ends of the master spring are formed into loops called spring eyes. One end of the spring ____ with the frame through a spring bolt passing through the spring eye. The other end is secured through a shackle.

The shackle helps in accommodating the change in length of the spring. When the wheel encounters a bump, the spring expands and increase in length ____ which is accommodated by the shackle. Similarly the reverse process of contraction ____. Bronze bushes are generally fitted into the spring eyes and through the bush, bolt passes. In some cases rubber is used ____ bushes. The rubber bushes are quiet ____ and require no lubrication.

Ⅳ. Translate the following sentence into Chinese:

1. Even though the tires and wheels must follow the road contour, the body should be influenced as little as possible.

2. In order to provide a rigid structural foundation for the car body, and to provide a solid anchorage for the suspension system, a frame of some sort is essential.

3. In the integral type frame (also called unit or unibody), the various body sections are used as structural strength members to help support and stiffen the entire unit.

4. In some cases, the rigid body has reinforced points to which the suspension system is attached; others use a partial frame, front and rear, to which the engine and suspension systems are fastened.

5. The cost of major repairs to the body of an integral chassis construction vehicle is quite high although the shock to the passengers is reduced due to absorption of collision impact by the body crumbles.

6. This system incorporates two air adjustable shock absorbers, attached to the rear suspension and connected with flexible tubing.

Ⅴ. Translate the following passage into Chinese:

Car bodies must be suspended on some type of spring devices to isolate them, as much as possible, from the irregularities of the road. The body and frame unit must be rigid and strong to provide secure anchorage for the suspension system, and also to provide positive alignment and the securing of all parts.

Some cars use separate frames, while others use the integral frame and body type of construction. Where the separate frame is used, it is constructed of steel channels and cold riveted together. It has various cross members to provide mounting and bracing points.

There are four types of springs used to suspend the car: leaf spring, coil spring, torsion bar and air spring.

Modern practice uses individual wheel suspension on the front of the car. This is accomplished by mounting the wheel assembly on the ends of pivoting control arms. Any of the four springs can be used in this system.

Common practice is still utilizing the solid rear axle housing with oil, leaf or air springs. Various combinations of control arms are used, depending on the type of drive. The individually suspended swing type rear axle is finding increased application, especially among foreign imported cars.

Hydraulic shock absorbers are used to control spring oscillation. Stabilizer bars help prevent tipping or rolling on corners. Track bars keep the body and rear axle in alignment.

# Chapter 5   Computerized Automotive-Control Systems

## 5.1 Computerized Engine-Control Systems

### 5.1.1 Electronic Fuel Injection Systems

Electronic fuel injection (EFI) has made conventional carburetors about as out of date as the Model T. A carburetor has to have several systems built into one body that include the following provisions:

1. Providing fuel and air to the engine in the proper proportions for idling
2. Some method of enriching the mixture for cold starting and running until the engine warms up
3. Providing a richer fuel mixture in the acceleration mode to avoid stumbling when the throttle is suddenly opened
4. Providing fuel and air properly mixed for steady cruising speed.

Designing a carburetor for each of these modes of operation required power valves, venturies, floats, metering jets controlled by throttle openings, choke systems, idle mixture-adjusting screws, and vacuum "kicks", along with plenty of bent-wire linkage.

All fuel systems can be broken down to three subsystems:

1. Fuel-supply system: Includes the fuel pump, lines, and filters that feed clean fuel to the fuel-metering system
2. Fuel-metering system: Includes all parts that control the correct amount of fuel entering the engine
3. Air-intake system: Includes air filters, ducts, and valves that control how much clean air enters the engine (Figure 5-1).

Electronic fuel injection, like carburetion, is a way of delivering the correct air/fuel mixture to the engine at the correct time under different operating conditions. Electronic fuel injection, however, is much simpler, more precise, and more reliable because it is controlled electronically rather than mechanically.

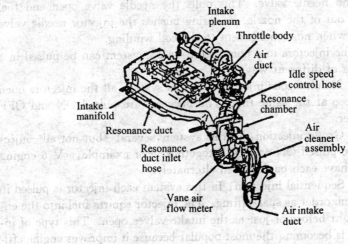

Figure 5-1 Typical air-intake system

Essentially, all EFI systems function alike, with some minor differences, such as cold start, air-flow measurement, and air-management control. All that is needed is a high-pressure electrically operated fuel pump, a fuelpressure regulator to maintain a specified line pressure, and fuel injectors each with a nozzle valve that opens and closes a small opening in its tip to permit a finely atomized fuel spray. Because fuel pressure is a constant, but fuel demand is not, the system includes a fuel-return line, which allows excess fuel to flow back through the regulator to the fuel tank. Of course, an onboard, preprogrammed microcomputer is needed to trigger injector solenoids.

There are different types of gasoline fuel injection systems used in automobiles. The two basic arrangements are port fuel injection and throttle body injection (TBI). Port fuel injection (also called multiple-point) systems use one injector per cylinder. A solenoid fuel injector uses a coil to open and close the needle alve. When energized by the computer, the coil's magnetic field attracts the armature and needle valve. This pulls the needle valve open and fuel sprays out of the nozzle. A spring pushes the injector-needle valve closed when no signal is sent to the coil winding.

The injectors in a port fuel injection system can be pulsed in a number of different ways:

1. Simultaneous injection: In this system, all the injectors open and close at the same time. The injectors are pulsed ON and OFF together.

2. Group injection: In this system, several—but not all—injectors are pulsed ON and OFF together. For example, a V-6 enging might have each bank pulsed alternately.

3. Sequential injection: In this system each injector is pulsed in the same order as spark firing. The injector squirts fuel into the engine right before or just as the intake valves open. This type of injection is becoming the most popular because it improves engine efficiency.

Fuel filters provide extremely fine filtration to protect the small metering orifices in the injector nozzles. The nozzles cannot normally be easily cleaned; if they become clogged, the injector may have to be replaced. For this reason, filter replacememt at recommended intervals is critical. Also, fuel pumps and pressure regulators are usually highly reliable factory-sealed units not meant to be adjusted or overhauled but, instead, replaced.

TBI (also called single-point injection) utilizes a central fuel-mixing feature similar to a carburetor along with an electronically controlled injector valve (Figure 5-2). Some TBI systems use only one injector (smaller engines), while two injectors are required for larger, more powerful V-6 and V-8 engines. The injector or injectors, located inside what amounts to a carburetor body, sprays the fuel, on command, into an essentially conventional intake manifold. The advantage of TBI over a conventional carburetor is the elimination of a float system, idle, acceleration, and main metering systems, and the choke assembly; these systems are replaced with accurate fuel metering through the injector(s). Just as throttle body injection improved fuel delivery compared with a carburetor, port injection improved throttle body delivery by metering fuel directly to each cylinder, reducing problems caused by intake manifold shape.

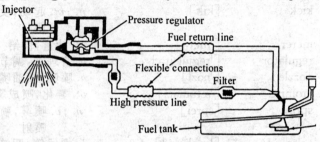

Figure 5-2 Throttle body fuel injection

The injector on-time or pulse width, is the length of time (measured in milliseconds) that the injector sprays fuel or stays open. The on-time of an injector is determined by the microcomputer. A microcomputer receives electrical signals from sensors that monitor different operating conditions. It evaluates the sensor information and, based on this, signals the fuel injectors, thereby controlling their ON and OFF pulses. On-time of an injector is increased when the engine is cold, during acceleration, and under load and wide-open throttle. During idle speed and steady throttle (cruise) with a warm engine, on-time is reduced.

## NEW WORDS

provision   [prə'viʒən]      n. 供应,防备,规定
stumble     ['stʌmbl]        vi. ;n. 迟疑,滞后;错误
throttle    ['θrɔtl]         vt. ;n. 压制,节流;节流阀,节气门
venture     ['ventʃə]        n. ;vt. 冒险,投机;冒…的

| | | |
|---|---|---|
| | | 危险,敢于 |
| choke | [tʃəuk] | n. 节气门,节流口,挡板 |
| vacuum | ['vækjum] | n. ;adj. 真空,真空装置;真空的 |
| essentially | [i'senʃəli] | adv. 本质上,基本上 |
| kick | [kik] | n. ;vt. 起动,反冲,后座力;踢 |
| meter | ['mi:tə] | vt. 计量,供给 |
| regulator | ['regjuleitə] | n. 管理者,调节器,稳定器 |
| nozzle | ['nɔzl] | n. 喷嘴,喷油嘴 |
| atomize | ['ætəmaiz] | vt. 雾化,喷成雾状 |
| spray | [sprei] | n. ;v. 喷雾,喷嘴,喷雾器;喷射 |
| solenoid | ['səulinɔid] | n. 螺线管,圆筒形线圈 |
| microcomputer | ['maikrəukəm'pju:tə] | n. 微型电子计算机 |
| armature | ['a:mətjuə] | n. 盔甲,电枢,衔铁 |
| simultaneous | [ˌsiməl'teinjəs] | adj. 同时的,一齐的,同时发生的 |
| alternately | [ɔ:l'tə:nitli] | adv. 交替地,轮流地 |
| sequential | [si'kwenʃəl] | adj. 连续的,有顺序的 |
| filtration | [fil'treiʃən] | n. 过滤,可滤性 |

## PHRASES AND EXPRESSIONS

| | |
|---|---|
| fuel-metering system | 燃料计量供给系统 |
| the same…as | 与…相同 |
| squirt…into… | 将…喷射入… |
| simultaneous injection | 同时喷射 |
| sequential injection | 顺序喷射 |
| electronic fuel injection | 电子燃油喷射 |
| multiple-point injection | 多点喷射 |
| fuel filter | 燃料滤清器 |
| single-point injection | 单点喷射 |
| main metering system | 主供油系统 |
| pulse width | 脉宽 |

throttle body injection　　　节流阀体燃油喷射

## NOTES TO THE TEXT

1. Electronic fuel injection, like carburetor, is a way of delivering the correct air/fuel mixture to the engine at the correct time under different operating conditions.

电子燃油喷射与化油器一样,是一种可以在不同的工况下供给发动机合适的混合气的方式。

like carburetor 做状语；delivering the …engine 现在分词短语做 of 的宾语,与 of 一起构成介词短语,修饰 way,做 way 的定语。

2. Because fuel pressure is a constant, but fuel demand is not, the system includes a fuel-return line, which allows excess fuel to flow back through the regulator to the fuel tank.

因为油压是恒定的,但是所需的油压并不如此,所以该系统有一个回流管允许过多的油通过调节器由油管流回油箱。

which allows excess…to the fuel tank 做非限制性定语从句,修饰 line；allow…to…允许…做…；to flow… 不定式短语做宾语补足语。

3. Fuel filters provide extremely fine filtration to protect the small metering orifices in the injector nozzles.

燃油滤清器可以防止小的物体进入喷嘴以免发生堵塞。

to protect the …nozzles 动词不定式短语做目的状语。

### 5.1.2 Computerized Ignition

Some vehicles are equipped with a computer that controls specific ignition system functions. Computerized systems often contain many of the same components found in electronic ignition systems. The fundamental difference between electronic ignition and computerized ignition is the way that each system advances the ignition timing. Electronic ignition systems use traditional centrifugal and vacuum advance systems. Computerized systems use sensors to monitor various operating conditions. The computer constantly adjusts the timing in response to these conditions. Many computerized ignition systems have selfdiagnostic capabilities.

**Electronic Engine Control**

Electronic ignitions have undergone periodic change and improvement since their introduction and now operate as part of an electronic engine-control system. All the functions that used to be done mechanically can now be done through electronics. Centrifugal and vacuum-advance mechanisms in the distributor have been eliminated, and ignition timing is controlled by the engine computer.

Figure 5-3 shows an overview of a Ford Thick-Film Integrated-IV (TFI-IV)ignition, which was introduced in 1983. A TFI-IV ignition module is attached to the distributor and operates to turn the primary ignition circuit ON and OFF. The distribut contains a profile ignition pickup (PIP)sensor(Hall-effect switch), which generates a signal that indicates the crankshaft position and speed (base timing).

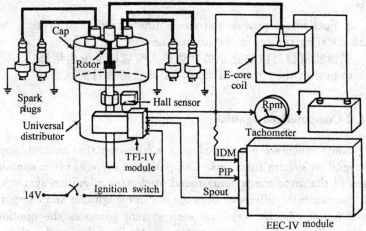

Figure 5-3    TFI-IV Computer Controlled Ignition System

The electronic control/computer assembly (ECA) receives the

PIP signal by way of the TFI-IV ignition module. The PIP signal is one of many inputs processed by the computer. The computer, after taking into account all the input sensor information, produces a new signal called the spark output (SPOUT) signal. SPOUT is a digital signal that represents the engine operating condition electronically. The SPOUT signal is sent to the TFI-IV ignition module and used by the module to turn the ignition coil ON and OFF. If the SPOUT signal fails to arrive at the TFI-IV ignition module, the module operates the ignition from the PIP signal that equates to base timing. No centrifugal or vacuum-advance mechanisms are used and all adjustments of timing and dwell are accomplished electronically. The IDM (ignition diagnostic monitor) signal generated by the ignition module tells the computer the ignition coil has fired and is used to operate the vehicle tachometer.

Figure 5-4 shows a crankshaft-triggered computer-controlled ignition system. The distributor is used only to switch the high

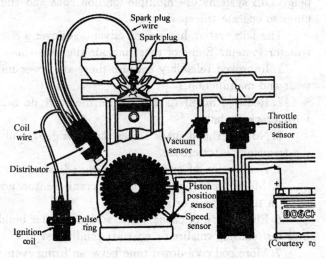

Figure 5-4  Crankshaft-triggered computer-controlled ignition system

· 331 ·

voltage to each spark plug wire and does not contain a pickup unit. Instead, a magnetic pulse generator reads engine speed from the flywheel teeth or pulse ring, transmitting one pulse per tooth. In addition, a second magnetic pulse generator is necessary to read the crankshaft position. The reference mark sensor is like the speed sensor except that it is triggered when a pin or a bore passes the sensor. Play in the timing chain and distributor drive gear is eliminated as a problem that could upset ignition timing. This results in more precise control of ignition timing.

### Distributorless Ignition Systems

Distributorless ignition system (DIS) refers to any ignition system that does not use a distributor. Most distributor ignition systems use a single ignition coil and a rotary switch (distributor) turned by the camshaft to distribute the high voltage to each spark plug. DIS systems use multiple ignition coils and the engine computer to operate the spark plugs.

The DIS system has several advantages over a conventional distributor system. Some of these include the following:

1. Improved reliability because there are fewer moving parts to wear and malfunction.

2. Reduced maintenance because there are no cap and rotor to burn, crack, or fail.

3. No underhood spark across the rotor gap, resulting in less radio-frequency interference.

4. Elimination of mechanical timing adjustments.

5. More precise spark control (crank sensor not affected by slack in timing chain or gears).

6. Elimination of ozone/nitric acid and water buildup in distributor cap, causing misfire or no-start conditions.

7. More coil cool-down time between firing events.

8. Improved packaging and mounting flexibility because DIS uses less space.

A distributorless ignition system uses an all-electronic system to replace the distributor as a means of switching ignition voltage from one spark plug to another. They all operate on the same basic principle—that is, elimination of the distributor. One style even eliminates the spark plug wires. Figure 5-5 shows the ignition components for one example of distributorless ignition called integrated direct ignition, or IDI. Under the protective cover are the coil pack and the ignition-control module. Note that this system does not use spark plug wires. Instead, the ignition coils and spark plugs connect through a small coil sparing conductor and are insulated by very heavy boots.

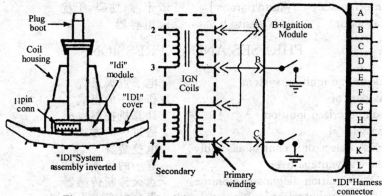

Figure 5-5 Integrated direct ignition (IDI) system

In Saab's direct ignition (DI) system, each spark plug has its own small, high-output coil built into the spark plug cap. The system is a capacitive dischargetype direct ignition system. It stores 400 V in capacitor, which then releases the voltage to the ignition coils, where it is stepped up to a full 40 000 V.

## NEW WORDS

| computerize | [kəm'pju:təraiz] | vt. 用电子计算机计算 |
| ignition | [ig'niʃən] | n. 点火,发火,发火装置 |
| module | ['mɔdju:l] | n. 模数,微型组件 |

| | | |
|---|---|---|
| diagnostic | [ˌdaiəg'nɔstik] | adj. ;n. 诊断的;特征,症状 |
| monitor | ['mɔnitə] | n. 传感器,监控器 |
| periodic | [ˌpiəri'ɔdik] | adj. 间歇的,周期的 |
| eliminate | [i'limineit] | vt. 排除,清除 |
| distributor | [dis'tribjuːt] | vt. ;n. 分发,把…分类,区分;分电器 |
| rotary | ['rəutəri] | adj. ;n. 旋转的;旋转运行的机器 |
| multiple | ['mʌltipl] | adj. ;n. 复合的;并联,多路系统 |
| interference | [ˌintə'fiərəns] | n. 干涉,妨碍,干扰 |
| capacitor | [kə'pæsitə] | n. 电容器 |

## PHRASES AND EXPRESSIONS

| | |
|---|---|
| electronic ignition system | 电子点火系统 |
| as part of | 作为…的组成 |
| computerized ignition | 计算机控制点火 |
| by way of | 通过…的方式 |
| ECA (electronic control assembly) | 电控装置 |
| have advantage over | 有…的优点 |
| IDM (ignition diagnostic monitor) | 点火诊断传感器 |
| DIS (distributorless ignition system) | 无分电盘点火系统 |

## NOTES TO THE TEXT

1. The fundamental difference between electronic ignition and computerized ignition is the way that each system advances the ignition timing.

电子控制的点火系统与电脑控制的点火系统的区别主要是点火提前方式不同。

that 引导的定语从句修饰 the way;difference 做主语;between electronic…ignition 介词短语做定语。

2. The computer, after taking into account all the input sensor information, produces a new signal called the spark output signal.

电脑接收由各传感器传来的信号经过分析计算产生一种新的

信号叫火花输出信号,它是一种描述发动机各种工况的数字信号。

　　after taking into account…information 是由连词 after 加上现在分词一起做时间状语;called the spark output signal 是过去分词短语修饰 signal,做定语。

　　3. Under the protective cover are the coil pack and the ignition-control module.

　　在保护罩下是线圈部件和点火控制模块。

　　under the protective cover 介词短语做表语;整个句子是倒装语句,the coil pack and the ignition-control module 是真正的主语。

## 5.1.3. Electronically Controlled Emission Systems

**Catalytic Converter**

　　The catalytic converter is the single most effective device for controlling exhaust emissions. A catalyst is a substance or material that causes a chemical reaction or change in another substance or material without a change in itself. The catalytic converter is a muffler-shaped device placed downstream in the exhaust system. Essentially, the catalyst agents in the converter reduce the concentration of undesirable exhaust gases coming out of the tail pipe relative to engine-out gases (the gases coming out of the exhaust manifold).

　　There have been different types of catalytic converters used on automobiles. The three-way catalytic converter is the one most often used for modern emission-control systems. It is called three-way because it simultaneously reduces the concentration of all three major undesirable exhaust gases (HC, CO, NOx) by about 90%. The conversion efficiency of the three-way catalytic converter depends mostly upon air/fuel ratio. A computerized converter depends mostly upon air/fuel ratio. A computerized engine-control system controls the exhaust emission by modifying fuel delivery to achieve, as nearly as possible, an air/fuel ratio of 14.7 to 1. This allows the three-way catalytic converter to operate at peak efficiency (Figure 5-6)

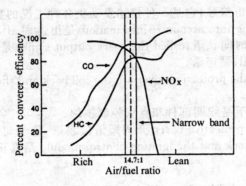

Figure 5-6 Efficiency chart for a three-way converter

A computer-controlled catalytic converter system uses the engine computer to operate its air injection system. The addition of air into the exhaust manifold helps the catalytic converter burn engine exhaust pollutants. The air injection system uses a belt-driven air pump, control valves, and connecting lines to force outside air into the catalytic converter or the exhaust manifold. The extra oxygen in the air promotes burning or oxidation or HC and CO in the exhaust system.

In a typical computerized air management control system. The reduction of exhaust emissions is aided by supply air to either the catalytic converter, engine exhaust manifold, or air cleaner. The air is directed to these different points by control valves on command from the computer (ECM) as required. The introduction of air into the exhaust manifold during the closed-loop mode would yield false signals to the oxygen sensor. At the same time, the addition of air into the exhaust manifold is of benefit in heating up the exhaust system, oxygen sensor, and catalyst during warm-up (open loop). Therefore, during start-up, air is directed to the air cleaner. After initial start-up, while the system is in the open-loop mode, air is directed to the exhaust manifold. After warm-up, when the system is in the closed-loop mode, air is directed to the converter.

## Exhaust Gas Recirculation (EGR)

Another subsystem of the emission-control system is the exhaust gas recirculation (EGR) system. Research has found that $NO_x$ is formed any time that engine combustion temperatures reach approximately 2 140°F; however, it is not produced in excessive amounts until combustion temperatures are at 2 500°F or above. The EGR system controls the production of $NO_x$ by diluting the air/fuel mixture with small amounts of inert exhaust gases, which do not burn. By diluting the mixture, peak combustion temperatures are reduced, reducing the amount of $NO_x$ formed during combustion.

The EGR system can be electronically controlled by a computer according to different engine operating conditions. At idle, where combustion temperatures and fuel consumption are low, the EGR is not allowed to dilute the fuel mixture. At wide-open throttle or when the demand on the engine is high (high loads), maximum power is desirable, so EGR is again turned OFF. Since the EGR is a temperature-related function, the absence of EGR will increase peak combustion-chamber temperatures and may cause costly engine damage.

A typical computer-controlled EGR system is illustrated in (Figure 5-7). This system directs burned exhaust gases back into the engine intake manifold. It uses the engine computer to control the opening and closing of the EGR valve. The EGR valve is vacuum-operated pintle-type common to most EGR systems. The pressure feedback sensor (electronic feedback EGR) is a ceramic capacitivetype that converts exhaust system pressure or vacuum into an analog electrical input signal to the computer (ECC-1V module).

The electronic vacuum regulator (EVR) is an electrically operated valve used to control the amount of vacuum applied to the EGR valve diaphragm. The computer monitors the pintle position of the EGR valve and varies the amount of exhaust gas recirculation according to engine operating conditions. Control of the amount of exhaust gas recirculation by the computer is accomplished with the EGR vacuum regulator. This device applies or bleeds off vacuum according to commands received from the computer.

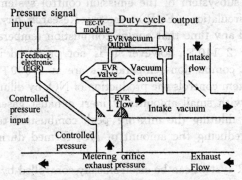

Figure 5-7 Typical computer-controlled EGR system

Small, hand-held vacuum pumps can be used to provide correct diagnosis of and to solve problems in vacuum-control devices. Most consist of a simple hand pump for producing vacuum and a gauge for measuring vacuum. The pump creates the proper vacuum on the device to be tested, allowing most to be tested without removal of the part form the vehicle.

**Engine Boost Control**

The power developed by an engine is largely dependent on the amount of air and fuel put into each cylinder. While putting more fuel in is a fairly simple matter, putting more air in is more difficult. The amount of air that can be put into the cylinder is normally limited by atmospheric pressure. Bends and restrictions throughout the air-intake system limit the amount of air that actually reaches the cylinder. This means the engine is not drawing in the full amount of air that it is capable of drawing in. The mixture of air and fuel is often called an air/fuel charge. Without external help, an engine receives only a partial air/fuel charge. An effective solution is to pump air into the engine, giving it a supercharge. By forcing more air into the cylinders, an engine can burn more fuel and produce more power.

A comparison of the amount of air that an engine could draw in to the amount that it actually draws in under normal operating conditions is called volumetric efficiency. The power output of an engine is directly linked to its volumetric efficiency. Most naturally aspirated engines (those that rely on atmospheric pressure to fill the cylinder) fill the cylinder only to about 85% volumetric efficiency. By pumping air through the intake system, volumetric efficiency can be increased. This method of pumping air into an engine is called supercharging. There are two different devices used for supercharging an engine: a turbocharger and a supercharger. The difference between the two is the power source that drives them.

A turbocharger is basically an air pump driven by otherwise-wasted heat energy in the exhaust system. When the exhaust gas is introduced in the turbine housing, it strikes the turbine wheel blades, turning the turbine wheel (Figure 5-8). Since the compressor wheel is connected directly to the turbine wheel by a shaft, the compressor wheel turns along with the turbine wheel. Clean air from the air cleaner is drawn into the compressor housing, where it is compressed by the compressor wheel blades and delivered to the intake manifolds.

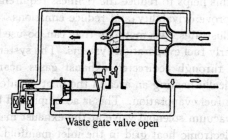

Figure 5-8 Waste gate control of boost pressure

As the engine speed rises, the amount of exhaust gas entering the turbine housing also increases, causing the speed of the turbine and turbocharging pressure (boost pressure) to rise. As the turbocharging pressure rises and the pressure acting upon the diaphragm chamber of the actuator rises above 8.89 lb/in$^2$. (0.63kg/cm$^2$), the waste gate valve is pulled open by the actuator, and part of the exhaust gas is diverted from the turbine wheel. This suppresses the turbine speed within an appropriate range and prevents the turbocharging pressure from overrising and causing possible engine damage.

The engine computer also controls the turbocharging pressure. On command from the computer, a vacuum switching valve (VSV) turns ON and OFF, according to engine conditions, to change the turbocharging pressure.

The only difference between a turbocharged and a supercharged engine is in the method used to drive the compressor. In a supercharged engine, the supercharger is driven mechanically by the engine instead of by exhaust gases.

**Early Fuel Evaporation**

Early fuel evaporation (EFE) systems apply heat to the area just beneath the throttle valves to prevent throttle blade icing and to enhance fuel evaporation during engine warm-up. During the warm-up period, this helps to reduce the richness requirement of the air/fuel ratio, improve drivability, and reduce emissions.

Figure 5-9 illustrates two methods that can be used for computer control of early fuel evaporation systems. The system provides a means — either through redirected exhaust gases near the inlet manifold of electrically heating an area in the inlet manifold — of enhancing cold-start fuel evaporation. This is accomplished by an electrically operated vacuum solenoid valve at the exhaust manifold or a relay controlled electronic heat grid in the inlet manifold. Both options are computer-controlled. The EFE solenoid/relay is energized when both coolant-temperature and engine-load criteria are met. These criteria are established to energize the system only when the engine is at low-load or low-temperature conditions.

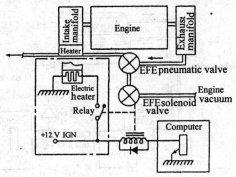

Figure 5-9  Typical computer-controlled EFE system

**Evaporative Emission Control**

An evaporative emission-control system is used on cars to reduce fuel vapors that would normally escape into the atmosphere. To reduce these HC emissions, a canister filled with active charcoal absorbs the fuel vapors when the engine is not running. When the vehicle is running, captured fuel vapors are purged (using engine vacuum) from the canister into the engine and consumed during the combustion process.

On computer-controlled engine canisters, the purge is activated after the engine has warmed up and gone into closed loop. In the closed-loop mode, any additional fuel from the canister can be compensated for, still maintaining a 14.7 to 1 air/fuel ratio.

Figure 5-10 shows the block diagram of a typical computer-controlled canister-purge system. Fuel vapors are collected from the fuel tank, throttle body fuel injection system (TBI), or carburetor fuel bowl during periods when the engine is OFF. When the vehicle is in closed-loop mode, a command from the computer opens the valve in the purge line that connects the canister to the manifold vacuum. This allows delivery of the rich mixture to the inlet manifold for closed-loop compensation at the catalytic converter.

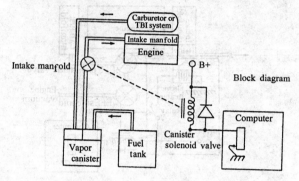

Figure 5-10　Typical computer-controlled canister-purge system

# NEW WORDS

| | | |
|---|---|---|
| substance | ['sʌbstəns] | n. 物质,本质,主旨,实体 |
| muffler | ['mʌflə] | n. 消声器 |
| concentration | [ˌkɔnsen'treiʃən] | n. 集中,浓缩 |
| downstream | ['daunstriːm] | adj.;adv. 顺流的;顺流地 |
| manifold | ['mænifəuld] | adj.;n. 多样的;歧管,复式接头 |
| promote | [prə'məut] | v. 促进,引起,发起 |
| undesirable | ['ʌndi'zaiərəbl] | adj. 不希望的,不合需要的 |
| initial | [i'niʃəl] | adj.;vt. 最终的;标注,草签 |
| dilute | [dai'ljuːt] | vt.;adj. 冲淡,稀释;淡的 |
| ceramic | [si'ræmik] | adj.;n. 陶瓷的;陶瓷制品 |
| analog | ['ænəlɔg] | n. 类似物,同源语 |
| pintle | ['pintl] | n. 枢轴,针栓 |
| boost | [buːst] | n.;vt. 增加,加速器;提高,升压 |
| restriction | [ris'trikʃən] | n. 限制,约束 |
| volumetric | [ˌvɔlju'metrik] | adj. 测容量的,容积的 |
| chamber | ['tʃeimbə] | n.;vt. 房间,腔;装,充入 |
| actuator | ['æktjueitə] | n. 调节器,传动机构 |
| appropriate | [ə'prəupriit] | adj.;vt. 适当的;占用,拨出 |

## PHRASES AND EXPRESSIONS

| | |
|---|---|
| catalytic converter | 催化转化器 |
| exhaust system | 排放系统 |
| EGR (exhaust gas recirculation) | 废气再循环 |
| three-way catalytic converter | 三元催化转化器 |
| air/fuel ratio | 空燃比 |
| oxygen sensor | 氧传感器 |
| open (close)-loop | 开(闭)环 |
| emission-control system | 排放控制系统 |
| EVR (electronic vacuum regulator) | 电控真空调解器 |
| boost control | 增压控制 |

## NOTES TO THE TEXT

1. A catalyst is a substance or material that causes a chemical reaction or change in another substance or material without a change in itself.

催化剂是一种可以引起其它物质发生化学反应而自身不发生变化的物质。

that 引导定语从句,修饰 material (substance); A catalyst is a substance or material 是主句。

2. This system directs burned exhaust gases back into the engine intake manifold.

(电控进气)系统将燃烧的废气排到发动机进气歧管。

burned 是 burn 的过去分词,在此做定语,修饰 gases。

3. While putting more fuel in is a fairly simple matter, putting more air in is more difficult.

虽然充进油是一件很容易的事,但充入空气却困难得多。

while 引导让步状语从句,在此处的意思是"虽然,尽管"; putting more air 是动名词短语做主语;more difficult 是形容词的比较级。

**5.1.4 Idle-Speed Control**

The basic purpose of the idle-speed control is to provide control during all periods of closed-throttle operation. Controlling idle RPM by means of the engine computer has the following advantages:
1. Reduces the occurrence of engine idle-stall
2. Permits substantially lower idle speeds, which saves fuel and reduces emissions while the car is idling in traffic or at stop lights
3. Reduces creep and load on automatic transmissions
4. Reduces drops in speed that occur when loads such as power-assisted steering, putting the automatic transmission in drive, or switching on the air conditioner occur.

With precise computer control, idle speeds are smoother and lower than ever before. Virtually all electronic fuel injection systems require some form of idle-speed control. The two methods used are: air metered around the throttle plates and air metered through and by the throttle plates. In both methods, the computer relies on inputs from various sensors such as RPM, temperature, air conditioning switch, and power steering switch to control idle speed.

Again, different idle-speed control systems are used by different manufacturers. One system uses a small, reversible DC electric motor that attaches to the side of the carburetor and changes the throttle opening by acting as a movable idle stop. The computer sends commands to the ISC motor to maintain the idle speed required for the particular operating condition sensed. A throttle switch is a part of the ISC motor. Position of the switch (open or closed) determines whether the ISC or the driver controls engine speed.

Engine idle speed may also be controlled by means of an idle air control valve. This system functions by controlling additional air around the throttle plate. Figure 5-11 shows a typical idle air bypass control unit. The engine computer monitors different vehicle operating parameters and outputs a signal to drive the air bypass actuator/stepper motor mechanism mounted on the throttle body. By extending and retracting the actuator pintle, a proportional amount of air is diverted around the throttle plate. If engine speed is lower than desired, more air is diverted around the throttle plate (motor retracting). If engine speed is higher than desired, less air is diverted (motor extending). When the engine is cold, idle speed is increased, much as with a standard carburetor choke. As the engine warms, idle speed is reduced. In order to be able to provide the required cooling power of the air conditioner, it may be necessary to increase idle speed. It is also often necessary to reduce the idle speed when drive is engaged in vehicles with an automatic transmission.

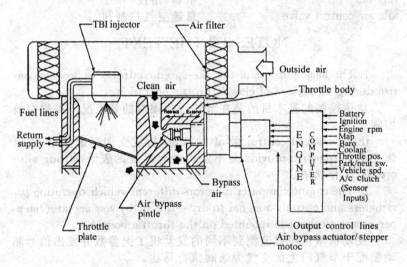

Figure 5-11  Typical idle air bypass control unit

## NEW WORDS

| | | |
|---|---|---|
| occurrence | [əˈkʌrəns] | n. 发生, 出现, 存在 |
| substantilly | [səbˈstænʃəli] | adv. 物质地, 实质, 大量地 |
| parameter | [pəˈræmitə] | n. 参数, 参词, 参量 |
| creep | [kri:p] | n. 滞缓, 位移, 蠕动 |
| occur | [əˈkə:] | vi. 发生, 出现 |

| retract | [ri'trækt] | vt;vi. 缩回;收回,撤消 |
| extend  | [iks'tend] | vt. 伸,伸出 |
| choke   | [tʃəuk]    | vt. ;vi. ;n. 阻塞;窒息,阻塞气门;阻气门 |

## PHRASES AND EXPRESSIONS

| power-assisted steering | 助力转向 |
| idle speed | 急速转速 |
| rely on | 依靠,信任 |
| idle air control valve | 急速空气控制阀 |

## NOTES TO THE TEXT

1. The basic purpose of the idle-speed control is to provide control during all periods of closed-throttle operation.

急速控制的基本目的是在节气门关闭时的各工况下提供有效控制。

the idle-speed control 做 of 的宾语,构成介词短语做定语,修饰主语 purpose;to provide 是不定式短语做 is 的表语;during all… operation 作状语。

2. The engine computer monitors different vehicle operating parameters and outputs a signal to drive the air bypass actuator/stepper motor mechanism mounted on the throttle body.

发动机微机可以监测到不同的发动机工况参数并发出信号驱动装配于节气门上的空气旁通阀执行马达。

to drive… 做目的状语;actuator/stepper motor 做 drive 的宾语;mounted on the throttle body 过去分词短语做定语。

### 5.1.5 Electronically Controlled Transmissions

Many automobiles equipped with automatic transmission use an electronically controlled torque converter clutch (TCC), or lockup clutch. The purpose of the torque converter clutch is to improve fuel mileage by eliminating the power loss in the torque converter stage when the engine is at cruise speed. This allows the automobile to have the normal convenience of an automatic transmission and the fuel economy of a manual transmission. The engine computer sends out a command to energize a solenoid inside the automatic transmission, which causes the hydraulic pressure to apply the torque converter clutch once cruise speed has been reached. The result is a straight-through mechanical coupling from the engine to the transmission output.

The transmission and engine can be electronically controlled as a unit in response to the driver's demand for more power. Precise computer control of the power train is illustrated in Figure 5-12 Sensors are used to keep track of transmission and engine speeds as well as engine loading. Gear-shift programs can be selected by the operator for economy, performance, or manual shifting. On the basis of all these items of information, the electronic control unit selects the most appropriate gear for the conditions at hand. The control signals from the electronic circuitry are converted into hydraulic control variables by an electrogydraulic control unit mounted directly on the automatic transmission. This type of control improves fuel economy, provides smooth shifts, and increases a given transmission's torque capacity as well as its life expectancy.

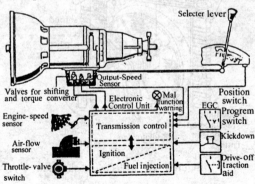

Figure 5-12   Electronic transmission control

## Electric Engine-cooling Fans

Electric engine-cooling fans are used on all transversely and some longitudinally mounted engines. Small, permanent-magnet, high-torque motors are used for this application. They are able to move large amounts of air independent of engine speed. Conventional electric cooling fan circuits incorporate a relay and engine-coolant temperature switch. Figure 5-13 shows a typical electric engine-cooling fan circuit for a vehicle equipped with air conditioning. When engine coolant temperature increases above 230°F or 100°C, the cooling fan switch closes to energize the relay coil and switch the cooling fan motor ON. The coil is also energized to switch the cooling fan motor ON any time the air conditioning unit is turned ON. On some vehicles the temperature-switch circuit is hot at all times, allowing the fan to continue to cool the engine compartment and the radiator coolant even if the ignition switch is OFF. For this reason, you should always disconnect the fan motor when working under the hood near it in case it comes on without warning.

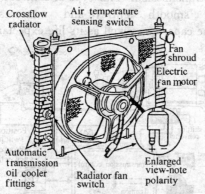

Figure 5-13   Electric cooling fan

Cooling fan motors are also controlled by on-board computer-based electronic control modules. A temperature sensor provides the input information used by the computer to determine the exact coolant temperature. Based on this information and other instructions programmed into it, the computer outputs a signal that switches the fan circuit ON and OFF.

One advantage of this type of control circuit is that the computer may be programmed to turn the fan OFF automatically when the car is traveling at speeds above approximately 35 mi/h. This puts less load on the alternator. The fan is not normally needed when the car travels at road speeds because of forced air flowing across the radiator.

## NEW WORDS

| | | |
|---|---|---|
| transmission | [trænz'miʃən] | n. ;vt. 变速厢,传动装置;传导,传动 |
| lockup | ['lɔkʌp] | n. 锁,闭,锁住 |
| mileage | ['mailidʒ] | n. 哩数,哩程 |
| convenience | [kən'vi:njəns] | n. 便利,方便 |
| hydraulic | [hai'drɔ:lik] | adj. 水力的,液力的 |
| coupling | ['kʌpliŋ] | n. 偶合器,联轴节 |
| illustrate | ['iləstreit] | vt. 用图说明,图解 |
| loading | ['ləudiŋ] | n. 载荷,载重 |
| operator | ['ɔpəreitə] | n. 驾驶员,操作者 |
| appropriate | [ə'prəupriit] | adj. 恰当的,合宜的 |
| mount | [maunt] | v. 设置,安放,制作 |
| defrost | [di'frɔst] | vt. ;vi. 除去…的冰霜;解冻 |
| resistor | [ri'zistə] | n. 电阻器,电阻 |
| alternator | ['ɔltə(:)neitə] | n. 交流发电机 |

## PHRASES AND EXPRESSIONS

| | |
|---|---|
| torque convertor | 液力变矩器 |
| send out | 发出,发送 |
| in response to | 响应,反应 |
| keep track of | 保持接触或联系 |
| on the basis of | 基于,根据,以……为基础 |

at hand 近处,当前,即将到来
in most cases 在大多数情况
instead of 代替,而不是

## NOTES TO THE TEXT

1. The purpose of the torque converter clutch is to improve fuel mileage by eliminating the power loss in the torque converter stage when the engine is at cruise speed.

扭转变矩器的目的是通过消除当车辆在稳定的巡游车速的扭矩变换器内的能量损失来改善燃油经济性。

整个句的主语是 purpose;of 构成的介词短语做定语修饰主语;by 是介词短语做方式状语用于修饰 improve;when 引导的是时间状语。

2. The transmission and engine can be electronically controlled as a unit in response to the driver's demand for more power.

变速器与发动机可由电脑控制,做为响应满足驾驶员对更多动力的需求的元件。

谓语 can be controlled 是被动语态;in response to 介词短语做定语,修饰 unit。

3. A temperature sensor provides the input information used by the computer to determine the exact coolant temperature.

温度传感器把输入信号传送给电脑,电脑决定准确的冷却温度。

used by… 动词过去分词短语做定语,修饰 information;to determine…temperature 是动词不定式短语做补语

### 5.1.6 System Diagnosis And Service

With computerized engine-control systems, a service manual that applies specifically to the vehicle being serviced is a must. Such a manual will provide you with accurate information on the following:

1. Location of engine and emission-control parts
2. System wiring and block diagrams

3. Description of the various components
4. Operation of the various subsystems for fuel, spark, and emission control
5. Safety precautions and recommended service procedures
6. Specifications for sensors and actuators
7. Accessing of self-diagnosis codes
8. Interpretation of diagnostic trouble codes
9. Tools and instruments necessary for diagnosis and repair.

Almost every automobile manufacturer uses some type of assembly line communication link (ALCL) or assembly line data link (ALDL) to test the system's operation as it leaves the assembly line. Special automotive diagnostic scanners are available for accessing information from computerized vehicles through connections to this serial data link. Information on inputs and outputs to the computer, such as fault codes, coolant temperature, RPM, timing retard/advance, vacuum, manifold absolute pressure, and oxygen sensor output can be retrieved using these devices. This information can be displayed on a screen, shown as a digital readout, or printed on a piece of paper and used for troubleshooting the system.

A diagnostic breakout box (Figure 5-14) can be connected to provide an easy way to access all electrical circuit connections to the engine computer. When used with a digital multimeter, resistance and voltage measurements are easily accessible from all circuits of the computer through the remotely located box. The data from the tests are compared with available diagnostic and voltage charts to indicate the problem. These are the same tests you would be performing without a breakout box, only now the tests are easy to do.

In some cases, diagnosis of the fuel injection system may lead you to suspect that there is something wrong with the fuel injectors. For example, if the engine misses or lacks power, it could mean that one or more of the fuel injectors has become clogged with a tar-like residue. Generally, this condition results from the use of fuel that does not have sufficient detergent additives or from frequent city driving. Most diagnostic trouble codes relate to the computer input voltages or signals and must exist for a specific period of time to be recognized as a hard fault.

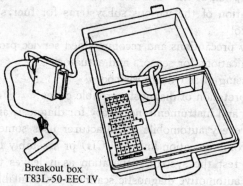

Figure 5-14  Typical breakout box attachment

Before beginning to troubleshoot a system, take time to discuss the problem with the driver. The driver can be an excellent source of information on problems, especially intermittent ones. It is important to understand the symptoms fully and know what conditions occur that cause the driver to complain.

When diagnosing engine performance, the sensitivity of electronic control systems makes organized troubleshooting a must. The following troubleshooting plan will give you a logical approach for diagnosing any problem:

1. Verify the complaint. Ask the driver; then check the vehicle. Make sure the problem actually occurs by using an operational check.

For example if the complaint is hard starting, check the starting performance.

2. Determine related symptoms. Know how the problem system should work. Related symptoms are identified by operation checks on circuits or components connected to the problem circuit.

For example, a rough idle could be caused by an electrical or a vacuum problem.

3. Analyze the symptoms. Think! What did the driver say?

What did the operational checks show? Consider the symptoms and their possible causes. Positive symptoms (things working as they should) rule out certain causes, whereas negative symptoms (things not working as they should) indicate certain causes.

4. Isolate the trouble. Be logical and systematic. Start with knowing the system. Then, test from the general to the specific. The split-half method of testing can save a lot of time. The trouble lies between a positive symptom and negative symptom. Start halfway between. If a positive result is obtained, split the next half, going toward the problem. If a negative result is found, split the other half, going back toward the area where the positive symptom was found. Always check the obvious before assuming something complicated is the cause. Most of the time, it is not the computer.

5. Correct the trouble. Repair wiring problems, replace faulty components, and service of adjust parts if necessary.

6. Check for proper operation. Make sure that the problem is fixed. Is the specific complaint corrected? Has the cause of the problem been identified and corrected? (A blown fuse, for example, is a simple problem that may require more than another fuse to repair). What may cause the problem to happen again? Are all the symptoms now positive? Have any new problems shown up in other circuits?

In diagnosing a problem on a computerized engine-control system, it is helpful first to pinpoint the problem as being related to the fuel system, the ignition system, a mechanical problem, or a problem with the components of the electronic control system. All fuel injection systems consist basically of a fuel pump, supply lines, fuel filter, injector(s), pressure regulator, and return line. Basic checks include proper fuel pressure, delivery of fuel by the injector, and the amount of injector ON time. Common fuel related problems include blocked fuel line or filter; inoperative fuel pump; incorrect system fuel pressure; defective, dirty, or sticking injectors; and contaminated fuel.

A computer-controlled ignition system consists basically of a pickup sensor and the device it is sensing, engine computer-timing circuitry, an electronic ignition-control module, ignition coil(s), and connective wiring. The first thing to check in the ignition system is whether spark is coming out of the plug wire; then work back from this point. Common ignition-related problems include fouled or faulty spark plugs, defective distributor cap or rotor, open or shorted ignition coil(s), defective high-voltage cables, faulty pickup sensor, defective electronic ignition-control module, and bad connections.

The mechanical system includes such nonelectrical components as vacuum hoses, intake air system, exhaust system, engine head and block, belts, oil pump, camshaft, crankshaft, timing chain or belt, nuts, and bolts. Mechanical problems can often be spotted by a good visual inspection. In fact, a visual inspection should always be the first step in troubleshooting any system. A seemingly unrelated mechanical problem such as a cracked or disconnected vacuum hose can have a direct impact on the performance of the system.

The electronic control system consists basically of the computer or electronic control module, engine wiring harness, input sensors, and output actuators. The electronic troubleshooting principles used are similar to those used on other automotive electrical and/or electronic systems. If a check engine or service engine soon light is ON, then deal with it immediately. Each vehicle manufacturer has its own way of retrieving diagnostic codes from computer memory and also its own system of code numbers.

The presence of trouble codes dose not always mean the computer is defective; usually these codes indicate that a specific input to the computer is missing or incorrect. Some technicians overlook this fact and are tempted to replace the computer first. Similarly, at times, drivability problems may occur in the system even when there has been no check engine light or trouble code signal. Remember that most trouble codes relate mainly to inputs; few outputs are monitored. Even if the input does not deviate from the normal reading long enough to be recognized as a problem, this does not completely eliminate it as a source of the problm.

It is important when troubleshooting to understand how the different inputs and outputs react with the computer to achieve the desired engine control. Each vehicle manufacturer has its own control process or way of retrieving sensor information and issuing commands to various solenoids and relays.

## NEW WORDS

| | | |
|---|---|---|
| description | [dis'kripʃən] | n. 描写,形容,绘制,说明 |
| precaution | [pri'kɔːʃən] | n. 谨慎,小心,预防(措施) |
| interpretation | [inˌtəːpriteiʃən] | n. 解释,翻译 |
| code | [kəud] | n. 代码,码,记号 |
| remotely | [ri'məutli] | adv. 远距离地,间接地,遥控地 |
| scanner | ['skænə] | n. 扫描器 |
| digital | ['didʒitl] | adj. 数字的,计数的 |
| residue | ['rezidjuː] | n. 残余,渣滓 |
| clog | [klɔg] | n. 阻碍,障碍物 |
| positive | ['pɔzətiv] | adj.;n. 确实的,积极的;确实 |
| detergent | [ditəːdʒənt] | n.;adj. 清洁剂;净化的 |
| negative | ['negətiv] | adj. 否定的,消极的 |
| diagnose | ['daiəgnəuz] | v. 诊断,断定 |
| monitor | ['mɔnitə] | n.;v. 监控器,记录器;监控,检查,控制 |
| retrieve | [ri'triːv] | vt. 复得,弥补,纠正 |

## PHRASES AND EXPRESSIONS

| | |
|---|---|
| self-diagnosis | 自动诊断 |
| hard fault | 严重的错误,严重的故障 |
| approach for | 接近,靠近 |
| block diagram | 框图,简(草)图 |
| make sure | 查明,使确定,确信 |
| vacuum hose | 真空管 |

## NOTES TO THE TEXT

1. With computerized engine-control systems, a service manual that applies specifically to the vehicle being serviced is a must.

随着电控发动机系统的产生,对于特定车辆的维修手册也是必须的。

with…systems 是介词短语做状语。

2. It is important when troubleshooting to understand how the different inputs and outputs react with the computer to achieve the desired engine control.

当我们对电控系统检查时,弄清输入和输出信号如何与电脑相互作用以获得正确的发动机控制信息是很重要的。

It 是形式主语,真正的主语是不定式短语 to understand…engine control;when troubleshooting 现在分词做时间状语。

## EXERCISES

Ⅰ. Answer the following questions according to the text:

1. All fuel systems can be broken down to three subsystems, What are they? What parts does each subsystems consist of?

2. How many types of gasoline fuel injection systems used in automobiles? Please give two basic types and each of character.

3. How does a electronic engine control work? Please say the main advantage of electronic engine control compared to mechanisms?

4. What advantages does the distributorless ignition systems has? Please answer the question base on the distributorless ignition systems' instruction.

5. What is the function of catalytic converter? What advantages does the electronically controlled emission systems has after applying catalytic converter and exhaust gas recirculation?

6. Where is the fuel vapors absorbs in? Does the fuel vapors useful?

7. What advantages does the idle-speed control has? Please say the process of the idle-speed control.

8. What advantages does the electronically controlled transmissions has? Do the transmission and engine can be electronically controlled as a unit? Why?

9. What differents are there between electric engine-cooling fans and conventional engine-cooling fan?

10. How do we use system diagnosis and service? Please say the logical approach for diagnosing problem.

Ⅱ. Fill the blank in each sentence with one of the four words or phrases which correctly completes the sentences:

1. The operational program for a specific engine and vehicle is stored in the computer's ___.
   A. logic module
   B. programmable read-only memory(PROM)
   C. random-access memory (RAM)
   D. keep-alive memory(KAM)

2. An exhaust gas oxygen (EGO) sensor is an example of a ___.
   A. resistor        B. potentiometer
   C. generator       D. solenoid

3. An engine detonation sensor uses a ___.
   A. piezoresistive crystal  B. voltage divider pickup
   C. potentiometer           D. thermistor

4. The binary system used by a digital computer consists of ___.
   A. 10 numbers      B. 5 numbers
   C. 3 numbers       D. 2 numbers

5. The computer can read but not change the information stored in ___.
   A. ROM             B. RAM
   C. KAM             D. none of these

6. An onboard computer can do all of the following except ___.
   A. ignore sensor input under certain conditions
   B. respond in different ways to the same input
   C. accept an input signal from another computer

· 357 ·

D. ignore its program instructions under certain conditions
　　7. When the onboard computer is in open loop operation, it ____.
　　A. controls fuel metering to a predetermined value
　　B. ignores the temperature sensor signals
　　C. responds to the EGO sensor signal
　　D. all of the above
　　8. ____ of the following is not true of a fuel-injected engine.
　　A. the computer controls the air-fuel ratio by switching injectors on or off
　　B. the pulse width is increased to supply more fuel
　　C. lean the mixture, the computer opens the air bleeds
　　D. engine speed determines the injector switching rate
Ⅲ. Choose a phrase from the list for each space in the passage below:

　　1. in which　　　　5. must be changed to
　　2. on/off　　　　　6. is provided
　　3. is sent to　　　 7. evolved into
　　4. respond to　　　8. are used in

　　Every computer has four main functions: input, processing, storage, and output. Computers can operate on analog or digital signals. An analog signal is infinitely variable. A digital signal is an ____ or high/low signal. In automobile applications, most variable measurements produce analog signals which ____ digital signals for computer processing.

　　Digital computers use the binary system ____ on/off or high/low voltage signals are represented by combinations of 0s and 1s.

　　Onboard computers ____ automotive fuel metering control systems. The control system regulates the operation of the vehicle's fuel system and operates in open loop or closed loop modes. In an open loop mode, the system does not ____ an output feedback signal. In a closed loop mode, the computer responds to the feedback signal and adjusts the output value accordingly.

　　Computer input ____ by sensors. Sensors can be switches, timers, potentiometers, piezoresistors, transformers, or generators.

Computer output ____ actuators, which transduce, or convert, the electrical signal to mechanical action. Most actuators are solenoids or relays, but some are stepper motors. The first feedback fuel metering system was Volvo's Lambda-Sond system in 1977. Ford and GM followed in 1978 with their own versions, which quickly ____ integrated engine management systems.

Ⅳ. Translate the following sentence into Chinese:

1. These data are programmed into the engine computer and used along with other information received from sensors to produce optimum engine performance.

2. Although there is considerable variation among the configurations of computerized engine-control systems used by various manufacturers over various model years, the basic operating principles are the same.

3. The current trend is toward a more integrated system, in which several subsystems are operated as separate functions of the same computer.

4. The main objective of any computerized engine-control system is to allow the vehicle to give good fuel mileage and clean emission but not at the expense of good acceleration and smooth operation.

5. Basically, the engine computer takes sensor readings and responds with signal outputs to control devices.

6. Sensors can update the computer every 100 ms for general information and every 12.5 ms for critical emissions and drivability information.

Ⅴ. Translate the followng passage into Chinese:

Electronic fuel injection (EFI) is far more common than the earlier mechanical injection represented by the Bosch K-Jetronic. EFI integrates the injection system into a complete engine management system which includes control of EGR, ignition timing, canister purging, and various other functions.

The EFI computer uses various sensors to gather data on engine operation. Intake air volume is determined by measuring airflow speed, manifold pressure, or the mass of the air drawn into the engine. This data is added to information about throttle position, idle speed, engine coolant and air temperature, crankshaft position, and other operating conditions. After processing the data, the computer signals the solenoid-operated injectors when to open and close. Injectors may be fired in vari-ous combinations, but all use the principle of pulse width modulation, in which the computer varies the percentage of on-time in each full on/off cycle according to engine require-ments. In this way, the amount of fuel injected can be varied instantly to accommodate changing conditions.

## 5.2 Other Automotive Electronic systems

### 5.2.1 Electronic Antilock Braking Systems

The purpose of an electronic antilock, or antiskid, braking system (ABS) is to prevent wheel lockup under heavy braking conditions on virtually any type of road surface. The most efficient braking takes place when the wheels are still revolving. If the driver slams on the brakes and the wheels lock, the following occur:
1. Driving stability is lost, and the vehicle skids.
2. The vehicle cannot be steered.
3. The braking distance increases.
4. The risk of an accident increases.

The basic principle of operation of an antilock braking system is fairly simple (Figure 5-15). It is a hydraulic braking system with a hydraulically assisted power booster/master cylinder. A sensor at each wheel indicates rotational speed. When the computer or antilock brake control module detects one wheel slowing much more quickly than the others, it operates solenoid valves to reduce hydraulic pressure and braking to that wheel to minimize chances of a skid. When that wheel's speed approaches the others, brake pressure is reapplied. The computer samples wheel speed data hundereds of times per second. It interprets not only the wheel's rotational speed but also its rate of change. Its ultimate goal is to achieve a controlled stop, in the shortest distance, without wheel-lock.

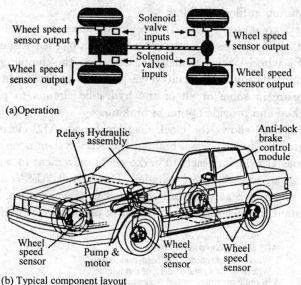

Figure 5-15  Four-wheel antilock brake system

The hardware used in an ABS system and the method of operation of the system vary with each vehicle manufacturer. Some provide skid control at the rear wheels only, whereas others provide control at all four wheels. The following are some of the major hardware components of an antilock brake system:

1. ABS wheel speed sensors  ABS wheel speed sensors are installed at each wheel; they transmit wheel and tire speed information to the computer. A small AC signal voltage is generated in the sensor, through magnetic induction, by passing a toothed excitor ring past a stationary magnetic sensor. The frequency of the signal varies directly with the wheel's rotation rate. This signal is used by the computer to determine the speed of the wheel.

2. ABS hydraulic actuator  The ABS hydraulic actuator regu-

lates the amount of fluid pressure appled to each wheel brake assembly during antilock braking. It is controlled by the ABS computer and provides pressure modulation for each of the wheel circuits as required during antilock braking.

3. ABS computer   The ABS computer uses the signals from the wheel speed sensors to control the operation of the hydraulic actuator. If a wheel-locking tendency is detected, the computer commands appropriate wheel circuit valve positions to modulate brake fluid pressure in some or all of the hydraulic circuits to prevent wheel lockup and provide optimum braking.

Figure 5-16 shows the block diagram for an ABS closed-loop control circuit. Under normal braking the ABS system is not used, and the master cylinder reacts to brake-pedal movement to send fluid pressure out to each wheel cylinder. During full, ABS-controlled braking, pressure is automatically adjusted to prevent wheel lockup with constant brake-pedal force. The three processes involved are as follows:

ABS closed-loop control circuit.
1 Wheel-speed sensor    4 Road conditions
2 Wheel-brake cylinder  5 Hydr·modulator
3 Braking pressure      6 Brake master cyl.

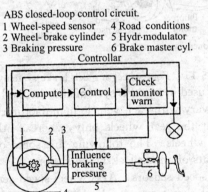

Figure 5-16   ABS closed-loop control circuit

1. Maintaining braking pressure   If a wheel speed sensor signals severe wheel deceleration to the electronic controller—that is, the wheels are likely to lock up—the braking pressure at the wheel

involved is initially kept constant as opposed to being further increased.

2. Reducing braking pressure   If the wheel still continues to decelerate, the pressure in the wheel brake cylinder is reduced so that the wheel is braked less heavily.

3. Increasing braking pressure   The wheel accelerates again as a result of the reduced braking pressure. Upon reaching a specified limit, the controller registers the fact that the wheel is now not being braked sufficiently. The formerly reduced pressure is then increased so that the wheel is again decelerated. The control cycle begins anew. There are approximately 4 to 6 control cycles per second, depending on the state of the road surface. This rate is made possible by rapid electronic signal-processing and the short response times of the solenoid valves.

**Electronic Cruise Control**

The basic function of electronic cruise, or speed, control is to keep a vehicle's speed at a preset range automatically. A curise-control system enables the driver to select a fixed cruising speed without maintaining throttle position by foot pressure on the accelerator pedal. The driver can override the cruise control at any time simply by depressing the accelerator or brake pedal or by turning the system OFF. The following are some of the advantages of cruise control:

1. Reduces driver tension and fatigue on a long journey

2. Eliminates speedups and slowdowns, yielding better fuel economy

3. Allows precise control of vehicle speed at whatever speed the driver wishes (above a minimum of about 30 mi/h, or 48km/h), even when climbing hills or facing a head wind.

Although specific designs vary, all electronic cruise-control systems share certain functional parts:

1. Controlling switches   The ON/OFF switch feeds current to the electronic cruise-control module to activate and ready the system for operation. The driver accelerates to the desired speed and mo-

mentarily presses the speed-set control button to allow the computer system to take over and hold that speed.

2. **Vehicle speed sensor**  The speed sensor produces voltage pulses that vary with the speed of the vehicle. The electronic control module uses this signal to determine the vehicle speed. Many cruise-control systems use the vehicle's speed sensor input to the engine-control computer for speed reference.

3. **Electronic control module**  The electronic control module houses a microcomputer. This can be a stand-alone device or a function of the engine control computer. The computer receives sensor input information about the system and outputs pulses to control the throttle servo actuator.

4. **Throttle servo actuator**  The throttle actuator physically moves the engine throttle lever to control engine power and resulting vehicle speed. It can be vacuum or motor-operated and moves the throttle valve by means of a linkage. Its movement is controlled by the electronic control unit to maintain the desired speed.

5. **Canceling switches**  Canceling switches are used to signal the computer to deactivate the cruise control. A brake-pedal-operated switch siganals the computer to shut off the cruise control when the brakes are applied. A clutch-pedal-operated switch signals the computer to shut off the cruise control when the clutch pedal is depressed. A neutral safety switch signals the computer to shut off cruise control when the shift lever is moved out of drive to prevent engine racing.

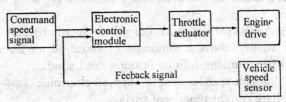

Figure 5-17   Simplified curise-control block diagram

Fingue 5-17 shows a simplified block diagram of a cruise-control system. The electronic control module has two inputs: the command speed signal, which indicates the desired speed, and the feedback speed signal, which indicates the actual vehicle speed. The electronic control module detects the difference between the two inputs and produces a throttle-control signal, which is sent to the throttle servo actuator. The throttle actuator sets the engine throttle position, which alters the engine speed to correct for the difference between the set speed and actual speed. The control system is operated in closed-loop mode because the speed signal from the vehicle speed sensor is fed back to the electronic control module to be compared to the command signal.

## NEW WORDS

| | | |
|---|---|---|
| slam | [slæm] | v. 猛踏,猛击 |
| skid | [skid] | vi. (汽车等)打滑,滑向一侧 |
| stability | [stə'biliti] | n. 稳定性,安全性 |
| booster | ['buːstə] | n. 助力器,加力器 |
| sample | ['saːmpl] | vt.;n. 从…取样检查;样品,试样 |
| ultimate | ['ʌltimit] | adj.;n. 最远的,最终的;极限,顶点 |
| install | [in'stɔːl] | vt. 安装,设置 |
| transmit | [trænz'mit] | vt.;vi. 传送,传递,传达;播送信号 |
| magnetic | [mæg'nitik] | adj. 磁性的,可磁化的,能吸引的 |
| induction | [in'dʌkʃən] | n. 感应,感应现象 |
| toothed | [tuːθt] | adj. 带齿的,使成锯齿状的 |
| excitor | ['iksaitə] | n. 激励器,励磁机,激活剂 |
| stationary | ['steiʃənəri] | adj. 固定的,不变的,紧配合的 |
| regulate | ['regjuleit] | vt. 调整,调节 |
| fluid | ['fluː(ː)id] | adj. 流动的,流体的,不固定的,易变的 |
| modulation | [ˌmɔdju'leiʃən] | n. 调整,调节 |
| optimum | ['ɔptiməm] | adj.;n. 最适的;最适度,最适条件 |
| diagram | ['daiəgræm] | n. 图解,图表,简图 |
| schematic | [ski'mætik] | adj. 图解的,纲要的 |

## PHRASES AND EXPRESSIONS

| | |
|---|---|
| antiskid braking system | 防滑制动系统 |
| apply to | 适用,把…应用于 |
| priving stability | 操纵稳定性 |
| take over | 接收,接管 |
| shut off | 关掉,切断 |
| reducing braking pressure | 减压过程 |
| increasing braking pressure | 增压过程 |

## NOTES TO THE TEXT

1. When the computer or antilock brake control module detects one wheel slowing much more quickly than the others, it operates solenoid valves to reduce hydraulic pressure and braking to that wheel to minimize chances of a skid.

当计算机或防抱死控制模块发现有一个车轮比其它几个车轮的转速慢时,便命令电磁线圈阀减小液压而使该车轮产生滑移的可能性减小。

when 引导时间状语;detects 做谓语;much more quickly than … 是形容词的比较级;to minimize chances of a skid 做目的状语。

2. If the wheel still continues to decelerate, the pressure in the wheel brake cylinder is reduced so that the wheel is braked less heavily.

如果车轮仍然持续减速,制动缸内的压力便降低,这样车轮不能抱死。

If 引导条件状语从句;is reduced 的被动语态做谓语;so that 以致于,以使…,做目的状语。

3. The throttle actuator sets the engine throttle position, which alters the engine speed to correct for the difference between the set speed and actual speed.

此机构能设置节气门的位置,这样改变发动机的转速并调整汽车车速。

which 引导非限制性定语从句,代替 position。

## 5.2.2 Active Computerized Suspension Systems

An active computerized suspension system incorporates various sensors, a computer, and shock-absorber actuators to control ride stiffness (Figure 5-18). The effeqct of the system can be felt immediately when the vehicle is driven. Steering, handling, ride, and down-the-road stability are greatly enhanced over conventional, passive suspension systems.

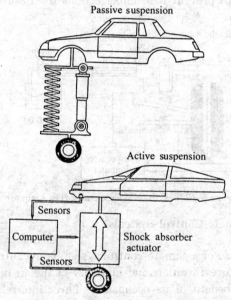

Figure 5-18  Active and passive suspension systems

Figure 5-19 illustrates the operation of a hydraulic shock absorber actuator as part of an active suspension system. Like a shock absorber, the cylinder end of the actuator is mounted to the body. Inside the cylinder is a piston-and-rod device. If hydraulic fluid is pumped into the upper portion of the cylinder and out of the lower portion, the piston and rod move downward. If, on the other hand, fluid is pumped into the lower portion of the cylinder and out of the upper portion, the piston and rod move upward. The suspension computer controls the direction and speed of piston motion by controlling the action of the four-port valve. Information on movement of the suspension system is provided by the load sensor, position sensor, and acclerometer. Hence, when wheels drop into potholes or rise due to bumps, the hydraulic actuator is directed to lower or raise the wheel while keeping the vertical position of the body fairly constant. This helps prevent road imperfections from causing as much body movement.

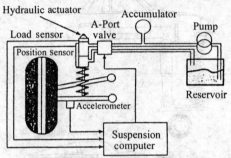

Figure 5-19  Hydraulic shock-absorber actuator

## Electronic Climate-Control Systems

The purpose of a climate-control system is to control the circulation, temperature, filtration, and humidity of the air in a vehicle to the maximum benefit of its occupants. Three interrelated subsystems can be controlled by a computer to provide the desired air temperature and quality. These include the air-distribution, or ventilating, system, the heating system, and the air-conditioning (AC) system.

The air-distribution system on most vehicles draws air from the outside, or recirculates it from the passenger compartment, and directs it to the cooling and heating systems. Heated and cooled air are mixed and distributed to ducts that connect to vents inside the car (Figure 5-20). Air enters through the intake door, which is

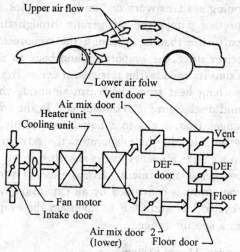

Figure 5-20  Typical air-distribution system

usually controlled by the computer through a vacuum actuator. The intake door opening determines the ratio or iresn air to recirculated air. The fan motor draws the air into the system, with the fan speed determining how much air is drawn in. The outlet doors determine which ducts deliver air to the car. Depending on the system design, the air flow can be directed to provide upper-level circulation, lower-level circulation, or both.

The heating system is designed to operate in conjunction with the air-distribution system to provide heat. It uses heated engine coolant delivered to a heater core (similar in design to radiator construction) located in the air-distribution system. The air-mix door controls the temperature of the air delivered to the car by regulating the amount of air that passes through the heater core. The door is computer-controlled and is normally in the intermediate position so that air is heated and then mixed with cold air.

Integrated with the car's heating and ventilating systems is the air-conditioning (AC) system, which cools and dehumidifies the air. All air-conditioning systems work on similar principles.

The compressor pumps the refrigerant through the system in the standard pattern — that is , through the compressor, the condenser, the receiver drier, the evaporator, and back to the compressor. While making its rounds, the refrigerant cycles from gas to liquid to gas, absorbing heat from the warm air inside the passenger compartment and discharging it to outside air. In the condenser, the refrigerant changes from a gas to a liquid; as a result, heat is discharged to the outside. In the evaporator, the refrigerant changes from a liquid to a gas; as a result, heat is absorbed from the warm air inside the passenger compartment. Evaporation of the refrigerant through the evaporator is controlled by an expansion valve, and the compressor is cycled ON and OFF to maintain the evaporator temperature within a specific range.

## Electronic Security Alarm Systems

At one time there was little need to worry about cars being broken into. However, auto thefts and burglarizations are commonplace today, making it necessary to take security precautions that were unheard of years ago. A vehicle security alarm system is designed to do one or more of the following:

1. Scare away would-be thieves by sounding the horn or warning siren an flashing the outside car lights

2. Attract attention to the break-in while alerting someone to call the police

3. Disable the ignition, fuel, or starter system, preventing the vehicle from being driven away by a thief

4. Send a message through a paging transmitter and receiver warning the driver that someone is tampering with his or her car.

Figure 5-21 shows a block diagram of a vehicle security alarm system. Various switches and sensors are used to detect a break-in. Once a swith or sensor is activated, a signal is sent to the electronic control unit. The electronic control unit then responds by issuing commands to activate alarm devices.

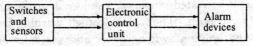

Figure 5-21  Alarm system block diagram

Vehicle alarm systems detect tampering and break-ins by monitoring the perimeter of the car with pin switches, motion detectors, sound discriminators, and voltage-drop sensors. Other sensors and detectors trigger an alarm only after the thief is inside the car. This sort of protection is called space, or area, protection. Figure 5-22 shows the layout of a typical perimeter detection system. The alarm is triggered if a thief tries to force entry to any door, the hood, or the trunk. The alarm consists of the horn sounding and the headlights, taillights, and side-marker lights flashing ON and OFF.

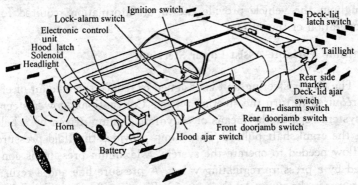

Figure 5-22  Typical perimeter detection system

## Audible Warning Devices

Audible warning devices are used to alert the driver to operating conditions such as seatbelts not fastened, door open with key in the ignition, and lights left ON with engine OFF.

Buzzers are often used as audible warning devices. The key warning buzzer is activated whenever the key is in the ignition and the driver's door is open. The fasten-seatbelt warning buzzer is activated when the ignition switch is ON and seatbelts are not engaged. A thermal timer circuit is built into the seatbelt buzzer by winding a heater coil around an internal circuit breaker. The heater coil is connected directly to ground through the ignition switch. When the coil is hot enough (4 to 8 s after the ignition switch has been closed), the contacts of the timer open, switching the buzzer OFF even if the seat buckle switch is still closed.

Electronic tone-generator modules are used to produce audible warning signals that are applied to a speaker. They are more pleasant sounding than buzzers but equally effective.

Electronic voice warning modules are used to provide audible warning messages. The voice is produced by a voice-synthesizer chip contained within an electronic control module. Sensors located throughout the vehicle provide the input information required for the operation of the system.

**Electronic Variable-Assist Power Steering**

The power steering unit is designed to reduce the amount of effort required to turn the steering wheel. Conventional power steering systems operate by means of a hydraulic pump driven by a belt from the crankshaft pulley. This pump provides the fluid pressure and flow needed to operate the system. Maximum pressure is controlled by a pressure regulating valve. A pressure line and a return line connect the pump to the system. Figure 5-23 shows a typical conventional power rack-and-pinion steering gear operation. The hydraulic pressure provides most of the force needed for steering. The remaining steering effort provides needed driver feel for good steering control.

The basic purpose of an electronic variable-assist power steering system is to provide maximum power assist for light steering effort during low-speed vehicle maneuvering, such as parking, and minimum power assist for firm steering wheel control and directional stability at higher speeds.

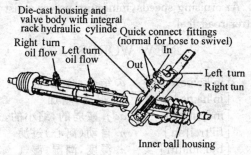

Figure 5-23  Typical power rack-and-pinion steering gear operation

Figure 5-24 shows the major components of a typical electronic

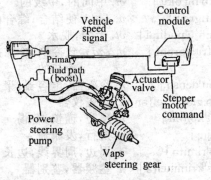

Figure 5-24  Electronic variable-assist power steering system

variable-assist power steering system. Essentialy, the system is made up of a microprocessor-based control module that receives information on vehicle speed from a vehicle speed sensor. The control module processes this information and signals an electrically controlled actuator valve in regard to the amount of assist required. During parking and low-speed operation, the control module sends a signal to the actuator valve stepper motor, positioning the valve spool to allow for maximum power assist. As vehicle speed increases, the control module signals the actuator valve spool to open gradually, diverting an increased amount of fluid, therefore providing less power assist. At cruising speeds, minimum power assist is supplied, providing better road feel.

## NEW WORDS

| | | |
|---|---|---|
| incorporate | [in'kɔ:pəreit] | v. 结合,合并,混合 |
| enhance | [in'ha:ns] | vt. 提高,增加 |
| imperfect | [im'pəfikt] | adj. 减弱的,缩小的,未完成的 |
| filtration | [fil'treiʃən] | n. 自动(离心)过滤 |
| humidity | [hju:'miditi] | n. 湿度,潮湿,湿气 |
| ventilate | ['ventileit] | v. 使通气,使换气 |
| duct | [dʌkt] | n. 管,输送管 |
| conjunction | [kən'dʒʌŋkʃən] | n. 同时发生,同处发生,连同 |
| intermediate | [intə'mi:diət] | vt. 中间的,中级的 |
| integrate | ['intigreit] | v. ;adj. 使结合;综合的,完整的 |
| dehumidify | [,di:hju'midifai] | vt. 干燥,脱水 |
| refrigerant | [ri'fridʒərənt] | n. ;adj. 致冷剂,冷冻剂;致冷的,冷却的 |
| condenser | [kən'densə] | n. 冷凝器,电容器,聚光器 |
| burglarization | ['bə:glərai,zeiʃən] | n. 防盗仪器 |
| precaution | [pri'kɔ:ʃən] | n. 预防,谨慎,警惕 |
| issue | ['isju:] | v. 发行,发布命令 |
| perimeter | [pə'rimitə] | n. 周边,周界线,边长 |
| discriminator | [dis'krimineitə] | n. 鉴频器,鉴别器 |
| trigger | ['trigə] | n. ;v. 起动装置;激发起,引起 |
| maneuver | [mə'nu:və] | n. ;v. 机动,调动;演习 |

## PHRASES AND EXPERESSIONS

| | |
|---|---|
| shock absorber | 减震器 |
| on the other hand | 另一方面 |
| drop into | 落入,偶然进入(某地) |
| air-distribution system | 空气分配系统 |
| mix with | 用⋯混合 |

| | |
|---|---|
| enhance over | 提高,增加 |
| break into | 破门而入,突然…起来 |
| tamper with | 损害,削弱,窜改 |
| break in | 闯入,破门而入 |

## NOTES TO THE TEXT

1. This helps prevent road imperfections from causing as much body movement.

这样,路面的不平度不会过度影响汽车的运动。

prevent … from doing 防止…做…,在这里做谓语;This helps 在句中做主语。

2. The door is computer-controlled and is normally in the intermediate position so that air is heated and then mixed with cold air.

为了能使空气加热然后和冷空气混合充分,通常将该门安置在通风系统的中间位置。

so that 为了…,在句中引导目的状语。

3. Essentially, the system is made up of a microprocessor-based, control module that receives information on vehicle speed from a vehicle speed sensor.

实际上,该系统是由能接来自车速传感器的车速信号的微电脑,处理控制模块组成。

be made up of 由…组成,在句中做谓语;that receives information… 引导定语从句。

## 5.2.3 Air Bag Restraint Systems

Air bags supplement the protection provided by safety belts by protecting the head and chest in moderate to severe front-end collisions. If a vehicle collides with a solid object, the occupants are thrown forward against the dashboard, windshield, and protruding objects, particularly the steering wheel. In the event of a moderate to severe front-end collision, tough nylon bags, similar to large balloons, inflate in a fraction of a second so that the driver and passenger are cushioned as they are thrown forward. As a result, the air bag absorbs the energy of the forward motion of the occupants with little or no injury to them.

Figure 5-25 illustrates typical driver side and passenger side air bag inflator module assemblies. Each air bag module contains an inflator, an igniter, and the folded air bag. When electrical current flows through the igniter, it produces heat, which ignites the generant material within the inflator. This solid generant burns in an enclosed chamber to produce harmless nitrogen gas. This gas is cooled and filtered prior to inflating the air bag.

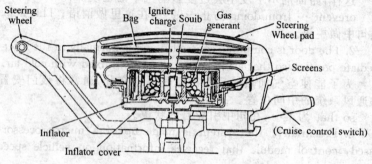

Figure 5-25   One type of air bag inflator module

The system performs three main functions:
1. Detects an impact
2. Provides a ground to the air bags for deployment
3. Monitors system readiness.

If an air bag should inflate by error under normal driving conditions, it could cause an accident. Similarly, should it fail to inflate as expected in a collision, occupants could be injured. To prevent either from happening, the system utilizes five electromechanical crash sensors (three front crash sensors and two safing sensors) to monitor and respond to appropriate impact forces. The three front crash sensors are mounted across the front of the vehicle to differentiate between moderate crashes that do not warrant air bag deployment and severe crashes that do. The system will not deploy the air bags unless it gets confirmation from one of the two safing crash sensors that there is sufficient vehicle deceleration to warrant deployment. The purpose of these safing crash sensors is to make sure that the air bags will not deploy inadvertently in the evnt of an electrical short in one of the crash sensors or wiring.

A backup power supply is provided by a capacitor unit. The purpose of this power supply is to enable deployment of the air bag, even if the battery cable is severed during a crash.

The diagnostic module microcomputer monitors the electrical system components and connections. When the vehicle's ignition is turned ON, the module self-checks the microcomputer's internal circuits and the air bag electrical system. It also energizes the air bag-readiness indicator light for approximately 6 to 8 s to indicate normal system operation. If a fault is detected after the self-check, the lamp will either light continuously or in a coded, flashing mode.

**Power Seats**

Power seats are electrically adjustable seats that can be designed to move in several ways. A six-way power seat includes up, down, forward, back, tilt forward, and tilt rearward seat movement. Four-way systems do not provide tilt adjustments. In addition, some power seats have a lumbar adjustment that uses a small air pump to inflate a bag or bags on the lower back of the seat to serve as a pillow. Figure 5-26 shows the construction of a typical six-way power seat assembly. Three reversible permanent-magnet motors in one housing provide the various seat movements. The motors are coupled to transmission gear-boxes that change rotating motion from the motor into linear motion for the seats.

Power seat switches located on the seat or door panel control current flow to the seat motors. Power is supplied from the battery at all times through a 30-A circuit breaker to the power seat control switch. In its normal OFF position, the circuit is open to each of the three motors. When any of the switches is closed, battery current will flow through that switch contact to the appropriate motor brush. Depending on the switch position and the direction of current to the armature, the appropriate motor will either revolve clockwise of counterclockwise to produce the desired seat movement. The permanent-magnet motors are grounded through the switch and are protected by an internal circuit breaker.

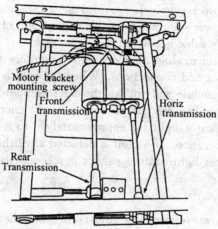

Figure 5-26  Typical six-way power seat assembly

Some power seats have a memory feature that will return the seat to a previously programmed position. Figure 5-27 shows the principle of operation for a typical programmable power seat-positioning system. The system is controlled by a microcomputer-based electronic control unit. The best seat position is selected using the manual adjustment buttons and then stored in the memory by pushing the memory button. Seat position sensors feed data to the module on the instantaneous position of the seat. The electronic control unit processes the signals coming from the keyboard, stores and compares the seat positions, controls the seat adjustment, and monitors the entire system.

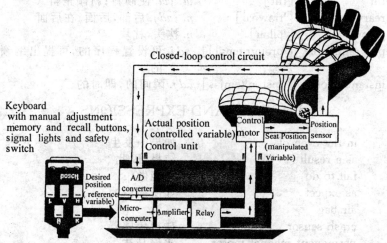

Figure 5-27　Programmable power seat

## NEW WORDS

| | | |
|---|---|---|
| supplement | ['sʌplimənt] | v. ;n. 增补,补充;增补 |
| moderate | ['mɔdərit] | n. ;v. 缓和,缓冲;减轻,节制 |
| occupant | ['ɔkjupənt] | n. 占有人,占有者 |
| dashboard | ['dæʃbɔːd] | n. 车辆的挡泥板 |
| protrude | [prə'tʃuːd] | vt. 使伸出,突出 |
| inflate | [in'fleit] | v. 充气,膨胀 |
| fraction | ['frækʃən] | n. 片断,片刻,小部分 |
| cushion | ['kuʃən] | v. ;n. 使减少震动,缓和…的冲击;垫子 |
| inflator | [in'fleitə] | n. 充气机,打气筒,增压泵 |
| fold | [fəuld] | vt. ;vi. 折叠,笼罩;对折起来 |
| differentiate | [ˌdifə'renʃieit] | vt. ;vi. 区分,分别;使变异 |
| deploy | [di'plɔː] | v. 展开,调度 |
| warrant | ['wɔrənt] | v. ;n. 认为正当,担保;正当理由,根据 |
| inadvertently | [ˌinəd'vəːtənt] | adj. 不经心的,疏忽的 |

| tilt | [tilt] | vt.;vi. 使倾斜;斜倾歪斜 |
| rearward | ['riəwəːd] | n.;adj. 后部,后面;在后面 |
| pillow | ['piləu] | n. 枕头,枕块 |
| programmable | ['prəugræməbl] | adj. 可设置程序的,可提出纲领的 |
| instantaneous | [ˌinstən'teinjəs] | adj. 瞬间的,即时的 |

## PHRASES AND EXPRESSIONS

| in the even of | 如果…发生 |
| as a result | 结果,因此 |
| fail to do | 不能做… |
| as expect | 如所期望的 |
| air bag | 气囊 |
| crash sensor | 碰撞传感器 |
| permanent-magnet motor | 永磁马达 |
| electronic control unit | 电控单元 |

## NOTES TO THE TEXT

1. Air bags supplement the protection provided by safety belts by protecting the head and chest in moderate to severe front-end collisions.

安全气囊作为安全带的附助保护装置用来在汽车发生碰撞时使司机头部和胸部免受伤害。

Air bags supplement 与 the protection 是同位语,在句中做主语;provided 过去分词短语做后置定语,修饰主语。

2. When electrical current flows through the igniter, it produces heat, which ignites the generant material within the inflator.

当电流流过点火器时,它产生热量去点燃膨胀器内的某种物质,该物质在燃烧室内燃烧。

When 引导时间状语;it 做主语;which 引导非限制性定语从句,修饰 heat。

3. Seat position sensors feed data to the module on the instantaneous position of the seat.

座椅位置传感器向座椅中的瞬时位置模块传送数据。

Seat position 做主语；feed data to 向…传送数据，做谓语；on the instantaneous position 介词短语做定语。

### 5.2.4 Self-Diagnosis Systems

Most computerized automotive control systems are equipped with built-in self-diagnostic systems that conduct a multitude of tests of the system. The basic microcomputer self-diagnosis system is designed to monitor the input and output signals of the sensors and actuators and to store any malfunctions in its memory as a trouble code. In general, checks are made for open and short circuits and illogical sensor readings. The number of codes stored and the meaning of the code numbers varies from one manufacturer to another. Figure 5-28 illustrates a typical trouble-code decoding chart.

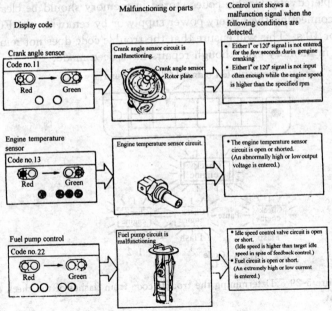

Figure 5-28　Trouble-code decoding chart

The method used to activate the self-diagnosis mode varies with each manufacturer. For example, on the General Motors computer command control (CCC) system, when a malfunction is detected, the check engine or service engine soon light illuminates on the instrument panel. If, for example, the engine-temperature sensor is supplying illogical readings, the light will come ON and the computer will substitute a fixed value from its programmed memory so the car can be driven. The light turning ON also means a trouble-code number has been stored in the electronic control module (ECM) memory to record the detected failure. The service technician can, at a later time, ground a test terminal under the dash and retrieve the trouble code, or codes, stored in memory. The stored codes are displayed in a series of flashes of the check engine light (Figure 5-29). If the problem is intermittent, the check engine light will go out, but the trouble code will remain stored. After all service is completed, any trouble codes stored in memory should be cleared by disconnecting the battery power supply or by removing the ECM fuse for 10 s. This will ensure that the trouble code does not remain stored in memory even though repairs have been made.

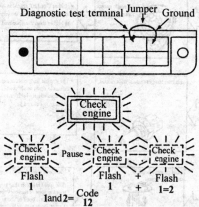

Figure 5-29  Determining the trouble code from flashes of the check engine light

The Chrysler electronic spark advance (ESA) on-board computer can be put into any one of its three self-test modes with a diagnostic readout tool. The diagnostic test mode is used to retrieve fault codes that are stored in the computer memory. In the circuit actuation rest mode, the operator selects a particular actuator circuit to be checked. The microcomputer then turns that circuit ON and OFF at short intervals for 5 min to allow it to be checked for proper operation. The switch test mode is used to test switch circuits to verify that their signals are being received by the microcomputer.

## NEW WORDS

| | | |
|---|---|---|
| multitude | ['mʌltitjuːd] | n. 大批,众多,大量 |
| malfunction | ['mælˈfʌŋkʃən] | n. 故障,失灵;发生故障 |
| manufacturer | [ˌmænjuˈfæktʃərə] | n. 制造厂,制造商 |
| terminal | ['təːminl] | a. 末期的,晚期的,末端的 |
| retrieve | [riˈtriːv] | vt. 收回,恢复 |
| substitute | ['sʌbstistjuːt] | n. ;v. 代用品代替 |
| intermittent | [ˌintəˈmitənt] | adj. 间歇的,周期的 |
| illuminate | [iˈljuːmineit] | vt. ;vi. 照明,阐明,照亮 |
| actuator | ['æktjueitə] | n. 促动器,调节器,螺线管 |
| feedback | [fiːdˈbæk] | n. 反馈,回复,反应 |
| target | ['taːgit] | n. ;vt. 目标,指标;把…作为目标 |

## PHRASES AND EXPRESSIONS

| | |
|---|---|
| open circuit | 断路 |
| short circuit | 短路 |
| trouble code | 故障码 |
| vary from… | 不同,变化 |
| switch test mode | 开关检测调试 |
| self-diagnostic system | 自诊系统 |

## NOTES TO THE TEXT

1. Most computerized automotive control systems are equipped

with built-in self-diagnostic systems that conduct a multitude of tests of the system.

大部分微机控制自动化汽车都装有自诊系统,用于检查微机系统的多数部件。

automotive control systems 做主语;be equipped with 被安装做谓语;that 引导的定语从句修饰 systems.

2. This will ensure that the trouble code does not remain stored in memory even though repairs have been made.

这样确保汽车修理好后,错误码完全消除。

that 引导宾语从句;the trouble code 做宾语从句的主语;remain 是宾语从句的谓语。

## EXERCISES

Ⅰ. Answer the following questions according to the text:

1. What is the purpose of an electronic antilock system? What will happen when the wheels lock?

2. What are the basic principle of operation of an antilock braking system?

3. Why do we use electronic cruise control system? How many types does electronic cruise-control has?

4. As part of an active suspension system, How does the hydraulic shock absorber actuator work?

5. What is the purpose of a climate-control system? What is the electronic climate-control systems composed of?

6. Today auto thefts and burglarization are commonplace, what is the purpose of a vehicle security alarm system?

7. What is the basic purpose of an electronic variable assist power steering?

8. What functions does the air bag restraint system performs? How does the air bag restraint system prevent inflating by error or failing to inflate as expected from happening?

9. What movements does a six-way power seat include? How do we select the best seat position?

10. How can we determine the trouble code from flashes of the

check engine light? After all service is completed, should any trouble codes stored in memory be cleared? How to do?

II. Fill the blank in each sentence with one of the four words or phrases which correctly completes the sentences:

1. The reference value sent to a sensor by the computer must be ____.
   A. above battery voltage
   B. exactly the same as battery voltage
   C. less than minimum battery voltage
   D. either A or C

2. A variable resistance sensor is called a ____.
   A. potentiometer    B. thermistor
   C. transformer     D. generator

3. The percentage of time a solenoid is energized relative to total cycle time is called the ____.
   A. pulse width modulation (PWM)    B. frequency
   C. duty cycle                      D. KAM

4. Most onboard computers work with ____.
   A. binary numbers    B. voltage signals
   C. both A and B      D. neither A or B

5. An engine coolant temperature sensor ____.
   A. receives reference voltage from the computer
   B. is a potentiometer
   C. provides the computer with a digital signal
   D. contains a piezoelectric crystal

6. The first electrically controlled fuel metering system with a 3-way converter and EGO sensor was the ____.
   A. C-4 system           B. Lambda-Sond system
   C. Ford FEEC system     D. none of these

7. ____ is the most efficient way to reduce $NO_x$ without adversely affecting fuel economy, driveability, and HC emissions.
   A. engine mapping       B. adaptive memory
   C. spark timing delay   D. exhaust gas recirculation

8. ____ of the following is not true of a late-model full-function control system.

A. the computer controls timing electronically
B. the computer changes the air-fuel ratio within the range of 14∶1 to 17∶1
C. fuel metering is controlled with a carburetor MC solenoid or by pulsing fuel injectors
D. the car can be driven in a limited operational strategy

Ⅲ. Choose a phrase from the list for each space in the passage below:

1. sends…to          5. is running
2. acts on           6. to account for
3. is compared to    7. takes…to
4. results from      8. are digitized by

All computers must perform four basic functions: input, proccesing, storage, and output. Engine control computers use various sensors to receive input data. This data ____ lookup tables in the computer's memory.

Some data may be stored in memory for future use. The computer output ____ the form of voltage signals ____ its actuators.

A control system operates in an open loop mode until the EGO sensor is warm enough, then the computer switches into the closed-loop mode. In open loop, the computer ignores feedback signals and functions with a predetermined set of values. Once the system switches into closed loop, the computer ____ the feedback signals and is constantly "retuning" the engine while it ____. The most recent computers have the ability to adapt their operating strategies ____ a number of conditional changes, including the wear that ____ engine operation.

System sensors generally measure analog variables. Their voltage signals ____ the computer, which compares the signals to its program and ____ an output signal ____ the actuators. Actuators change the computer voltage signal into electromechanical motion. Sensors are generally switches, resistors, transformers, or generators. Actuators are usually solenoids and stepper motors.

Ⅳ. Translate the following sentence into chinese:
1. An electronic full-time four-wheel-drive control system im-

proves vehicle traction and handling on surfaces with good traction and when inclement weather or road conditions reduce traction.

2. Electronic instrument clusters use an instrument computer, sometimes called a body computer, to process input information from sensors and to operate electronic displays.

3. An automatic load-level control system is used to keep the rear of the vehicle at a predetermined level position regardless of vehicle load.

4. In automobile applications, most variable measurements produce analog signals which must be changed to digital signals for computer processing.

5. A change in the car's height caused by a bump, for instance, is detected and the computer changes the shock damping.

6. When slippery conditions cause a loss of traction that results in a variation in the front and rear output shaft speeds, inputs from the front and rear speed sensors signal the electronic module to lock up the electromagnetic clutch assembly.

7. Any time the brakes are applied, the clutch is unlocked by the computer if the vehicle speed is 5 mi/h or faster in order to allow operation of the rear antilock brake system.

V. Translate the following passage into Chinese:

The electronic control system consists of five major components connected by wiring harnesses: electronic control unit (ECU), throttle position sensor, speed sensor, range selector, and control valve body. The throttle position sensor, speed sensor, and range selector transmit information to the ECU. The ECU processes this information and then sends signals that actuate specific solenoids located on the control valve body in the transmission. The action of the solenoids affects hydraulic circuits which in turn control the upshifts, downshifts, and lockup functions.

In addition to controlling the operation of the transmission, the ECU monitors the system for conditions that could result in damage to the transmission or improper vehicle operation. When one of these conditions is detected, the ECU is programmed to automatically respond in a manner that will ensure safe operation of the vehicle and transmission.

The torque converter is identical in design and function to those used in nonelectronically controlled units covered earlier. The lockup clutch is also similar in design, but is engaged and released in response to electronic signals from the ECU. The ECU can also disengage the lockup clutch at any time if it detects certain undesirable conditions.

# Chapter 6   Automobile Design

## 6.1 The design objective

"Why did they build a car that way?" is a common question asked by many students.

To understand the reasons why a vehicle is built in a certain way, it is necessary to know some of the questions a manufacturer must answer before he has his engineer design a car.

The first thing a manufacturer must consider is the specific job the vehicle, that is to be designed, should be capable of doing. This is called the design objective. For example, is the vehicle going to be required to carry a heavy load at low speeds or a light load at high speeds? Each of these operations obviously requires a different type of vehicle. The design objective may be more vivid if the reader considers a race car. A race car is not designed to operate on the highway and would be very difficult to drive in city traffic. The two car, on the other hand, will operate satisfactorily in traffic, but would be a very poor race car. When discussing which car is best, a person must always state what type of operation the vehicle is designed for.

When designing a vehicle, the engineer must consider maximum required acceleration, speed, economy, load to be carried, ride and handling characteristics, size, etc., that will be expected from the vehicle. The finished vehicle is a blend of these components, one feature traded off against another, to produce the final product. The maximum limits of these features are called the design parameters.

The next step to be considered is durability. How many miles should the vehicle operate before service is required? For example, a passenger car is designed to operate 100,000 highway miles before major service is required. An Indianapolis race car needs to complete only 500 racing miles. A dragster can make 100 quarter mile runs in 25 miles of driving. Each part of the vehicle has a specific design life, which takes into account its operating load, speed, temperature, lubrication, etc. For example, ball bearing manufacturers provide tables which list the ball bearing life expectancy based on operating speed and load. Overloading reduces bearing life expectancy and underloading increases life expectancy.

Once the design requirements are known, the manufacturer must consider cost. Therefore, one of the major design objectives is to lower the price without compromising the design parameters. In some cases, a large reduction in cost can be accomplished with only a slight compromise in a design objective and all keep the vehicle competitive.

One method of reducing cost is to change the manufacturing method. A forged part may be replaced by a cast part and a cast part is often replaced by a stamping or sintered metal part. In this way, the cost of part is reduced by reducing the number of manufacturing operations that are required to be done on the part before it can be used in the vehicle.

Plastics are replacing metal for non-structural parts having complex shapes. In some cases, entire vehicles are made from fiberglass and plastic. Plastic parts generally reduce manufacturing costs when made in quantity, as well as reducing weight.

Many product features are the result of the engineer's preference. These preferences are usually based upon previous satisfactory performance of the design. There is a tendency to continue those features until they becomes uneconomical or unpopular, or until new engineering management takes over. Engineering preference has generally been pushed into the background by the other design requirements that the vehicle must meet.

Vehicle design must start with occupant seating. No matter what the designer wishes, the vehicle must have room for the driver, passengers and load. The vehicle must have enough engine power to move the load at the desired speed and enough braking power to safely stop the vehicle. While moving, the vehicle must be controllable, so it can be driven to follow changes in the roadway and traffic condition.

## NEW WORDS

| | | |
|---|---|---|
| vehicle | ['viːikl] | n. 车辆,机动车,机械器具,运载工具 |
| vivid | ['vivid] | adj. 活泼的,生动的 |
| blend | [blend] | vt.;vi.;n. 混合;混合一体;融合 |
| parameter | [pə'ræmitə] | n. 参数,参项,结晶 |
| durability | [ˌdjuərə'biliti] | n. 耐久性,耐用性,持久性 |
| lubrication | [ˌljuːbri'keiʃən] | n. 润滑,润滑法,注油 |
| expectancy | [iks'pektənsi] | n. 希望,期望,预期 |
| compromise | ['kɔmprəmaiz] | v. 损害,妥协 |
| cast | [kaːst] | vt. 浇铸,铸造 |
| stamp | [stæmp] | vt. 冲压,用印模冲压 |
| sinter | ['sintə] | n. ;v. 熔渣,烧结物;使烧结,熔结 |
| fiberglass | ['faibə'glaːs] | n. 玻璃纤维,玻璃丝 |

## PHRASES AND EXPRESSIONS

| | |
|---|---|
| trade off | 交替使用,交替换位 |
| on the other hand | 另一方面 |
| manufacturing method | 制造方法 |
| replacing metal | 替代金属 |
| take over | 接收,接管 |
| as well as | 和…,也,又 |
| start with | 作为开始 |
| braking power | 制动力 |

## NOTES TO THE TEXT

1. Each part of the vehicle has a specific design life, which takes into account its operating load, speed, temperature, lubrication, etc.
汽车的每个部分都有特有的设计寿命、工作载荷、速度、温度、润滑等都应考虑在内。

which takes into account…是由 which 引导的定语从句修饰 design life；take into account 考虑,重视。

2. In some cases, a large reduction in cost can be accomplished

with only a slight compromise in a design objective and all keep the vehicle competitive.

某些情况下,大幅度地降低成本可通过在设计目的上稍微妥协而保证车的竞技性。

a large reduction in cost 在句中做主语;accomplish 的被动式做谓语;be accomplished with 伴随…。

3. There is a tendency to continue those features until they becomes uneconomical or unpopular, or until new engineering management takes over.

这是一个继续采用,直到它不经济或不流行或直到被其它新的技术替代的趋向。

take over 接替,接管;until they…or until…是两个并列连词由 until 分别引导时间状语从句。

## 6.2 The Design of the Basic Components

**Body and Frame**

The occupants should be provided with a comfortable ride to minimize fatigue. The seats must be firm with adequate support. Driver visibility must be excellent in all directions. Noise level and vibration should be as low as possible.

Different construction methods are used among the manufacturers and their vehicle models. Separate body and frame construction has been used for the longest time. In this type of construction, the engine, drive line, and running gear are firmly fastened to the frame; then the body is mounted to the frame with insulators to minimize noise and vibration transfer.

A second type of construction is the unitized body, in which the frame is part of the body structure. Body panels add strength to the frame pieces that form part of the structure. The running gear and drive line are attached with large soft insulators to minimize noise and vibration. If the insulators are too soft they tend to give the vehicle a spongy ride, and if they are too hard they do not insulate properly. Careful insulator design and location will produce a vehicle that is satisfactory to drive and ride in.

A third type of construction combines features from both of the preceding types. It uses a stub frame from the fire wall forward and a unitized body from the fire wall back. The unitized portion is very rigid, while the stub frame provides an opportunity for good insulation. This construction method is generally applied to larger body styles.

Manufacturers select their construction method by deciding which type is most economical for them to build, while still providing the noise, vibration, and ride characteristics they want to have in their vehicle. The largest number of standard-size vehicles use separate body and frame construction. The majority of small vehicles are unitized construction.

**Engine**

Most automobiles use a gasoline fueled reciprocating engine mounted ahead of the passengers. This location seems to provide the most room for occupants and load, as well as being a safety factor in a head-on collision. It also allows placement of the cooling radiator at the front of the car with a minimum of ducting and hoses. Engines have been placed behind the rear axle (rear engine), and between the occupants and the rear axle (midship). Neither has extensive application in domestic automobiles.

Some specialty automobiles use a different type of engine. The diesel engine is used in some taxicab fleets, because it uses considerably less fuel than the gasoline engine when operated at low speeds. It is quite common in Europe, where fuel costs are much greater than in the United States. The rotating combustion chamber engine is gaining popularity in small European and Japanese cars. Its use will probably increase. Turbine engines show promise, especially in commercial vehicles. They are powerful, light weight, and low on harmful emissions. They are ideally suited to replace some diesel engines in over-the-road load carrying vehicles.

## Drive Line

The drive line carries power to the drive wheels. A clutch or torque converter is connected to the engine crankshaft to provide a means to effectively disconnect the engine from the drive line, so the engine can idle while the vehicle is stopped. It is engaged to drive the vehicle.

A transmission is located directly behind the clutch or torque converter. Its function is to provide gear reduction for high torque to start the vehicle moving and drive it up steep grades. The transmission will also provide a reverse gear for backing the vehicle. Gear range selection may be either manual or automatic.

In front-engine vehicles, the transmission is located under the front floor pan. A propeller shaft is required to carry the engine power to the rear axle. It has universal joints on each end to provide flexibility as the suspension position changes.

A differential on the rear axle splits the incoming power to each drive wheel. This also allows the drive wheels to turn at different speeds as they go over bumps and around corners.

Vehicles with front wheel drive, or with midship or rear engines usually combine the transmission and differential, so they do not have a propeller shaft.

## Running Gear

The four tire footprints are the only place the vehicle touches the road. All of the engine power, steering and braking forces must operate through these tire-to-road contact footprint areas. Any time the tire does not contact the road or skidding begins, vehicle control is reduced or lost. The suspension's job is to keep the tire in contact with the road as much of the time as possible even on rough roads, while supporting the vehicle.

The suspension consists of springs, shock absorbers, and linkages or arms. The suspension system must be strong enough to resist axle twisting from high engine power and from brake reaction.

Brakes are mounted inside the wheels. Hydraulic force from the brake pedal pushes the brake shoes against a cast iron surface with enough force to slow wheel rotation. This, of course, slows the vehicle. Brake designs are either drum type or disc type. Most applications using disc brakes have disc brakes on the front and drum brakes on the rear.

The running gear is supported with either coil, leaf, or torsion bar springs. Coil springs are most popular. They require links and arms to hold the axle in position. Leaf springs can hold the axle in position without an additional device. Torsion bars require the same type of support as coil springs.

## NEW WORDS

|  |  |  |
|---|---|---|
| fatigue | [fə'ti:g] | n. ;vt. 疲劳,劳累;使疲劳 |
| firm | [fə:m] | adj. 坚固的,稳固的 |
| visibility | [ˌvizi'biliti] | n. 可见度,视界 |
| vibration | [vai'breiʃən] | n. 振动,振荡,摆动 |
| insulator | ['insjuleitə] | n. 绝缘体,绝热体,隔离物 |
| minimize | ['minimaiz] | vt. 使减至最少,把⋯估计得最低 |
| strength | [streŋθ] | n. 强度,体力,力量,浓度 |
| spongy | ['spʌndʒi] | adj. 海绵状的,松软的 |
| location | [lou'keiʃən] | vt. 定位,位置,地点 |
| combine | [kəm'bain] | vt. 兼备,兼有,使结合 |
| preceding | [pri(:)'si:diŋ] | adj. 上述的,以前的 |
| stub | [stʌb] | n. 连杆头,短管,管接头,凸缘 |
| reciprocate | [ri'siprəkeit] | vt. ;vi. 往复运动;往复移动,报答 |
| collision | [kə'liʒən] | n. 碰撞,冲突 |
| commercial | [kə'mə:ʃəl] | adj. 大批生产的,商业的,工厂的 |
| radiator | ['reidieit] | n. 散热器,散热片,水箱,冷却器 |
| duct | [dʌkt] | n. 导管,管道,线渠,风道 |
| hose | [houz] | n. ;vt. 软管,皮带管;用水龙浇水 |
| domestic | [də'mestik] | adj. 本国的,国产的,地方的,局部的 |
| taxicab | ['tæksikæb] | n. 出租汽车 |

| ideal | [aidiəl] | adj.;n. 理想的,标准的,典型的;理想 |
| disconnect | ['diskə'nekt] | vt. 分离,拆开,断开 |
| universal | [ˌjuːni'vəːsəl] | adj. 万能的,通用的,多方面 |
| flexibility | [fleksə'biliti] | n. 挠性,挠度,柔软性 |
| footprint | ['futprint] | n. 足迹,轨迹 |
| drum | [drʌm] | n. 鼓,鼓状物 |

## PHRASES AND EXPERESSIONS

| running gear | 行动装置,行走机件 |
| in all direction | 在所有的方向 |
| head-on | 迎头的,正面的 |
| be fastened to | 被紧固于 |
| harmful emissions | 有害排放物 |
| universal joints | 万向节 |
| drum type | 鼓式 |
| disc type | 盘式 |

## NOTES TO THE TEXT

1. Manufacturers select their construction method by deciding with type is most economical for them to build, while still providing the noise, vibration, and ride characteristics they want to have in their vehicle.

制造厂通过确定最经济的车型来选择汽车结构方式,同时,考虑噪音,振动和乘坐特性。

by deciding… 是介词短语做方式状语,while … 是现在分词短语做状语,同时还包含了一个定语从句 they want to have。

2. This location seems to provide the most room for occupants and load, as well as being a safety factor in a head-on collision.

这种放置形式可为乘坐者和货物提供更大的空间,同时也增加了迎面碰撞时的安全系数。

as well as 与 not only 同义,不但,即…又,是并列连词,它连接的是动名词短语,做并列句。

3. A clutch or torque converter is connected to the engine crank-shaft to provide a means to effectively disconnect the engine

from the drive line, so the engine can idle while the vehicle is stopped.

离合器或者液力变扭器与发动机曲轴相连,提供有效地切断从传动系与发动机的传动方式,从而使车辆在停车时,发动机可以怠速运转。

to effecting…drive line 是不定式短语做目的状语;so the engine… so 是连词引导结果状语从句,while … 是时间状语从句。

4. All of the engine power, steering and braking forces must operate through these tire-to-road contact footprint areas.

发动机的全部动力、操纵和制动都必须通过轮胎与地面的有效印迹面积来实现的。

through 是介词,介词短语做状语;stering and breaking 分别是现在分词做定语,修饰 forces。

## EXERCISES

Ⅰ. Answer the following questions according to the text:

1. As a automoble manufacturer, What questions does he must consider?

2. In order to reduce cost, How many methods does a manufacturer apply?

3. During design the body and frame, What conditions must the occupants meets?

4. How many types of construction are used in vehicle? What character does each type has?

5. Why is the combines construction applied to larger body styles?

6. How many types of engine are used in automobile? Where are they used? What advantage does each type has compared the others?

7. Explain the basic function of drive line?

8. Where is the transmission located? What is the function of transmission?

9. What are the suspension consists of?

10. What is the purpose of the suspension?

II. Fill the blank in each sentence with one of the four words or phrases which correctly completes the sentence:

1. The escape of air and the loss of heat both ____ a lower temperature at the end of compression.
   A. result from        B. result in
   C. give off           D. come back to

2. The starter solenoid is ____ operated heavy-duty switch.
   A. an electromagnetically    B. an electrically
   C. a hydraulically           D. an automatically

3. The solenoid switch opens and closes the circuit between the battery and ____.
   A. the engine             B. the generator
   C. the starting engine    D. cranking motor

4. The battery must supply ____ current flow to the starter before it can crank the engine.
   A. a little           B. little
   C. a great deal of    D. very few

5. In the modern automobile the starting switch is part of the keyed ____ switch.
   A. battery    B. ignition
   C. fuel       D. safety

6. Many solenoids also shift the cranking pinion into ____ the flywheel ring gear.
   A. mesh with            B. contact with
   C. holding out against  D. touch with

7. The current producing the magnetic field in the windings ____ the battery via the ignition switch.
   A. passes on      B. comes from
   C. is stored in   D. forms part of

8. The starter motor is energized ____ a key-operated starter switch.
   A. make use of    B. help through
   C. as a means of  D. by means of

III. Choose one of the four words that best matches the definition given below:

1. An alternate path for a flowing substance
   A. channel    B. bypass    C. tube    D. conduct
2. Process of changing from a liquid to a vapor
   A. evaporation           B. expansion
   C. ventilation           D. radiation
3. Products of combustion that are discharged through exhaust system of vehicle
   A. carbonization         B. oxidation reaction
   C. contamination         D. exhaust emissions
4. Pipe connecting engine to muffler to conduct spent gases away from engine
   A. propeller shaft       B. differential gear
   C. exhaust pipe          D. suction line
5. A device designed to remove suspended impurities or particles of foreign matter from intake air, fuel system or lubricating system
   A. filter    B. muffler    C. cleaner    D. sweeper
6. A pump which injects or inserts a fluid or gas, usually against pressure, into a cylinder or chamber
   A. distributor           B. injector
   C. carburetor            D. accelerator
7. An antifriction bearing using a great number of rollers of small diameter in relation to their length
   A. journal bearing       B. rolling bearing
   C. maintenance-free bearing   D. needle bearing
8. A pressure less than atmospheric pressure
   A. vaccum    B. charge    C. exhaust    D. suction
9. Cloudlike bodies made up of very small drops of water floating in the air, near or reaching to the ground
   A. steam    B. frog    C. mist    D. smog
10. To thin or reduce the concentration of a solution
    A. diluent    B. dilute    C. mixture    D. compound

Ⅳ. Choose a phrase from the list for each space in the passage below:

　　1. are equipped for        5. according to

  2. such as      6. are divided into
  3. may be provided with   7. are classified as
  4. aside from     8. are subdivided into

  The automobile is a self-propelled transport vehicle. ____ their application, automobiles ____ trucks, passenger, and special-purpose vehicles. Cargo carriers include trucks, truck tractors, trailers, pole trailers, and semitrailers. The trucks ____ beds to transport different goods or with special-purpose bodies ____ dump bodies to transport loose and viscous cargo, tank bodies for liquids, refrigerator vans for perishables, etc. ____ a body type, trucks are classified according to their load-carrying capacity and cross-country capability.

  The passenger vehicles ____ cars seating from one to six men, and buses. The buses ____ city and intercity ones. Touist buses make a separate group. According to their length buses are classified as minibuses (up to 5m), small (up to 7.5m), medium (up to 9m), large (up to 12m), and articulated (over 16.5m).

  The special-purpose automobiles ____ performing particular tasks. Among them are fire and garbage trucks, ambulances, tower, water tank, repair trucks, etc.

Ⅴ. Translate the following sentence into Chinese:

  1. The automatic level control is designed to maintain a nearly constant rear curb height (distance from bumper, frame, etc., to ground) regardless of load changes (to 500 lbs. or 227 kg) over the rear axle.

  2. You know that the modern auto does ride well, its ability to negotiate rough roads and handle well at freeway speeds is a direct result of a properly designed suspension system.

  3. The correct ratio is determined by a careful consideration of the car weight, the type of service it will have, the engine horsepower, transmission gearing, and whether or not an overdrive is incorporated.

  4. Like the standard transmission, the automatic transmission is designed to adapt the power of the engine to meet varying road and load conditions, and to produce an infinite number of ratios between engine and wheels.

5. The clutch is designed to connect or disconnect the transmission of power from one working part to another in this case, from the engine to the transmission.

6. Modern brake systems utilize a device that automatically adjusts the drum-to-lining clearance as the linings wear down.

Ⅵ. Translate the following passage into Chinese:

The car wheels are suspended on springs that support the weight of the vehicle. The springs absorb road shock as the wheels encounter holes or bumps and prevent, to a large extent, any consequent jarring action or up-and-down motion from being carried through the frame and body. Springs are coil type, leaf type, torsion bar or rod or air suspension. The coil spring is a heavy steel coil. The weight of the frame and body puts an initial compression on the spring. The spring will further compress when the wheel passes over an obstruction in the road.

The leaf spring has been made in a number of forms, but the one that has been most commonly used is the semielliptical type. The leaf spring is made up of a series of flat plates, or leaves, of graduated length, one on top of another. The spring assembly acts as a flexible beam and is usually fastened at the two ends to the car frame and at the center to the wheel axle. Some cars have used only one leaf spring at the rear and one at the front, each spring supporting two wheels. With this design, the center of the spring is attached to the frame, and each end of the spring supports a wheel. The action is similar on all leaf springs. When the wheel encounters a bump, the spring bends up-ward to absorb the blow. When the wheel drops into a hole, the spring bends downward. Thus, the leaf spring does the same job as the coil spring in the vehicle.

## MEASURING SYSTEMS
### ENGLISH        METRIC

### LENGTH

| | |
|---|---|
| 12 inches = 1 foot<br>36 inches = 1 yard<br>3 feet = 1 yard<br>5,280 feet = 1 mile<br>6 feet = 1 fathom<br>320 rods = 1 mile | 1 kilometre = 1000 metres<br>1 hectometre = 100 metres<br>1 dekametre = 10 metres<br>1 metre = 1 metre<br>1 decimetre = 0.1 metre<br>1 centimetre = 0.01 metre<br>1 millimetre = 0.001 metre |

### WEIGHT

| | |
|---|---|
| 27.34 grains = 1 dram<br>438 grains = 1 ounce<br>16 drams = 1 ounce<br>16 ounces = 1 pound<br>2000 pounds = 1 short ton<br>2240 pounds = 1 long ton<br>25 pounds = 1 quarter<br>4 quarters = 1 cwt | 1 tonne = 1,000,000 grams<br>1 kilogram = 1000 grams<br>1 hectogram = 100 grams<br>1 dekagram = 10 grams<br>1 gram = 1 gram<br>1 decigram = 0.1 gram<br>1 centigram = 0.01 gram<br>1 milligram = 0.001 gram |

### VOLUME

| | |
|---|---|
| 8 ounces = 1 cup<br>16 ounces = 1 pint<br>32 ounces = 1 quart<br>2 cups = 1 pint<br>2 pints = 1 quart<br>4 quarts = 1 gallon<br>8 pints = 1 gallon | 1 hectolitre = 100 litres<br>1 dekalitre = 10 litres<br>1 litre = 1 litre<br>1 cecilitre = 0.1 litre<br>1 centilitre = 0.01 litre<br>1 millilitre = 0.001 litre<br>1000 millilitre = 1 litre |

### AREA

| | |
|---|---|
| 144 sq. inches = 1 sq. foot<br>9 sq. feet = 1 sq. yard<br>43,560 sq. ft. = 160 sq. rods<br>160 sq. rods = 1 acre<br>640 acres = 1 sq. mile | 100 sq. millimetres = 1 sq. centimetre<br>100 sq. centimetres = 1 sq. decimetre<br>100 sq. decimetres = 1 sq. metre<br>10,000 sq. metres = 1 hectare |

| TEMPERATURE ||| 
| FAHRENHEIT | | CELSIUS |
| --- | --- | --- |
| 32 degrees F | Water freezes | 0 degree C |
| 68 degrees F | Reasonable room temperature | 20 degrees C |
| 98.6 degrees F | Normal body temperature | 37 degrees C |
| 173 degrees F | Alcohol boils | 78.34 degrees C |
| 173 degrees F | Water boils | 100 degrees C |
| 212 degrees F | | |

## METRIC TABLES

### SOME COMMON ABBREVIATIONS/SYMBOLS

| ENGLISH | | METRIC | |
|---|---|---|---|
| UNIT | ABBREVIATION | UNIT | SYMBOL |
| inch | in | kilometre | km |
| hectometre | hm | feet | ft |
| dekametre | dam | yard | yd |
| metre | m | mile | mi |
| decimetre | dm | grain | gr |
| centimetre | cm | ounce | oz |
| millimetre | mm | pound | lb |
| cubic centimetre | $cm^3$ | teaspoon | tsp |
| kilogram | kg | tablespoon | tbsp |
| hectogram | hg | fluid ounce | fl oz |
| dekagram | dag | cup | c |
| gram | g | pint | pt |
| decigram | dg | quart | qt |
| centigram | cg | gallon | gal |
| milligram | mg | cubic inch | $in^3$ |
| kilolitre | kl | cubic foot | $ft^3$ |
| hectolitre | hl | cubic yard | $yd^3$ |
| dekalitre | dal | square inch | $in^2$ |
| litre | L | square foot | $ft^2$ |
| square mile | $mi^2$ | square yard | $yd^2$ |
| millilitre | ml | centilitre | cl |
| dekastere | das | Fahrenheit | F |
| square kilometre | $km^2$ | barrel | bbl |
| hectare | ha | fluid dram | fl dr |
| are | a | board foot | bd ft |
| centare | ca | rod | rd |
| tonne | t | dram | dr |
| | | bushel | bu |
| | | Celsius | C |

· 404 ·

# INDEX

## A

aC, three-phase
accumulator piston
actuators
air bleed
air check valves
air cleaners
    dry type
    oil—wetted polyurethane
air conditioning
    air flow
    wiring circuits
air distribution manifold
air horn
air injection system
    dual flow
    pulse
    tubes
air pump
air spring
air temperature cut-off switch
    ambient
air-cooled engines
airflow meter
airflow sensor
    plunger
airflow valve
alignment, front wheel
alternator
    construction
    operation
    single unit regulator
altitude compensation
antibackfire valve
antifriction bearing
atoms
automatic choke circuit
automatic leveling control
automatic transmissions
    basic construction
    clutch
    different types
    fluid coupling
    fluid coupling efficiency
    locking converter
    lockup operation
    lubrication
    oil cooling
    oil pump
    shifting
    split ring
    torque converter
    torus
automobile brakes
    hydraulics
    piston assembly
auxiliary gap
axles

## B

balk ring

ball and trunnion universal
    joint
ballast resistor
battery capacity
    capacity ratings
    chemical action
    discharge rate
    dry-charged
    electrolyte
    functions
    negative plate
    positive plate
    voltage
bearing, clearance
block
bodies
booster failure
brake bands
brakes, automobile
    anti-skid system
    check valves and
    siston springs
    double anchor
    double anchor
    double cylinder
    drum
    dual master cylinder
    dual "split"
    emergency
    fade
    fluid reservoir
    hydraulic principles
    lining
    master cylinder
    release

    parking
    power
    ratio
    self-adjusting
    servo action
    self-energizing
    shoe arrangement
    shoe assembly
    single, self-centering
bronze-bushed shackle
bTU (British Thermal Unit)
buelding an engine

## C

calipers
cam angle
cam ground
camber
camshaft
canister construction
carbon monoxide
carburetor
circuits
    downdraft
    dual
    four-barrel
    functions, others
    icing
    mixture-control solenoid
    sidedraft
    single barrel
    updraft
    variable venturi
caster

negative
catalytic converter
center link
centrifugal advance
cetane number rating
check valve
    liquid
    rollover
chisels
choke
    automatic
control
    stove
    thermostatic coil
    vacuum piston
    valve, offset
circuit
    parallel
    series
    series-parallel
    simple
circuit breaker
closed loop system
clutch
construction
cooling
    definition
    disc
    overrunning
    pedal "free travel"
    pedal linkage
    release lever operating mechanism
    riding
    roller

    self-adjusting
coil, ignition systems
coil construction
coil springs
cold start injector
combustion chamber
    design
    hemispherical
    wedge shape
compensator valve
compression ratio
compression rings
compression stroke
compressor
    discharge pressure switch
    muffler
    superheat switch
computers
    hardware
    ignition systems
    software
    trouble codes
condenser
construction
conduction
connecting rod
    bearing
construction
construction, canister
construction, engine com-ponents
continuous injection
    mechanical type
control circuits, hydraulic
convection

converter
    air injected three-way
catalytic
    dual bed, three-way
catalytic
    dual bed, three-way
    multiple
    two-way, monolith
    (honeycomb) type
    two-way, pellet type
coolant temperature sensor
cooling
classification
closed system
    pressurized
    system
    system, care of
crankcase
cranking performance
crankshaft
    position sensor
    hall effect
    magnetic type
    optical type
crescent wrench
cruising speed
current
cycle classification
cylinder
    bore and piston stroke
classification
    head
    head, removable
    sleeves

# D

dC generator circuits
dC generator polarity
dC generator regulator
design, engine components
detonation
dial calipers
diaphragm clutch
dies
    special
diesel fuel
    characteristics
    injection pump
    injection system
dieseling, run-on
differential
    carrier and bearings
    planetary gear
    special traction
dimmer switch
dipstick
direct fuel injection
direct ignition system, General Motors
disc brake
distributor cap
distributor type injection pump
diverter valve (bypass valve)
dividers
double anchor, double cylinder brake
double anchor brake
downdraft carburetor

drills
    sharpening
    using
drive axle assemblies
    axles
    construction
differential
    housing
    lubrication
    transaxle
drive lines
    ball and trunnion universal joint
    Hotchkiss drive
    propeller shafts
    slip joint
    torque tube drive
    universal joints
dry sleeves
dual carburetor
dual cylinder
dual exhaust system
dual flow air injection system
dual master cylinder
dual metering rod control

## E

eccentric shaft
eCS operation
efficiency
    mechanical
    practical
    thermal
    volumetric

electric fan relay
electic fuel pump
electric fuel pump relay
electric test instruments
electrical circuits
    cuit breakers
electrical fuel shutoff
electrical system
    battery
    circuits
    fundamentals
    generator
    insulators
    test gauges
    voltage drop
electrolyte
    specific gravity
electromagnet core
electron theory
electronic fuel injection
emergency brakes
    drive line
emission control
engine
    block
    classification, parts identification
    clutches
experimental
    four-stroke cycle
    four-stroke cycle diesel
    gas turbine
    horizontal-opposed
    in-line
    internal combustion gasso-

line
    slant, inclined type
    two-stroke cycle
    two-stroke cycle diesel
    V-type
engine components
    application
    construction
    design
engine mounting
engine oil service classification
engine size, displacement
engine tests, measurements
engines, water-cooled
EGR system
evaporation control system
evaporator
exhaust gas recirculation
    vacuum modulated, ported
exhaust manifolds
exhaust pipe
pipe to manifold connection
exhaust systems
    dual
emission controls
    hangers
    heat shielding
    other connections
    single
expander devices
expansion tube
expansion valve

## F

fast idle
feeler gauges
files
    cut and shape
    rotary
filters
    operation
    system, bypass
    system, full-flow
firing or power stroke
firing order
first gear, transmission
    transaxle
flash point
float circuit
flooding
flow meter potentiometer
fluid coupling
fluid coupling, efficiency
flywheel
    ring gear
four-barrel carburetor
four-stroke cycle
frames
free electrons
friction, bearing
friction, bearing construction
friction, definition
friction, reduction
front and rear wheel alignment
front end suspension system
front wheel hubs

fuel, preparing
fuel accumulator
fuel bowl
fuel charge, warming
fuel classification
fuel distributor
fuel filters, types
fuel injection
    closed loop feature
    continuous
    continuous
    continuous, mechanical type
    direct and indirect
    electronic
    intermittent electronic
    intermittent (non-timed)
    intermittent (timed)
    mechanical
fuel injector
fuel intake and exhaust
    passages
fuel lines
fuel pulsation
fuel pump
    electric
    mechanical
    pressure source
fuel pump and vacuum pump
    combination
fuel pump efficiency
    measurements
fuel pump, serviceable and non-serviceable
fuel systems
    carburetion

fuel injection
full pressure lubricating system
fuses

## G

gaskets and seals
gasohol, alcohol
gasoline
    breaking up
    definition
    pickup pipe
    premium
    regular
    tank
    unleaded
gear oil pump
gear ratio
gears, timing marks
general Motors direct ignition system
generator
    alternating current
    armature
    brushes
    commutator
    cooling and lubrication
    direct current
    polarizing
    pole shoes
    regulator
glow plugs
governor
governors
ground symbol

## H

hacksaws
hammers
hammers
head construction
head shape
headlamp switch
headlights
    bulbs
    fuses
heat control valves
heat dam
heat transference, air conditioning
heat value
high gear
horns
horsepower
    brake
    definition
    formula
    frictional
    indicated
    potential
    ratings, gross and net
hoses
hotchkiss drive
hubs, front wheel
hubs, rear
hydraulic brake fluid
hydraulic system
hydraulic valve lifters
hydro-boost, hydraulic power booster
hydrocarbon
hypoid gearing

## I

idle compensator
idle speed motor
idle speedup control for air conditioning
idler arm
ignition systems
    coil
    components, battery
    module
    switch
ignitions, electronic to computerized comparison
impact wrench
independent front suspension coil spring
indirect fuel injection
injection system, diesel
injector pulse width
injector pump delivery valve
injector types, diesel
in-line injector pump
in-line injector pump metering control
intake air, heated
intake manifolds
intake stroke
integrated direct ignition
intermittent fuel injection
    airflow meter type

    digital closed loop type
internal gear

### J

jets

### K

knock sensor

### L

latent heat
leveling control
    electric compressor
linkage train
liquefied petroleum gas
liquid check valve
liquid fuel control
liquid-vapor separator
load strength
low gear
lubrication systems
    combination splash and pressure
    full pressure
    splash

### M

magnetic clutch
magnetic lines of force
magnetism
main bearings
    crankshaft
main discharge tube

manifold absolute pressure (MAP) sensor
manifold air temperature sensor
manifold design
manifolds heat control valve
manifold to exhaust pipe
manifolds, intake
manual control valve
manual transmissions and transfer cases
mass airflow (mAF)
master cylinder, reservoir level
matter
mean effective pressure
measuring tools
mechanical efficiency formula
mechanical fuel injection
mechanical fuel pump
mechanics
metering rod control
metering valve
micrometer
molecule
muffler design
multi-grade oils
multiple converters
    Neutral, transmission
    Newton's Law

### O

Octane rating
oil pan
oil pickup
oil pressure gauges

oil pump
    gear
    plunger
    rotary
    vane
oil seals
oil viscosity
overdrive construction and operation
    advantage
    constant drive
    controls
    definition
    direct drive mode
    direct freewheeling
    drive stages
    exploded view
    locked out
    mode
    roller clutch
overhead camshaft
oxygen sensor

## P

parking brakes
    dise type
partial skirt piston
parts identification
pCV control valve
pin installation
pinion engagement
pipe wrenches
pistons
    assembly

cam ground
expansion problems
head construction
head shape
lengthen
materials
partial skirt
pin
pin boss
pump
positive crankcase ventilation
power booster
    bellows type
    diaphragm
    failure
    hydraulic
piston type
    vacuum reservoir
power steering
    in-line unit
    offset gear
pumps
    rack and pinion
    self-contained unit
power stroke
practical efficiency
precision thin wall casting
preignition
pressure differential warning switch
pressure plate
    spring
pressure relief valve
pressurized cooling system
primary circuit

proeller shafts
proportioning valve
pull rod and return spring
pullers
pulsation damper
pulse air injection
pulse width, controlling
pulse width, injector
pump charging cycle
pump circuit acceleration
pump construction
pump discharge cycle
pumpr fuel return circuit

## Q

quadra-Trac transfer case
quick take-up master cylinder

## R

radiation
radiator
random access memory
reamers
rear hubs
rear suspensior
receiver-dehydrator
refrigeration system
    oil
    principles
r-12
regulator, single unit
regulator, transistorized
relay
removable cylinder head

resistance
resistor
resistor spark plug
resonators
reverse, transmission
reverse gear
ring and pinion
rocker arm and link
roller clutch
roller lifters
rollover check valve
rotary engine operation
    carburetion and exhaust
    compression ratio
    cooling
    emission control
    performing four-strok
    peripheral port intake
    side port intake
rotary oil pump
rotator
positive type
release type
rotor
rubber-bushed shackle

## S

safety
    battery
    brakes
    electric drills
    engine
    fan
    fire

gasoline
gasoline tank
radiator
refrigerant
steering system
suspension system
    tire inflation
    voltage
    wheels
screwdrivers
second gear
secondary circuit
    ignition systems
self-adjusting brakes
self-adjusting clutch
semielliptical leaf springs
sensors
    coolant temperature
    crankshaft position
    knock
    manifold absolute pressure
    manifold air temperature
    mass airflow(MAF)
    oxygen
    throttle valve
series-parallel circuit
service vaives, discharge and suction
shift mechanism
shifter
shock absorber construction operation
    control action
sidedraft carburetor
single anchor, self-centering
brake
single barrel carburetor
single exhaust system.
single leaf spring
slip angles
slip joint
socket attachments
    handles
    wrenches
soldering equipment
solid axle
spark plug
    heat range
    insulators
    projected core nose
shells
special shocks
spiral bevel gearing
splash lubricating system
split ring
split skirt
spring, torsion bar
spring oscillation
springs
    air
    coil
    semielliptical leaf
    single leaf
sprung weight
spur bevel
Stablizer bar
starter
    actuating switches
    drive
solenoid

starter system
    armature loop
    commutator segments
    electrieal circui
static electricity
stator
steel strut
steering arms
steering axis inclinatior
steering gear reduction
steering gearbox
    manual or standard
steering geometry
steering linkage
steering shaft universal joints
steering system
    caster angle
    knuckle angle
stoichiometric air-fuel mixture
stroke
    compression
    exhaust
    firing
    intake
    power
sulphur content
sump
sun gear
superheat switch
sure-Grip differential
suspension system
    automatic leveling control
    front end
    independent front wheel
    lubrication
    manual leveling control
    rear wheels individually
suspended
solid axle
    torsion bar front
swing axles
switch
    ambient air temperature
    dimmer
    fan
superheat
synchronizier devices
synchronizing mechanism

## T

taps
special
temperature gauge
test gauges
thermal efficiency
thermostat
    closed
    function
    pellet type
threaded shackle
three-speed synchromesh
transmission
three-way dual bed converter
throttle position sensor
throttle positioners
throttle return dashpot
throttle valve
tie rods
timing

    gear cover
    setting basic
tire
    balance, static
    construction
    excessive wear
    inflation
    pressure chart
    radial lead/pull
    radial waddle
    rotation
    runout
    size
    special
tubeless
toe-in
toe-out on turns
tools
    cleaning
    identification
    material
    special purpose
torque
torque converter
    curve
    multiplication
    multiplication curve
torque wrenches
torsion bar front suspension
transaxle, construction torsion
bar spring
torus
transaxle, construction
transfer cases
    four-wheel drive

    full-time, construction
    full-time, operation
    other designs
    part-time, consturction
    select drive
transistor
    consturction
    operation
transmission/transaxle
    cross section
    five-speed
    four-speed
    gear ratios
    gears
    overdrives
three-speed synchromesh
trunnions
t-slot
turbochargers

## U

universal joints
    constant velocity
unsprung weight
updraft carburetor

## V

vacuum advance
    diaphragm
vacuum controlled metering roc
vvacuum modulator
vacuum pump
valve guide
valves

air check
antibackfire
check
classifications
classifications, F-head
classifications, I-head
classification, L-head
  classifications, overhead
valve adjustment
classifications, T-head
classifications, valve train
deceleration
diverter
exhaust gas recirculation
high pressure relief
lifters (hydraulic type)
lifters (mechanical type)
Liquid check
manual control
metering
overlap
ports
proportioning
rollover check
scats
shifter
springs
timing
train
Vane
oil pump
supercharger
vapor lock
variable pitch stator
venturi

  secondary
variable
vibration damper
viscosity
  index
vise
voltage
  computerized regulation
  electromotive force (EMF)
  equal
  regulator
volumetric efficiency
vortex flow

## W

wankel rotary piston engine
  advantages
  classification
  construction
  end housings
  intermediate housing
  rotor
  rotor housing
waste gate valve
water detector
water heated manifold
water-cooled engines
wear-in, piston rings
wet sleeves
wheel brake assembly
wheel cylinder
wheel hubs
  attaching
  front

· 419 ·

tires
wheels,quick-change,special
hubs
wrenches

## 参考文献　REFERENCES

1 Mathias F. Brejcha. Automatic Transmissions and Transaxles,Regents/Prentice Hall,Englewood Cliffs,1993

2 Frank D. Petruzella. Automotive Electronic Fundamentals, Glencoe Division Macmillan/McGraw-Hill. Columbus,Ohio. U. S. A. 1991

3 Martin W. Stockel and Martin T. Stockel. Auto Mechanics Fundamentals, The Goodheart-Willcox Company. Inc. U. S. A. 1990

4 Frank J. Thiessen and Davis N. Dales. Diesel Fundamentals, Prentice Hall,Englewood Cliffs, 1986

5 Roger Fennema. Engine Performance Diagnosis Tune-up, Harper and Row. Publishers, 1989

7 邓贤贵,徐达编著．汽车专业英语．北京:人民交通出版社,1995